PLAIN COUNTRY FRIENDS

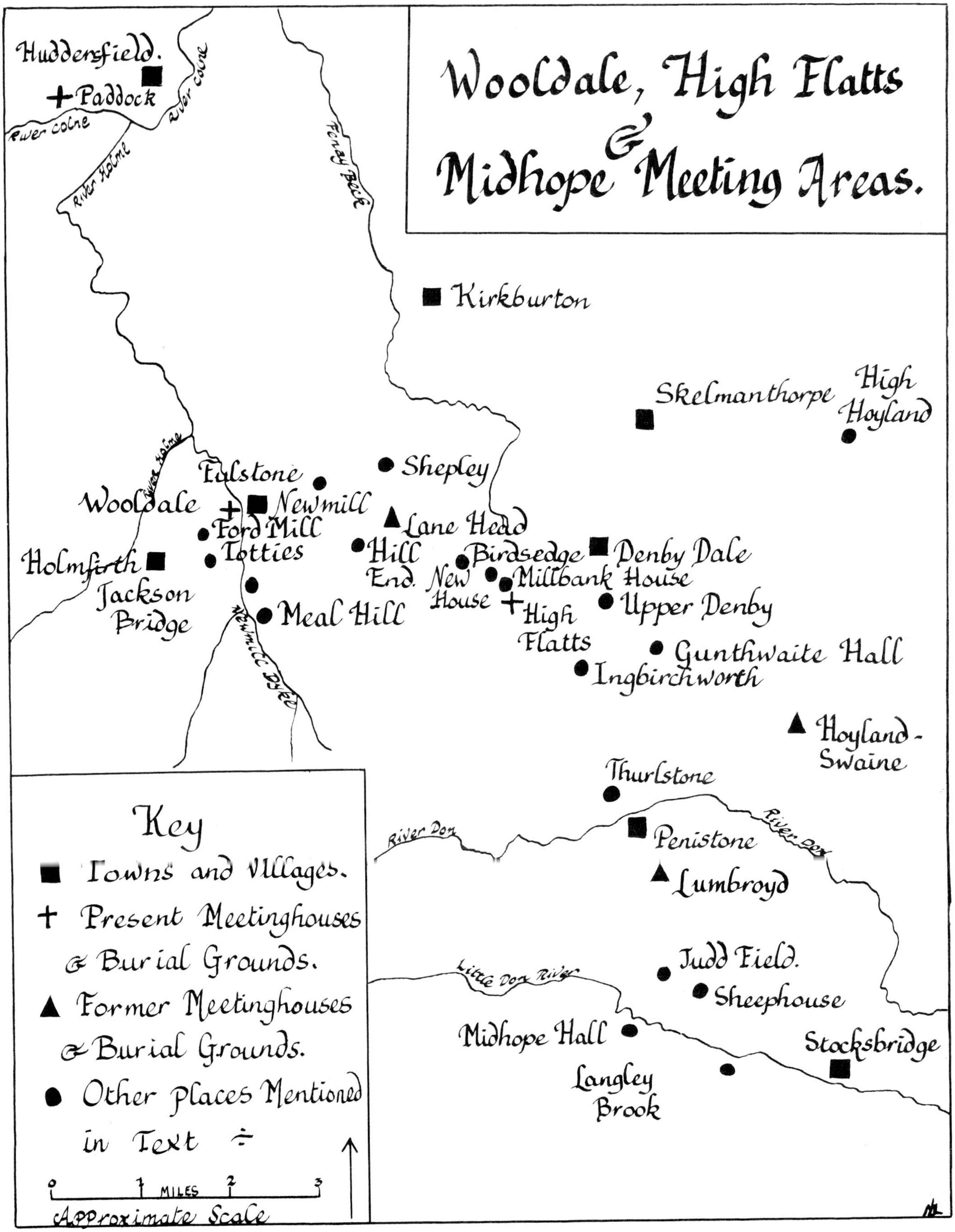
Wooldale, High Flatts & Midhope Meeting Areas.
Huddersfield.
Paddock
River Colne
River Colne
River Holme
Fenay Beck
Kirkburton
Skelmanthorpe
High Hoyland
River Holme
Shepley
Fulstone
Wooldale
Newmill
Lane Head
Ford Mill
Totties
Hill End.
Birdsedge
Denby Dale
Holmfirth
Jackson Bridge
New House
Millbank House
Upper Denby
Meal Hill
High Flatts
Gunthwaite Hall
Ingbirchworth
Newmill Dyke
Hoyland-Swaine
Thurlstone
River Don
Penistone
River Don
Lumbroyd
Judd Field.
Sheephouse
Little Don River
Midhope Hall
Stocksbridge
Langley Brook
Key
Towns and Villages.
Present Meetinghouses & Burial Grounds.
Former Meetinghouses & Burial Grounds.
Other Places Mentioned in Text
0
1
MILES
2
3
Approximate Scale

PLAIN COUNTRY FRIENDS

The Quakers of Wooldale, High Flatts and Midhope

David Bower & John Knight

with a Foreword by
Edward H. Milligan

'...I went to High Flatts, and was at their meeting, it being first day, which was very large; it being composed of plain country Friends...'

JOHN GRIFFITH 1748

Published by Wooldale Meeting of the Religious Society of Friends (1987).

Plain Country Friends

© 1987 David Bower & John Knight
Reprinted 1993
Published by Wooldale Meeting of the Religious Society of Friends (1987)
Printed and bound in England by The Amadeus Press Ltd., Huddersfield

ISBN 0 9512633 0 7

This book is dedicated to all past, present and future Friends of Wooldale and High Flatts Meetings and in particular to Ruth Bower and Julie Knight.

CONTENTS

Acknowledgements	VIII
Foreword	1 & 2
Preface 1	3
Preface 2	4
Preface to Second Impression	5
Introduction	6

Quaker Dawn — 7-17

Early Persecutions	8
The Jackson Family	10
Henry Jackson I	10
Henry Jackson II	11
Henry Jackson III	16

Plain Friends — 18-65

Quaker Visitors	19
The Visit of John Griffith	21
Other American Visitors	23
John Woolman	24
Elders, Overseers and Ministers	24
Disowments and Testimonies of Denial	26
Marriage and Marital Difficulties	28
Marrying Out	30
Irregular Marriage	31
Quaker Courtship	33
Loose and Disorderly Conduct	33
Insolvency and Non-payment of Debts	36
The Unnecessary Frequenting of Alehouses	38
Non-attendance at Meetings for Worship	40
Admittance to Membership	42
Returning to the Fold	43
Resignations from Membership	45
Gravestones and Mourning	46
Entertainment	47
Tithes and Sufferings	49
Quaker Women	52
A Friend in Need	54
Removals from High Flatts and Wooldale	55
Servants	55
Visions and Dreams	57
Pheobe Haigh's Miracle	58
The Visiting of Families	59

Quaker Cameos in Shades of Grey — 66-105

John Brooke of Hagg	66
Elizabeth Morehouse of Mount	67
Jonathan and Ann Green	68
Caleb Roberts of Wooldale	71
Joshua Woodhead of Mount	72
Uriah Brook of High Flatts	74
Joseph and John Broadhead of Wooldale	75
Joseph Brook of Wooldale	77

CONTENTS (continued)

George Lee of Wooldale	79
John Haigh of Moor Royd Nook, High Flatts	80
Elihu Dickinson the Tanner	83
Elihu Dickinson the Clothier	84
Daniel Collier and Edward Dickinson	88
The Last Disownment	89
Joseph Wood of Newhouse — 'Fisher of Men'	91
Quakers and Luddites	97
James Jenkins at High Flatts	103

The Growth of Concern — 106-117

Education	106
Quaker School Days — A Letter from Ackworth	107
First Day Schools	107
Adult Schools	109
Poor Relief and Charities	110
Upholding the Peace Testimony	113
Local Friends and Politics	115
High Flatts Sanatorium	115

Friends at Work — 118-120

Occupations	118
Wood and Burtt	118

The Families — 121-135

The Dickinsons of High Flatts, Sheephouse and Thurlstone	122
The Firths of Shepley Lane Head	127
The Woods of Newhouse	131
The Broadheads of Wooldale	134

Epilogue — 136-138

Bricks and Mortar (A Supplement) — 139-153

The Origins of Wooldale Meeting	140
Wooldale Meeting House	140
High Flatts Meeting House	145
Hoyland Swaine	148
Shepley Lane Head	148
Midhope, Sheephouse and Judd Field	149
Lumbroyd	151
The Origins of Friends Meeting House in Paddock	152

Appendices — 155-195

Bibliography — 195-198

Index of Places — 199-201

Index of Names — 202-207

ACKNOWLEDGMENTS

The authors wish to extend their deepest thanks to everyone who gave so freely and patiently of their time in helping this history to be written. Our sincere apologies are also extened to anyone we have been negligent in omitting by name in the ensuing list.

We wish to thank the decendants of the Wood family without whom we would have been unable to provide such detailed information. We are deeply indebted to: James Wood of Newton Mearnes, for the kind loan of the very extensive Joseph Wood Manuscript Collection; Freya Wood and Catherine Walton for the use of later Wood family sources, notes and photographs. To Catherine Walton we are especially indebted for information about the later Firth family. At the same time we wish to express our sincere thanks to Thea Backhouse and John S.G. Wood who helped to put us in touch with various members of the family.

We would also like to thank Corma and Arthur Chapman of Utah, Mr. H.G. Wood and Mr. Herbert Senior for information concerning the Dickinson family, Helen J. Adamson about the Pontefract family and John Wynne concerning the Broadheads of Wooldale. Our thanks are also extended to Mrs. Ainley, her brother Mr. J.Brook and Evilene and Margaret Sarfas for information about the Brooks of Wooldale and High Flatts.

Quite a large part of this book would not have been completed without the help received from Malcolm Thomas and the staff of Friends House Library, Betty Limb, the Archivist at Ackworth School and the staffs of the Special Collections Department of the Brotherton Library in Leeds, the Huddersfield Local History Library, the Sheffield Local History Library, Harverford College Library and the Wakefield County Records Office. Additionally, the staffs of Ford & Warren Solicitors (in particular Edward Brown) and Friends Trusts Ltd. (in particular Donald Robertson). Our grateful thanks are also extended to: W. Pearson Thistletwaite, Mary Hooper, Russell Mortimer, Thomas Walker and Richard Woodall.

To persons living in the locality we wish to thank Mr. David Mallinson and Mrs. Jennifer Needham for information concerning Newhouse, Frank Lindley concerning Ford Mill, Michael Fitton concerning Midhope, Mr. Brittain concerning Hoyland Swaine Burial Ground and the present owners of Mill Bank House, Meal Hill, Folly, Bellroyd, Sheephouse, Judd Field, Midhope Hall, Oakes, Lane Head, Shepley-Woodend, Ebson House, Hill End and all the other houses that we visited and where we were most kindly received.

The authors wish to specially mention the help, information and support they received from the membership of the two meetings in this project, particularly: Frank Cook, Gladys Netherwood and Eileen Williams of High Flatts Meeting, Ruth Bower, Edward Darke and David Hoyle of Wooldale Meeting. To John and Margaret Lawton, for the cover design and map, and Steve Dixon, for the many patient hours he expended upon creating an alphabetically ordered list of visitors, our most sincere thanks for their whole-hearted and enthusiastic efforts. To Julie Knight, for her patient encouragement, assistance with initial-proofing and constructive comments, our very deepest and sincerest thanks.

Finally, we wish to thank the following. Lisa Dearman (for patiently wading through our typescripts checking errors in the text). Lynn Brayshay (for reading through the manuscript to provide us with a non-Quaker historian's perpetive). The staff of Netherwood Dalton for their technical advice. Edward Milligan for his meticulous reading of the manuscript, helpful comments and suggestions. The Barnsley Friends Adult School Trust Fund, the Edith M. Ellis Charitable Trust, the W.F. Southall Trust, the C.B. & H.H. Taylor 1984 Charitable Settlement and the Edward Cadbury Charitable Trust for their financial help in meeting the cost of publication.

FOREWORD

'For Art and Science cannot exist but in minutely organized Particulars.' And neither, for that matter, can history. Here, in this story of Quakerism in a cluster of tiny country meetings in South-West Yorkshire, are exactly the *'minutely organized Particulars'* that we need. Here are the individual men and women who received Truth in the mid-seventeenth century and here, too, the women and men who across the centuries sustained the meetings now represented by Wooldale and High Flatts. It is one of the many triumphs of the authors that they have been able to provide so many compelling vignettes of Friends; it is another that they have led us so lucidly (and painlessly) through the complex ramifications of the families which substantially made up the meetings — families which understandably but confusingly tended to adopt in every generation and in every branch the same limited range of Christian names.

Inevitably, in small and isolated meetings such as these, meeting relationships and family relationships are inextricably interwoven. The woman Friend who was a thorn in the flesh of the meeting was equally an exercise in the home. The problems of the meeting, moreover, were accentuated by its distance from the rest of Pontefract Monthly Meeting. The Quarterly Meeting at York was a weighty but remote assembly, the Yearly Meeting at London, yet more weighty, was vastly more remote.

'The intent and design of our annual assemblies, in their first constitution' runs the Yearly Meeting Epistle of 1718, *'were for a great and weighty oversight and Christian care of the affairs of the churches pertaining to our holy profession and Christian communion.'* This oversight was expressed, in large measure, through the visits of Friends travelling in the ministry. David Blamires, in his 'A History of Quakerism in Liversedge and Scholes' (1973), the story of another Yorkshire meeting of comparable remoteness, is able to show from a list kept by Mary Crosland that no less than forty-three ministering Friends visited Liversedge meeting between 1741 and 1757, coming from York and Kendal, Gloucester and Ipswich, Ireland and Pennsylvania. These women and men came not only with the ministry of the word but with the ministry of the family visit, the sharing of news in days long before The Friend, and the broader experience which so often enabled local Friends to see their problems in perspective.

From the smallest and remotest of meetings (Wooldale and High Flatts among them) Friends were raised up with a gift in the ministry — a gift exercised not only in their own meetings but very often, under a compelling personal concern tested in the corporate life of the Monthly Meeting, in journeys (often lengthened and arduous) to other parts of Great Britain and beyond the sea. Ministering Friends returned home to the smallest and the most isolated of meetings bringing glimpses of the life and the thought and practices of other Friends in other places.

And what of Yearly Meeting's *'great and weighty oversight'* expressed in the counsel of minute or epistle — counsel codified in 1738 (at the instance of Yorkshire Quarterly Meeting) in *'Christian and brotherly advises'* and subsequently in the printed editions of the Book of Extracts? It is perhaps safe to say that, on any subject from *'Covetousness'* through *'Love and Unity'* to *'Tithes'*, if Yearly Meeting advised against it then a lot of Friends were doing it; and if Yearly Meeting counselled it, then a lot of Friends were not doing it. Otherwise, why bother to issue minutes on the subject? David J. Hall, fifteen years ago, tabulated for us the advices Yearly Meeting felt constrained to make between 1738 and 1861. One of our needs now is to understand what were the deficiencies in the Quarterly Meeting answers to the queries that demonstrated the need for Yearly Meeting's counsel — or, very often, renewed counsel. And, behind the Quarterly Meeting's summary answers, which were the deficient Monthly Meetings? And, behind the Monthly Meetings answers, who, just who, were there recalcitrant Friends?

It is over sixty-five years since the publication of Rufus Jones' two-volume 'Later Periods of

Quakerism'. It was a monumental and impressive labour but, unlike the two William Charles Braithwaite volumes, 'The Beginnings of Quakerism' and 'The Second Period of Quakerism', it is not susceptible to a straight reprint with additional notes. It must stand as a classic of its time, noteworthy for some magnificent insights and for its memorable passages, such as that on the character of eldership (pp.125-7). But it must be replaced in due time by a series of volumes. And before they can be written we need a whole host of detailed studies, some of which are now completed or in prospect, on a wide range of aspects of Quaker life in the eighteenth and nineteenth centuries.

Amongst the detailed studies we need are descriptions of the day to day life of local meetings. We have been fortunate that since the Second World War there have been some seventy such studies. But we need more. And too often, alas, supposedly local histories have in fact been local chronicles, relying far too much on copious quotations from Besse's Sufferings and random uncoordinated extracts from Preparative and Monthly Meeting minutes. There may be no harm in this, but it is not enough. It is another of the triumphs of this book that it makes use of so wide a range of source material. In particular, of course, there is the magnificent journal of Joseph Wood, and it is to journals and, perhaps, even more to letters that we must turn if the minutes of meetings for church affairs are to come alive. In journals and letters, above all, we see the triumphs (and the quirks) of individual personality. And it is about the interplay of personality that we need, and in this book rejoice in, *'minutely organized Particulars.'*

Edward H. Milligan
July 1987

PREFACE 1

I have spent all my life associated with Quakerism and in particular Wooldale Meeting. My earliest memories were of being brought into meeting for the final fifteen minutes — we had no childrens meetings then. As I grew older I attended Quaker boarding school in York. From there I went on to finish my education at Leeds University. I returned to take an active part in the life of the meeting. My family have been associated with the meeting for a number of generations. I have been priviliged and excited to see the growth of the meeting from what was essentially a gathering of my own mainly elderly family to the active, vital group that it is today.

Given this background and my general interest in history it was probably inevitable that at some point I should attempt to write a history of the meeting. In fact I began collecting snippets of information about fifteen years ago as I came across them just out of interest. It was not until about three years ago that I decided that I must put pen to paper and record what information I had collected.

At this point my idea of the eventual result was of a short booklet dealing mainly with the history of the building. Never having attempted to do anything like this before, and not really knowing the best way to go about it, nothing much happened for a time other than further research. It was then that my co-author, John, appeared at Wooldale and within a few months he had joined the Society. We found we shared a common interest in history and one evening when visiting him and his wife, Julie, we went through all the research I had previously done. John and I then decided to cooperate on the project. Then started a fairly intensive eighteen months of research and writing. It soon became obvious that the book could not be limited to Wooldale and must include High Flatts and associated meetings because of their close inter-connections.

I was able to contribute my inherited knowledge of Quaker organization: knowing where to go, who to ask, what documents to consult. John brought his enthusiasm and academic knowledge of history and writing to the book, which ensured that it turned out in this format. As well as thoroughly enjoying being a part of the project I have learned a tremendous amount about both Quaker and local history. I was delighted to find that some of my ancestors included Gervas Kay of Fulstone and Meal Hill and Thomas Ellis of Wooldale. They were amongst the earliest convinced Friends in the locality. Two things that I was completely unprepared to discover were the numbers and influence of the *'Plain Country Friends'* on this small rural area over the years.

DAVID BOWER (1987)

PREFACE 2

'Time and chance govern all' wrote the author of the Book of Ecclesiastes (Ch. 9:11) and it has sometimes seemed as though time and chance were responsible for directing my steps to Wooldale on an unusually warm and sunny Spring evening in 1985. More often I consider the words of Proverbs Ch.20:24 to be more appropriate since it seemed at the time that I could not really account for a reason for being there that particular evening beyond having a strong desire to see where the old meeting house was situated. Standing in the tranquil grounds, knowing very little about Quakerism, I found myself realizing I needed to return on the Sunday to attend a Meeting for Worship. I would like to think that the idea of writing this book began then during that first brief visit. In a sense, I suppose, that it did: for my presence there had reasons that I had long ago sought to conceal in the recesses of the mind and had almost managed to forget. I had neglected a special relationship and like the prodigal had come to a sense of my failings. That following Sunday proved to be a home-coming. Amongst the Quakers of Wooldale I found a worshipping community and a personal spiritual renewal which in a few short months led me to make a clear committment to the Religious Society of Friends.

It also now seems somehow quite inevitable that with my professional background as a historian I should find myself drawn to learning something of the past history of the meeting and the people who had formed this worshipping community over so many generations. In David Bower I found not only a kindred spirit to share my enthusiasm and curiosity about the past but a rather special friendship and working relationship. This rapport and unity of purpose set us firmly on reconstructing a picture of people seeking to walk more closely with God.

Researching the past is like trying to find the pieces of a jigsaw puzzle, scattered by careless children in the most unexpected places, whilst having only a vague idea of the complete picture and even less idea of the size of the canvas and the number of pieces involved. All too often those pieces that are recovered result in a far from complete picture: some portions are re-assembled in detail and others are so hopelessly lost that we are left with gaping blanks in the recreation of this canvas of the past. At the end of the day the final result can never be satisfying or conclusive. In the case of 'Plain Country Friends', the size and the detail of the canvas has proved to be so intimidatingly large that portions will need to be left to a follow-up work. There still remains much that needs to be recorded about the Quakers of this area. Their contribution to this locality has been neglected too long by local historians. Even as I write the true impact and influence of the Religious Society of Friends generally is beginning to emerge in the light of modern historical scholarship.

Having now expended considerable time and energy reliving the past I am frequently made mindful in our local Quaker gatherings how the past and the present are a dynamic and living continuum. Friends still meet in fellowship as a worshipping community and they continue, even with their individual human frailties, to strive to live in that life which expresses their love of God and their neighbours.

'Whatever is has already been, and what will be has been before' (Ecclesiastes Ch. 3:15) now seems so appropriate to me when I consider the past. I believe that in helping to write this book I have come to understand that, *'there is nothing new under the sun.'*

JOHN KNIGHT (1987)

PREFACE TO SECOND IMPRESSION

Six years after publishing this book we find ourselves in the surprising position of preparing for a second print-run. The 850 copies produced in 1987 have all sold. Copies have been sent to many parts of the world. There has been tremendous interest in the contents of the book, in particular from family historians. Thus Wooldale PM have decided to commission a further 500 copies to be printed to satisfy the continuing demand and interest.

This is not a second edition, as the original text has been left unaltered, but it is worth drawing readers' attention to some salient points.

The first is to correct the statement on page 152 concerning the site of the former meeting house and burial ground at Lumbroyd. Subsequent research has shown that the site was never sold and in fact remains the property of Friends to this day. (During 1991 memorial stones were erected at both Lumbroyd and at Hoyland Swaine (see page 148) to commemorate these former Quaker sites).

Secondly readers may be interested in some research undertaken into the location of graves at Wooldale burial ground. This was carried out, by dowsing, during 1990 by some Wooldale Friends assisted by a member of the British Society of Dowsers. The research indicated that, as had been deduced by the authors (see page 144), there was a section in the north of the graveyard (part of the 1914 addition) that was still unoccupied. As stated in this book the rest of the graveyard is full, the dowsers confirmed this. However there were other discoveries that were unexpected. They found that there were burials underneath the meeting house, the drive, the gateway and part of the road, Pell Lane. The earliest date of internment was 1623 (prior to Quakerism). Also the original entrance was dowsed to be a set of steps leading up from Pell Lane to the east side of the meeting house. A site plan was drawn up at the conclusion of the research showing the findings. One copy is lodged with Wooldale PM clerk and a second copy with MM archives at Ackworth School. All this research was undertaken by dowsing both on site and from a plan. There has been no attempt to prove the findings by either documentary or archaeological evidence. (Perhaps a project for the future?).

Thirdly it should be noted that all but the most recent records, that were formerly kept at Ackworth School, have been transferred to the County Records Office in Wakefield. They are freely available for public research.

New source material has been brought to our attention by people who have read the book. This has included much genealogical information and also extracts from personal diaries. For example the diary of John Pickford of Ingbirchworth, kept between 1797 and 1802. This is a unique collection of the thoughts and events of a Friend's religious life within the Society of Friends, during the later part of the eighteenth century.

In conclusion Wooldale PM would like to acknowledge the financial assistance it has received in enabling it to produce this second impression. A number of Quaker trusts have given generous grants. Particular mention should go to The Barnsley Friends Adult School Trust Fund whose continuing support and generosity have been crucial. Thanks should also go to High Flatts PM for their encouragement and financial support.

It is hoped that for years to come the book will continue to stimulate interest in not only Quakers of the past, but also in the activities and people of the Society of Friends of today and tomorrow.

DAVID BOWER (1993)

INTRODUCTION

This is a history of the Religious Society of Friends (Quakers), from 1651 to the present, encompassing an area that is today represented by the meetings of Wooldale and High Flatts. It also covers the former meetings of Shepley Lane Head and Lumbroyd (between Midhope and Penistone) along with meetings that were held in private houses throughout the area.

Quakers are a religous body within the Christian fold. They have no clergy, no creeds, no sacraments and no consecrated buildings. They seek for, *'that of God in everyone.'* They worship together in silent waiting upon God, out of which ministry may arise from anyone present. Their testimonies, including those on peace, social injustice and conduct in business, are guiding influences in their daily lives.

It will be helpful at this stage to define the terms used in the text to explain the structure of Quaker meetings:

Recognized Meeting — a local meeting for worship recognized by the MM (e.g. Lumbroyd Meeting). Before 1967 such meetings were known as Particular Meetings save for smaller ones known as Allowed Meetings.

PM (Preparative Meeting) — a recognized meeting holding business meetings (e.g. High Flatts PM).

MM (Monthly Meeting) — a number of PM's grouped in a geographical area meeting together for business. (e.g. Pontefract MM).

QM (Quarterly Meeting) — the grouping of a number of MM's meeting for business (e.g. Yorkshire QM). The name was changed to GM (General Meeting) in 1967.

YM (Yearly Meeting) — the national grouping of Friends (e.g. London YM).

Until 1792 High Flatts PM included the various recognized meetings and private houses used as places of worship that existed in the area prior to that date. These were: High Flatts, Wooldale, Shepley Lane Head, Lumbroyd, Judd Field, Midhope, Sheephouse, Lockwood and Longroyd Bridge. In 1792 Wooldale became a PM in its own right within Pontefract MM and Paddock (Huddersfield) a PM within Brighouse MM in 1794. Lumbroyd remained a part of High Flatts PM and the other meetings mentioned no longer existed. The records of all the meetings mentioned and the individual Friends associated with them are so interwoven and inextricably linked that they form part of the same story, hence the definition of the area covered. The single exception to this is Paddock Meeting whose story after 1794 is linked with Brighouse MM and which, except for its origins, has not been covered in this work.

It is hoped that the book will give some idea of the overall history of ordinary rural Quakers illustrated by the specific stories of the meetings and individuals in our immediate locality. The book commences with sections dealing with the earliest days when Quakerism came to the area, the times of persecution and the influence of one particular family in this period. The story of the eighteenth and early nineteenth century is illustrated by sections based on the various Quaker 'disciplines' that preoccupied the lives and conduct of Friends. Biographical 'cameos' concerning individual Friends of note supplement this period. The latter part of the nineteenth and the present century are dealt with in a framework of separate sections that span the years under a variety of headings including occupations, education, the peace testimony, poor relief and charities. Families connected with the local meetings through succeeding generations are also covered. The various places used for meetings throughout the 330 years are then covered in considerable detail in 'Bricks & Mortar'.

In addition to the main text there are comprehensive appendices which might prove to be of further interest. These appendices contain, amongst other items, one of the most detailed surviving lists of visiting Friends to any group of meetings, personal testimonies, accounts and subscriptions relating to building and renovation work undertaken in connection with the meeting houses, as well as sundry lists pertaining to membership.

All original quotations are reproduced as they appear including the 'thorn' rendering of yt., ym. and ye, as well as abbreviations such as Mg. (Meeting) and Mo. (Month). The system of dating employed follows the Quaker pattern of numbering months and readers should refer to Appendix [1] for dates prior to 1752 when calendar changes were made.

QUAKER DAWN

The backdrop to the early part of our local history is of a country in the midst of political, economic and religious crises. In brief outline the seventeenth century saw the installation of the Stuart dynasty with the cornonation of James I. A bitter civil war waged between King Charles I and Parliament ending in his execution and followed by the establishment of Cromwell's puritan Commonwealth. Then came the restoration of the monarchy with the return of Charles II and finally William and Mary's acceptance of the Crown after the 'Glorious Revolution'.

In religious thinking there was still tremendous dissatisfaction with the corruptions of the Established Church which had first manifested itself in the previous century. The organization, doctrines and forms of worship were under severe criticism from many dissenting groups such as the Presbyterians, Baptists, and Independents (Congregationalists). George Fox's arrival on the scene during the 1640's and 1650's saw a formidable preacher of stature and intense spiritual conviction. He found many like minded people, of whom the Seekers are perhaps best known, already practising along the lines that he was advocating, eager to listen and ready to join him.

It has not proved possible to establish with any certitude or accuracy when the earliest convincements took place in this area. George Fox is known to have visited Yorkshire in 1651.

'Then passing into Yorkshire I preached repentance, through Doncaster and several other places, and then came to Balby; where Richard Farnsworth was convinced and several others. So I passed through the countries to several places, preaching repentance and the word of life to them, and went into the country about Wakefield where James Nayler lived, where he and Thomas Goodaire and William Dewsbury and many more were convinced.' (1)

It is conceivable that on his way from Balby to Wakefield George Fox may have passed through Midhope and High Flatts and made converts. It is equally conceivable, given the proximity of Wakefield, that some of the earliest local convincements might have taken place on his visit there. The probability, however, is that local convincements happened after 1651 and 1652. It is also highly likely that those who were amongst the very earliest to become converts to Quakerism became convinced as a direct result of the preaching of men like William Dewsbury, Richard Farnsworth, Thomas Aldam, Thomas Goodaire and James Nayler. The close relationship between William Dewsbury and Henry Jackson would seem to realistically suggest such a possibility. (See 'Henry Jackson II').

A large number of early local Friends from the 1650's can be named: Henry Jackson of Meal Hill, Richard Battye, Thomas Ellis and Thomas Roberts of Wooldale, Gervas Kay of Fulstone, Joshua Marsden of Shepley, John and Henry Dickinson of High Flatts, John Turner, Richard Priest and Thomas Crowder of Denby, John Swift and Ather Brooksbank of Gunthwaite, John Blackley of Gunthwaite Hall, Amor Moxon of Hoyland Swaine, William Wordsworth of Penistone, John Woodhouse of Midhope Hall, Joseph Hinchcliffe and Ralph Sanderson of Upper Midhope, Jonathan West of Oakes (nr. Midhope), Henry Dickinson of Sheephouse and Thomas Crossley of Hunchill. The detailed circumstances surrounding their convincements are purely conjectural as no written accounts appear to be extant. It is only by comparing births, deaths and marriages in Church records with similar early Quaker records that it has been possible to identify some approximate dates of convincement.

According to Kirkburton Parish Registers Thomas Ellis of Wooldale was married in 1653. Neither his eldest son, Thomas (b.1654) nor Simeon (b.1656) are mentioned as being born or baptized. Details of their births are recorded solely in Quaker registers. It is therefore a reasonable assumption that Thomas Ellis became a Friend sometime between his marriage in 1653 and the birth of his eldest son, Thomas, in the 3rd month 1654. Likewise Thomas Roberts of Wooldale who married Dorothy Roebuck on the 12th of the 3rd month 1656 and became convinced before the birth of their first son, Joshua, in the 10th month 1657. Gervas Kay of Fulstone married Sarah Thewlis in a civil ceremony conducted by Sir John Saville in the 9th month 1654. Their first two children, Mary (b.1655) and John (b.1656), are recorded in Parish records as being baptized but their subsequent children continuing with Josiah (b.1658) are not mentioned. Gervas and Sarah Kays convincements can thus be placed sometime between 1656 and 1658. Applying the same form of analysis to Joshua Marsden of Shepley we can date his convincement as occuring after the birth of his daughter Elizabeth (b.1658) and Martha (b.1661). Interesting though such studies are they can be misleading for they take no account of those Friends who may have been married for some years and whose children were somewhat older than baptismal age. Nor is there any allowance for those who were single during this period and married later, like Henry Jackson, or who remained single. Therefore, without firmer and more positive evidence and employing the above analysis of marriages and births, it would appear that in the vicinity of Wooldale the earliest convinced Quaker could have been Thomas Ellis sometime in 1653 or 1654. There are, however, some unsubstantiated reasons to suggest that he was not alone and that Henry Jackson (II) of nearby Meal Hill may also have been convinced at about this time.

An essential requirement of these earliest Friends would have been places where they could meet together and share their particular form of worship. These needed to be not only venues for the sharing of religious experiences but also places where there could be a social and supportive contact between Friends. The more remote and unlikely a building that could be used the better. Up until the Act of Toleration (1689) there would be the constant threat of the authorities descending on these 'illegal' meetings and causing suffering upon those taking part. Thus, before 1689, there were very few purpose built meeting houses: the homes and barns of Friends being the most common meeting places. The need for a place to bury their dead was more pressing and often resulted in burial grounds being established many years before meeting houses. Often Friends would meet, in the open air, on these plots of land to hold their meetings for worship.

Locally, this pattern of meeting place development can be traced. Many of the original buildings and plots of land have now been identified. The sections at the end of the narrative part of this book, under the heading 'Bricks and Mortar', detail the establishment and growth of the buildings.

(1) JGF p.73.

Early Persecutions

Whilst still in its infancy Quakerism and its adherents were persecuted for their beliefs by various post-Restoration Acts of Parliament such as the Conventicle Acts and the 'Five Mile' Act. The Conventicle Acts were introduced to prevent Quaker and other religious dissenters from convening their meetings for worship. The 'Five Mile Act' attempted to prevent 'ministers' either preaching, living, or earning a livelihood within five miles of any parliamentary borough unless they had sworn an oath never to try to change the government, Church or state. Punishable offences under these and more specific Acts like the Quaker Act included; the refusal to swear the Oath of Allegiance, holding religious meetings not conforming with the Established Church, refusal to pay Church tithes and being absent from Church services. Punishments included fines, confiscations of property, imprisonments and transportation.

Local Quakers may have been persecuted during the Commonwealth period but no records of such persecutions have yet come to light. The earliest specific examples of the sufferings undergone by local Friends can be traced to 1660 when Richard Batty, Thomas Ellis and Thomas Roberts, all of Holmfirth, along with Henry Jackson, were imprisoned in York for refusing to take the Oath of Allegiance and for holding meetings. The same three were again imprisoned in York in 1661 for the very same offences. These three Friends appeared to be prime targets of the authorities as their names are frequently to be found in the lists of of sufferings. In 1665 along with Joshua Marsden of Shepley they spent twelve weeks in York prison for refusing to swear the Oath of Allegiance. Then again in 1666 we read of them being sent to prison for ten days for *'refusing to pay towards ye Repair of Steeple-house.'* The local priest was John Briggs who sued many Friends for the non-payment of tithes and appeared to be particularly active in this capacity. (1) (See also 'Tithes and Sufferings'). There are a number of instances recorded of meetings being broken up in the locality about this time. The following Friends were imprisoned for three weeks in 1660 for being at a meeting: John Moxon (or Mogson) of Hoyland Swaine, Richard Priest of Denby, William Wordsworth of Penistone, Joseph Blackley of Gunthwaite, John Marsden of Denby and

Joseph Clark of Cathill. (2) These raids on meetings appear to have been sporadic as Joseph Besse records in his, 'Collection of the Sufferings of the People called Quakers'. After discharge of these prisoners early in 1661 meetings were able to continue in peace for some months. Reading through the sufferings of these troubled times it seems that one's hopes of being left in peace remained largely in the hands of local Justices or Informers. William Thornaby, for example, carried out a very concentrated campaign in 1670-71. This was in the North Riding of Yorkshire against the Quakers principally for his own personal gain. The amount of fines raised upon his information in this fourteen month period amounted to £1999 5s 0d.

The number of fines and other sufferings imposed on our area is small by comparison. This must in part be due to its remoteness but perhaps also to the fact that the local population appears to have been fairly sympathetic to non-conformist sects as witnessed by the strength of the Presbyterians, Baptists and (later) Methodists in this region. However, the sufferings that were caused, in many cases, were of such a nature that livelihoods of whole families could be threatened as that of the Ellis family was in 1665:

'Thomas Ellis of Wooldale taken from a meeting to Sessions at Wakefield, both imprisoned 6 months & fined goods worth £9 10s 0d, including 2 pieces of cloth and tools.
Note. Is not there the fruits of the Devill & Satan who is a destroyer, & did not these goo about to destroy him & his family, in takeing away his shears, his presse & appurtences so that he was disabled to follow his calling to gitt a livelihood for himself & his family, now thus to destroy him. Oh Righteous God Take thee notice of these things.' (3)

Another family to suffer were the Kays of Meal Hill. In 1681 Gervas Kay had two pewter dishes worth 5s 6d confiscated against a fine of 3s 0d imposed upon his wife for not attending Church. This was collected by *'Daniel Lindley and Willm. Littlewood...Officers in Holmfirth.'* At this time Gervas Kay had been in prison for seven years *'for 3s 6d Demanded by Jos. Briggs parish priest.'* At the same time his son John Kay had cloth worth 2s 6d confiscated and another son, Josiah Kay, wool worth 4s 0d. (4)

However Friends were not always the complete losers as sometimes those who caused the sufferings appeared to meet their just ends! The case of William Downing (d.1670) of Midhope in 1664 illustrates this:

'William Downing of Midduphall was also fined £5 and had two Cows taken away worth £8. The Bayliff, a common Informer, who made this Distress (by Name Thomas Wildsmith) boasted that he would live upon the Quakers three years, and raise his Fortune by them. Accordingly he procured their Imprisonment, spoiled their Goods, and drove away their Cattle unmercifully; but in the Midst of his Career he was cut off by an untimely Death, being run through the Body with a rapier by an Attorney of Barnsley. Thus fell a violent Persecutor, in so remarkable a Manner, that his Fellow-Informer took it as a Warning, and said, He would never meddle with the Quakers Goods.' (5)

Terms of imprisonment varied and could be as short as a few days. In other cases terms of imprisonment could last for a number of years as for these Friends in 1684 who had refused to swear the Oath of Allegiance:

'On the 29th of December this Year were remaining Prisoners, Joshua Green of Denby...who together with Mathew Burdett of Nether-Denby had been committed above two Years...' (6)

The story continues that Matthew Burdett finally took the Oath and was set free. Joshua Green remained in prison for a longer time. One of the other laws that Quakers fell foul of was being absent from *'National Worship.'* At the Rotherham Sessions in 1683 John Firth became a victim and had goods confiscated to meet his fine:

'From the said John Firth, five Pieces of Kersey, Wood, Bedding, Hay, Corn and Household Goods, to the Value of £29 10s. They turned the said John Firth out of Doors and beat one of his servants unmercifully, for attempting to remove his own Chest of Clothes.' (7)

Goods were also taken in kind when Friends refused to pay tithes. John Crowder of Denby suffered particularly badly as between 1675 and 1683 he had goods taken on thirteen occasions valuing in total £6 0s 10.5d. He was liable to pay the tithe gathers of both Emley and Hoyland. John Crowder was a farmer and usually oats, wheat or barley were the goods distrained. (See also 'Tithes & Sufferings').

In 1689 the Act of Toleration was passed which, although it gave no relief from tithes, greatly reduced the persecution suffered by Quakers. It allowed dissenting worship. By the Affirmation Act (1696) Friends were able to make affirmations instead of swearing an oath. From this time onwards the number of public meeting houses being licenced and built rose dramatically.

(1) Morehouse
(2) Yorkshire QM Sufferings Vol.I Pt.I (1651-95)
(3) Thistlethwaite p.34 (quoted)
(4) Ibid (1)
(5) Besse's Sufferings p.109
(6) Ibid p.109
(7) Ibid p.152-3

The Jackson Family

The Jackson family was amongst the most influential, long established and prominent families in the Graveship of Holme. The social structure of the day, excluding the nobility and titled ranks, can be broadly divided into four groups: the gentry, the yeomanry and merchants, the craftsmen and the rural and urban poor (husbandmen, wage earners and the destitute). The Jacksons can be classed as very wealthy yeomen or minor gentry whose position in local society enabled them to wield considerable influence. It was largely due to their influence that Quakerism took such an early and strong hold on many of the local populace.

The family seat was at Meal Hill in the township of Hepworth and it was this same family that gave its name to the village of Jackson Bridge. They built the bridge to facilitate easier travel between their properties at Meal Hill and Totties. Humphrey Jackson, who married Margaret Crosland of Cartworth in 1591, was the father of Henry Jackson I (1593-1667) with whom this Quaker history must begin. Henry I was the father of Henry II (1633-1710) and the grandfather of Henry III (1680-1727). (1) Each was to play their part in bringing and rooting the Quaker message to these Pennine communities.

Henry Jackson I (1593-1667)

Henry Jackson married Elizabeth Tyas, the daughter of George Tyas and the widow of Oliver Roberts of Wooldale. They had two children: Henry II and Elizabeth. The Kirkburton Parish Registers record the marriage *'by licence'* of his daughter Elizabeth to Jarvis Leek, gentleman of Horbury, in 1662. As early as 1632 Henry Jackson, James Genn and Joshua Earnshaw (whose families all joined the ranks of religious dissent), were in dispute with John Binns the curate of Holmfirth Chapel. (2) The Chapel had just been enlarged and they refused to pay a levy based upon the number of seats towards the curate's stipend. The dispute dragged on till 1639 when Henry Jackson was forced to pay fifty seven shillings in arrears to John Binns by the Commission under the great Seal of England. He was also among the 128 local persons in this period who signed a petition to have the Chapel at Holmfirth *'severed, and divided from the said Churches (Kirkburton & Almondbury), and be made a parish church.'* There were many in the district who believed that they had been *'compelled and oppressed'* and made to *'pay all such assessments as the Churchwardens of Kirkburton and Almonburie have been pleased to impose upon them.'* (3) Considering his radical attitudes it seems strange that when the Civil War broke out, instead of siding with many of the local people who were religious dissenters, disatisfied with the Establishment and ardently pro-Parliamentarian, Henry Jackson identified himself with the Royalist cause. He became a cornet, the lowest rank of commissioned officer in a cavalry troop, who carried the standard in Captain Joshua Castle's Troop in the service of King Charles I. (4) This body of men served under the command of Sir Francis Mackworth and later under Col. Thompson principally in the North. (5) Nothing is known about this wartime period of his life. It is almost certainly the case that Henry Jackson did not suffer the sequestration of his estate, as did some Royalists at the end of the Civil War, for his son Henry inherited them upon his death.

There can be little doubting that Henry Jackson was a man of considerable local importance. He served in a variety of capacities in the Wakefield Manor Court before and after the Civil War. In 1639 he served the Leet Court as a juror. He is recorded as one of the jurors *'on the panel of the Lord of the Manor'* of Wakefield on the 16 February 1665 as well as a leet juror for the Manor *'court leet'* held a year earlier. (6) Henry Jackson is described as a gentleman. So is his step-son, Oliver Roberts. In the period 1664-1665 he is also cited as a *'lord's tenant,'* qualifying for this position as a copyholder of land, on numerous occasions. This points conclusively to his very extensive holdings since the number of conveyances he had to witness were considerable. As he had to swear an oath to perform the various duties it is clear that he did not become a Quaker. In fact, at one stage of his life, Henry Jackson actively disapproved of his son's religious convictions. In the records of Yorkshire Sufferings the following entry appears:

'Henry Jackson of Mealhill was put out of his fathers house because he Denyed to Goo to heare ye Nationall priests; And afterwards in ye year 1660 he was taken by two Souldjers & Carried before one called Justice Kay & because he Refused to Swear in obedience to Christs Comands he was sent to Yorke Castle, & there kept prisoner 20 weeks.' (7)

However, it is interesting to note that by the time of his death his son had been a Quaker for at least seven years and had suffered a number of terms of imprisonment for his beliefs yet his father never disinherited him. Having regard to Henry Jackson I's early stance for local religious freedom it is conceivable that there was some sympathy with his son. This only became a problem when Henry II made it obvious to his father that he was quite prepared to defy the law of the land and take whatever consequences resulted. This would have put the older man in a very difficult position. He had now become a respected figure in the locality, holding legal offices. This was probably the only course of action left to him particularly considering his advanced years. A few years later Henry Jackson died at the age of 74 and was *'buried att Chapell the VIth day'* of May 1667 in Holmfirth.

(1) Clay & QBBREG1.
(2) Morehouse p.179. He states that Henry Genn was 'connected with the Society of Friends.' The authors have found no evidence to confirm this statement during their research.
(3) Morehouse p.156-159. Also KPR Vol.1 for full list of 128 petitioners. Those Named include Thomas Roberts, Thomas Ellis, Richard Batty and John Firth.
(4) Morehouse p.177. A Cornet was the lowest rank of cavalry officer corresponding to the modern day rank of 2nd Lieutenant. Joshua Castell (b.1596) was the son of Godfrey Castell of Cartworth in the Graveship of Holme.
(5) Sgt. Major-General Sir Francis Mackworth was a professional soldier who commanded 'seven divisions of Newcastle's foot at Marston Moor' in 1644.
(6) 'Wakefield Court Rolls' for 1639-1640 p.107 & p.114-118. Also for the period 1664-1665 p.42, p.146-150, p.200-202, p.204/5. YAS
(7) Yorkshire QM Sufferings Vol.I Pt.I (1651-95)

Henry Jackson II (1633-1710)

Henry Jackson lived his childhood through the turbulent times of the Civil War witnessing at close quarters the horrors of warfare. In 1643 the Earl of Newcastle, who was garrisoned at Wakefield with a large army, entered Holmfirth with five regiments of infantry, three of cavalry and two of dragoons. They burnt thirty houses, killed, took prisoners and plundered goods from the township. Detachments of his troops were also sent into the parishes of Almondbury, Kirkburton and Penistone in order to quell the strong support given by the local population to the Parliamentary cause. (1) Henry Jackson would also have been aware of the religious controversies that then raged. Given these circumstances it is not surprising that as a young man he became convinced by the preaching of George Fox and the early Quaker leaders. It is also highly likely that he was in some way acquainted with George Fox who is known to have first travelled through Yorkshire in 1651-1652.

Henry Jackson was among the *'First Publishers of Truth'* in Yorkshire. He became a personal friend of William Dewsbury of Wakefield, who had been convinced by Fox in 1651 and was one of the earliest leaders of the movement. Dewsbury, described as *'one of the sweetest and wisest of the early Quakers,'* and Jackson spent long terms of imprisonment together. (2)

In these early years many Friends suffered persecution for their beliefs. Henry Jackson spent a number of years in prison and the records left from these experiences are an insight into his character and the conditions surrounding him. In 1660 he was one of 535, along with Richard Batty, Thomas Ellis and Thomas Roberts of Holmfirth, imprisoned in York Castle, *'for the cause of meeting together and for refusing to take the Oath of Allegiance'* (3) At the Assizes held in 1661 all were released except 27 of the most prominent Friends. These 27 included Henry Jackson and William Dewsbury. Later, in 1661-2, he was sent to Newgate Prison in London, once again with William Dewsbury. They were committed there by the Lord Mayor, Richard Brown, who was particularly anti-Quaker and caused many to suffer for their beliefs. (4) It was during this period of incarceration that twenty prisoners died including Richard Hubberthorne and Edward Burrough, two of the most prominent of that band known as 'the Valiant Sixty'. Considering *'the throng was so great, and the air so vitiated'* in Newgate Henry Jackson's physical capacity to survive such an ordeal must have been considerable.

It was common practice for Friends, when in prison, to write to other Friends to exhort them to keep faith with their testimony. As many of the leaders were frequently imprisoned in different parts of the country it must have been very demoralizing for Friends still at liberty to continue without inspired leadership. Copies of two such letters written by Henry Jackson during his imprisonment illustrate his dedication and faith in helping to keep the Quaker testimony alive. The first is dated the 12th of the 9th month 1661:

'To Friends and Bretheren The Prisoners in York Castle...and dearly doth greet you my dear Friends and fellow Sufferers...that they which suffer with him (Christ Jesus) shal Reigne with him...' (5)

The second dated, the 5th of the 1st month 1662, is in a similar vein:

'Dear Lambs be diligent in meeting together to wait upon the Lord, that his living presence you may feel in all your holy Assemblies and the operation of his Spirit, power and life in your hearts... Deare William Dewsbury my endeared companion and fellow prisoner...life and peace doth greet you...' (6)

A letter written by Henry Jackson from Lincoln Castle, dated the 28th of the 5th month 1663, typical of many such letters written by imprisoned Friends, is prefaced: *'...where I am a prisoner for ye testimony of Christ Jesus & for keeping his commandments.'* (7) Upon his release from Lincoln Henry Jackson travelled to Warwick. His aim was to visit his friend William Dewsbury who was confined in prison once again. Dewsbury had been imprisoned with others for giving thanks before supper at an inn. The authorities, seeking any kind of an excuse to arrest him, treated this as a form of preaching at a Conventicle. Henry Jackson was also clearly a target. Whilst staying at a Friends house in Warwick he was almost immediately arrested for being at an unlawful meeting and found himself in gaol with Dewsbury. The date of Henry Jackson's imprisonment in Warwick has been wrongly recorded in Besse's work which states that it started in 1661: the correct date being 1663. (8) The case proceeded in the following way:

'After some Time of Confinement they were sent to a Justice at an Inn, who, for their refusing to Swear, sent them to Prison as under Sentence of Premurie...though never legally tried or convicted.' (9)

It was during this period that he wrote 'A Visitation of Love to the Tender Plants of Gods Vineyard'. This was addressed to the Friends in southern counties including: Essex, Suffolk, Norfolk and Kent. He had been planning a visit to these Friends *'with my dear and honourable Brother and companion in the Lord, W.D. (William Dewsbury).'*

Incarcerated at Warwick it was nearly three years before Henry Jackson was able to petition the King in 1666 about his release. In the petition he described in detail his unlawful arrest and the subsequent attempts to ensnare him by requiring him to take the Oath of Allegiance. He further added that he was not formerly indicted at the Sessions and could therefore not enter a plea of innocence. According to the current law he should not have been kept unjustly in prison for longer than three months. In his petition he mentioned his loyalty to the King and repudiated the authority of the Pope. Throughout this petition Henry Jackson also pleads the case of other Friends who were imprisoned with him. There is one striking paragraph that leaves a vivid description of the conditions which he and and others experienced inside Northgate Street gaol in Warwick:

'In which time of imprissonmt great hath been the cruelty inflicted upon mee (& others of my friends here) by being thronged up in Stincking roomes & somtimes in one roome above twenty of us, where we could not all ly downe at once, & no straw allowed us to ly upon; Except wee would pay 2s 6d for one Bolting, wch. was sould to ye felons for 2d; And no maner of victuals allowed to bee brought to us Except we would pay 6d for one penny Loafe of bread, & as much for a quart of milke, & 3d for a quart of water, &c. Which unreasonable rates wee was not willing to pay & our friends & relations was not oney kept from us, but what they brought to minister to our necessityes, was taken from them, & given to other prissonrs & this was continued for 4 to 5 days togeither at one time, insomuch yt moderate people in ye towne (although not of our iudgmt) heareing of this cruelty inflicted upon us, was stirred up in tenderness to throw bread over a house top, into the Dungeon Court, for our prsent reliefe, to ye frustrateing of the Exspectation of our cruell opprssors. Our Beddcloathes also & other goods & necessaryes was taken away from us, & lockt up by ye Gaoler, & mee & others hee struck wth. his Staffe, & naked staunchion, & severall times hath chaynd mee wth fetters to another man, & lockt mee to a Post, & many more inhuman & seldome heard of crueltyes & incivillityes hath hee inflicted upon mee, & others of my friends (& all this for serving ye lord & keepeing of Christs comand). And yet nevertheless, I do not hereby seeke revenge against him, nor ye worst of my persecutors but rather yt they may repent, & turne to ye Lord yt hee may forgive them. Onely its upon heart at this time to spread it before the King, that hee may not be altogeither ignorant of ye multiplyed sufferings & crueltyes inflict upon many honest inocent & peaceable Subjcts. & yt for no evill doeing as aforesayd.' (10)

(During this period prisoners were required to pay for the necessities of life including food, fuel and 'chamber rent').

Henry Jackson's wife, Katherine, wrote a note to the King supporting her husband's case. The matter was passed on to Lord Arlington. In 1666 Henry Jackson wrote an address to this nobleman to further clarify his situation. The following quotations are taken from this and help to build up our picture of Henry Jackson's character:

'...I came to this place to vizit my friend & Countreyman...And so mee also they cast into prison...' 'I am a Christian, & Christ Jesus has comanded to Love one another, & to vizitt one another in afflictions & adversity.'
'...I was A Prisoner when I was a Youth, about tenn years of Age, taken by the Kings adversaryes & I never bore armes against the King in all my life, for my Principle is, To live peaceably with all men & to seeke the good peace welfare & prosperity: both of the King & all his subjects.'
'As to ye Pope; his power and suprmacye I do utterly deny & all his adherents.' (11)

The reference to being a prisoner when ten years old clearly refers to the Civil War. We already know that his father was a staunch Royalist serving in the King's army: therefore, the arrest of the son in a pro-Parliamentarian area with other members of the family cannot be surprising. As the Jackson family were Royalists their dissension must have been for purely religious rather than political reasons. This is in contrast to many who became Friends and who had sided with and fought for Parliament, expressing their dissatisfaction with the monarchy.

The results of these various petitions is not revealed. It seems that they fell largely upon deaf ears because Henry Jackson remained in prison until 1672. In that year he was released in the General Pardon for Warwick. (12) According to the extant records he had been a prisoner there for more than seven years.

His life during his years of imprisonment was not without periods of personal happiness. He was married in 1666 to Katherine Cooke, daughter of Charles Cooke of Hatfield, whilst a prisoner. They eventually had eleven children, including two, who died in infancy, whose birth place is recorded as Warwick: Henry (b.1671) and Samuel (b.1673). The notion of being married and having children born in prison may strike readers with disbelief. However, events such as this were far from unusual during this period.

Friends appeared to be subjected to two broad categories of imprisonment. The first of these was close confinement where conditions were appalling as in the above description of Warwick gaol. Secondly, there was also a much more lenient category of imprisonment which many long term prisoners were allowed following periods of close confinement. We hear of William Dewsbury visiting and staying a night with Thomas Salthouse in Ilchester gaol. Also how Dewsbury's grand-daughter, Mary Samm, when only a child of twelve years came and stayed with him, and in fact died there, while he was in Warwick gaol. Of the nineteen years Dewsbury spent in Warwick gaol only four were in close confinement. (13) Thus Quakers were frequently granted varying degrees of 'freedom' whilst theoretically incarcerated. George Fox was allowed out of confinement on more than a few occasions and even managed to continue preaching. Somersetshire QM was allowed, for a number of years, to hold its meetings inside the County Gaol at Ilchester. Friends were permitted to write minutes and other documents, to handle Friends monies, to have visitors and even to leave prison and make visits themselves. (14) Friends of Pontefract MM, jailed in York Castle, are recorded as being allowed to return home 'on parole' to attend to family matters. Many other notable instances are recorded in the annals of Quaker history. Even in these early days of the movement Friends had already managed to prove that they were as good as their word.

There were to be further shorter terms of imprisonment for Henry Jackson after his release from Warwick Gaol usually for *'resorting to unlawful conventicles and absenting himself from church.'* In 1682 he was arrested by Edmund Blackburn and accused at the Wakefield Sessions of being a *'Ring Leader of ye Quakers.'* (15) He was even convicted of riotous assembly at Hoyland Swaine at the Barnsley Sessions in 1684 with twenty others:

'For kneeling down & Calling upon ye name of ye Lord in prayer with Divers friends & other People after ye buriall of ye Corpse of a friend some weeks before ye said Sessions...was fined for a Riot one hundred pounds.'

As well as this crippling fine he was caught in the usual trap of being asked to swear the Oath of Allegiance and was sent to York Castle. (16) This incident was the subject of a letter written by George Fox addressed *'to Friends at York.'* Henry Jackson was amongst the last to be released under the King's General Pardon of March 1686. George Fox pointed out to Friends that the punishment was technically illegal since *'when he was praemunired his estate was the King's estate and £100 is more than the Conventicle Act allows of and it is hard to make a riot out of a burial...'* (17) During one of these spells in York Prison he was forced to lie in a large oven in the Castle yard wall with Richard Robinson as the prison was so full of Friends. (18) His prominence within the Society is again illustrated in two of these later imprisonments in York. In 1682 he was one of the five signatories of a letter to Meeting for Sufferings outlining their sufferings on behalf of the two hundred and forty Friends held prisoner. Then later in 1684 he was one of fourteen signatories, on behalf of two hundred and twenty seven prisoners, to an address to the King stating their plight. (19) He was released from prison for the last time in 1686 under the King's General Pardon of that year.

Throughout those years, spent in different prisons, Henry Jackson continued to try to lead as normal a family life as was possible. His children were born at irregular intervals. Apart from the two sons who died at Warwick five other children never reached adulthood: Hilkiah (b.1674), Hannah (1675-1682), Tabitha (1679-1682), Benjamin (1681-1682) and Tabitha (b.1682). Still preserved at Wooldale Meeting House are the gravestones of Hannah and the first Tabitha who both died of smallpox and of Hilkiah and the second Tabitha. The latter two stones are part of the structure of the building and hidden from view. (See 'Bricks and Mortar — Wooldale Meeting House'). He was a man who loved his children with the deepest affection. On the death of Tabitha in 1684 this grief stricken father wrote a nine page poem mourning his daughter's loss yet being reconciled that she was now *'with the Lord.'* As literature it may possess little grace but its poignant words permit us to be favoured with a precious insight into the personality of Henry Jackson:

'My Tabitha is left me and is gone
Her outward Absence now I may bemone
She was a Child to me lovely and dear
I greatly did desire her Presence here
But in submission to my Fathers Will
For he is worthy to be served still
And to dispose of me and mine forever
....

She with the Lord forever shall remain
And unto us shall not return again
My Care concerning her is now at an End
My Prayer is answered I need not spend
One Minutes Time a Position to prepare
For Her: for that my Lord hath taken Care
And given her a Position far more great
Than earthly Riches or a Princes Seat...' (20)

The children who survived were Elizabeth (b.1668), Elihu (1669-1730), Abel and Henry III. Elizabeth married Gervase Seaton of Blyth in 1693. It may, perhaps, reflect some measure of the esteem and respect that Pontefract MM held Henry Jackson, that the records of the intention of marriage of his daughter to John Seaton's son were recorded in an uncharacteristically elaborate and detailed manner. Later, Elizabeth is named as Alsop in her father's will and so it must be assumed that she was widowed and remarried. Elihu, the eldest son, became a physician. He built Wooldale Hall about 1714 but then removed to Doncaster. Elihu's relationship with his father appears to have been stormy at times as indicated by a dispute over some land settled on his younger brother, Henry III. The eldest son felt aggrieved over this and took the matter to MM for them to mediate upon it in 1703. (21) Little is known about his youngest son, Abel, except that he became a merchant in London. When his wife died the Kirkburton Parish Registers recorded the event: *'Katherine pretended wife of Henry Jackson of Totties buried in the Quaker's burying place the 26th day (June).'* Though the Act of Toleration gave some legal security it did not alter the Church's hostility to the Quakers.

Despite Henry Jackson's frequent absences from home he still managed to find time to be prominent in the affairs of local Friends. He was one of the first Yorkshire Friends to be involved in attending Meeting for Sufferings which began in 1675-6.

'This mtg: hath concluded & agreed that John Whitehead, Tho: Killam, Richard Robinson & Henry Jackson or any 2 of them be in a readiness to Attend friends meeting att London...' (22)

He was also regularly appointed for dealing with important tasks including deciding which meeting places should be registered under the Act of Toleration (1689). (23) He was also involved in several disputes. In the case of Samuel Poole and Thomas Cooper, who were disputing over a debt in 1679, he was actually accused of being a Jesuit by one of the parties. (24) The most serious dispute that involved him was one that broke out at High Flatts in 1708-1709.

Joseph Bayley (Bailey) had by deed of gift conveyed the meeting house and burial ground to Friends in 1701. However, he had imposed some restrictions upon its use. The matter was finally referred to MM who offered their suggestions for the resolution of this problem. Since no further mention was made of the matter it appears to have been concluded satisfactorily.

Henry Jackson also found time to write various letters and addresses pleading the Quaker cause. Two lengthy documents were printed in the form of epistles: 'A Testimony to Truth with an Exhortation of Love' in 1662 and 'A Visitation of Love' in 1663. These were written in prison and were mainly exhortations to other Friends, both in and out of prison, to stand by their Quaker testimonies. In these Henry Jackson urged Friends to *'...not be negligent in the work of the Lord but meet often together to wait upon him in the Spirit...'*

Between 1682-1684 Henry Jackson built Totties Hall and made it the new family seat. Yeoman houses of the size and grandeur of Totties Hall, which Henry Morehouse described as *'a substantial mansion'* having *'the appearance of a manor house,'* are very rare in this part of West Yorkshire and reflect the station of their builder and his family within the local community. (Further details of Totties Hall are supplied in the section on Henry Jackson III). Henry Jackson inherited substantial estates from his father as well as from his half-brother, Oliver Roberts II of Wooldale, who died without issue in 1668. He owned Meal Hill, Totties Hall and possibly Langley Brook near Midhope to the south of Penistone. He lived at all three at different points in his life. His family association with the Midhope area could conceivably date back to the Civil War days when Penistone was a Royalist stronghold. Sir Francis Wortley made the Church at Penistone a Royalist garrison. The high density of early Quaker converts in the area might be explained by the Jackson influence. George Fox records in his journal for 1669 visiting Henry Jackson's (probably at Meal Hill):

'I visited most of the meetings in Yorkshire and came up to the Wolds and Holderness. I passed through the country till I came to Henry Jackson's where I had a great meeting.' (25)

Henry Jackson II died aged 77 in 1710 having lived a full and active life. He was an important figure in local society and had a strong influence on the spread of Quakerism not only in the immediate locality but in other parts of the nation as well. His son Henry was to continue the work of spreading the Quaker testimony.

(1) Morehouse p.21
(2) CFPESofF
(3) Besse's Sufferings Vol.II
(4) Ibid Vol.I
(5) MSS Collection FHL
(6) Ibid
(7) Ibid
(8) 'Letters to William Dewsbury & Others' edited by Henry J. Cadbury.
(9) Ibid (3)
(10) 'Extracts from State Papers relating to Friends 1654-72' edited by Norman Penney
(11) Ibid
(12) Ibid
(13) 'The Life of William Dewsbury' Edward Smith
(14) 'The Somersetshire QM of the S of F 1668-99' edited by Stephen C. Morland
(15) Yorkshire QM Sufferings Vol.1 Pt.1 (1651-1695)
(16) Ibid
(17) Thistlethwaite p.49
(18) 'The First Publishers of Truth' edited by N.Penney
(19) Besse's Sufferings Vol.1
(20) MSS Collection FHL
(21) MMMB 1703
(22) Thistlethwaite p.328.
(23) Ibid
(24) Ibid (4)
(25) JGF

Henry Jackson III (1680-1727)

By the time Henry Jackson had reached his teens the days of persecution were over. Tithes remained as the last instrument of repression and Friends still faced fines and distraints for their non-payment. It must have been very difficult for the young man to follow his father who had been so involved in the harsh realities of the sufferings of early Quakers. However, young Henry did follow in the family tradition and became prominent not only in local Quaker affairs but was also a respected minister and travelling preacher throughout England and Ireland. We have a record of his life from an unknown source:

'Jackson, Henry of Tottys in Wooldale, Yorkshire, was one who yielding obedience to the visitation of Divine love in early life, experienced a growth in grace, until under the preparing hand of his Divine Master, he was fitted for the reception of a gift in the ministry. His labours for the promotion of the gospel were not confined to many parts of England, but in 1723 were extended into Ireland. At Limerick he is said to have had remarkable service in preaching in the streets; for which he was apprehended by order of the Recorder, but was shortly afterwards discharged at the instance of the Mayor.
He was sincerely desirous to train up his family by good example as well as precept and was in life and conversation a pattern of humility greatly beloved by his circle of acquaintances. He was suddenly attacked with illness which in a short time terminated his life in the twenty second day of the tenth month 1727' (1)

Some idea of his journeying as a travelling preacher may be obtained from the MM minute of the 11th month 1719:

'Henry Jackson having this day Laid an Intended Jurney (before us of) visiting the Churches in the north parts as Bishoprick of Durham, northumberland Cumberland (viz.) & he haveing the full unity of the particular meeting, this meeting giving a Certificate along with him, of good unity with him Desires the Lord may strengthen him in that Great Work & Service he hath called him to be Concerned in for ye honour of his great name.' (2)

Henry Jackson married Barbary Lupton of Bradley near Addingham. They had seven children. The only surviving son was Ebenezer (1715-1775) who never married and died at Farfield Hall in Addingham. Shortly after Ebenezer had been born Barbary Jackson died. (See Appendix [9]). Henry Jackson married again. His second wife was Mary Elwood, the daughter of Thomas Elwood of Kirby Kendal.

When Henry died in 1727 Yorkshire QM issued his testimony. This was unusual as testimonies normally originated from MM. In the history of Yorkshire QM there have only been six occasions when such testimonies have been issued. These included, as well as Henry Jackson, John Woolman and John Wilhelm Rowntree. The testimony, though short, carries very similar sentiments to the record of his life quoted above.

A probate inventory for 1727 of the content of Totties Hall also survives. It confirms that the Jackson's were still amongst the wealthiest families in the Graveship of Holme and shows that they were not involved with textiles as were many yeoman of the day. Their income was entirely from rents and the profits from agriculture. Totties Hall, by design and size, was a much grander home than that of the typical yeoman. The number and nature of the rooms is revealing. A first floor chamber was used exclusively as a withdrawing or sitting-room contrasting sharply with the combined living and sleeping quarters of a more typical yeoman's house. Henry Jackson's Best Chamber was furnished with *'a Chest of Drawers a range a little square table 9 chairs a close stool 2 stands a Looking Glass 2 little stools & Window Hangers.'* His total inventory was valued at £1646 1s 3d which included livestock and monies owing on mortgages. (3) This was a very considerable estate.

Henry Jackson's death brings to an end an era in the history of Quakerism locally. The family had been a driving force and guiding influence on the local meetings from the earliest murmurings of dissent to the beginnings of the Quaker Quietist period. Their refusal to bow to conformity and pursue their pathway to religious freedom without concession makes them part of the valiant age of the Society of Friends.

(1) MSS Collection — Friends House Library
(2) MMMB 1719
(3) Quoted in 'Peasants & Clothiers' Holmfirth High School

PLAIN FRIENDS

The closing years of the 17th century witnessed Quakerism slipping into a lengthy period of 'Quietism'. The incredible expenditure of energy in the Publishing of Truth and the resulting persecutions (both at home and abroad) led to a gradual, if grudging, acceptance of Quakerism after the Act of Toleration. With this acceptance came a new generation of Friends intent upon securing their Society throughout the land. The zealous missionary ideals of George Fox and his early followers began to fade. Friends became more concerned in the way in which they should live their lives and, furthermore, to be seen to live them.

'Friends are also advised to be careful of their conduct at all times, and on all occasions, that no stumbling-block be laid in the way of honest inquirers, nor offence given to tender young friends. 'Let your light so shine before men, that they may see your good works, and glorify your Father which is in heaven.' (Matt. v.16).' (1)

Concern with outward appearance and manner dominated the lives of eighteenth century Friends. Quakers became easily identifiable from their neighbours by their sober dress and 'plain speech'. This concern with appearance had earlier been condemned by Margaret Fell who, surviving her husband George Fox, had lived to see these changes commence and had commented:

'Christ Jesus saith, That we must take not thought what we shall drink or what we shall put on; but bids us consider the lilies, how they grow in more royally than Solomon. But, contrary to this, we must not look at no colours, nor make anything that is changeable colours, as the hills are, nor sell them, nor wear them...This is a silly, poor Gospel.' (2)

Friends chose to ignore her words. They became more puritan in their outlook, outward appearance and conduct than the Puritans had been. From being outward in spreading the Truth, they now turned inwards becoming a 'peculiar' people living in closed groups, bound by kinship and heredity. Nowhere can this be better exemplified than in these rural and isolated Peninne meetings. Repeatedly the same dominant family names appear in the minute books and records. Repeatedly, the same preoccupations, as elsewhere within the Society of Friends, with 'plainess' or 'peculiarity'. This increasing concern with 'plainess' is well documented in both a handwritten 'Book of advices & disciplines' belonging to Pontefract MM (1765) and in various printed editions of 'Rules of Discipline and Advices'. It is also well documented in the PM minutes.

In 1708, the following advice was given from YM with regards to plainess:

'...That Parents be exemplary to their children, in keeping out of ye Vain Fashions, Customs & Pride of the World, by adorning themselves Modestly, and to the simplicity in plainess According to the Truth received by us in the beginning.' (3)

It is an interesting exercise to compare how, only ten years later, these strictures found themselves to be in need of further elaboration. It seems that not all Friends were readily prepared to give up vain and fashionable ways of the world. In 1718, YM felt it necessary to issue a more detailed advice.

'...The way of truth is evilly spoken of, and our Holy Profession greatly reproached by many among Us putting on extravagent Wiggs & wearing their Hats & clothes after ye Vain Fashion; Unbecoming the Gravity of Religious People; And too many Women decking themselves in the gaudy & Costly apparel, Gold Chains, Lockets; necklaces & Gold Watches; exposed to open view which shews more of Pride & Ostentation than for use & service. Besides their Vain imitation of that Immodest Fashion of going with Naked Necks & wearing hooped petticoats; inconsistant with that Modesty, which should Adorn their sex; and did Adorn the Holy Women of Old.' (4)

Professing Quakerism was not to be taken lightly. By pursuing the latest changes in fashions, Friends were likely to lose their sense of spiritual direction with their thoughts growingly pre-occupied with trivial materialistic matters that allowed less time for their faith and its observance. Neither did Friends of this period merely concern themselves with sombre grey clothes lacking in lace and frills. Nor simply with matters of 'plain speech' as *'... a light and vain conversation would tend to alienate their minds from the love of virtue and sobriety.'* (5) Their homes had also to lack ostentatious furnishing. Furniture had to be plain, functional and lasting otherwise it would lead to *'a mind engaged with trifles, and a fondness for show which is inconsistent with the Christian character; and it disqualifies for duly advising such as may rush into further degrees of extravagance.'* (6)

Personal conduct had to be above criticism. Each Quaker had to be a shining example of Christian life and virtue to his non-Quaker neighbours. The frequenting of ale-houses, dubious places of entertainment such as the theatre, pleasures such as music and dancing, reading novels, vices like gambling, sports such as hunting and other worldly pleasures were regarded as distinctly ungodly and un-Quakerly. These activities would do little for promoting the Truth and had to be avoided. In their business dealings with Friends and non-Friends alike Quakers had to be honest and beyond reproach. Only the best goods and workmanship were to be permitted, and the price quoted would be the only price that was to be accepted. To have allowed haggling would have been to show dishonesty. A Friend who did not conduct his business affairs properly and went bankrupt could find himself disowned for causing financial distress to others. Frugality, temperance and honesty were to be cultivated, frivolity and ostentation to be avoided at all cost so that *'...the simplicity of truth in these things may not wear out, or be lost in our day, nor in those of our posterity...'* (7) Simplicity was the key to the Quaker lifestyle of this 'Quietist' period; and simplicity did not end with death. Quakers were even denied a gravestone. (See 'Gravestones and Mourning').

By and large the Meetings at Wooldale, High Flatts and Lane Head pursued a path of quietist conformity. Visitors from more distant meetings in the land would have found them no different from their own. And visitors there were, largely travelling ministers with a particular concern. This much had not altered since the days of George Fox and the Valiant Sixty. It is through their visitations that we are able to ascertain that our meetings were bedrocks of Quietism.

(1) RDA 1834 p.38 No.9 1731
(2) Quoted in CFPSofE No.401 1960 YM
(3) MS Transcription 1765 of YM RDA
(4) Ibid
(5) RDA 1834 p.38 No.10 1809
(6) Ibid p.212 No.13 1809
(7) Ibid p.206 No.2 1691

Quaker Visitors

The journeys George Fox undertook in the preaching of the Truth saw him travel the length and breadth of the British Isles and overseas to the West Indies, North America and Europe. He established, by personal example, the idea of a travelling ministry which has endured. During and after his lifetime Friends heeded his words to: *'... spread yourselves abroad, that ye may be serviceable for the Lord and his Truth.'* (1)

The minister with a travelling 'concern' (particular objective arising from the promptings of the Spirit) was a common sight to Friends everywhere from the earliest days of Quakerism. Many of these travelling ministers kept journals reflecting both their physical and spiritual journeyings. Like George Fox they were prodigious in their feats of distances travelled and numbers of meetings attended. John Griffith (1713-1776), an eminent eighteenth century Welsh/American Friend who travelled as an intinerant minister throughout Britain and North America claimed to *'on a moderate calculation'* have travelled *'11,875 miles, and was at about 560 meetings.'* (2) This was not at all unusual.

Ministers and travelling Friends could expect to be warmly received by Friends wherever they travelled. They would be accommodated in the homes of local Friends, attend their meetings for worship, as well as PM's and MM's, and then continue their journey. Thomas Story (1662-1742), a prominent minister, recorded in his journal how he visited High Flatts in 1717:

'On the 20th I was at an appointed Meeting at High Flatts, which was large and pretty open, there being several People of the Neighbourhood of various notions present, who were generally satisfied; and that evening I went about three miles with Daniel Broadhead, where I staid till the 22nd, it proving very rainy & stormy.' (3)

His host on this occasion was Daniel Broadhead (d.1735) who resided at Moorside, Wooldale which is only three miles distant from High Flatts. In the 5th month 1728 Thomas Story stopped off *'at a Meeting near Pennystone.'* Thomas Story returned again to the area in 1731:

'On the 9th (7th month)...that Evening went to the Widow Mary Jackson's at Totis; and the next Day was at the Meeting at Woodhouse (Wooldale), the Village adjacent, which consisted, for the greater Part, of Friends, and pretty open: though it is observable, in these Days, that our Meetings are generally brightest and most open, and the necessary Truths of the Gospel most clearly and powerfully opened, where the People are invited by Friends, and come freely in; whereby Friends themselves become further informed and edified...On the 12th I was there again, Forenoon and Afternoon; when the meeting was much larger and opener; many of the Neighbours being there.'

In 1732 he returned again and recorded:

'On the 16th I went to Tottis (Totties), to the widow Mary Jackson's, where I was respectfully entertained, as she used to do generally to such as travelled on like account; and on the 18th I was at their meeting at Lane Head. That evening I returned to Totis.' (4)

On the 20th he went to a meeting at *'Meadop near Pennyston'* where *'the Lord gave us a good Time in his holy Presence.'*

Through visitors journals and through the records kept by local Friends it is possible to construct an interesting picture of the life of each of these meetings. Between 1718 and 1820 there were several hundred visitors to Wooldale, High Flatts, Lane Head, Judd Field and Lumbroyd. (See Appendix [16]). They came from every part of England, Wales, Scotland, Ireland and, of course, North America. Many of these travelling or *'Publicke Friends'* are known to us only by name. Others came with, or established, lasting reputations. The Meetings were visited by many famous and distinguished Friends including Thomas Story (1717, 1728, 1731 and 1732), Samuel Bownas (1720), John Fothergill the Elder (1725), Benjamin Holmes (1739 and 1743), Samuel Fothergill (1745), John Griffith (1748, 1753 and 1761), William Backhouse (1752), Esther Maud (1764) and her husband to be William Tuke (founder of The Retreat for the insane in York) who came in 1770 on a QM visit (and again in 1785, 1792 & 1802), and John Woolman (1772), as well as Sarah Grubb (1783), Thomas Scattergood (1799), Thomas Shillitoe (1807), Stephen Grellet (1812) and Elizabeth Fry (1818). Other visitors included William Rowntree and the members of his family. There were travelling Friends of lesser stature but equally deserving of mention like Mary Slater who came at least seven times between 1736 and 1760. Her husband William came on at least six occasions during this same period. Jane Crosfield (1748) of Westmorland, May Drummond (1749) of Edinburgh and William Impey (1742 and 1752) also visited. So too did James Clothier (1751) of Street who was lame but did not allow his disability to prevent him from travelling in the ministry. Another regular visitor to these meetings was Samuel Spavold (1708-1774). He had been a Yorkshire carpenter who had become a ship's captain and had then travelled regularly in the ministry even visiting America in 1757.

Some were not entirely well received, as this rather interesting extract suggests:

'On ye 1st day of ye week ye 1st day of ye 12 mo:1740-1 our Friend Mary Smith & Mary Ellinton Came to Visit us at our Meeting held at Wooldale.' (5)

Following this entry, in the same hand, but obviously an adddition due to the darker colour of the ink, this rather cryptic but telling comment: *'and continued till 4 in ye afternoon.'*

To travel as a minister, a Friend had to *'go in the unity of the meetings to which they belong, and with certificates therefrom....'* (6) This was a precaution to discourage all but the truly dedicated. (There were still those who rambled up and down the country). It was by no means an easy undertaking to launch oneself on an itinerant journey of ministry. Travel in the eighteenth century could still be dangerous and difficult. There were highwaymen and ruffians ready to mete out violence. Inns were of a variable standard. Roads were now slowly beginning to improve upon the rutted cart tracks that most people had to contend with on their journeys. This was the century of road builders like Metcalf, Telford and MacAdam, of new toll roads, turnpike trusts and improvements. It must be remembered that it took most of that century before it was possible to reap the benefits in the transformation of road transport.

Local Friends also undertook such journeys. We read in a minute of 1752 that:

'...Sarah Marsden hath acquainted this Meeting that it hath weighed, some time upon her Mind to Visit Some Meetings South-wards on to London And having a Suatable Companien Frds. hath Given her a Certificate from this Meeting along with her Till one Can be had from our next monthly meeting which is Intended to be sent after her.' (7)

As Quaker women had equality in matters of ministry with their menfolk they too could be called to the travelling ministry. They required the necessary approval of their local meetings just like the men but their sex was never regarded as a barrier even though Sarah Marsden did confess that *'she set forwards In great Fear.'* (8)

Sarah Marsden was certainly not a rarity in being a woman minister with a concern. The records include many visitations to this area by Quaker women accompanied by one or more travelling companions. The granting of a certificate was no formality for any minister. The certificate was a credential to other Meetings recommending a Friend with sound spiritual views. Its granting was done only after prayerful deliberation by the PM and MM.

Sarah Marsden was not alone in this area in travelling beyond the bounds of the local meetings. Later, William Earnshaw of Totties was to undertake such visits to Lancashire and North Yorkshire. Like Henry Jackson II and Henry Jackson III the tradition of a local travelling ministry was maintained throughout the eighteenth century and well into the next by others particularly Joseph Wood.

Friends, more than any other group in a community, were generally prepared to travel abroad from their locality. It was a part of their Quaker inheritance from the days of George Fox. Even if journeys of no great length were made then some would still regularly travel to MM and also to QM usually held in York.

(1) 'No more but my love' ed. C.Sharman QHS 1984 Ep.64 p.30
(2) 'The Journal of John Griffith' pub. London 1779 p.203
(3) 'The Journal of Thomas Story' pub. London 1753
(4) Ibid
(5) Appendix [16]
(6) RDA 1834 1834 p.163 No.17 1720
(7) PMMB 1752
(8) MMMB 1752

The Visit of John Griffiith

From about the 1720's travelling ministers began to arrive from North America. Many would have been the descendants of Friends who had emigrated during the seventeenth century to William Penn's Quaker colony of Pennsylvania. John Griffith (1713-1776), one of the earliest recorded American visitors to this area, came from Derby Meeting in Chester County, Pennsylvania. Born in Radnorshire, Wales, he had emigrated to America at the age of 13 with his parents. Upon the death of his wife he had returned to England and eventually settled at Chelmsford. His arrival for the first time is recorded in the visitors booklet with a brief and understated two lines:

'On ye 1 day of ye week on ye 31 5 mo:1748 our Friend John Griffith Came to visit us at our meeting held at Lainhead from America.' (1)

Griffith, who was travelling northwards from Sheffield, certainly made a point of detailing his visit to High Flatts in his journal (although he made no mention of visiting Lane Head).

'From thence (Sheffield) I went to High Flatts, and was at their meeting, it being first day, which was very large; it being composed of plain country Friends. The Lord was pleased to favour us with a precious opportunity together, in the comfortable enjoyment of his love shed abroad'... (2)

High Flatts Meeting would have been the most geographically convenient meeting to visit in this locality. Friends travelling north or south, by way of Sheffield, would encounter High Flatts rather than the remoter meetings. The large size of the meeting could be due to the fact that Friends from the other local meetings, all no more than three to four miles equidistant, would regularly come together at one or

21

the other in turn. It could be even larger still if Pontefract MM was being held. He visited High Flatts a second time in 1753 without passing comment. However, it is his third recorded visit of the 25th of the 5th month 1761, that proves to be the most intriguing, for if the first and second visits did not cause a stir then the third one certainly did.

'...The next meeting I had was at High Flatts, which was large, there being a numerous body of plain Friends, as to the outward appearance belonging there unto. It was a laborious meeting, but through divine favour, there was strength afforded, to lay before them, in a close pressing manner, the great danger of resting contented in a decent form of religion, without the life and power thereof. I hope it was a profitable time to many.' (3)

Griffith together with other Friends had been appointed by YM to visit various meetings. For several years prior to 1760 concern had been exhibited amongst Friends at *'slackness and unfaithfullness...in some weighty branches of our Christian testimony.'* YM (1760) troubled about a general state of laxity in maintaining the Discipline, *'appointed a large and weighty committee'* of fifty-eight *'zealous Friends'* to visit QM's and MM's throughout the land. In 1761, John Griffith, Matthew Mellor, Thomas Corbyn, Joseph Row and others, forming one of several such groups, began their visits to *'help in promoting good order and discipline in the several parts.'* (4) This interesting rememberance of his third visit is not his only account of that particular meeting. Many pages later in his journal Griffith elaborates on that memorable meeting.

'The 25th (5th mo: 1761) we visited Pontefract Monthly Meeting, held at High Flatts. Here was a very numerous body of Friends, whose outward appearance was very becoming our self-denying profession; and I really believe this plainess, in a considerable number amongst them, was the genuine product of a well regulated mind; yet I fear, in too many, it was more the effect of education, which, however, I would not condemn, where people are not prevailed upon by the subtlety of Satan, to take their rest therein; since the form must follow the power, and not the power the form. We had close labours, in order to rouse those who had settled down in a false rest, and also to promote a better regulation in some respects; yet I think it might be said that discipline, in most of its branches, was pretty well maintained in that meeting. It was a time of high favour; counsel and admonition was plentifully extended.' (5)

Griffith was a *'seasoned'* minister and his companions all *'weighty'* Friends. Very little would have escaped their attention. From the earlier observations on matters of *'peculiarity'* and *'plainess'* it would not be an unreasonable assumption that *'the form was not following the power'* in all cases. Perhaps, too many local Friends of this period were more concerned with living appearances than with spiritual living. The PM minutes also prove revealing.

'We have this day Received An acct. in writing of the State of Affairs the Mo. Meeting, as they appeared to the following Frds. in their late visit thro this County w. some advice & Remarks made by John Griffith, Matthew Mellan, Jona. Rains, Thos. Corbyn, Joseph Roe & Joseph Taylor who amongst other things Frds. were under the appointment of the Yearly Meeting to Visit the Monthly & Quarterly Meetings in this Nation, which amongst other advices Contained in the said paper, is Recommended that where there is not a distinct appointment of Elders & overseers that such Meetings would take the same into consideration. This Meeting only having Elders appointed, it seems to be the desire of some friends, that some proper persons be Chose & Appointed as Overseers, the consideration of which is left to our Next Meeting...' (6)

The overseers were concerned with the pastoral welfare of Friends. The elders were concerned with maintaining sound religious principles, discipline within the meeting and the spiritual life of the Society in general. The lack of overseers had obvious implications which Griffith had immediately detected. Whatever else the visit did or did not achieve the PM found itself revitalized. One has only to compare the minutes before 1761 with those immediately after the visit to realize the effects. The short complacent minutes with their greater concern for monetary details become lengthier, more positive, filled with the affairs, problems and concerns of local Friends. Much of this was undoubtedly due to the appointment of the five overseers in the 11th month of 1761: Edward Dickinson, Enoch Dickinson, Joseph Firth, William Radley and Joshua Marsden.

(1) ATF(MS)
(2) 'The Journal of John Griffith' pub. London 1779
(3) Ibid p.234
(4) 'Quaker Organization & Business Meetings' L.Hugh Doncaster p.31
(5) Ibid p.325-326
(6) PMMB 1761

Other American Visitors

John Griffith was by no means the only American Friend to visit these parts. (See Appendix [16]). The first recorded visitor from the New World was John Eston of New Jersey who came to High Flatts in 1721. Between 1721 and 1820 there were 53 American visitors to the local meetings. Amongst these many visitors was John Churchman and his travelling companion John Pemberton who came to Wooldale and Judd Field (1753). This same John Pemberton was to walk in sackcloth and ashes through the streets of Londonderry in 1784. (1) Other eminent *'Publicke Friends'* from America included John Woolman (See next section), Rebecca Jones, George Dillwyn, Joseph Cloud and Stephen Grellet. Abstracted details of these visitors are presented here:

Visiting American Friends 1721-1820 (2)

John Eston	NJ.	1721 H	Sarah Morris	Penn.	1772 H
John Cadwalliter	Penn.	1722 W	Deborah Morris	Penn.	1772 H
Esther Clarey	Penn.	1723 W	Thos. Carrington	Penn.	1776 W
John Sawkill	Penn.	1726 W	Robert Valentine	Penn.	1780 H
Robert Jordan	Vir.	1729 H	Rebecca Jones	Penn.	1784 H
Rebecca Marshall	Penn.	1736 W	Nicholas Waln	Penn.	1784 H
Lisel Harper	New Eng.	1737 H	Rebecca Wright	NJ.	1785 H
Esther White	Penn.	1743 H	Geo. Dillwyn	NJ.	1785 H
Ebeneezer Large	NJ.	1746 H	Ann Jessop	NC.	1786 H
John Griffith	Penn.	1748 H	James Thornton	Penn.	1786 H
Peter Davis	Rh. Is.	1748 W	Samuel Smith	Penn.	1790 H
David Stainton	Penn.	1749 W	Sarah Harrison	Penn.	1796 H
Thos. Nicholson	NC.	1750 H	Phebe Speakman	Del.	1799 H
Phebe Dodge	Long Is.	1752 L	Hannah Barnard	NY.	1799 H
John Pemberton	Penn.	1753 W	Elizb. Coggeshall	Rh. Is.	1799 H
John Churchman	Penn.	1753 W	Tho. Scattergood	Penn.	1799 H
William Brown	Penn.	1753 W	Charity Cook	SC.	1801 H
Margaret Ellis	Penn.	1753 H	Mary Swifte	NJ.	1801 H
Margaret Lews	Penn.	1753 H	Joseph Cloud	NC.	1803 H
Peter Andrew	WJ.	1755 L	Wm. Jackson	Penn.	1803 H
Mordecai Yarnell	Penn.	1757 H	David Sands	NY	1803 H
Joseph White	Penn.	1761 H	Benjamin White	Penn.	1809 H
William Horn	Penn.	1763 W	Henry Hull	NY.	1811 H
Thomas Goodin	Penn.	1763 W	Stephen Grellet	NY.	1812 H
William Hunt	NC.	1772 H	Hannah Fields	NY	1818 H
John Woolman	NJ.	1772 H	Willott Hicks	NY.	1820 H
			Nathan Hunt	NC.	1820 H

(1) JofFHS Vol.53 No.1 1972 p.34
(2) ATF, Joseph Wood's Visitors Bks. and various Journals of Travelling Friends. See Appendix [16].

John Woolman

By far the most prominent American Friend to visit this area was the noted Quaker minister, John Woolman of Mount Holly (West Jersey) who came in 1772 on foot to High Flatts. He was then nearing the end of his life and was making his way from London to York. On Wednesday 5th August he arrived from Sheffield at High Flatts to attend the weekday meeting. The following description of him was recorded by the twenty two year old Joseph Wood:

'Friends Travelling in the Ministry High Flatts MM 1772
John Woolman, New Jersey.
John Woolman appears to me to be a man of a very deep experience in the things of God, and comming up in obedience to the Light of Christ was led out of all superfluity in meat, drink and apparel, being a pattern of remarkable plainess, humility, and self denial. His dress as follows:
A white hat; a coarse raw linen shirt, without anything about the neck; his coat, waistcoat and breeches of white coarse woolen cloth with wool buttons on; his coat without cuffs; white yarn stockings and shoes of uncured leather with bands instead of buckles, so that he was all white.' (1)

The diary of another visitor to High Flatts on this same day further confirms this visit as well as providing some interesting information. Deborah Morris and her aunt, Sarah Morris, were staying at neighbouring Birdsedge with Joshua and Hannah Marsden when John Woolman arrived. (2) The Morris's were both acquainted with him and Deborah recorded the following brief details:

'...went to their meeting which was large for a country meeting. Here we met J.Woolman who had a fine time, my Aunt also, though short. Dined at Edward Dickinson('s) (3) close by the meeting house, and after dinner John (Woolman) and Aunt had a seasonable and uniting time with the young folk and a few others. A solemn parting time indeed. He then went to Huddersfield and we to Hollingthorp.' (4)

John Woolman died tragically some weeks later in York of smallpox on the 7th October 1772.

(1) JofFHS Supplement No.31 'John Woolman in England 1772' by Henry J.Cadbury. p.96-7. As H.J. Cadbury rightly pointed out this passage has been wrongly ascribed to Pontefract MM minutes where there is no mention of Woolman's visit. It was written by Joseph Wood in one of the visitors books that he had compiled.
(2) Sarah Morris (1703/4-1775) of Philadelphia. Travelling Minister. Her niece, Deborah (1723-1793) accompanied her to England and kept a diary of the visit. Joshua Marsden (b.1735).
(3) Edward Dickinson (1708-1773) was the son of Elihu Dickenson & Mary Firth and the father of Elihu Dickinson the Clothier.
(4) JofFHS Supplement No. 31 p.97

Elders, Overseers and Ministers

From the early days of Quakerism outstanding personalities arose from amongst Friends to fill those positions where leadership was required. Friends had (and have) no separate, much less paid, ministry believing that in a rightly gathered meeting utterance might be given to any one of the worshippers. It was, however, recognized that to some the ministry of the word was given in greater measure than to others and these, women and men, became known as *'Publicke Friends'* and, later, as *'acknowledged'* or *'recorded'* ministers. Their gift was recognized by the MM and recorded in its minutes. In due time (and practise varied in different places) the custom grew up of recognizing Friends with other gifts as elders and overseers. As the Society of Friends entered the eighteenth century and its age of quietism a gradual change was wrought in the influence extended over the Society by the elders, the overseers and the ministers. The elders were charged with the maintenance of the spiritual welfare of their meeting and the overseers with the pastoral care. Initially the roles of eldership and oversight were combined and there does not appear to have been a distinction made between the two. It was only after 1750 that the distinctions and separation of the functions appears to have become complete. Certainly, with regard to our local meetings, the role of overseer was frequently combined as part of the the work of an elder. Only in 1761, after John Griffith's visit, were overseers formally appointed. (See 'The Visit of John Griffith').

Elders came to dominate the decision making processes of the Society and exercised considerable authority within their PM's, MM's and QM's, especially at Meetings for Discipline. The following description of elders in this period is worth quoting for it appears to have been applicable not only as a general statement but also as one fairly specific to our local meetings:

'They acquired the power to sit through the longest meetings without stirring or moving. They never seemed to look at anything and yet they saw everything that happened. If anybody fell asleep they knew it. If any person was present and yet not 'gathered', they were aware of it. They never looked at a timepiece and had no hour-glass and yet they knew by a kind of infallible click when it was time to close Meeting. They seemed unmoved as the desert-sphinx while some Minister was preaching and no change of facial muscle betrayed in the least their approval or disapproval, but if the Minister made the slightest slip in quoting scripture, or if he deviated from 'truth', or his garb, or voice, or manner revealed that he was not 'seasoned' or 'savoury' or 'in the life', he would would know it himself before he got home, or in the near future... They were meek and gentle to look upon but somehow they acquired an extraordinary mastery over the membership. What they meditated on in silence sooner or later became a fact. They shaped the development of the Discipline. They wove the dead past into the living present and kept the 'truth' as nearly as possible unaltered. They were guardians of custom and they used their position and authority to preserve the plain speech and the type of garb which their fathers had honoured.' (1)

Those recorded as ministers were further encouraged to travel to other meetings both near and far, at home and abroad, if a concern arose. This resulted in a strong and dynamic travelling ministry. The recognition of such Friends with a gift in the ministry did not preclude other Friends from speaking or *'dropping a few words'* if moved to do so. Friends continued to recognize that God could speak through any member of the meeting no matter how young or old.

Recognition in ministry had little to do with intellectual or academic abilities. Quite a few local Friends who were recorded as ministers during the eighteenth century came with slender academic qualifications. Henry Dickinson of Strines and John Bottomley (1759-1820) were Friends from *'lowish circumstances'* who proved their worth in the ministry without any high academic standing. The following extract concerning John Bottomley is quite revealing:

'In the 2nd Month 1790 and in the thirty first year of his Age he first dropped a few Words in publick Testimony in the Meeting at Highflatts, He professed only a small share of human learning; but we were satisfied that he had the superior advantage of being instructed in the School of Christ wherein he learned humility and Self denial and gradually experienced a preparation for increasing usefulness in the exercise of his Gift. His Ministry we esteemed lively and edefying and his affectionate Labours amongst us we trust will be long and profitably kept in our Rememberance.' (2)

John Bottomley was Joseph Wood's servant, close personal friend and protege. Joseph Wood helped to educate him and encouraged him to develop his 'gift in the ministry'. They frequently travelled together preaching at the same meetings.

William Earnshaw of Totties was in complete contrast to both John Bottomley and Henry Dickinson of Strines. He was an educated Friend who taught school as well as pursuing employment as a clothier. We are fortunate to possess an account of William Earnshaws labours as a minister. On a visit to Paddock Meeting House, in the company of John Bottomley of Newhouse, on the 18th of the 11th Month 1798, a young Friend recorded his ministry. A brief extract is herein quoted to provide some idea of the nature of ministry given in this period.

'He had much to say, on the subject of silent waiting upon the Lord, mentioning for our encouragement, that many whose minds had been centred, in the truly solemn silence of all flesh, had at times & seasons experienced the Lord to break in upon them, & reduce them into tears of joy, contrition & tenderness, when that no outward testimony had been delivered; exhorting us, not to have our attention too much outward, upon what others might have to declare, shewing us, that the Lords true & dedicated servants, had nothing at their own command, to offer unto the people, beautifully shewing, that it was not human learning, nor any other acquirement that would do us good, but it was life, the life of religion, which alone could satisfy the soul. He was particularly led towards the youth then present, in which number I class myself, expressing disires, that we might, while in the flower & bloom of life, bow down our necks under Christs yoke, adding 'for truly

his yoke is easy, & his burden is light'. He had to revive the advice given by Solomon formerly, Remember now thy Creator, in the days of thy youth, while the evil days come not, nor the years draw nigh, when thou shalt say I have no pleasure in them Eccles. 12.1.' (3)

Perhaps the most outstanding minister of this period was Joseph Wood. (See 'Joseph Wood of Newhouse'). Whereas Henry Dickinson of Strines rarely ventured beyond the boundaries of West Yorkshire and William Earnshaw a little more frequently, Joseph Wood was a *'Publick Friend'* of some note. He journeyed almost continuously from the age of about seventeen until his death.

Ann Broadhead (?1685-1763) and Sarah Marsden (1706-1762), the wife of Caleb Marsden an elder of High Flatts, were both inspiring and respected ministers. (See Appendix [10]).

The practice of recording ministers was discontinued by London YM in 1924 when it was felt that it had outgrown its usefulness and might serve to discourage others from vocal ministry in meeting. The roles of elders and overseers have been retained.

(1) 'The Later Periods of Quakerism' Rufus M. Jones Vol.1 p.126-7
(2) John Bottomley's Testimony(HF)MMMB2 1813-1824.
(3) Joseph Wood Collection. Misc.Papers.

Disownments and Testimonies of Denial

Any Friend who was not in 'unity' with the rest of the meeting could find him or herself disowned from the Religious Society of Friends by a 'Testimony of Denial' being issued against them. This was a written exclusion disassociating the Society with the person involved. It denied that Friend's further involvement in the Society's affairs as well as safeguarding the meeting and the Society from any further excesses committed by that same Friend. A special book of 'Testimonies of Denial' was maintained by Pontefract MM detailing the reasons why the disownment had taken place.

For a 'Testimony of Denial' to be issued and a disownment to take place a complaint first needed to be laid before the local meeting by Friends. The meeting would then appoint suitable Friends (usually elders and/or overseers) to visit the person concerned and investigate the truth of the complaint. If the complaint was found to have grounds the 'accused' Friend would have opportunity to explain him/herself and offer a 'defence' at the next PM. If no satisfaction could be offered, or the accused did not turn up, the case would be forwarded for consideration to MM where a decision would be deliberated. Friends who felt that they were being wrongly disowned had the right to appeal to QM and even YM.

The raising of a complaint against a Friend was a serious matter. It was a graver matter if it reached the stage where a 'Testimony of Denial' was likely to be issued. Families who had members disowned would be placed in a difficult situation. As parents were regarded by the Society of Friends as being responsible for the bringing up of their off-spring they could even be held personally responsible for that disownment having taken place.

'And ye parents, be ye solicitous to discharge your important and aweful duty, with scrupulous attention. It is often too late to warn the youthful mind of danger, when your own negligence, or indulgence hath suffered your offspring to deviate from that path of simplicity, in which you have thought yourselves bound to walk...having failed to rule your own house well, can you expect duly to 'take care of the church of God', by performing that too much neglected admonition therein?' (1)

A disownment tended to be seen as a failure on the part of the meeting to communicate with a delinquent member. Elders and overseers were especially entreated to be diligent in their *'extensive duties.'* It was their task to ensure that *'the ignorant may be informed, the weak strengthened, the tender encouraged, the scattered sought out, the unwary cautioned, the unruly warned; and that such as act in opposition to the testimonies required of us by the Spirit and doctrines of Truth, may be treated with in love and meekness, yet with holy firmness.'* (2) Friends were encouraged to *'watch diligently over the flock, and deal in due time, and in a spirit of Christian love and tenderness, with all such as walk disorderly amongst you, in order to reclaim and restore them by brotherly counsel and admonition...'* (3) Reading the minute books for Wooldale and High Flatts there is a realization that on the whole this is how local Friends did conduct themselves. This might not appear to be so from the number of disownments that appear. However, we must try to remember that Quakers were expected to live up to the highest ideals (even if the ideals were overly puritanical). In a society that allowed a greater laxity of personal, moral and religious behaviour they undoubtedly did not have an easy time. A fairly typical testimony of denial is quoted below.

A Testimonies of Denial issued against
Richard Johnson of Hilltopp, Shelly 1708

Forasmuch as it hath pleased ye Great God in his Infinite mercy & goodness to call a people out of the Worlds spirit with its ways fashions & customs to be a people unto him zealous of & for that w.ch is good: we find it our Duty to give of Testimonyes against loouse & libertine Spirites who altho They may proffess to know god in words yet in works deny him such so longe as They remain in Their loouse walking we cannot owne according to that w.ch is held forth by ye apostle If any man that is called a brother Be a fornicator or Covetous or an Idoliter or a Railer or a drunkord or an Extortioner not to keepe Company with such an one no not to eat.. These are therefore to Certifie all persons home the Same may Concerne that whereas Richard Johnson of Hilltopp in Shelly hath professed himselfe to be one of ye people called Quakers & did Pretty often come to their meetings yet his life & Conversation hath not been answerable to ye Prinsiples of Truth as Professed by them First in running into Debt beyond his ability by 2 in Breaking his word & promises about ye Payment thereof by 3: In Company keepeing att Alehouses & Drinking to excess Dayes & nights togeither Lastly his Foolish talkeing & useing his tongue at his pleasure All w.ch are expressly Contrary to ye Principles w.ch Through the mercy of god we have Reed & also are Delivered unto us in ye holy Scriptures which hath beene cause of great trouble & Sorrow unto us & the Occation of opening ye mouthes of many to Speak evel of ye Truth as Professed by us & the great dishonour of god & ye sd. Richard Johnson hath beene many times admonished and advised Concerning ye aboves Matters Privately & Publickly w.th great tenderness that if possable he might break of from yt. w.ch is Evel & Retire to ye witness of god in him w.ch would bring him if his day of Visitation be not over to Repentance & amendment of life, Thus friends haveing waited for Several years but Still hee continueing in his former Course of Life Wee Think Our Selves Concerned according to ye Doctrine of Christ Jesus our Lord & the practice of ye primitive Christians to give out this Testimoney against his unfare accons and disorderly walkeing and Talking and to Lett all our friends and other People Concerned Know that as he hath Rejected the truth of God to be Ledd and guided thereby togeither with ye Evidence of it in the hearts & mouthes of Its witnesses even So wee disown and deny to have all fellowship with him so longe as he remains in his unfruitfull words & works of darkness that so no person or persons for Time to Come may Charge us with his disorderly accons. & bad Coversation or any of ye Society of People call Quakers so w.th desires yt. may please god Still to shew him a day of Visitation & that he may accept thereof & come through Judgement & mercy to obtain forgiveness we conclude & subscribe ourselves heartily well wishers unto ye whole Creation of god. Signed on the behalf of our Monthly Meeting holded at Burton: 9 o ye 10 mo: 1708. Elihu Dickenson Nathan Rhodes Francis Harrison Hen. Jackson Jr. James Nayler Richard Ward Jr.'

A disownment did not mean total exclusion from the meeting. Those disowned could, and frequently did, continue to attend Meeting for Worship but were excluded from meetings for discipline. In the course of time they could apply to be re-admitted. Friends endeavoured to ensure that the children of disowned parents received a Quaker based education. Rawdon School near Leeds was specially established to serve this purpose.

(1) RDA 1834 p.196 No.20 1800
(2) Ibid p.183 No.4 1780
(3) Ibid

Marriage & Marital Difficulties

In the ninety-eight year period between 1701-1799 there were about 150 intentions to marry recorded in the MM and PM minute books relating to the local meetings. Of this number forty-eight were instances of local Friends marrying Friends from beyond the area of their local meetings. Most of the marriages in the locality of Wooldale and High Flatts were between local Friends which accounts for the very close ties of kinship between local families. (See Appendix [11]).

The unique form of marriage ceremony practiced by Friends posed problems for Friends during the early days of Quakerism. The lack of a *'hireling Priest'* to officiate at the ceremony frequently caused the legality and validity of Quaker marriages to be called into question. Non-Quaker relatives could claim that children born from such marriages were illigitimate and wills could be contested on those grounds. By the eighteenth century this had been largely overcome and Quakers could marry one another without legal hinderance in a way that was acceptable to them: to take one another in marriage before a gathered meeting of Friends witnessing and attesting the marriage. (Case Law judgements from 1661 had held that Quaker marriages were legal but there was no security in statute law until 1753).

Just as within other churches the solemnization and institution of marriage was a serious undertaking. It could not be lightly entered into and had to follow a prescribed pattern. To begin with: it was necessary to have full parental consent by both parties since *'parents have a natural right to approve of, and consent to, the marriage of their children.'* (1) Furthermore it was expected that all *'children would consult and advise with their parents and guardians, in that great and weighty point so essential to their happiness and comfort...'* (2) Young Friends were further cautioned to:

'...seriously wait upon the Lord for counsel and clearness in this weighty concern, before they make any procedure with any, in order to marriage; that they may not be led by any forward or uncertain affections in this great concern; to their own hurt, the grief of their friends, and the dishonour of truth.' (3)

Equally, parents were also expected to *'wait upon the Lord...'* before giving *'any encouragement thereunto.'* If and when consent was granted parents were also expected to ensure that the marriage went ahead once it had been arranged. Parents were further cautioned, when deciding upon their children's futures:

'...not to make it their first or chief concern to obtain for their children large portions or settlements of marriage; but rather to be careful that their children be joined in marriage with persons of religious inclinations, suitable dispositions and temper, sobriety in manners, and diligence in business, (which are things essentially necessary to a comfortable life in a married state); and carefully to guard against all mixed marriages, and unequal yoking of their children.' (4)

Whilst many of the local marriages did appear to be successful, and certain cases highly successful, living up to such high standards was difficult. Certainly Friends in the local meetings of Wooldale, High Flatts, Lane Head and Lumbroyd found that marriages could sometimes be trying and testing experiences.

A popular historical misconception is to regard the breaking up of marriages as an endemic ailment of this century. Marital breakdowns also happened on more than one occasion amongst local Friends in the eighteenth century. In the 11th month of 1783, a particularly bad year for marriages breaking down, the following complaint was laid before the PM:

'...John Green & Wife hath violated the solemn Covenant of Marrage by a Continual discord one with another, so as to bring a reproach upon our Profession...' (5)

(See 'Jonathan & Ann Green.' (John Green b.1755 was their grandson)).

The meeting sent out Godfrey Woodhead, George Chapman and Thomas Roberts to investigate the complaint. It appears that they managed to achieve very little because they reported back that they had *'Visited John Green & his Wife but met with no satisfaction having no hope of a Reconcilliation betwixt them...'* They also found their general conduct to be *'reproachful.'* The couple must have been quarreling bitterly and incessantly, not only in private but, worse than that, in public.

'...for some time past (they) hath lived at continual variance & in some respects seperated from each other & that their Conduct in many other respects is very inconsistent with the Truth.' (6)

In modern parlance, there must have been 'an irretrievable breakdown' in the relationship. What makes this case so much more interesting is the fact that John Green had only recently married Hannah Earnshaw in 1781. The wedding declarations stipulated that a marriage had to endure *'until it shall please the Lord by death to separate us.'* (7) There seemed to be little chance of this happening. The PM had little option but to present the case to MM with the inevitable consequence of disownment.

Preceeding the case of the Greens by five months, was the case of Mary Ward. She was abandoned by her husband. The separation was swiftly brought to the attention of the PM because she was visited in the 6th Month of 1783 and was *'found to be in Necessatous Circumstances'* without an earlier mention in the minutes. Her husband had left her and had made sure that she was almost penniless. The PM straightaway forwarded 10s 6d for her immediate use. Once again, the PM appointed a band of 'weighty' Friends, (very 'weighty' Friends one might hasten to add), consisting of Tobias Mallinson, Henry Dickinson, Joseph Firth and both Elihu Dickinsons to visit Mary Ward's husband to see if they could *'prevail with him to allow his Wife something towards her future support.'* The next minute reports that they failed to speak with him. (Undoubtedly not through a lack of trying). So, in the meanwhile, Benjamin Dickinson was dispatched with a further 10s 6d to tide her over in the interim until the matter was resolved. The elders and overseers eventually caught up with the elusive Joseph Ward sometime during the 9th Month. Elihu Dickinson the Tanner reported that they had visited *'Joseph Ward the Husband of Mary Ward'* where they managed to 'learn' that he was *'willing to allow her 6/- (a) week...'* as maintenance money. Six shillings was quite a tidy and generous sum: Joseph Ward seemingly had no intention of ever effecting a reconciliation with Mary. As in the previous instance the case was *'laid before the next Monthly Meeting.'*

John Roberts (b.1768) and his wife Hannah (nee Beaumont of Denby) were married in 1784 and lived at Springhouse, Totties. For twelve years their marriage appeared to have been sound until he became insolvent. Upon investigation of his affairs, by Godfrey Woodhead and Elihu Dickinson the Tanner, certain things came to light that went beyond the bounds of mere debt and insolvency. The following MM minute for 1796 records:

'We advised them to give up their effects to be equally divided amongst their Creditors, he expressed his willingness to do so but she appeared very averse to it; we then enquired into the cause of their insolvency and found that notwithstanding they had some small losses, it principally proceeded from a want of a proper attention to business & extravagancy: we also enquired into the truth of some disagreeable reports which was spread concerning them & found that he had been guilty of some reproachful conduct towards a young Woman; and she had been too frequently overtaken with drinking to excess upon the whole it was our judgement that they were equally blamable.' (8)

Whatever we might like to think about marriages in the past the reality is probably a good deal closer to our own age. Although divorce did not exist in the sense that we understand it this does not mean that marriages did not break down and end in separation. Quite possibly the fewer instances recorded amongst Friends could point to a greater stability but it does not indicate that Quaker couples lived happier married lives than those of other religious persuasions. Separations may have been rare but then the strong stigma of a separation between husband and wife almost certainly led to some couples suffering in dutiful silence.

(1) RDA 1834 p.94 No.24 1723
(2) Ibid p.95 No.4 1723
(3) Ibid p.94 No.1 1690
(4) Ibid p.94 No.3 1722
(5) PMMB 1783
(6) MMMB 1784
(7) See RDA 1834
(8) MMMB 1799

Marrying Out

In a time when there was no civil marriage ceremony Friends could find that if they wished to marry someone who was not in 'unity' as a Quaker it would mean having a Church wedding and being *'joined by a Priest.'* Since Friends could only marry Friends this was a step to be taken in desperation. Friends did not simply marry Friends because they wanted to remain exclusive. Although a major reason it is not the only reason. Quakers had always objected to and had successfully resisted being married by clergymen. However, their actions were technically contrary to the law of land. Lord Hardwicke's Act against Clandestine Marriages of 1753 allowed Quakers and Jews to marry without the need of a 'priest'. Unfortunately, the law stated that a marriage could only take place if both parties were in membership. Marrying out nearly always resulted in disownment. It has to be remembered that marriage by a priest would be conditional. By agreeing to a Church wedding a Friend was indicating his desire to accept the teachings and ways of that Church and thereby denying his Quaker beliefs. The case of Joseph Kay in the PM minutes for the 3rd month 1762 well typify this:

'This Meeting being informed that Joseph Kay of Shepley who had his Education amongst & in his young years frequented our Meetings till he got Married by a Priest w. a woman not of our Society since which he hath not attended our Meeting but joined himself in society w. that whom his wife Joins with. Therefore we as People don't look upon him as one of us, as he by his Conduct hath denied our Profession & dismembered himself from us as a People...' (1)

The case of John Parkin of Wooldale Meeting is all the more interesting. He had been an exemplary Friend participating in the Societies affairs as well as attending PM and MM regularly. Then a MM minute of 1773 records that he *'met with some unexpected Tryalls.'*

'...for want of a patient waiting and putting his trust in the Lord, that never failed, he became much unsettled and sought after a Woman not in profession with us, and at last prevailed with one of that sort, and hastily married her by assistance of a Priest.'

James Haigh, the son of Ann Haigh of Wooldale, knowingly and insistantly married out in 1775 despite *'much Labour & Pain'* that *'had been taken with him, to disuade him therefrom, both by Friends & his Mother his only surviving Parent, but without effect.'* Another reason why Friends might choose to be *'joined by a Priest'* was a ruling forbidding marriage of near kin such as first cousins.

'It is our living sense and judgement, that not only those marriages of near kindred, expressly forbidden under the law, ought not to be practiced under the gospel; but that we in our day ought not take first cousins in marriage...And though some, through weakness have been drawn into such marriages (which being done must not be broken) yet let not their practices be a precedent or example to any others amongst us for the time to come.' (2)

This injunction, dating back to 1675, was violated by Joseph Haigh and Susannah Haigh in 1784. Having no recourse they decided that their future happiness could only be achieved by marrying out of the Society in a church under the auspices of a *'hireling priest'*.

'Complaint hath been made to this Meeting that Joseph Haigh & Susanah Haigh late of Wooldale — being first cousins have Contrary to the repeated advice of their friends Joined themselves together in Marrige by a Priest the Representatives are desired to lay their case before the MM.' (3)

The couple had obviously been advised against their course of action by family and Friends according to a ruling of 1747:

'...this (Yearly) Meeting desires all friends, whenever they know and hear of any first cousins designing or intending to marry, that they immediately advise against it.' (4)

In the eyes of the meeting everything that could be done had been done to end this romance. Their efforts failed. Both Joseph and Susanah Haigh knew what the consequence of their marriage would be and it was a penalty they were prepared to take. As a result of the intermarrying that went on between local families in close communities Friends were only too aware of the dangers of in-breeding. It was no wonder that they were reluctant about such marriages.

It was not until 1873 that the Quaker marriage became open to all who desired it and who won the approval of their meeting. In the eighteenth century Friends had two courses of action, neither of which was entirely satisfactory: either to *'marry out'* or *'keep the discipline.'*

Marrying out and sexual misdeeds formed the largest group of disownments by far according to the minute books of the three meetings. In a twenty nine year period between 1763 and 1792 there were 17 cases of *'marrying out'* at Wooldale and High Flatts. There were only two instances of a request to be re-united with the Society. The first was that of Samuel Green who married out in 1784 and then in 1798, after fourteen years exclusion, requested to be re-admitted. (5) The second, and far more interesting case, was John Mallinson (the son of Tobias Mallinson of High Flatts) who married out in 1786. (6) Twelve years later, in 1798, John Mallinson requested to be reunited with the meeting together with his wife, not then a member of the Society. He was allowed back into the fold largely one suspects because of his father's dedication and long standing service to the local meetings. Within two years the meeting minutes record that he was chosen as a representative to MM. He served regularly in that capacity from about 1800 onwards. (7) He also undertook many other tasks such as the distribution of money to those in distress and to the sick. Unfortunately, some twenty years later he was disowned again: this time for insolvency. Children born of disowned parents, or even on the rare occasion of parents of mixed marriage who had not been disowned, received special consideration as this memo from the Committee for the County of York and Durham (1769) shows:

'...Children born after the denial of their Parents & who duly attend our Meeting for Worship, being also of an Orderly Conversation, should be tenderly regarded...if they express a desire to be esteemed Members of our own Society they ought to be admitted at the discretion of the Monthly Meeting.' (8)

Although the local meetings agreed with this in principle, the following minute indicates that they tended to take a harder line:

'It is our opinion, that Children born of Parents who have been disowned ought to be registered upon Application made for that purpose, to which this Meeting agrees, and further decides that making such registers, it should be noted that those Children were born of Parents out of Unity with us, and that it shall in no wise be esteemed a title of membership; and if Friends shall see Meeting at any time, to admit persons to be intered in friends burial grounds, who assent in Unity with us, or have been Testified against, it should always be noted in the register.' (9)

When the matter of admitting children of mixed marriages into the Society was raised in 1789 it is recorded that *'...we do not find that there is any within the compass of the Meeting.'* (10) This would hardly be surprising since the children would have adopted the new faith of their parents.

(1) PMMB 1762
(2) RDA 1834 p.97 No.10 1775
(3) PMMB 1784
(4) RDA 1834 p.98 No.12 1747
(5) PMMB 1798
(6) PMMB 1786
(7) PMMB 1800
(8) PMMB 1769
(9) Ibid 1769
(10) Ibid

Irregular Marriage

There are few recorded details to be found in the minutes of the local meetings concerning clandestinely contrived or irregularly contrived marriages. The case which appears to have caused the only major scandal in this respect, and which was sufficiently well documented at the time, transpired in 1773. At its centre was William Earnshaw (b.1741), the son of Joshua and Mary Earnshaw of Judd Field, *'who set his Mind & set his Affections on a young woman of a different Education & Profession in matters of Religion.'* This in itself was neither unusual nor uncommon. In these circumstances one either married out of the Society or the non-Quaker party became convinced and became a member of the Society. William Earnshaw initially decided that the latter approach was the most favourable to be pursued. He appears to have *'prevailed'* with his intended to attend meetings for worship at Lumbroyd. Then some short time later, as MM recorded, he *'made Application for her to be admitted a Member of our Society & to be married amongst us.'* However, to become a member of the Society of Friends in this period was no easy matter. (See 'Admittance to Membership'). When the young woman was visited it must have been transparent to Friends that her sole reason for desiring to be admitted to membership was not primarily spiritual. According to MM minutes:

'...upon mature & deliberate Consideration, together with proper enquiry we found too much Cause to believe the only inducement was that of getting married amongst us, without any apparent Convincement of the Truth of our Principles, and therefore could not admit her.' (1)

The prevention of this marriage by denying admittance to this unnamed young woman resulted in William Earnshaw undertaking a most 'bizzare', inexplicable and contrary course of action.

'In a little Time after, the said Wm. Earnshaw & the young Woman in a clandestine Manner appeared in one of our Meetings held at Lumbroyd near Penistone & there repeated a Ceremony about taking each other in Marriage & brought wth. them several Persons not of our Society, one of whom read something in imitation of our marriage Certificates; all of which was & is contrary to the Rules of good Order established amongst us in relation to Marriage.' (2)

It was inevitable that such a clandestinely performed marriage could not be long concealed. When it came to light, as the couple must surely have expected to happen sooner or later, they could expect little from the Society.

'...such Proceedings was not with our knowledge or Consent, & that we have no Unity with such Clandestine Transactions...' (3)

The Society's rules governing the conduct of marriages were strict and had to be beyond reproof. The Quaker manner of marriage was more open to the possibility of abuse by 'deceptions' than the customary Church procedure familiar to non-Friends. This clandestine marriage, between William Earnshaw and the unknown young woman, could have no legality. Only members of the Society could be legally married in the Quaker way according to the law of the land. Quite what they hoped to gain from it remains unclear. Life would have been simpler for them had they just decided, out of impatience, to marry out. The less attractive alternative might have been to wait longer for the young woman to be considered a more suitable candidate for membership. This travesty of a wedding ceremony resolved nothing. Their motives for undertaking it must remain at very best conjectural, the full truth of the matter now long since having gone to the grave with those involved in it.

William Earnshaw was disowned for this very contrary action with the following, and in his case, final comment from MM held at Pontefract:

'... we sincerely desire he may so come to see himself as to come into sincere repentance for his Proceedings & by his future Conduct will be found worthy of being restored into membership again.' (4)

Not surprisingly, William Earnshaw of Judd Field, never applied to be re-admitted to the Society of Friends.

(1) MMMB 1773
(2) Ibid
(3) Ibid
(4) Ibid

Quaker Courtship

There is very little detail with regard to Quaker courtship that is extant. Friends appeared to have been most reticent in committing to writing the details of how they initiated their first contacts with one another with a view to marriage. The following letter from the Catherine Walton Collection is reproduced here in full without further comment to shed a glimmer of light on the topic.

Letter to Susannah Wood of Newhouse (dated 1784)

*'Respected Friend,
I hope theese will find Thee in good health as the(y) leave me. Not having the opportunity of seeing Thee at this time I take the liberty of writing thee a few lines which I hope thou'l Parden having considered a little of what passed when Together thou might think me forward at that time it being the first I ever saw thee but being as it were Struck at the first sight meeting with so likely a companion save this a great deal to good for me but I could wish for such a One that I might be made better thereby upon Enquiry Respecting thee my Friend I understand thou was disengaged from any & so was encouraged to take the first Opportunity to have a little of thy company which Pleased me well & got a good sleep that night which kept me awake all the day After if I had mist of this I might have been asleep in meeting and dreaming of Thee before I had tumbled headlong of seat I wish to live worthy to see thee again I Remember a Caution which dropt from thy sweet lips that thou should not Engage hastily with any in this great Affair I thought thee prudent & hopes I may learn something thear from when I came to consider it for myself I find it is a Matter of great Importance & to be equally yoked ought to be our chief concern Now to Attain this to begin right must we not first seek the Kingdom of God & the Righteousness thereof & then nothing will be a wanting he will lead us right & point out the way that is best shall not be Ensnared as Dinah was with Shechem & Mislead for he knows what & who is best for us & will shew us what to do if we strain & do not Practice as I ought yet I often wish I may & hopes at length to close in with divine Visitation I Believe Thou my Dear art far Preferable to me in that which is good so I am not capable of giving thee my Advice but thou may be helpful to me through Divine assistance till I overtake thee & then we can go hand in hand through this world of Trouble I am afraid I shall tire thee with so much Nonsense but let me beg pardon & humbly request one favour that if there be an Engagement between thee & a nother or otherwise that I can have no room or place in thy heart I say if this be the case let me prevail purely to desire thee not to explore this in the least to no mortal but commit it to the Burning flames which will put an End to the vanity of it I do not mean to trouble thee any more as yet while I see my way farther & more clearer shall be very glad of a line from thee from thy Affectionate Frnd.'* (?)

An unknown Friend admirer.

'Loose' & Disorderly Conduct

Friends could also be denied membership of the Society for pre or extra-marital sex and even 'loose' behaviour with the opposite sex. To fall to such immoral behaviour was to deny the testimony of Truth held by Friends with regard to their faith and its observance. Interestingly, as the case of Joseph Kay's disownment was brought up at Wooldale so too was the case of Abraham Beaumont of Totties.

'This Meeting also being Informed that Abram Beamont Jun. a Member of this Meeting hath given to much Cause for his Neighbours to believe that he is guilty of Fornication, Since which no Notice hath been taken of him by this Meeting therefore Friends desire that Henry Dickinson, Caleb Marsden would take an opportunity w. him & make Report...' (1)

There seemed to be no sign of repentance from Beaumont as the minutes for the PM of the 31st of the 3rd Month 1762 would seem to indicate.

'The Persons Appointed to speak to Abram Beamont Jun. Report that they took an opportunity w. him & acquainted him w. the Proceedings of this Meeting against him & that by the discourse they had w. him, had

no Satisfaction, neither did there appear any tokens of Sorrow in him. The Representatives are desired to lay the Case before our Next Meeting.' (2)

The case of Abraham Beaumont is worthy of further consideration because according to the minutes of the PM held at High Flatts in the 8th Mo: 1769:

'Abram Beamont Jun. presented to this Meeting a paper of Acknowledgement of his past misconduct, which was here read, this Meeting allows him to lay the same before our next Monthly Meeting.' (3)

Loose and disorderly behaviour did not always merit an automatic disownment. Some, like John Broadhead, were merely censured for their conduct and then simply moved out of the area without informing the meeting of their whereabouts. The following two minutes taken from 1775 tell an interesting and complete story:

'This Meeting hath been now Informed that John Broadhead, Son of Joshua Broadhead late of Biggin, deceased, hath for some years ago left these parts and no clear Acct. have been lately heard where he is, nor whether he be alive nor dead, but Friends considering, his loose & disorderly conduct, before his going, and that he merited the Censure of the Society, the Representatives are desired to lay the case before next Monthly Meeting.' (4)

'Henry Dickinson gives Acct. that the Case of John Broadhead was laid before our last Monthly Meeting, and a Minute made certifying Friends disunity with him and that if he be living is looked on as no Member of our Society.' (5)

Broadhead, once having left the area, made no effort to contact the meeting in his new area. He had obviously opted out of the Society altogether so that he could continue 'his loose and disorderly conduct' without hinderance. The local meeting would eventually become aware of this fact when no certificate of transfer was requested by his new meeting. It would then act according to the ruling:

'If an offender cannot be found, the meeting to which he belongs, shall issue a testimony against him; if the nature of the case require it...and in all cases a copy is to be delivered to the person disowned, if access can be had to him.' (6)

The consequences of *'fornication'*, in an age where contraception was not generally practiced, was bound to lead to illegitimate births. There is only one explicitly recorded instance of an illegitimate birth being recorded in PM minutes between 1752 and 1812: Elizabeth Haigh of Ingbirchworth in 1786. (7) However, this single instance is not indicative of the fact that Friends were not confronted with such problems. On the contrary: MM minutes disclose that illegitimate births were far more common than we might have been led to believe. Generally, illegitimacy was concealed or avoided by timely marriages as in the case of Joshua and Lydia Woodhead and Wm. Jepson and Mary Green cited below. Or more commonly the man or woman in question was disowned for an act of fornication before the birth. In the case of Elizabeth Haigh, who somehow managed to conceal the birth without being disowned for *'the sin of fornication'*, we have a notable exception. She was disowned after the birth of her child. Perhaps her family history had some bearing on her misconduct. (See 'John Haigh of Moor Royd Nook, High Flatts').

The following cases illustrate the necessity of some 'timely marriages'. Joshua Woodhead and Lydia Dickinson laid their intention to marry before the Women's PM on the 31st of the 6 mo: 1737. The marriage took place but the couple had committed an 'indiscretion' prior to their wedding. According to the Women's PM minute book the couple admitted their guilt before being called upon to do so:

'...we had a paper presented to this meeting from Joseph & Lydia Woodhead who had caused sorrow & grief to faithful Friends, that such foul accions should be committed in ye Dark, that they having a child to soon after marriage maid they having expressed their great sorrow for the same in the said paper but she not being there was desired to appear at our next MM.' (8)

Joshua Woodhead appears to have hoped to spare his wife the distress of being present for this acknowledgment but the couple's joint liablity was in question. She was made to appear at the next MM. The young couple's moving and heart felt letter of acknowledgement is minuted in MM records:

Dear Friends
We do sincerely and heartily confess and Acknowledge we have sined and done which Caused us to have our Child and is in doing that we ought to have had it According to the time of our marriage but O the sorrow & the excecieses we have undergone on that Account often Lying Down in Sorrow So that we have been made to water our pillow with tears so that we thought ourselves unworthy of ye loves merceys we Desier your Secret prayers for us and to be as Charitable towards us as you can (need?) pass by this offence as you see us worthy of forgiveness so shall leave it to your Consideration Desireing ye Lord may still mercifull towards us as we keep truly humble before him and give us truely to repent So as to witness forgiveness of him that he may lift up to the Light of his Countenance upon us againe which is the Sincere desire of us

Joseph Woodhead Lydia Woodhead
ye 13 of 5th Mo: 1738 (9)

Possibly because they admitted their guilt so readily before being called upon to do so Friends were willing to accept their sincere repentance. No Testimony of Denial was issued against the pair.

William Jepson and Mary Green (daughter of John) were both in membership. In 1776 the minutes state that they decided to marry out and that *'they were guilty of fornication'* (10). The 'evidence' for the said act of fornication was physically visible to all who saw the young Mary Green. The young couples reasons for marrying, as well as marrying out, would also be quite obvious. When Godfrey Woodhead visited William Jepson he received *'no answer'* to his questions, nor for that matter did William Jepson bother to appear at the next PM to defend himself and his new bride. Their position in the eyes of Friends was completely indefensible. This would also have appeared to have been the case with Hannah Sanderson in 1741 who was disowned *'chiefly for the filthy sin of fornication'* and likewise in 1742, Mary Dickinson of Sheephouse (the daughter of the already disowned Caleb Dickinson). (11) We can safely assumed that where a charge of fornication was levelled against a person it was done so if pregnancy was the outcome.

The only recorded case of adultery within the local Quaker community happened in 1734 and concerned a woman Friend from Shelley.

'Mary Broadhead of Grice Coming again before us at this meeting and friends Considdering the great reproach that such Unclean Accions and Adultery bringeth upon truth professors, And that the said Mary hath not been so much Concerned as (to) think she ought to have been to give forth a testimony against her filthy Accion.' (12)

How and with whom the said adultery was committed by Mary Broadhead is something that is not disclosed. Neither are we made aware of how the adultery came to be disclosed. We must assume that the affair resulted in the birth of a child. MM minutes show that she was disowned.

(1) PMMB 1762
(2) PMMB 1769
(3) Ibid
(4) PMMB 1775
(5) Ibid
(6) RDA 1834 p.252 No.2 1754
(7) PMMB 1786
(8) WMMB 1737
(9) Ibid 1738
(10) PMMB 1786
(11) WMMB 1742
(12) Ibid 1734

Insolvency and Non-Payment of Debts

Insolvency and non-payment of debts could and did lead to disownment. In 1758 the PM held at Wooldale had to consider the case of Joshua Marsden which was brought before them on the 31st of the 5th month.

'Some Friends report to this Meeting that Joshua Marsden hath fallen short of paying his Just debts. Jona. Bottomley to request him to appear at our next Preparative Meeting.' (1)

Joshua Marsden duly presented himself at the next meeting (which was held two months later at Lane Head). *'...not giveing Satisfaction'* (2) to the Meeting it was decided that his case should be laid before the next MM by the PM's representatives. Two months later, in the PM minutes, we find recorded that *'...Agreeable to ye Directions of our Last this Meeting is to Send a Testimony of Denial Against Joshua Marsden and his wife.'* (3) On the surface a harsh judgement seeming to lack in Christian charity meted out to an unfortunate man and his wife. By the standards of today we could be forgiven for thinking this an unwarranted and unjust expulsion. However, since we are not privy to the full details of the affair it is necessary to be a little more circumspect. Also we need to appreciate the religious climate of Quakerism as it then existed.

'We recommend to friends in their respective quarterly and monthly meetings, to have a watchful eye over all their members; and where they observe any deficient in discharging their contracts and just debts in due time, so as to give reasonable suspicion of weakness or negligence, that friends do earnestly advise them to a suitable care and necessary inspection into their circumstances, in order that they may be helped; and if any proceed contrary to such advise, and by their failure bring open scandal and reproach on the society, that then friends justifiably may and ought to testify against such offenders. Nevertheless it is not intended to prevent monthly meetings from exercising the discipline in cases which no advice may have been given prior to insolvency.' (4)

Quakers were expected to be totally honest in all their financial dealings and transactions. *'Maintain strict integrity in all your transaction in trade, and in your other outward concerns, remembering that you will have to account for the mode of acquiring, and the manner of using your possessions'*, was an advice to all Friends to remind them of their conduct before the eyes of God. (5) A prudent God-fearing man would take all precautions to ensure that no one suffered financial distress because of his lack of forethought or business acumen.

When Joshua Marsden's case was raised before the PM held at Wooldale, it has to be realized that any decision reached would be achieved by religious not ethical principles, after prayerful deliberation. The Meeting would discuss and evaluate the case. This decision would not be reached by a crude system of voting. The clerk of the meeting would gauge the spirit of the meeting as voiced by its members. This would not be done hurriedly or with a lack of care but with due gravity. The decision was by no means a foregone conclusion although admittedly Joshua Marsden would have had to put forward a very good reason for being wrongly judged. In this instance it is doubtful that Joshua Marsden had acted prudently in the matter of his debts. His wife's joint disownment would strongly point to her involvement. She would not otherwise have been denied membership. The case of Joshua Marsden and his wife appears to have provoked a further tightening of the strictures. A year later, in 1759, at MM held at Wakefield, the following concern presented by an unnamed Friend, was duly recorded:

'...some such Prosperous have had wives who have rather been Instruments of furthering or bringing about than hindering this scandalous Affair, & consequently have been disowned by this Mtg., & yet when such have come under the dealings of Friends the said Friends hath observed that such wifes do generally alledge that they have been keept ignorant of their Husband's Affairs and did not think Things were so bad with them as they now find they are, in Consideration of which the said Friend saith he hath for some Time had a Concern upon his Spirit to give forth the following Testimony...

...any husband finding his Circumstances declining & he is so imprudent as to conceal the same from his wife, and consequently deprive himself of that helpful Assistance Counsel & Succour which he ought to receive

from a comfortable Helpmate And also so obstinate that he will not comply with the Rules of our Society by opening his Condition to some Friend or Friends who he may think most likely to Advise and assist him therein: And as it appears to the aforesaid Friend to be every Womans natural right as well as Duty to be acquainted with her husbands Affairs as a matter of great consequence to her and her offspring as well as for the Honour of God and reputation of Truth especially if she suspect that they are declining or going backward in the World...' (6)

There can be little doubt that this concern evolved as a result of the case of Joshua Marsden and his wife. The concern then became policy with these few brief words *'...that every such Wife ought to be judged an offender & may be testified against along with her husband.'*

Extravagance in the face of unpaid debts was a charge levelled at Joshua Broadhead in 1761 when his son's marriage took place. The following extract is recorded in the minutes:

'...at the Late Marriage of Matthew Broadhead, great entertainment was suffered and made by his Father Joshua Broadhead whose Circumstances in the World is such, that he hath Neglected paying his Just Debts, some of which is of an old stand, & he having been before said Marriage advised to the Contrary very Closely...' (7)

Joshua Broadhead seemed to take some exception to this allegation as he was present at Wooldale Meeting in person to defend himself the following month when his case was raised:

'Joshua Broadhead happening to be at this Meeting & seem'd to say a deal on his own Behalf concerning the late Marriage of his son & which is but Little Satisfaction to Friends, this Meeting leaves the further Consideration thereof to our next.' (8)

Whatever he had to say on the topic on that 6th day of 1st Month of 1762 did little to impress local Friends. They were probably only too aware of his misconduct in over-spending on a wedding. In a closely knit society like that of the Quakers in High Flatts and Wooldale it would be almost impossible to hide a sumptuous affair like a large wedding feast. When the matter was raised again the following month at next PM a decision was finally deliberated unfavourably, as this entry minutes:

'The Affair of Joshua Broadhead being Reconsidered & he also being present, & seem'd again to Vindicate his former Proceedings & not Rightly sensible of his Situation, which being no Satisfaction to this Meeting the Representatives are desired to represent the Case at our MM.' (9)

Friends felt that it was necessary to have Joshua Broadhead reprimanded for his conduct by the authority of the MM since he was obviously not prepared to accept their enforcement of discipline. Whatever his debts and worldly circumstances, he must have managed to clear them because no further mention is made in the next few years. The minutes record a statement directly from MM condemning extravagant behaviour at weddings:

'Some acct. has been given to this Meeting by some particular persons that in their opinion some extravagancy hath Lately been committed at Marriages in their Particular Meeting of High Flatts, both w. respect Provision & Invitations which is much discouraged by this Meeting who desires the Representatives to Publish same, & desires the Elders will be Careful to give timely advice for the Future.' (10)

Joshua Broadhead was reprimanded as the above minute details — but in this instance there was no sterner measure brought against him. Presumably he had cleared himself of the said debts before the matter could be taken more seriously. One also has the impression that the case was rather more zealously brought before the meeting than might have been so a year or two earlier. 1761 was the year of John Griffith's visit to the area. (See 'The Visit of John Griffith'). The suspicion that Joshua Broadhead was 'deliberately' hauled up for censure cannot be entirely dismissed. (The local meetings had received *'plentiful admonitions'* concerning their lack of 'oversight' in that year). The fact that he is not specifically named in the MM statement and that the extract refers to *'marriages'* would seem to indicate that he was not alone in being guilty of extravagance when catering for his son's wedding. There is also a criticism of the lack of care shown by the local elders who appear not to have advised Joshua Marsden against his unwise and extravagent marriage arrangements. In this instance the whole matter appeared to have been blown out of all proportion to the problem. Contrasting the cases of Joshua Marsden and Joshua Broadhead one can see the extremes that it was possible to fall into when it came to matters of debt. The two cases are not the only ones brought before the meetings, but they are each typical of the treatment that could be expected if one strayed beyond the bounds of what was permissable under the rules of 'plain behaviour'.

(1) PMMB 1758
(2) Ibid
(3) Ibid
(4) RDA 1834 p.274 No.14 1732
(5) Ibid p.2 Advices
(6) MMMB 1759
(7) PMMB 1761
(8) Ibid 1762
(9) Ibid
(10) Ibid

The Unnecessary Frequenting of Ale Houses

The consumption of alcholic beverages in moderation was not regarded as an offence by Quakers in the eighteenth century. Considering that beer was more of a staple drink than tea or coffee the reason is plainly clear. Temperance was a Victorian institution promulgated by Evangelical Friends. However, the consumption of alcohol was one thing whilst the *'unnecessary frequenting of Alehouses'* was something else entirely.

'Bretheren, we caution you against resorting to places of public diversions, unnecessarily frequenting taverns and alehouses, and mixing yourselves in such company and conversation, as having a tendency to corrupt your hearts...We especially warn you to beware of the too frequent use of spirituous liquors, and intemperance of every kind...' (1)

The alehouses of this period would bear no resemblance to the public houses of today. Some would be the haunts of the disreputable, criminal and low, as well as being *'dens of iniquity and vice.'* It is no wonder that they would arouse strong feelings in Friends. Frequenting alehouses unnecessarily was bound to lead to censure by the meeting. Friends would not be alone in shunning these places of worldly corruption. Other churches had similar attitudes.

The policy of censure played a far more important role with regards to *'frequenters'* than did the ultimate sanction of disownment. A certain degree of latitude was allowed in dealing with offenders who suffered with a 'weakness' for regular visits. Friend's forbearance with a 'fallen' member could reflect the patience of Job — and did in the case of George Cartwright. His long but sorry tale is worth recounting in full to see how patient Friends of this period could be with one of their community. The first mention of George Cartwright's misconduct is recorded in the minutes of the 5th day of the 8th month 1753 for PM held at Lane Head:

'The bad Conduct of Geo. Cartwright in frequenting Alehouses over much without needful occasion which have Led ye Geo. to Act much Contrary to Frds. known rules ye same being reported & considered of in this Meeting and Frds. in regard to ye said Geo. ask for advice Requests Jn. Broadhead, Jo. Firth and Caleb Marsden to speak to George...and report what answer Geo. gives them.' (2)

So, the Friends delegated to do their duty visited George Cartwright to see what he had to say in his own favour. From the next minute, recorded just two months later, it seems as though George had been going through a 'bad patch' and asked Friends to allow him time to sort himself out:

'Agreeable to Request ye aforementioned Frds. spoke to Geo. Cartwright relating his past misconduct and he seems to Desire that Frds. would see how to behave a little further. So this Meeting agrees to his request.' (3)

For the next eight years the minutes remained silent, George Cartwright appearing to have mended his ways. Not at all. The reputation of Wooldale Friends appeared to have had a hard time as a result of George's continuing misconduct, as this minute for the 12th month 1761 shows:

'...Nothwithstanding the Long forebearance of Friends that Geo. Cartwright Still Continues to frequent Alehouses Unnecessarily. His behaviour there is very unbecoming & a scandal to our Society...' (4)

When interviewed by representatives of the meeting to explain himself George appeared to have laid on the charm and to have made quite a performance of his act of contrition. Four months later the minutes record:

'Geo. Cartwright appearing agreeable to request & readily acknowledges his fault, & seems to take the advice of his Frds. kindly, So Frds. out of a Tender regard to said George, Refer the Consideration thereof a little longer, to see whether or no his Conduct will be better & desires he may put the better in Practice.' (5)

Eight months later, in a minute of 1762, George's drinking habits did not seem to have yet fully resolved themselves and the meeting requested that the newly appointed overseers *'take an opportunity with him in order to Encourage him to amendment.'* Four months later the overseers, having seen George, reported that they *'have hopes of some amendment.'* Whatever hopes Friends had for *'some amendment'* proved short lived. Five months later George was in trouble again for the self-same reasons:

'Some Frds. appointed by this Meeting have this Day taken an opportunity with George Cartwright, who finds he is not yet clear of unnecessary frequenting of Alehouses as he ought to be which he confesses & takes Friends Care over him kindly, & desires that Friends would continue their Care over him a little longer. this Meeting at present complies therewith.' (6)

It is all beginning to sound a little bit too familiar and repetitive. One can almost picture George Cartwright's 'solemn' contrition straining the credulity of the meeting. When this 'roguish' character is seen by Joseph Firth in his capacity as an overseer, the PM minutes of the 12th month 1764, quote George as having said to him that *'his conduct was not so bad as was reported.'* (7) Friends were of course appointed to investigate the truth of this statement. The following month, the first of the new year, saw *'Fresh complaints brought to this Meeting concerning the conduct of George Carwright...'* with a further team of Friends, headed by William Earnshaw *'to make enquiry into George's conduct.'* They were by this time past being taken in by penitent contritions:

'The Frds. appointed to speak to George Cartwright report they took an opportunity with him, but reapt little or no satisfaction therein, & found he could not altogether clear himself of the reports laid against him, especially in unnecessary frequenting of alehouses & Drinking to excess, the Representatives are desired to lay the same before our next Monthly Meeting.' (8)

He had obviously been liked and tolerated by local Friends but his total abandonment to drink, despite their protracted forbearance, could only have one inevitable consequence. Surprisingly, MM gave him one last chance to repent. Before the ink had even dried on the paper, as this final minute written at High Flatts in 1766 records, George managed to 'blot' his copy book for the very last time:

'In a minute of this Meeting 10 mo: 1765 the Representatives were to Lay the Misconduct of Geo. Cartwright before the Monthly meeting which was accordingly done, & hoping the Monthly Meeting expectation of being more Circumspect for the present time to come, he was left under the care of this Meeting. And as now a fresh complaint is made that he still continues in Unnecessary frequenting of alehouses & no hope of amendment, the Representatives are desired to inform Monthly Meeting.' (9)

Not all Friends received the tolerant treatment which George Cartwright received. Where George Cartwright had a weakness for drink which must have been seen in purely simple terms as a personal drink problem, protracted patience was understandable. Thomas Lister was not so fortunate for he manage to combine the vices of drinking to excess and fornication. This was a far graver matter:

'The conduct of Thos. Lister as mentioned in a minute of Last Month hath been here considered, and we find by accts. given by several friends present, that he hath for most part of the time since he came into these parts, been too much in practice of unnecessarily attending of Alehouse and sometimes in drinking to excess, which several friends hath spoak to him about, who gave him such advice as they thought necessary, but to them he pretended such reports were many of them without foundation; but to our Sorrow we have reason to believe that instead of reforming, he hath of late been drawn into more excess in spending his time and money at Alehouses & we are doubtful often in drinking to Excess, and as one Evil leads to another, may have reason to believe that he is guilty of Fornication, all of which hath brought a reproach upon the Truth, and us as a People; wherefore this Meeting desires the Representatives to lay the same before our own next Monthly Meeting.' (10)

Thomas Lister was not the only Friend to have found himself in such circumstances. Other instances are to be found in the minute books for the three meetings. However, the two cases colourfully illustrate the dangers of wrong social conduct for Friends.

(1) RDA 1834 p.252 No.2 1754
(2) PMMB 1753
(3) Ibid
(4) Ibid 1761
(5) Ibid
(6) Ibid 1762
(7) Ibid 1764
(8) Ibid
(9) Ibid 1765
(10) PMMB 1770

Non-attendance at Meeting for Worship

Meeting for Worship was, and still is, the focal point of all religious activity for Friends. Today, Friends' Meetings for Worship are usually only of an hours duration. It is not mandatory to attend every Sunday meeting: though most Friends would consider it very important to attend on a regular basis. In the eighteenth century Meetings for Worship were considerably longer (sometimes 3-4 hours in length) and members were expected to attend conscientiously. Most Friends in this period would attend twice on a First Day (Sunday); once in the morning and then again in the afternoon. At most meetings there would also be a mid-week Meeting for Worship. As a result of its fundamental importance to the observance of the faith irregular and non-attending members would soon find themselves in trouble. Prolonged absence was not to be recommended as we shall shortly see.

The Meeting for Worship was not just a corporate expression of faith, it was also a social gathering of Friends. After worship Quakers would have the opportunity to be more informal. Local problems and difficulties could be discussed. Family groups would also have occasion to meet. Frequently, a meal would follow, especially when one considers the distances that some members might have had to travel in order to attend. Many a courtship and marriage started as result of this social interaction. A protracted absence by a Friend would not only be noticeable, it would be commented upon. Eventually it would reach the point where the absent Friend or Friends would be visited and questioned about their non-attendance. If they continued to avoid attending after such a visitation then the whole affair could end up being brought up at MM. As we are by now aware this type of confrontation was best avoided. Visitation was, as usual, done according to Quaker practice and its after effects, if any, were dealt with in a prescribed manner by a meeting for discipline:

'Persons proffesing with us, who absent themselves from our religious meetings, and disregard the repeated advice and endeavours of friends to stir them up to this necessary duty, are to be dealt with by the monthly meeting to which they belong, even to disowning, if the case require it.' (1)

In 1761 the minutes record that Daniel Brook found himself in trouble over non-attendance. Whatever his personal motives were for not attending we shall never fully know; they are not stated in the minutes. The logical assumption seems to point to a lack of spiritual interest rather than to idleness.

'This Meeting having under its serious Consideration the Conduct of Daniel Brook of High Flatts, with respect to his neglect of Attending our Meeting for Religious Worship, which he hath done for a long time, & altho' he hath been spoak to heretofore by Appointment from this Meeting. Yet as he continues in his Neglect, of that Necessary Duty; this Meeting thinks proper to desire Jn. Broadhead, Caleb Marsden w. any other Frd. or Frds. who may be willing to attend them in order to make him as sensible of the neglect of his Duty in that respect...' (2)

John Broadhead and Caleb Marsden made no progress. They reported back to the meeting the following month (5th of the 8th Mo.) that *'they had not that satisfaction with him, with respect to his neglect of attending our Meetings for Religious Worship...'* (3) Now it seems apparent that Daniel Brook had been absenting himself for some considerable period of time. He had been advised repeatedly prior to the visit and had still refused to reform his ways. Surprisingly, the meeting did not at that point decide to present his case before MM. True to the forbearance of local Friends he was paid yet another visit — this time by one of the leading members in the area: *'Henry Dickinson Reports that he and some other Frds. had an opportunity with D.Brook but had no satisfaction with him...'* (4) Even the weighty Henry Dickinson of Strines failed to impress upon Daniel Brook the significance of his failing. Much more likely is the possibility that at this point in time Daniel Brook did not feel it necessary to explain his reasons. Inevitably, according to the formula, the *'matter was to be laid before the next monthly meeting.'* Daniel Brook could expect nothing more under the circumstances of his blatant neglect. His lack of *'satisfaction'* could be indicative of the fact that he probably offered transparent excuses for not attending which may possibly have masked a deeper reason. Nothing more is recorded in the minutes about the outcome of the case but we do know that he was not disowned in this instance. In a later entry we are informed that he had removed to Brighouse with his wife (c.1766-67) and had asked for his certificate to be sent to his new meeting. As this could only be done when someone was still in full membership we must make a tentative assumption that he mended his ways when the matter came before MM and so he was not disowned.

In another instance in 1791, Joseph Brook of Longroyd Bridge found himself in trouble with his meeting over the matter of non-attendance:

'Joseph Brook reports that he hath visited Joseph Brook of Longroydbridge, and he gave him to expect he should be more diligent in the attendance of Meetings which we understand hath been of late the Case, a Certificate on his behalf being now produced & read is with some Alterations approved and ordered to be laid before the Monthly meeting.' (5)

At this time those living in Longroyd Bridge were still counted a part of Wooldale Meeting. They were not yet counted as members of Paddock Meeting in Huddersfield. As Huddersfield was now becoming a rapidly growing industrial township, which was swallowing up small hamlets like Longroyd Bridge and Paddock, and the boundaries of the meetings were not adjusted to take account of this, some 'distant' members would take advantage of the situation. Joseph Brook was very near the recently established meeting at Paddock. He could justifiably claim that it was nearer for him to attend Paddock. However, it appears that he was not regularly attending Paddock Meeting. The implication seems obvious by the fact that he requested a certificate of transfer (presumably to Brighouse MM) as soon as he came under investigation. Hence the comment that *'Alterations'* had been made to the certificate. One cannot help wondering if these *'Alterations'* pointed out that he had been avoiding both meetings. It is likely that he was caught out in a cross-check between the two meetings. (This could have happened when the relevant certificates were being exchanged between the meetings).

(1) RDA 1834 p.141 No.38 1770
(2) PMMB 1761
(3) Ibid 1761
(4) Ibid
(5) PMMB 1791

Admittance to Membership

Membership of the Quaker fold has until this century been either by convincement or by admission in childhood whether by birth or as a minor at the request of the parents. Birthright membership was abolished in 1959. The term convincement is still applied today to those persons who have realised that their spiritual and religious life needs to be shared and expressed in the Quaker way. Birthright membership was a straight forward matter in the eighteenth century. If you were born of Quaker parents you were considered to be a Quaker. Without a formal ceremony like a Baptism to admit children into 'unity' it was necessary to permit the existence of birthright membership to satisfy certain legalities.

To become a member by convincement was altogether a different matter. Whilst the actual convincement might be very brief in itself the process of joining the Society of Friends was deemed to be a lengthier process. The entire proceedings were naturally set down. Quoting one of the typical advices from this period (1764) makes this particularly cautious approach more readily understandable:

'Advised, that monthly meetings lay hands on no man suddenly, nor speedily admit into membership, any who may come to friends' meetings as convinced persons, especially such as discover an earnestness for speedy admission into communion with us, without a seasonable time to consider their conduct. Let the innocency of their lives and conversation first be manifested, and a deputation of judicious friends be made, to enquire into the sincerity of their convincement of the truth of our religious principles, and let this appear to the satisfaction of the monthly meeting, previously to their admission.' (1)

Quite simply: having become personally convinced of 'the Truth', it was now necessary to convince Friends in the local meeting of a readiness to come into unity with them. Before placing a request for membership before the meeting it would have been an absolute pre-condition to have diligently attended Meetings for Worship for several years. Additionally, as an attender the prospective applicant would also have had to prove by conduct, conversation, manner and plainess that they were sincere in their profession of 'the Truth' and that they would never *'bring reproach to the Society.'* In the fullness of time, having broached the subject with local Friends, a request for membership could be submitted before the PM. The PM would then appoint suitable representatives, elders and overseers or other Friends to visit the applicant. The visitation would enquire into the applicants reasons for wishing to join whilst at the same time making an assessment of their understanding of Quaker testimonies and beliefs. If the applicant was successful in his endeavours the visitation would report back to the PM which in turn would lay the matter before the next MM.

The attainment of membership, as we can see, was no easy matter lightly gained. If the visitation appears to have been an ordeal, or some kind of Quaker inquisition, then this is a purely superficial understanding of the process. It has to be understood that for someone determined to join the fold in a sincere profession of faith this would not be a trial by fire. These visitations were governed by Christian tenderness and were preceded by an informal Meeting for Worship in the applicant's house. Membership was highly prized and cherished when obtained.

We can begin to understand why Quakerism was in decline during the latter part of the eighteenth century. The onus for becoming a Friend was always personal and there was never any pressure placed upon an attender to join. There could never be, and still does not exist, a casual system of membership primarily because becoming a Quaker demanded genuinely sincere committment on behalf of the applicant. There were few tangible gains to be made by becoming a member. Membership meant duty and placing yourself at the service of your fellow Friends.

'... after admittance into membership, you may not measure yourselves by others; nor take a rest short of the true rest. Seek rather an increase in the heavenly principle which comes by Jesus Christ, the true and holy pattern for his flock. Thus only, will your union with us contribute to your advantage; and thus only, will the increase of numbers produce an increase of the joy.' (2)

It thus becomes understandable how Quakers managed to perform deeds in all walks of life totally out of proportion to their numbers. Their committment was forged of stern stuff. Quakerism was and is still a way of life deeply rooted in spiritual faith. It may have softened in many respects but the onus today is still one of making a personal commitment to become a member.

Between 1774 and 1806 only 24 applications were made to join the meetings at Wooldale and High

Flatts. (Readers are referred to the Appendices). Fifteen of the applicants were men, the remaining nine were women. Of these 24 applicants in 32 years, there were only two cases of non-admission and one case of delayed admission (each worthy of examination).

A typical example of admission to the Society was George Chapman in 1774. The minutes record that he was *'a young Man, who for some Time hath attended our Meetings for Worship on first Days'* and that, *'he has made Application to be joined in Society with us.'* (3) However, what makes his case more interesting is that two years later in 1776 his brother, John Chapman, also joined with much the same sentiments being expressed *'that there appeared nothing to hinder his case.'* (4) There was a marked tendency for members of the same family to join round about the same time. (See Appendices). George and John Chapman became loyal, dedicated Friends serving the meetings in many capacities over the years. John Chapman and his wife Sarah (nee Wood) eventually removed to Cheshire in 1791.

Not all applicants found their entry into the Society as easily as the Chapman brothers. William Taylor joined in 1783 after attending *'Meetings for Worship for many Years.'* Like the Chapmans he was to prove to be a valuable acquisition. James Taylor tried to continue the family tradition in 1785 but upon being visited it is minuted by the representatives that they *'were unanimous in their opinion that he was not yet in a Proper situation of mind...'.* (George Chapman was one of the representatives sent). James Taylor tried again in 1792. He was finally accepted. Even though it took him so long to convince local Friends he too proved an asset. His name is recorded in the minutes fulfilling many tasks on behalf of the local meetings in the early years of the nineteenth century.

The only two instances of deferment and failure to seek a further application are in the cases of Georgiana Carter (1783) and Mary Lockwood (1784). For Georgiana Carter the minutes record that Friends *'are of an opinion it may be best to suspend any further proceedings respecting her case at Present.'* No reason is supplied which makes her case very mysterious in view of an earlier statement saying *'she hath attended our meetings from a Child.'* One cannot help wondering how poor Georgiana did not manage to come up to Friends satisfaction under those biographical circumstances. (Georgiana Carter died in 1788 at the age of 29. She did not apply again in the intervening years before her death). Mary Lockwood was considered as *'not yet come to a State propper to be admitted into Membership.'* Her case was *'referred to further consideration at some other time when this Meeting may think proper.'*

There a noteworthy instance of a convinced Friend being accepted into membership and within a matter of only a few years being disowned. Joshua Roberts of Shepley who was made a member in 1792 was disowned in 1797 when his marriage to Judith Dickinson (married 1793) appears to have broken down.

Where Friends in this locality admitted attenders into membership they appear generally to have done so with great wisdom. Many of the attenders who joined proved to be very creditable gains doing a little to counter the losses being experienced through disownment and movement to the new industrial growth areas.

(1) RDA 1834 p.60 No.4 1764
(2) Ibid p.60 No.5 1799
(3) PMMB 1774
(4) Ibid 1776

Returning to the Fold

Disownment, although invoked as an ultimate sanction against delinquent members, always came after due warnings. Many disowned members never sought re-admission and left the Society of Friends for good joining other persuasions. However, disownment did not have to be final and irrevocable. It was possible to be re-admitted into membership after a passage of some years. Naturally, former Friends would be expected to show and prove true contrition to the meeting. According to Quaker discipline:

'Should any person having been disowned, coming to a just sense of his misconduct, be desirous of readmission into the society, he is to apply to the monthly meeting which disowned him; which if it think proper, is to visit him, or apply to the meeting wherein he resides, to do it, and make report. The monthly meeting which disowned him is then to proceed to accept or reject his acknowledgement...if readmitted, he is to become a member in the meeting to which he formerly belonged. The same course is to be pursued in the case of a friend who may have resigned his membership...' (1)

Equally, Friends who had been *'censured'* could come back into full membership of their meeting providing they had repented. The process of *'censuring'* was not as drastic as that of disownment since it was a serious reprimand without the full force of total denial. A Friend who had been *'censured'* still needed to pursue a similar course of action to the disowned member:

'Forasmuch, as some persons who by their ill-conduct, have justly deserved and come under the censure of the meetings to which they belong, have thought to get under the weight of that judgement, by signing a paper of condemnation, and thereby have supposed themselves discharged; it is therefore recommended to friends' consideration, that they be careful not to admit such persons too early into fellowship, or give them cause to think they are accepted before the meetings are satisfied of their repentance and amendment; nothwithstanding such paper be given.' (2)

The *'paper of condemnation'* was a written condemnation of past misconduct that was presented to, and read out at, the meeting. Wooldale, High Flatts and Lane Head had their fair share of such papers. The minutes record a number of such instances where penitent Friends were subjected to this form of ordeal. The paper of acknowledgment presented by Joshua and Lydia Woodhead cited earlier (See 'Loose and Disorderly Conduct') is typical of the contrition required for re-admittance. It can be no wonder that many did not seek to come back. The earliest case mentioned was that of Joseph Brook (b.1694) of Row in 1753:

'... hath this Day Presented a Paper listing his Past misconduct acknowledging and Expressing his Sorrow for ye same wch hath been here read and he is left to his Liberty to Present ye same at MM.' (3)

From that extract one can visualize poor Joseph Brook stood before the meeting going through this uncomfortable, disconcerting and personal agony. The experience was quite obviously meant to be salutary and no doubt well succeeded in its purpose. Only a truly repentant person would subject themselves to such abasement. Now it so happens that the said Joseph Brook had two daughters: Mary (b.1721) and Hannah (b.1729).

'We have rec.'d this day two Papers from Mary & Hannah Brook two daughters of Joseph Brook who some Time since Left Frds. Which Said Papers is a Condemnation for the Past misconduct which seems to the Satisfaction of this Meeting...' (4)

Having seen their father re-admitted, the daughters decided it was time to make their own joint reconciliation. No doubt the penitent and reformed Joseph Brook was a singular influence in their decision to return to the fold. They were obviously allowed to return since by being *'left to their Liberty to Send ye Same before MM'* it was clear that their own meeting was prepared to have them back and is confirmed by MM minutes. Examining the Womens Meeting minute books confirms that Joseph Brook of Row was held to be in part responsible for their disownments because it says of him that he, *'Some years since gave their Inclinations too much Liberty in getting married by a Priest and absenting from our assemblies.'* (5)

Jennet Barraclough's (nee Ratliff) experience in 1757 was decidedly more exacting. She had been disowned in 1752 for marrying out. Repenting her past misconduct with the usual *'paper'* her case lingered on for nearly three months more. For two consecutive PM's the minutes record that *'the Affair of Jennet Barraclough to be further considered at our next (meeting).'* Finally, in the fourth month, the *'Affair Concerning Jennet Barraclough is Left to ye ordering of Frds. Agreeable to her future Conduct.'* (6) It would seem that although she was given the benefit of the doubt concerning her past delinquency the feeling within the meeting was one of definite uncertainty concerning her future behaviour. Her future conduct would be well monitored for any likely signs of regression. As her husband makes no appearance in the records we must assume that he had no wish to be in *'unity'* with Friends and consequently they felt particularly reticent about the return of Jennet Barraclough to the meeting.

The following extract is worth quoting at length for it is an actual paper of acknowledgement recorded in the minutes for 1789.

*'To Friends of Highflatts Preparative Meeting,
& Pontefract Monthy Meeting.*

Dear friends,
I was decended from Parents Professing the Truth and had my Education within the compass of Wainfleet Monthly Meeting in Lincolnshire, being a member thereof, but for want of steadily adhearing to the principles wee profess; I let out my mind after unsutable company and was thereby drawn into a Conduct and Conversation inconsistent with the pure Truth, and for many Years wholly neglected the attendance of friends Meetings, but it having pleased the Lord to bring me to a sight and sence of any outgoings and a Godly sorrow for the same, I do not find that I can be easy without making an Acknowledgement thereof, and though I was never dealt with, I have and do look upon myself as disowned and therefore request to be admitted into full unity with friends, I am with the salutation of Love,
Your friend,
Anthony Kinsley,
Skelmanthorp 5th mo. 23 1789.' (7)

Accompanying this letter was a request that *'Leah his wife ... be admitted a member of our Society.'* No similar paper is to be found recorded in PM minutes. It is more usual to find such papers in MM records consequently this sole poignant example is interesting in several respects. Firstly, that Anthony Kinsley was not apparently disowned by his own home meeting, even though he regarded himself as effectively being disowned. This might indicate that members leaving their home area could avoid disownment. Secondly, he was an outsider in every sense of the word. He had come from another part of the country and was an unknown quantity to the local meeting. This would be an unusual happening. Finally, the minuting of the letter must have served an important purpose to be included in PM minutes. Perhaps, it was a safeguard in the event of Wainfleet MM ever disowning him after such a considerable time: this could still happen. The content of the paper also reflects the kind of statements that a Friend could be expected to make in such circumstances. Anthony Kinsley was allowed back into the Society of Friends and appears to have been a faithful servant from then on.

The interval between denial and re-instatement varied from individual to individual. Joseph Brook of Row sought *'unity'* after a mere three years. Jennet Barraclough took five. Caleb Dickinson was disowned in 1722 and left his acknowledgment for nearly thirty three years seeking to be re-united in 1755. (8)

(1) RDA 1834 p.141 No.36 1782
(2) Ibid p.140 N0.35 1708
(3) PMMB 1753
(4) Ibid
(5) WMMB
(6) PMMB 1757 & WMMB 1752
(7) PMMB 1789
(8) MMDRC c.1755

Resignations from Membership

Resignation from the Society tended to be by default. Generally, Friends appeared to do all in their power to prevent resignations usually by giving those concerned time in which to consider their decision. There are no real instances of formal resignations in the minute books of the PM. The only case where the parties indicated that they were no longer interested in being regarded as members occured in 1782. This concerned two of the sons and a daughter of John Sanderson. A brief sketch of the family might prove helpful in understanding how this situation arose.

The Sanderson family was one of the earliest in the vicinity of Penistone to become convinced Quakers during the seventeenth century. Since neither Penistone nor Midhope possessed a meeting house the Sandersons attended High Flatts. It is likely that they also held Meetings for Worship at Judd Field and possibly even Sheephouse when there was no PM. John Sanderson of Midhope was probably the wealthiest of the Quakers in the area during this period. His personal subscription to the building of Lumbroyd Meeting House in 1763 amounted to a very generous and sizeable £6 5s 0d: by far the highest individual donation. (1) This generous donation is easily understandable considering the nearness and convenience that the new Meeting House at Lumbroyd would provide to the Sandersons living at Midhope. Whilst he was alive his children diligently obeyed him in all respects. There is no note of any misconduct from them during his lifetime. However, their bond to the Society must have developed into a purely token one. When John Sanderson died at least three of his children started to live the kind of life that was more typical of wealthy non-Quakers living in the area. A few brief indications of this exist in the minute books but it is not until the 11th month of 1782 that the case comes to light when a deputation from the Mens Meeting was sent to visit the two brothers (Joseph and Joshua Sanderson) and another one from the Womens Meeting to see the sister (Hannah). According to the record they had *'for sometime neglected the attendance of our Religious Meetings for Worship...'* as well as *'joined with people of another Profession in their way and manner of Worship.'* (2) Hannah Sanderson seems to have particularly offended Friends by being baptised or *'sprinkled by a Priest.'*

It is doubtful that Friends expected to get the Sandersons back into the fold. They had probably been aware for sometime that the childrens allegiance would not be very long lasting after their father's death. Nevertheless, they had to confirm the worst:

'...friends have Visited Joseph, Joshua & Hannah Sanderson Children of the late John Sanderson but met with no satisfaction the sons expressing thay had no desire to be Continued as members of Our Society...' (3)

Financial considerations apart, the loss of a family like the Sandersons must have been deeply felt and their motives noted. Quite possibly someone delivered ministry round about this time, in one of the local meetings, on the theme of the *'evils of wealth and its temptations to worldly and vain pleasures.'* The Sandersons became Methodists. Whatever the Sandersons' reasons, they had their wish; their case went to the next MM where their decision to leave was formally recognized.

(1) See Appendix [5]
(2) PMMB 1782
(3) Ibid

Gravestones and Mourning

It is hard to believe, as you enter through the gate from Pell Lane into the grounds of Wooldale Meeting House, that it was ever used as a burial ground. A keen observer might notice the gentle bumps visible in these grounds and realize their significance. Most visitors, not conversant with Quaker history, would never realize that these are the unmarked graves of Friends long departed. Only the tell-tale, small headstones of this century, situated near the childrens meeting room, might indicate that this was a burial ground. A stark contrast indeed to the local church and chapel graveyards. Plainess in life also meant plainess in death. The idea of having a gravestone to mark one's resting place became as inconsistent with Quakerly principles as wearing lace or bright colours. The observance of this ruling must have tried some Friends as this particular advice of 1717 would indicate:

'This Meeting being informed that Friends in some Places have gone into the Vain & Empty Custom of Erecting Monuments of the Dead Bodies of Friends by Stones, Inscriptions, Tomb Stones, etc., & being Very desirous Friends should keep a commendable Plainess & Simplicity in this as well as other respects, it is therefore the advice of this Meeting that all such Monuments as are already in being over the dead bodies of Friends should be removed as much as many be with Discretion & Conveniancy: And that none be anywhere made or set up by or over the dead bodies of Friends or others in Friends Burying places for Times to come.' (1)

This was easier said than done. Human nature being what it is, then as now, the idea of being interred in an unmarked grave must have been most unappealing. It would have been carried out but probably more from a sense of Quakerly duty than anything else. At Wooldale even Henry Jackson's family gravestones were removed and put to a more practical use. (See 'Henry Jackson II' & 'Wooldale Meeting House'). However, like the periodic warnings on ornamentation and clothing, there was regular need to remind Friends of their austere duties to the dead as this advice from MM of 1765 suggests:

'As the practice of erecting Gravestones in some places appears to be continued, (not withstanding the advice of this Meeting to the contrary) I think it expedient to revive ye Minutes of 1717 (on it?), & earnestly recommend its observance to Friends in general.' (2)

The advice was either not properly communicated or, more likely, it went unheeded. The following year a further reminder on the subject had to be issued. It was not until 1850 that permission was granted for gravestones to be erected subject to the approval of the MM concerned.

Neither were Friends to *'imitate the vain custom of wearing or giving mourning...'* nor were there to be any *'... extravagant expenses about the internment of the dead.'* For a while, Friends even discouraged the attendance of female Friends at burials until in 1782 an advice was issued, stating that *'...it becomes both sexes to show for their deceased relations and friends...'* (3) This was a return to earlier principles and certainly more in keeping with distinctive Quaker testimonies such as equality of the sexes.

(1) RDA 1834 p.70 No.1 1717
(2) MMMB 1765
(3) RDA 1834 p.70-71 No.5 1782

Entertainment

To understand local Friends' attitudes towards *'diversions, sports and pastimes'* we must appreciate the significance of the key word *'diversions.'* Indulging in activities that had little spiritual uplift or no religious end in themselves was regarded as being wholly negative. It is necessary to treat every encounter of the word *'diversion'* as meaning to divert from the spiritual life. Equally, it is important to acquaint ourselves with the then current advice on the subject. Since the following advice of 1799 tends to be a fairly comprehensive embodiment of previous advices the relevant part is reproduced in full to help provide a further insight into Quaker thinking:

'This meeting has repeatedly testified against vain sports, and places of diversion, as so many allurements tending to draw the mind from its watch, and to lay it open to further temptation. The best recreation of a Christian is the relief of distress; and his chief delight to promote the knowledge, and exalt the glory, of his heavenly master: and this is most effectually done, under his holy influence, by a life of faith, purity, and general benevolence. False principles too, as well as wrong practices, may have their advocates for a time; but the unspotted lives of the faithful remain to be their best refutation, let none then start aside at the magnitude, or be too much dismayed because of the little progress they seem themselves to make in the way of holiness; but, trusting in the Lord, who giveth power to the faint, let us all press after ability to comply with the apostolic advice, 'Be ye holy in all manner of conversation.' (I Peter 15) (1)

If the above advice is coupled to the other advices regulating sober, virtuous and industrious patterns of behaviour we become aware of the totality of committment expected from Quakers of the Quietist age. To comprehend a life devoid of music, art, literature, the theatre and other forms of entertainment, is to enter the very heart, mind and being of eighteenth century Quakerism. Visualizing Quaker homes without pictures, ornaments, musical instruments, or literary works, is difficult. Our local records remain silent on homes and entertainments. We need to refer to accounts about Quakers written by outsiders like Thomas Clarkson whose 'Portraiture of Quakerism' provides vivid descriptions of the lifestyle of Friends. However, it is evident that the Friends of Wooldale and High Flatts frequently found it difficult to lead such untainted and austere lifestyles on many occasions. An interesting minute of 1766 records:

'In this Meeting friends were closely & unanimously concerned to advise friends not to suffer their Children & servants to go to Fairs & other places of diversion without having any substantial business.' (2)

So how did local Friends entertain themselves in their leisure hours if they were prohibited from the usual popular activities? Surveying the extensive libraries at Wooldale and High Flatts the answer appears strongly to indicate reading. Levels of literacy were generally better among Friends than those of similar groupings. (See 'Education'). Given Friends' preoccupation with education and that they were by and large of a well-to-do middle class background, reading as a recreational outlet is hardly surprising.

Reading content was naturally confined to works of a religious nature. This was engendered from the earliest age. Parents were, *'not to allow their Children to read play books romances of: but rather the holy Scriptures.'* (3) The Bible held the place of prominence, followed by religious tracts, pamphlets, devotional works and the journals of travelling Friends. Special provision existed to ensure that poorer

Friends were not denied the opportunities of reading. The Women's Meeting minutes for 1754 record that:

'The Representatives to York Considered to Purchase a number of Frds. primers for ye use of our poorer Friends.'

In 1771 the PM records show that copies of the Bible were distributed to poorer Friends. There were also donations made of popular works to be distributed to those less well-off as this minute of 1754 illustrates:

'Three books brought from Monthly Meeting to this acct. of ye life & travels In ye work of ye ministry of John Fothergill, two of the said being a Gift of Jn. Fothergill ye younger to be handed to Frds. of low circumstances in ye world.' (4)

The publication of new books or reprints was the responsibility of Friends. Usually the publication of a particular work was decided upon by a QM or even YM with terse minuted comments like *'the QM has ordered some books to be printed...Friends are desired to Consider what number they will be likely to take'* (1752). (5) Based on the returns an edition would be published. Quite a few instances of such subscriptions being raised and met are noted in the records of both MM and PM. By far the most interesting of these subscription records is one relating to the publication of John Griffith in 1765:

'Subscriptions for Jn. Griffith's Books are 48. Viz: Henry Dickenson, Jn. Broadhead of Wooldale, Thos. Roberts, Joseph Woodhead, Joshua Marsden, Wm. Radley, Jn. Bottomley, Joshua Broadhead of Wooldale, John Parkin, Tobias Mallinson Jr., Joshua Broadhead of Ridings, Joseph Firth, Jn. Wood, each of 'em one. Joseph Brook of Wooldale 13, Wm. Earnshaw 4, Sam Wood 2, Joshua Broadhead of Biggin 4. Jn. Broadhead of Meltham 2, Godfrey Woodhead of Penistone & James Dickinson 10.' (6)

The very large total number purchased, let alone certain individual purchases, only further serves to confirm the impact that this American Friend had on his visit in 1761. (See 'The Visit of John Griffith') It is also an indicator of the relative affluence of some members. This is further confirmed by a subscription the following year:

'Geo. Fox's Journals are Come to Pontefract, the friends that have subscribed are desired to give pay for them to one of our Representatives on first day next being 12/6d per book.' (7)

The high price of the Journal is most illuminating but considering that a copy of Thomas Story's Journal cost 12s 9d in 1752 we can be left in no doubt that local Friends were serious readers. Rather than attempt to exhaustively detail every title that was purchased by local meetings a brief list of typical titles is supplied for study.

(1) 'Reasons why the people called Quakers do not pay Tythes'
(2) 'The Great Case of Tythes Truly stated'
(3) 'Brief Remarks on the common arguments now used in support of divers Ecclesiastical Matters'
(4) 'The Way of Life revealed and the Way of Death discovered'
(5) 'Reasons for the necessity of Silent Meeting in order for the Solemn Worship of God'

Yet these titles were not the most popular items borrowed from the shelves of the libraries. Local Friends seemed keener to read the journals of travelling Friends: particularly those who had visited meetings in the vicinity. Thus the works and travels of George Fox, Thomas Story, John Fothergill, Benjamin Holmes, John Griffith, John Churchman and others were highly popular. However, the most popular work by far was Samuel Bownas's Journal which was repeatedly removed by *'diverse Friends'* for their edification. It was closely followed by John Fothergill's Journal. The content matter was undoubtedly lighter than of the type of material before mentioned. Perhaps, being able to read of the adventures of Friends in faraway places such as North America and the West Indies provided the only form of escapism that was allowed.

(1) RDA 1834 p.44 No.20 1799
(2) PMMB 1766
(3) WMMB 1754
(4) PMMB 1771
(5) PMMB 1752
(6) Ibid 1765
(7) Ibid 1766

Tithes and Sufferings

George Fox and the early Quakers totally rejected the concept of a clergy entirely on scriptural grounds: *'freely ye have received, freely give.'* (Matt. 10.8) Consequently, Friends refused to pay tithes to maintain local clergymen and their parish churches. It became a central tenet of Quakerism for nearly two hundred years until tithes and church rates were abolished. Since the gospel had been freely given it was not necessary to pay *'hireling Priests'* who had *'made a trade of saints' words, and the apostles' and prophets' words, and gotten a great deal of money by them.'* (1) There were various abuses within the Anglican Church of the seventeenth century and, by the eighteenth century the abuses had worsened. Absentee rectors and vicars derived large personal incomes to pursue the leisured life of country gentry. They seldom visited their parishes leaving the daily labours and ministration to curates. Robert D'Oyley, who succeeded Joseph Briggs upon his death in 1727 as the Vicar of Kirkburton, was a typical example of a non-resident. Vicar of Windsor, as well as Kirkburton for nearly forty years, he only paid three visits to this local parish leaving his curate, John Hardy, to attend to the spiritual needs of his flock. (2) A lesser, but equally more pernicious abuse, was *'the custom of buying and selling pews'* which *'was the only recognized way of obtaining a seat in God's house.'* (3) In Quaker eyes absentee vicars were beyond the pale. Neither did Quakers regard church buildings, or *'steeple-houses'*, with any special reverence: God's 'house' was everywhere. The selling of pews, as occured locally at Honley, only further convinced Quakers that there was a trade being made of religion. Hence their dissenting stand.

Inevitably such a stance provoked a wave of persecution initiated by the clergy who did not like to have their income whittled away and authority challenged. The reluctant Quakers found that their goods and possessions were distrained or seized when they refused to pay these church taxes. Incarcerations in prisons were the lot of those who did not pay and would not allow their valuables to be so seized: some even died in these prisons for their testimony against the injustice of tithes. By the eighteenth century the persecutions had almost disappeared. Tithes still continued to be demanded by the Parish and Quakers still continued to resist their payment. Local Friends diligently maintained their testimony against tithes in this period. In the Pontefract MM 'Book of Sufferings 1688-1793' we find recorded a comprehensive statement of resistance to tithes in this area for 105 years. The earliest case recorded is that of Samuel Naylor of Skelmanthorpe in 1691, who had wheat, barley, oats and pease to the value of £1 2s 0d seized by one, Robert Ouldham. At the same time George Dyson took barley worth 3s 6d. In 1697, Joshua Broadhead of Wooldale had goods taken *'by night, obtained by Joseph Briggs priest of Kirkburton'* worth 8s 6d *'for 6s 8d demanded.'* To fully catalogue every instance of such seizures is beyond the scope of this book. However, a few extracts from the early years of the eighteenth century are worthy of mention and are reproduced here for consideration.

'Taken from Daniel Broadhead for 3s 9d demanded by Joseph Briggs vicar of Kirkburton, & by notice of a warrent under the hand (sealed) of J. Farnsley and Godf. Boswell goods to ye value 6s 10d.' (1702)

'Taken from Richard Brook of Row (Lockwood) in ye Parish of Almondbury ye 22nd of ye 2 Mo:1706 by William Dyson Constable & William Swallow Churchwarden 5 pewter Dishes & 3 Brass ( )iggs to ye value of 12s 6d by warrant from from Sir John Kay & Jn. Anby for 5s 6d for Steeple house Repairs.'

'Taken from Hen. Jackson Jun. 25 5 mo:1710 by Godfrey Crossland Constable 11 poules or Small hens by virtue of a warrant under ye hand of Richard Witton and Jo. Anby for 4s 9d demanded by Jos. Briggs Professor — small ditto worth 14s 0d.'

'Taken from Henry Jackson by ye aforesaid persone (Joseph Swallow Constable & Joseph Hurst Churchwarden) for 3s 4d demanded by said Priest (Joseph Briggs) and 5d charges goods worth 10s 0d.' (1712)

'Taken from Wm. Earnshaw of Totties by the aforesaid persone for 2s 10d demanded by said Priest & 5d charges Brass & iron ( ) worth 12s 0d.' (1712) (4)

Joseph Briggs, the *'very troublesome and litgious'* vicar of Kirkburton for nearly sixty years, was particularly vigorous in ensuring that he obtained his full dues, prosecuting with the full weight of the law in support. His view on the *'schismatics'* were well known and voiced. Briggs viewed the role of the clergy, and specifically himself, as *'active instruments'* of a mission: that mission *'was to restore the dissenters again to the body of the church; and if his persuasions failed in their object, he did not scruple to call upon the civil magistrate to enforce obedience.'* (5)

The value of the goods seized in nearly every recorded instance was greater than the the actual amount demanded with legal charges thrown in for good measure. Even personal standing, position and wealth in the community were no immunity to these church demands as we can see from Henry Jackson's inclusion.

As the century progressed the seizures became an accepted facet of Quaker existence, an unvarying ritual of carefully noted lists of members and their individual and collective sufferings at the hands of the *'hireling Priests'* as this abstract of 1755 shows:

'The 22nd of the 5th Mo: Taken by Chris. Green Constable of Holmfirth by the above Authority (Wm. Radcliff & Jn. Smith, Justices) and for the same Priest (Robert Doyley of Kirkburton) Viz. From

	Seized	Value	Demanded
Sam Greenwood	Malt	8s 4d	3s 9d
Wm. Earnshaw	Meal	4s 9d	2s 4d
Jn. Broadhead	Cloth	9s 4d	4s 4d
Jo. Broadhead	Meal	6s 1d	3s 0d
Jn. Parkin	Meal	4s 8d	2s 4.5d
Robt. Broadhead of Meltomhouse	Wheat	11s 4d	5s 3d
Jn. Woodhead	A Range & Iron goods	6s 0d	2s 9d
Ab. Beaumont	Meal	9s 6d	4s 9d (6)

In the 5th month 1764, the case of Daniel Broadhead of Mearhouse contending with William Mountjoy, the vicar of Kirkburton, surfaced illustrating a rare but serious instance of tithe abuse which led to the involvement of MM. The following letter, recorded in MM minutes, is explicitly detailed:

Pontefract 10th 5th 1764

To Wm. Mountjoy Priest of Kirkburton

Respect'd Friend

Whereas we are inform'd that Tho: Littlewood Deputy Constable of Holmfirth came to the House of our Friends Robert and Daniel Broadhead of Mearhouse with a Warrant of Distress under the hand and Seal of a Majestrate for a demand of 3/1d upon the said Robert Broadhead at thy suit, and not withstanding it was told him again and again that the Goods he Distrain'd were not the property of the said Robert but Daniel's against whom he had no Authority and also the Goods of the said Robert was show'd to him upon which might have made Distress but refused and Illegally Seiz'd and carried away the Goods of the said Daniel upon which he applyed to an Attorney and order'd him to Write to the said Littlewood and let him know that if he did not return the said Goods so Distrain'd he might expect trouble from him the said Daniel upon that Acct. This affair being brought to our Cognisance by a Friend in that Neighbourhood who did not approve of the young Man Daniel's conduct we think it our duty to inform thee that we had no knowledge of it and if he had apply'd to us for advice if we cou'd not have persuad'd him to have submitt'd to the Distress as a Suffering upon a Religious Acct. we shou'd have derect'd him to have applyed to thee in the first place and if thou had refus'd to relieve him he might afterwards have complain'd to the Justices who granted the Warrent rather than have recourse to a Lawman for which we are sorry, who are with due regard thy well wishing Friends the people called Quakers.'

(Addendum to the Letter).

'The Priest had threatened to proceed according to the rigor of the Law but this Letter assuaged him. Robert Broadhead & Joseph Firth carried the Letter.' (7)

William Mountjoy, described as *'a worthy, pious minister, a good preacher'* with *'amiable and conciliatory manners,'* appears to have responded to this common sense apppeal with some grace. It is doubtful that, even if Mountjoy had proceeded, as he threatened to do with *'the full rigor of the Law'* that he would have been successful given the nature of the injustice. The publicity alone, resulting from a legal action, would ultimately have done very little for his reputation.

Towards the end of the century, in 1792, the seizures had become fully systematized. The formal language of distraint remained the same with only a few changes in names to indicate the passage of time as this abstract reveals:

'Taken by virtue of a warrant granted by Henry Zouch & Pemberton Millns. Justices by John Bray Deputy Constable of Holmfirth for Benjamin Kay Priest of Kirkburton for one year demand of small tithes

From:

	Seized	*Demanded*	*Value*
Thos. Roberts of Wooldale	*Oatmeal*	*1s 3d*	*3s 2d*
Joseph Brook of Wooldale	*Oatmeal*	*2s 0d*	*4s 7d*
Wm. Earnshaw of Wooldale	*Oatmeal*	*1s 0.5d*	*2s 0d*
Jn. Roberts of Totties	*Oatmeal*	*1s 2.5d*	*3s 0d*
Sarah Broadhead of Melthouse	*Oatmeal*	*3s 3.5d*	*7s 2d*
Daniel Broadhead of Mearhouse	*Oatmeal*	*1s 10d*	*4s 4d*
Matthew Broadhead of New Mill	*Oatmeal*	*1s 0.5d*	*2s 9d*
Godfrey Woodhead of Foulstone	*Malt*	*2s 10.5d*	*6s 4d* (8)

The information contained within these tithe details serves to illuminate some interesting points. The process of seizure in this area had, by 1792, ossified into a ritual which Friends continued to use unhesitatingly to defy this particular injustice. This was in sharp contrast to the notorious Lothersdale Tithe Case in 1791 when eight Quakers were imprisoned at York for refusing to make such payment. (9) The seizure of goods had become uniform in the type taken. It was easier, after all, for the Church authorities to dispose of whole consignments of a staple like oatmeal rather than an ill-assortment of personal possessions. There is also a decline in the amount demanded by the Church from Friends in the latter part of the century. The most likely explanation for the decrease is to be found in the large number of enclosures being carried out in this period. The system of parcelling land into fields created serious difficulties for the Parish in gathering its tithes. As compensation the Parish received grants of land which helped offset the amounts paid by the local inhabitants to the *'Mother Church.'* Church rates were paid instead and these were smaller. There is no evidence, despite the onset of an economic depression, that Friends were becoming poorer although this cannot be entirely discounted.

The only major irregularity in maintaining the testimony against tithes was bound up in a purely technical legality and involved a small number of Friends living in the Wooldale and Penistone areas. A few of them, for many generations, had paid a kind of tithe to the Duke of Norfolk Hospital in Sheffield. It was actually a *'Modus in lieu of Tithes.'* During the mid-1790's those Friends paying the modus were challenged by MM and their PM concerning these payments. The matter was never successfully resolved as Friends involved in the payment of the said modus refused to stop its payment claiming that it was more akin to rent than tithe. MM and PM always maintained that it was a tithe. (10)

(1) 'Wait in the Light' pub. QHS 1981. Quoted p.11 Ep.249 (1667)
(2) Morehouse p.68-69
(3) 'A History of Honley' Mary Jagger
(4) MMBS 1702-1712
(5) Morehouse p.67
(6) MMBS 1755
(7) MMMB 1764
(8) MMBS 1792
(9) For a detailed account see Thistlethwaite p.433 or MMMB
(10) MMMB 1798

Quaker Women

Women, within the Quaker fold, enjoyed a truer sense of equality with men than any other religious group in British society during the last three hundred years. Equality was based upon sound scriptural interpretation coupled to a profound insight into the natural and complementary functions and roles of both sexes.

'There is no such thing as Jew or Greek, slave and freeman, male and female; for you are all one person in Christ Jesus.' (Galatians 3.28 NEB)

The much quoted Pauline aberration (Ephesians 5.22-23 NEB) with its emphasis on female submission was largely and justly ignored by Friends. (1)

It is easy, in the latter part of the twentieth century, to be dismissive of this early Quaker equality given the paradoxical division of the men and women into separate business meetings. Our latter day perceptions need to become historically attuned and our prejudices need to be stilled if we are to appreciate the realities of an age long past. That age shares so little of our contemporary ethos and social climate as to be almost an alien landscape. We must be prepared to accept that separate meetings for business allowed an autonomy and expression of thought and life which might otherwise not have survived. Quakers were the products of their own time and society in which the position of women was one of subservience. (In such a context mixed meetings for business would have tended to see feminine growth stunted). The wider social conditioning of the age would have resulted in the women increasingly deferring to the decisions of men and to greater conformacy with society at large. In their own meetings women were free and unfettered, charged with the governing of their religious and social affairs, and capable of an unhampered spiritual growth without undue male influence. The number of recorded women ministers, both locally and throughout the land, testify so eloquently to this truly egalitarian mode of conduct. (2) (See Appendices (10), (13) & (16)) In no other circumstance could the women of this age have been allowed to travel freely as ministers, with their own special concerns, across the length and breadth of the land and even overseas.

Under the legal system of the day women were sorely constrained. The 'coveture' system ensured that married women lost their legal rights to own property, enjoy such wages as they could earn or even have a right to their own children. Men were expected to be solely responsible for financial matters. In this respect Quaker men conformed to the existing laws of the land. However, Quaker men readily acknowledged the indisputable and considerable strengths of women. Quaker women were charged with the responsibilities of the home and the bringing up of children. It was the women who were charged with ensuring 'plainess' of dress and home furnishing. It was their duty to curb extravagant domestic expenses. (See 'Debt & Insolvency' with regards to a wife's culpability in the cause of debt). To their keeping was commended the bringing up of the children to walk in Quaker ways. Thus by example children would learn plainess of speech and good 'plain' conduct. A minute from the Women's PM minute book records the importance of these task in 1719:

'...Friends should keep to plainess both in speech & habit & keep in ye moderation in all things that we may be good examples to our children & bring them up in ye way that ye should go; that we may adorn ye Gospel of our Lord Jesus Christ which we make profession of; And it hath allso been advised several times to keep to ye days of ye week according to scripture, and not as ye heathens.' (3)

Conduct beyond the boundaries of the home was also considered their rightful province as this extract from 1733 indicates:

'...to Advise one another to have a watchful eye over our Youth in their going to as Cumming from our meetings to see that they behave themselves orderly and that they may give no occation of offence to any.' (4)

It was also the duty of the women to bring about such education of their children as they could. This too needed to be right-minded as this minute from the same source records in 1730, advising:

'...parents not to allow their Children to read play Books romances of: but rather the holy scriptures which is to be ordered to be recorded in this Book for future services.' (5)

As an interesting aside, Quaker women of the eighteenth century were generally more literate than their contemporaries. Examining the Women's Meeting minute books discloses visual evidence of their progress. The earliest recorded minutes dating back to 1713 show childishly immature handwriting with little conception of spelling, grammar or style but by the middle of the century the writing is polished, composed and the equal match of the beautiful wrought copperplate scripts of the men. Nor was this ability limited to a few women. The number of different clerks of meetings appointed to keep these records, each with their own characteristic hand, testifies to this significant fact. To what extent this level of education permeated the entire membership we cannot be absolutely certain.

Where else, beyond the scope of their homes and their God given right to be ministers, did local Quaker women exhibit their natural equality? It is generally conceded, by most men today, that women are usually more empathetic to the social situations around them. It was the women Friends who were charged with the task of noting those in distress and need. It was they who were responsible for informing the men of the particular cases requiring attention.' The Quaker women were the true social workers. Wooldale and High Flatts Meetings, as a microcosm of the larger Quaker community, delegated the important first steps to those most capable of detecting distress or impoverishment as this minute of 1720 shows:

'...Martha Dickenson is appointed to Shephouse side to take care of ye poor And that all things be kept in good order as becomes the Blessed truth which we make profession of. and Mary Marsden is appointed to Hyflatts & Wooldale Meeting to take care of aforesaid...' (6)

A further short extract (1733) is also clearly revealing about how important the women's role was in this respect:

'...our men friends haveing some Interest money of the aforesaid Legacies Did a quaint us to confide who was most necessitous.' (7)

It was the men who had to ask the women *'to confide who was most necessitous.'* Even though the men initially regulated the purse strings, it was the women who kept the watchful eye and were always first to act. By 1740 the women had become so active that it became necessary for them to have their own funds readily at hand. So a further step towards a fuller equality was made:

'The Collection which was ordered by our women friends at our last monthly meeting for that end yt. we might have a Stock Amongst our Selves So we might Adminster of ye Same to our own poor women friends as we might see Ocation.' (8)

Nor was the relief of poverty confined only to Friends. The relief of poverty and distress is more fully dealt with in 'Poor Relief & Charities.' Suffice it that we appreciate the very tangible role of Quaker women in this respect.

Beyond their responsibilities as social workers Quaker women had other duties. They had to send representatives to Womens MM and QM. Usually this was done on the basis of a husband and wife making the journey together to the same MM, although this was by no means only for married couples. Widows and young single women could also be chosen as representatives. This kind of involvement and participation was virtually unheard of by women outside Quakerism.

Another important function of the women's meeting was that concerning marriage. Intentions of marriage were normally presented to the women's meeting before being passed to that of the men. It was the womens task to prove *'clearness'* from other commitments by the parties intending to marry. If the Womens Meeting approved the couples intention by finding *'clearness'* then it simply became a formality to obtain confirmation from the men's meeting.

It was also the women who tended to vet newcomers as this interesting little cameo from their minutes of 1772 reveals:

'A young man belonging to this Meeting having paid Visits to a Young Woman not of our Society in order to make her his wife and after some time prevailed with her to come to our Meeting which she hath now some time attended. She is now desirous of being taken into Membership with us and some Frds. have taken an opportunity with her and they believe She is not so much as we could desire in the profession of that which

gathered our Ancestors to be a people, and caused them to separate themselves from Amongst other professors to meet together to worship their father in Spirit & Truth. The affair having been under Frds. consideration for some time we have now laid it before the Mens Meeting.' (9)

In other respects women shared their equality more openly. Widows and single women were also liable for the payment of tithes and Church rates just like men. They shared their testimony with the men and their sufferings in this respect are to be found catalogued alongside those of the men. They expected no immunity and were granted none. (10)

At a time in history when women had few legal rights, were expected to rear large families, work outside the home or alongside their husbands, and lead lives of sheer drudgery in many instances, Quaker women enjoyed an enviable freedom and quality of life that their contemporaries did not. They also enjoyed the benefits of education, the powers of genuine influence in Quaker affairs, and the exercise of democracy, that was little evident to many men let alone women. Where else, but in their separate meetings for business, was there real democracy, as we today have come to understand it? In this respect and within this context our local women Friends were well in the vanguard of real equality at a time when there was great social and economic inequality.

(1) 'Early Lancaster Friends' See 'Early Quaker Women in Lancaster & Lancs.' p.43-53
(2) Ibid
(3) WMMB
(4) Ibid
(5) Ibid
(6) Ibid
(7) Ibid
(8) Ibid 1740
(9) WMMB 1770
(10) MMBS 1688-1792

A Friend in Need

Until recent years personal correspondence was the most important method of keeping in touch with family and friends especially when any distance separated them. The advent of the telephone and the motor-car in ever increasing numbers, enabling people to keep more readily in touch with one another, has reduced the importance of letter writing for many. How much personal detail will be lost for future historians with this decline in personal correspondence is imponderable. In the letter quoted below we have been left a a more permanent legacy in the form of written words expressing thoughts and emotions that allow us to be more empathetic in our understanding of individuals in the past.

'Wooldale 29th of 9th mo. 1800

Dear Friend,
Thy very kind Letter came safe to hand in acceptable time of need, though my dependance is on Divine Providence, yet I have of late passed through deep poverty of Spirit, and can readily adapt the Language of the Apostle, I have been in the deep, a night and a day in hunger and watchings often in Distress and nakedness. Dear Friend tho' we seldom see one another yet if thou find freedom to continue the same correspondence which is a strength in weakness, Make no excuse of thy Writing or Spelling for I can make all out. As thou requested an Answer I may inform thee that we have not seen Cousin T.Earnshaw nor heard anything from him a long time, never since thou was with us, my father thinks he disapoints him very much, and if we could have an opportunity with thee might have said much more than I write. We shall be glad to see thee and make our Habitation thy aboad if free, an so conclude in haste from thy well wishing friend,

Hannah Earnshaw

(To John Bottomley at Newhouse)' (1)

(1) Catherine Walton Collection — Misc. Correspondence.

Removals from High Flatts and Wooldale

The latter years of the eighteenth century were a time of great change not only nationally but also locally. From about 1787, as the Industrial Revolution gathered momentum, the meetings began to experience a gradual, long term, sapping decline in their size, strength and influence. A steady series of removals from these rural localities to Huddersfield and Brighouse, as well as to Sheffield, can be seen through the number of requests for transfer of membership to adjacent MM's. Over 80% of the total removals from 1787 to 1812 were to these rapidly urbanising industrial townships. The largest proportion of these removals were in the direction of Huddersfield. Given the very large number of Friends engaged in the textile trade as clothiers it cannot be surprising to find this trend. Perhaps more interesting was the almost equally large number who removed in the opposite direction towards Sheffield. (See Appendix (15)). High Flatts and Lumbroyd appear to have been significantly affected by these removals but Wooldale less so. In the case of Lumbroyd there was a fatal decrease in the size of the meeting from which there was little hope of recovery. By the late 1840's Lumbroyd could no longer be sustained and was closed.

The meeting at Wooldale, where the population increased during this period and new mills were built, saw fewer Friends removing. At High Flatts, the much more rural community, the effects were tangible and did not go unnoticed. Joseph Wood certainly noted and commented upon this in his personal writings when on a visit to Brighouse MM in the 2nd Month 1800.

'Went by Shepley & Almondbury to Huddersfield were we called to see my Cousin Susanna Mallinson who lives with her Son George having the week before left Wood & removed with her son Joseph into this Town, She was in the 72nd year of her age & not withstanding several friends appeared to be much concerned about their removal, some of whom freely imparted their minds unto them yet it appeared to have very little place with her. My mind hath oftens been affected with sorrow that so many of the members of our Society who are comfortably situated in the country, where they are favoured with everything which nature requires, leave these peaceful quiet, habitations, & flock into Cities & great Towns. I have oftens yea very oftens seen the sorrowful consequences thereof, for however they may have advanced themselves in the world thereby, very few according to my observation have advanc'd much in piety & virtue; Wherefore I cannot but much unite with many faithful friends who bore their testimony against it, & had to see even in their day the sorrowful consequences of it, For by entering into large concerns in trade many got so leavened into the spirit of this World as almost wholly to depart from the plainess & simplicity of the pure Truth...' (1)

However, the long decline of the meetings cannot be solely attributed to these removals. The large number of disownments must also have taken its toll combining to erode the influence of these historic country meetings in favour of those in the towns and cities. Throughout the nineteenth century there was a steady trickle away from the rural areas and a steady decline in membership.(See Appendix (15b)). By 1879 only 35 persons are recorded as connected with the meeting at High Flatts whilst at Wooldale, for the first time in its history, the numbers were slightly larger with 37 persons. From 1879 to 1917 the numbers of those associated with the meetings remained fairly stable with only a slight but perceptible loss until the end of the Great War. The ensuing two inter-war decades with their economic depression saw a further decline with Wooldale reduced to just 14 persons and High Flatts to 26 by 1941. (2) By 1967 both meetings had fallen into what appeared to be an irremediable decline with only 14 members and attenders at each. Meetings for Worship were frequently reduced to just a couple of Friends and even, on occasion, to a single Friend. From about the early to mid-1970's the long decline which commenced in Joseph Wood's day began to reverse.

(1) Joseph Wood Small Book No.32
(2) Membership figures taken from various pub. lists of members 1879-1967. (Yorkshire QM & GM).

Servants

The more wealthy Quaker families were no different from other families in the employment of the less wealthy to be their servants. We can dip into the records left by Joseph Wood (1750-1822) and gain an insight into the way servants were treated. Servants would often be members of the meeting. If they were not when commencing their service, then they often became so.

Joseph Wood usually referred to his servants as his family. At any one time he had a number of servants who would not only help in the house but on the land as well. They would share in many of his activities: joining in the daily worship at Newhouse, going to the local meetings and even accompanying him on his travels. On numerous occasions he also referred to his servants as *'beloved friends'* and that is exactly what they became. Another example is detailed in the section 'James Jenkins at High Flatts' when we learn how both James Jenkins and his mother were well cared for within the Fry family. The Frys recognized their responsibilities and stood by them. (James Jenkins was the illegitimate son of a servant Ann Jenkins and Zephaniah Fry).

The circumstances surrounding how John Bottomeley, Joseph Wood's closest friend and servant, arrived at Newhouse and the subsequent development of their relationship are revealing. (1) He came to live in the district from a neighbouring meeting and became seriously ill with convulsions. Local Friends were concerned for his health and asked Joseph Wood to take him into his own home which he did. Joseph Wood goes on to recount how his health took a remarkable turn for the better after the move and when fully recovered how he remained at Newhouse for many years. He often accompanied Joseph Wood on his travels and was a frequent attender at meetings where he developed his gift in the ministry. In the course of time he became a recorded minister as was his employer.

Joseph Wood's concern for the welfare of others was not just limited to his own servants. John Mallinson of Birdsedge, who was Joseph Wood's cousin, had in his employ (as a servant in husbandry) a young man named Joseph Grayham. Seeing that the young man was not able to read or write Joseph Wood spent many hours in teaching him. (2) Joseph Grayham became a frequent visitor to Newhouse and eventually a servant in his teacher's employ. The young man had his weaknesses and problems but throughout Joseph Wood supported and helped him. However, Joseph Wood made it his task to point out these weaknesses to Joseph Grayham in no uncertain terms. (3)

Concern for the welfare of servants was not just limited to their physical needs but was also directed towards their spiritual needs. In 1802 Joseph Wood wrote: 'An Epistle of the tender Love and caution to mine own family'. (4) At this time his *'family'* consisted of his servants: William Taylor, John Bottomley, Henry Marsden, Hezekiah Smith and Frances Field. The following extracts are from that epistle:

'Beloved Servants,

It has been the earnest desire of my mind that...me & my house may serve the Lord; & being now favoured with a family all of whom have been visited with the day spring from on high; & have seen the beauty & excellency of the pure Truth...my spirit hath felt a travail for your preservation, growth & establishment in pure righteousness: That, so we may be as a city set upon an hill, which cannot be hid; A family of Love; manifesting to others whose disciples we are, each one being preserved in that humility of mind, altho' our gifts may be different, our respective duties unto God & one another will be clearly manifested...We have all of us an unwearied enemy to war with...if one see the approach of the enemy how will his bowels yearn with compassion for his Brother or Sister & thus shall be enabled to speak a word in reason one to another which may prove as Apples of God in pictures of silver; Thus shall we be made truly helpful one unto another... I am with unfeigned love to you all, your Brother & companion in the tribulation of fellowship of the Gospel of Christ.

Joseph Wood.'

Joseph Wood still kept an interest in his former servants even when they moved on. He records in 1805:

'I went to see my old & beloved friends Henry & Elizabeth Marsden who were newly settled on a small farm at Haddenley were I hope & much desire they may do well as I do feel a sincere regard for their welfare, having lived so long with me I very much respect them as much so as if they were near Relations.' (5)

(1) Joseph Wood Memorandum Book No.19
(2) Joseph Wood Memorandum Book No.20
(3) Joseph Wood Memorandum Book No.28
(4) Joseph Wood Memorandum Book No.17a
(5) Joseph Wood Memorandum Book No.24

Visions and Dreams

Friends from their very earliest days have always been aware of their visions and dreams, believing them to be a manifestation of the leadings of the Spirit. One of the most important events in George Fox's life was the vision he had in 1652 on Pendle Hill of *'a great people to be gathered'* dressed in *'white raiment.'* Rufus Jones (1863-1948), the noted American Friend, described Quakerism as essentially a mystical religion throughout his writings. By mysticism he meant a personal, intuitive and experiential knowledge of God. Along with Fox early Friends in particular felt a closeness to God in their visions and dreams. Local Friends were no exception to this and we have recorded a number of instances that obviously made a deep impression upon them. Joseph Wood tells the story of how his uncle Joseph Green of Roydhouse, Shelley, when awake in bed one night was visited by his dead mother who: *'...came quite across the chamber floor & putting her mouth to his ear said 'Tell thy Father there is a God & a Devil, a Heaven & a Hell'.'* (1) This happened shortly after Joseph Green's father had been planning to make a pact with a friend that which ever one should die first should return and visit the other. Another event concerning death that Joseph Wood recounts was an experience he himself had. He tells how in 1798 he went to Mary Earnshaw's funeral at Wooldale. During the meeting:

'...I had to stand up & say, My mind had been deeply impressed with a belief that some present was near the close of their time, When I came out of the meeting Joseph Bower was standing near the gate coming out of the Burial ground, as soon as I saw him it appeared to me, that he was the person unto whom the foregoing testimony did belong.' (2)

Joseph Bower was from Wooldale, Townend, and a Methodist. However, he had met and been greatly influenced by William Earnshaw, a recorded minister of Wooldale Meeting, who lived at Totties. He started to attend meetings at Wooldale. Apparently, Joseph Wood had not met him before this day. It transpired that Joseph Bower had been unwell for some time. Joseph Wood visited him several times and had discussions which seemed to please him. However, within three months of Mary Earnshaw's funeral Joseph Bower had died at the age of 17. He is recorded as saying to his mother the night before he died that: *'...he had formerly had no apprehension that Heaven was so glorious a place as it now appeared to him.'*

On a number of other occasions when describing a Quaker meeting Joseph Wood tells how *'various states were opened'* and he then spoke to the condition of those present. Joseph Firth's vision, as recounted to John Nelson, was of a more mystical nature. (3) It seems that Joseph Firth had been wrestling with a problem on *'...perseverance of the Saints: whether a person once in Grace could finally fall?'* Sitting at home with his wife one evening, he heard a sudden noise and a voice saying: *'In a little time thou shalt be resolved of all doubts.'* A few days later he had a vivid vision. In this he found himself in a field full of weeds *'...the harder he laboured to pull up these weeds...the faster they grew.'* He finally got out of the field through a narrow hole in a wall. He had to remove his clothes before being able to get through the hole. He then met a being who acted as his guide. They experienced the broad road to hell before the narrow road to heaven. They saw that the worshippers who had their backs to God's throne *('hearts given to the world')* were not true. Those facing the throne *('given their hearts to God')* were true. Joseph Firth's problem was answered in the affirmative when he was shown a book in which the names could grow brighter or dimmer. He then realized that his guide was *'no other person than the Lord Jesus Christ.'* A few weeks after this vision Joseph Firth died. It had however altered his attitude to people he knew as he had been very surprised by whom he had seen in heaven and hell. Another vision which concerned heaven was experienced by Emanuel Brook of Delf, Honley. (4)

'...I was placed at the remotest Quarter from the East with my Face towards the East...and straight before me a Narrow paved path which I walked on...& by one side of this narrow path there was a great Descent downwards...and on it by me Dogs & evil Creatures...'

All along, despite the path becoming wider, he had to watch his footsteps so that he did not slip down the hill. Eventually, he came to heaven which was a *'white house'* and he went in. He was shown how: *'...Heaven was taken by Violence but these that took it thus by Violence might not enter therein...'* The interpretation of this by H.E., to whom Emanuel Brook had recounted his vision, ran as follows:

'...how Careful we ought to be in our Stepping along & it hath much Confirmed me in my small Experience of the great Danger there is of slipping aside or falling prey to the Enemy, if we do not walk steadily in this paved path.'

Our final example of a dream is again taken from the records left by Joseph Wood. (5) It is worth quoting in full as it clearly shows how Friends of that day still firmly believed in Joel's prophecy: *'And it shall come to pass afterward that I will pour out my Spirit upon all flesh; and your sons and your daughters shall prophesy, your old men shall dream dreams, your young men shall see visions.'* (6) It also shows that Friends did not take everything on its face value but were reaching for the deeper meanings that lay hidden waiting for discovery.

'A Dream

About the middle of the 3rd Mo. 1802. A Friend dreamed That Robbers broke into my house with weapons of different kinds, such as she never saw before, but exceeding sharp; some of them very long, & others shorter; that they slew two of my family & wounded the rest: she awakened in a very agitated state of mind & before she was well awake it ran through her; what can be the cause of this in this peaceable family. The same week she related the dream to me, & altho' I seemed to take little notice of it; It very much affected me; There appearing some heavy tryal was impending but, how or after what manner was entirely hid from me. The week following I attended our Quarterly Meeting held at Leeds; & both before I left home & on my way thither was very much exercised not knowing the cause: But endeavouring to get down low in mine own mind; It appeared to me that something was stirring in the minds of some (whatever their intentions might be) that would be very proving to me & some others. When I got to Leeds I went to the Select meeting exceedingly bowed in mind, where a friend moved something & was followed by some others, which unfolded my exercise, & the dream came into my mind. Clearly perciveing there were weapons of different kinds that was very sharp which was not outward, & that, there was a life, which might, be taken that, was not natural; & that many might be sorely wounded when their bodies was not hurt. And a cry run through me after this manner O Lord preserve the little ones in the patience whatever they may have to pass through; & keep them from thinking evil of those, who may ignorantly suppose they are doing their service. Open their understanding to see the Truth of thy declaration, left upon record in the Scriptures of Truth 'No weapon that is formed against thee shall prosper; & every tongue that shall rise against thee in judgement thou shall condemn, this is the heritage of the servants of the Lord, if their righteousness is of me saith the Lord.' On 1st of 4th Mo. 1802 I wrote the above, my mind being at the time covered with a sweet carm, & felt a degree of pure resignation to the divine will.

Joseph Wood'

(1) Joseph Wood Memorandum Book No.16
(2) Joseph Wood Memorandum Book No.7
(3) Friends House Library — Misc. MSS.
(4) Letter from H.E. (Hannah Earnshaw) to J.Wood 1783.
(5) Joseph Wood Memorandum Book No.23
(6) Joel Ch.2 v.28

Pheobe Haigh's Miracle

'...stopt about half an hour at Peobe Haighs who once told me, that before her convincement, she had been for many years so infirm that it was with difficulty she could get to & from bed or even walk up & down the house, in which state a desire was raised in her mind to get to a meeting of Friends, & being obedient there unto she set forward & was enabled to get to Highflatts on a Week-day, from that time forward she mended apace & not only became a diligent attender of our own meetings, but walked on foot to many others at a considerable distance, I thought this was worthy to be recorded amongst the many miracles the Almighty is working for his People inwardly & outwardly.' (1)

Pheobe Haigh (1731-85) resided at Heighmoor House (between Shepley and Shelley). She was the widow of James Haigh.

(1) Joseph Woods Small Notebook No. 14. (12th Month 1782)

The Visiting of Families

'We are concerned again to recommend to monthly meetings, the appointment of solid and judicious friends to visit the families of their bretheren in Christian love, and therein to inform, admonish, and advise, as occasion may be; and we beseech you, brethren, let the tender advice of such as shall undertake so brotherly an office, meet with a kind and open reception, that in the mutual giving and receiving of wholesome counsel and advice, you may co-operate to the help and furtherance of each other's faith, and the reviving of our ancient Christian testimony.'
'Rules of Discipline and Advices' 1752.

'...good service may arise from visiting the families of our bretheren, by rightly concerned friends...'
'Rules of Discipline and Advices' 1773.

The visiting of the families within each meeting played an important part in the life of every Quaker community throughout the eighteenth and early nineteenth century. The aims of such visits were to ensure that the religious life, as professed by Friends, was being maintained in all its aspects by the membership. The visits were concerned with the matters of regular attendance at meetings for worship, resistance to tithes and church rates, *'plainess of habit and speech'*, sound monetary dealings and the upholdings of the other testimonies held by Friends. The visits were held on the same basis as a meeting for worship and the varying *'conditions and states'* of the visited could be opened up to the visitors. The opportunity for spiritual counselling and guidance was a paramount part of the visitation.

Such visits might appear as rather undue intrusions by present day standards. However, as has already become evident, the Quakers of the Quietist age were *'a peculiar people'* (See 1 Peter 2:9 Authorized Version): a community with its own unique discipline within a wider community. The maintenance of the high standards of conduct set by Friends required methods of self-regulation. These periodic visits were one such method by which uniformity of conduct was maintained.

From Joseph Wood's records we have a detailed picture of several such visits paid to families in the area. Each of these provides its own fascinating wealth of information but the scope of this book prohibits an examination of these several accounts. The visit made to local families by Jane Burrow of Otley in the 8th month of 1778 is in many ways typical. The way in which this particular visit arose can be best explained in Joseph Wood's own words:

'Having had a desire on my mind for some time that a religious visit might be paid to the Families in our meeting, believing it might be of service; but a sense of my own weakness prevented my communicating it to any friends in our meeting; but happening to be at Otley & falling into conversation with Jane Burrow on the subject of visiting Families, I inform'd her how long it was since a visit of that kind was paid to us, & likewise the service I had seen in them, the next time I saw her she inform'd me of the concern that was on her mind to pay such a visit, & desired me to accompany her which in much weakness & fear I gave up to.' (1)

Arrangements for the visit were then made with High Flatts Friends and an itinary drawn up. For part of this visit Jane Burrow would be accompanied by another well known minister: George Conway of Southowram near Halifax. In addition to Joseph Wood, who was on the threshold of the ministry himself, the party would be joined by other local Friends who were recorded ministers, Mary Dickinson, Henry Dickinson of Strines and William Earnshaw of Totties, as well as by local elders including Caleb Marsden and Hannah Marsden. Other concerned Friends, recently entered into membership, such as George Chapman and Jeremiah Smith would also take part.

Rather than proceed with a lengthy account of people, places and dates, a summarized schedule of the entire visit is supplied at this point. It is based upon Joseph Wood's account in his writings for the 8th month 1778.

Jane Burrow's Visit to the Families of High Flatts PM (August 1778).

Summary of Visit

Under Convincement = C
Disowned but attending Meetings = D

Family/Individual	Location	Status

Thursday 13th

Jane Burrow of Otley and George Conway arrive at Newhouse where they will lodge. The fourteen day long visit begins with Samuel Wood's family that same evening.

    Samuel Wood   Newhouse

Friday 14th

The visit gets under way at 6 o'clock in the morning. The 6 a.m. start will occur on each day of the visiting. Those in the party include: Jane Burrow, George Conway, Henry Dickinson and Joseph Wood.

Tobias Mallinson	Wood	
Joshua Priest	Denby	D
Joseph Beaumont		
Samuel Haigh		
Joseph Stead	Toppett	C
John Green	Ingbirchworth	

After the first visit they breakfast with Tobias Mallinson's family. They are joined by Mary Dickinson at Joshua Priest's home. She is with the party for the next two visits. The party dine at Joseph Beaumont's. Jeremiah Smith joins the party at John Green's house and is with them all that day. The visiting ends at 6 o'clock with the party returning to Newhouse where Jane Burrow and George Conway lodge that night.

Saturday 15th

The party breakfast at Henry Dickinson Sr. (minister) after the visit to his family is completed.

Henry Dickinson	Strines	
Ann Dickinson	High Flatts	
Henry Dickinson Jr.		
Daniel Brook		
Ann Cartwright		
Elihu Dickinson		

After visiting Henry Dickinson Jr. the party dined at Ann Dickinson's. The party returned to lodge at Newhouse again that night completing their day's visiting at 6 o'clock.

Sunday 16th

Only a single visit on first day: Caleb Marsden's family. (Followed by Breakfast).

Caleb Marsden	Birdsedge
(+ Mary Wood)	
Mtg. for Worship (a.m)	
Mtg. for Worship (p.m)	

The party lodged at Newhouse once again. Visits to families in the immediate vicinity of High Flatts Meeting House completed.

Monday 17th

George Conway returns home. He is replaced by William Earnshaw of Totties. The party is also joined by Hannah Marsden and then sets out in the direction of families living at Ingbirchworth and Thurlstone (near Penistone).

James Dickinson	Folly	
Joseph Priest	Bellroid	
Thomas Dickinson	Bellroid	
Benjamin Dickinson	Thurlstone	
Jonathan Green		
Dorothy Roebuck		D

The party dined at Benjamin Dickinson's. At the end of the day's visiting they returned to lodge at Benjamin Dickinson's house. Joseph Wood returned to Newhouse for the night. (Hannah Marsden probably returned home too).

Tuesday 18th

The party returned to Jonathan Green's to see young Samuel Green and Joshua Roebuck's apprentice, Joseph Sanderson. Both young men had been absent the day before.

Jonathan Green		
(+ son and Joseph Sanderson)		
Godfrey Woodhead	Penistone	
Joshua Earnshaw	Judd Field	
Sarah Earnshaw		
John Sanderson	Midhope	
Thomas Earnshaw	Langside	
William Earnshaw	Bintcliffe	D

The entire party dined at Sarah Earnshaw's that day and returned to Newhouse to lodge the night at about 7.30 in the evening.

Wednesday 19th

A very busy day for the party. Much of the visiting took place in Skelmanthorpe where there were many convinced attenders who would eventually become members. Jeremiah Smith rejoins the party.

Daniel Collier	Cumberworth	
George Haywood	Lower Cumberworth	C
William Dyson	Powker (Clayton West)	C
William Stead	Silver-Ing	
(+ John Radley)		C
Martha Dyson	Skelmanthorpe	
(+ Benj. Dyson's family)		
Mary Dyson	Skelmanthorpe	C
& Patience Jakeman	Skelmanthorpe	C
Anthony Kinsley		D

The party dined at William Stead's. After the last visit they returned to Newhouse at 8 o'clock in the evening.

61

Thursday 20th

The visitors set out in the direction of Huddersfield, where the most distant members lived, stopping along the way to see the two Bottomley families living within the bounds of Thurstonland.

Hannah Bottomley	Thurstonland	
John Bottomley		
Robert Kay	Lane End	
John Brook	Row (Huddersfield)	
(+ Hannah Crosland)		D
Richard Brook		
(+ John Walker's Family)		

The party dine and lodge the night at Robert Kay's home at Lane End.

Friday 21st

After the usual early start the party commences the journey from Huddersfield visiting the families residing near Honley on their way to Wooldale.

Emmanuel Brook	Delf (Honley)	
James Brook		
Mary Brook		D
Joshua Broadhead	Ridings	
Sarah Broadhead	Wooldale	
John Parkin	Wooldale	D
(+ George Lee)		D

Another very busy day. Many of the disowned in the vicinity of Wooldale and the less conscientious members are part of the itinary. The party dine at Sarah Broadhead's in Wooldale. Jane Burrow and Caleb Marsden lodge with Sarah Broadhead. Joseph Wood and Jeremiah Smith spend the night at William Earnshaw's of Totties.

Saturday 22nd

The day's labours are concerned chiefly with visiting disowned members. Much of the visiting is within the bounds of Wooldale in the morning whilst in the afternoon their journeying takes them to New Mill, Biggin and Mearhouse before returning to Wooldale via Scholes or Totties.

Ann Haigh		
Thomas Robert Jr.	Wooldale	
Joseph Haigh	Wooldale	D
Joseph Brook	Pell Croft, Wooldale	
Alice Moorhouse	Hollingreave	D
James Broadhead	Biggin	D
Daniel Broadhead	Mearhouse	

Jane Burrow and Caleb Marsden are lodged once again at Sarah Broadhead's whilst Joseph Wood and Jeremiah Smith return to their respective homes.

Sunday 23rd

No visits on this first day. Both Meetings for Worship are very full and well attended each one lasting about 2 hours.

Mtg. for Worship (a.m.)	Wooldale Mtg. House
Mtg. for Worship (p.m.)	Wooldale Mtg. House

A social evening at Sarah Broadhead's for the party. Jane Burrow and Caleb Marsden lodge the night there once again. Joseph Wood and Jeremiah Smith go to William Earnshaw's at Totties.

Monday 24th

The party visit Friends living in the areas of Mount, Snowgatehead and Fulstone. They dine at Joseph Woodhead Jr.'s in Fulstone.

Sarah Broadhead	Meltom House	
Joseph Haigh	Epson House	
John Haigh		D
Joseph Woodhead Jr.	Fulstone	
Arthur Jepson		
Godfrey Woodhead		
Joseph Woodhead Sr.		

Quite a trying day for the party: not only in contending with the hilly terrain of this locality but also having a less than encouraging time with those they visited. Jane Burrow and Caleb Marsden spend the night once again at Sarah Broadhead's of Wooldale. Joseph Wood and Jeremiah Smith go once again to William Earnshaw's at Totties.

Tuesday 26th

George Chapman joins the party at William Earnshaw's house. He is with them for three visits later in the day.

William Earnshaw	Totties	
John Beaumont		
John Chapman	Leeside	
Ann Beaumont	Deershaw	
Ann Gouldthorpe		D
Abraham Beaumont		D
Matthew Broadhead	Upper Holmhouse	
(+ Elizabeth Birytops)		

This day the party dined at John Chapman's of Leeside. In the evening they made the return journey to Newhouse where they were to lodge that night.

Wednesday 27th

The final day's visiting in and around the village of Shepley.

Abraham Bottomley	Shepley-Woodend	
William Radley	Shepley	
Sarah Morton	Heymoor House	C
Joseph Firth	Shepley Lane Head	

The last of the visits was completed at about 3 o'clock in the afternoon. The party was back at Newhouse by 4 o'clock. Jane Burrow returned to Otley the following morning being accompanied all the way home by her son, Anthony. Joseph Wood, his mother, George Chapman and Jeremiah Smith travelled *'many miles"* with them to set them on their way.

This particular visit is interesting in several respects. Many of the Friends mentioned, if not already familiar to the reader at this point in the book, will in due course become familiar. The number of disownments for marrying out in the ten years preceeding and following this visit will total about twenty five people. Many of these are visited, for example: William Earnshaw of Bintcliffe (See 'Irregular Marriage') and John Parkin of Wooldale (See 'Marrying out'). Then there are those who have been, or who will be, disowned for other reasons such as: George Lee (See 'George Lee of Wooldale'), John Haigh (See 'John Haigh of Moor Royd Nook, High Flatts') and John Green (See 'Marriage and Marital Difficulties'). Joseph Wood records some fascinating comments upon visits to these. In the beforementioned William Earnshaw's case *'...we had a short & poor Opportunity...'* On visiting John Parkin they *'...had a poor opportunity with him & George Lee together...They was earnestly recommended to make a right preparation for that awful change which seem'd to be drawing near.'* In the case of the very recently disowned John Haigh, *'...Jane Burrow appeared first from Job C:5 v:7. Man is born unto trouble, as the sparks fly upward, setting forth in an extraordinary manner the difference betwixt that Trouble which brings death & that which leads to life, but feared the former was too much the case with this family...'* When they visited Ann Beaumont of Deershaw (disowned for marrying out in 1781) *'...we had a suffering season a state of insensibility seemed to prevail & Death & darkness appeared to cover the minds of some which was declared to them & they intreated to join in with the visitation if it was not already too late...'*

The way in which less dutifully attending families were dealt with is also quite interesting. Matthew Broadhead's family of Upper Holmhouse received *'...Weighty counsel & advice..'* which *'...was tenderly delivered both to Parents & Children which I desire may be remembered they was particularly cautioned against forsaking the Assembling of themselves together with their Brethren & Sisters.'*

The contrast in the *'counsel'* and *'advice'* given to the varying state of families is also quite instructive:

'...we had an Opportunity with William Earnshaws family of Tottis. which was a precious season. Jane Burrow appear'd therein from the language of Ahimaaz to King David 2 Sam: C:18 v:28. All is well: expressing her satisfaction with this visit, & how sweet it was to sit under a feeling sense of that which is good free from that painful exercise which we met with in many places, encouraging them to persevere in the way of well doing to the end.'

Those who tried to evade the net of the visit found it impossible to escape with the party returning to ensure that everyone was visited:

'...went first to Jonathan Green's were we got an opportunity with his Son Samuel, & Joseph Sanderson who was Apprentice at Joshua Roebucks, but both gone from home the day before Jane Burrow appear'd first, had hard work having a sharp Testimony to bear from Eccles C:11 v:9. Rejoice, O young man, in thy youth: & walk in the ways of thy heart, & in the sight of thine Eyes: but (k)now that that (sic) for all these things God will bring thee into Judgement. William Earnshaw appeared next, & afterwards Jane Burrow again had something very encouraging to the young Apprentice & he appear'd very tender. After the Opportunity was over, William Earnshaw & me got a little time with Samuel Green by himself (he having been lately guilty of some misconduct) in which we was enabled to discharge our duty.'

In the cases of those under convincement like William Dyson of Powker they *'...had a watering season together...'* Perhaps the most interesting of the convinced families visited was that of George Haywood's where they also saw John Ellis, a disowned member:

'...we had an opportunity with this family & John Ellis (D) of Woodnook Jane Burrow appeared first set forth the beauty & innocency of a Child apprehending she saw something of such a state present...& afterwards had close work with another state which appeared to her something like the fruitless Figtree to which our Saviour said Cut it down why cumbereth it the ground...'

It was on this visit that Joseph Wood appears to have made his first steps in the ministry as he records, for the first time in his writings, *'I dropt a few words.'* In 1779 he commenced his calling as a minister which was to last forty-two years.

Did the visiting of families in this manner achieve its aims and objectives? Did it serve a useful purpose? If the end result is to gauged by disownments then the answer must be a most emphatic no. Disownments continued to rise sharply in the following years as the discipline continued to be strictly maintained. (See

Appendix (12)). If the visiting of families failed tangibly in that respect was there an intangible way in which it was successful? There were certainly those who became convinced and became members like the Steads and the Dysons. Perhaps, there were even those who may have faltered or have been on the verge of faltering when such a visitation may have spoken with strength to their condition. If nothing more the visiting of families served to keep that sense of community and *'peculiarity'* alive amongst the Quakers of these meetings.

(1) Joseph Wood Small Note Book No.12

QUAKER CAMEOS IN SHADES OF GREY.

One of the many inherent dangers of writing a history is to concentrate solely on the *'heroes and villains'* and *'the saints and the sinners.'* It is generally the case that posterity is left with a detailed record of the famous and the infamous whilst the majority are forgotten. The following fourteen cameos inevitably contain their share of the more well known personalities associated with the meetings. However, the authors have consciously endeavoured to redress such an imbalance in the writing of these cameos by including the lesser well known Friends.

A cameo, by its very nature, can do no more than shed a little light on the life and times of an individual. Collectvely, such cameos can help to recreate a picture of the past. The lives of individuals can never be clearly coloured black or white: life is never like that. Life and history are matters of shades of grey.

John Brooke of Hagg

Very few recorded instances exist of local Friends leaving England for America during the turn of the seventeenth century. John Brooke of Hagg near Honley, in the parish of Almondbury, is the only case minuted. His brief story is worthy of inclusion. From information contained in a family Bible it appears that John and his wife had six children: Jonathan (b.1666), Abigail (b.1670), Elizabeth (b.1672), John (b.1676), James (b.1678) and Matthew (b.1680). Elizabeth, John and Matthew are recorded as having been baptised in the Kirkburton parish records. He became a convinced Friend probably some time after 1680 and must shortly have removed to Hagg, near Honley, thereafter. Only his wife and two youngest sons became Quakers, the older children apparently determined to stay with the Established Church. There is also a distinct possibility that he was forced to remove from within the boundaries of Kirburton parish to that of Almondbury due to the excessive demands and anti-Quaker activities of the Rev. Joseph Briggs. (The Vicar of Kirkburton at this period. See Section on 'Tithes'). Undoubtedly his experiences locally contributed to his decision to leave for the Quaker colony of Pennsylvania where he would enjoy religious freedom and avoid *'hireling priests'* determined to extract tithes at any cost and by any method.

John Brooke informed MM of his *'intention to remove himself and family into Pennsylvania'* after his departure from England early in 1699. A certificate was granted to him and his family on the 9th day of the 11th Month 1699. (1) However, by the time the certificate had been issued, John and his wife had died.

John, his wife Frances, and two sons, James and Matthew, had set sail for Philadelphia from Liverpool. During their voyage across the Atlantic on board the 'Brittania', commanded by Richard Nicholas, a contagious disease had broken out amongst the ship's company and passengers. The 'Brittania' was not allowed to land in Philadelphia and was eventually allowed to discharge its passengers at Gloucester, New Jersey about August of 1699.

Soon after their arrival, John and Frances Brooke died from this unknown disease contracted on board the ship. He and his wife were buried at Friends burial ground at Haddonfield in New Jersey. They never lived to see the 1500 acres of land he had purchased jointly with one Thomas Musgrove of Halifax from William Penn in 1698:

'The Prop'ry by Lease and Release dated 17th and 18th March, 1698, granted to Thos. Musgrave and John Brook 1,500 acres. (Thos. Musgrave of Halifax and John Brook of Holmfirth, in Coun. York) of which the heirs of John Brook since the Pro'rs arrival took up his share, viz, 750 acres.' (2)

The land he had purchased could have been taken from anywhere between the Delaware and the Susquehannah rivers. His two sons, James and Matthew, who had survived the contagious disease, chose to settle lands in the township of Limerick and County of Philadelphia (now known as Montgomery). There they apparently prospered and were successful. One of the descendants of James Brooke, Hugh Jones Brooke born in Radnor in Delaware (1805), became a Senator. By the terms of John Brooke's will, a copy of which is to be found in the Pennsylvania Archives, 2nd Series Vol. XIX dated the 17th and 18th March 1698 — duly signed and attested, he divided his share of the 750 acres between all his children.

There were conditions: namely, that the older children could only inherit the land if they came to America otherwise their portion would be equally divided and given to the two younger sons. Not one of those who remained in England took up the offer. (3)

(1) MMMB 1699
(2) KRP Vol.II (See Appendix ccccix).
(3) Ibid

Elizabeth Morehouse of Mount

Godfrey Morehouse of Mount (c.1664-1724) married his second wife Sarah Swift, the daughter of John and Jane Swift of Gunthwaite, in 1680. He appears to have been one of the poorer local Friends who did not feature prominently in local Quaker annals but who was called on in his younger days to serve the Society in various small capacities. We know for certain that he had three daughters: Mary (b.1676) and Sarah (b.1674) by his first wife (who also happened to be called Sarah), and then Elizabeth (b.1681) by his second wife. Mary married Caleb Marsden of Birdsedge in 1702. Sarah married John Woodhead just over a year later. However, Elizabeth, their younger half-sister, was a problem. When her father died at the advanced age of 82 she was left without any one to care for her needs. (Her mothers death is missing from the records but is likely to have been sometime before her father's).

'Friends of Highflatts have given us a relation of ye Daughter of Godfrey Morehouse who is Incapable of helping her self not having the Common Cappatis (capacities) of other people & her father being Dead and there not being a Competance for her livelyhood she became an Object of Charity to this meeting Friends of Highflatts meeting her necesitys to be supply'd by this mo: meeting...' (1)

The exact nature of Elizabeth Morehouse's disability is not made clear. It is evident that she could not fend for herself either because she had been born mentally retarded or because she was physically deformed in some way, or possibly even a combination of both. High Flatts Friends had endeavoured to look after her as best they could but when their means appeared limited they applied to MM for assistance. As an *'Object of Charity'*, and not of pity, she was made the responsibility of MM in 1724. They awarded her a monthly sum of between 4s and 4s 8d for the rest of her life. The women Friends of High Flatts were directly responsible for ensuring that she was properly looked after as these minutes quoted from their records show:

(a) 05/03/1731 *'...the pore Condition of Elizabeth Morehouse Comming before us Concerning her Clothing and a small quantity of money was Collected to Defray the Charges.'* (2)

(b) 03/09/1731 *'Att this meeting haveing under their Consideration the necessity of Eliz. Morehouse wanting Shooes and other necessaries and sumthing was Collected to relieve her and put in ye hands of Mary Marsden for the faire service.'* (3)

(c) 05/05/1732 *'...the poore condition of Eliz. Morehouse laid before this meeting concerning some Clothing & the men friends being acquainted did order five shillings for said use...'* (4)

(d) 03/11/1733 *'Att this meeting friends being informed that Elizabeth Morehouse wanted Shifts, Aprons and other things necessary, and the men friends being informed, sent us eight shillings...'* (5)

In this age the mentally retarded and physically handicapped were considered to be abnormal and the by-products of sin. They were usually cruelly treated and endured harsh conditions in terrible institutions like the infamous Bedlam. In this context we can be truly appreciative of the enlightened and caring attitude of Friends towards Elizabeth Morehouse. To be an *'Object of Charity'* cared for by local Friends was preferable to any alternative form of 'care' that might have been available. This same enlightened attitude would one day, later in that same century, lead William Tuke to establish The Retreat in York.

MM continued their care over Elizabeth Morehouse until her death in 1737 at the age of fifty-six. She was interred at Friends burial ground in Wooldale on the 26th of the 4th Month.

(1) MMMB 1724   (3) Ibid
(2) WMMB1731   (4) Ibid 1732   (5) Ibid 1733

Jonathan and Ann Green

In the 2nd month of 1726, Jonathan Green appeared before MM being held at Pontefract. According to High Flatts Friends he had managed to *'run himself into Debt beyond what he is capable to pay with'* and having been spoken to by them was *'Desired to appear at this monthly meeting to Certifie friends of the Circumstances of his affairs.'* (1) This was in accord with the discipline of the Society and the only proper action that could be undertaken by a Friend in such a situation if he were not to be disowned.

'We recommend to friends in their respective quarterly and monthly meetings, to have a watchful eye over all their members; and where they observe any deficient in discharging their contracts and just debts in due time, so as to give reasonable suspicion of weakness or negligence, that friends do earnestly advise them to a suitable care and necessary inspection into their circumstances, in order that they may be helped...' (2)

Having been made aware of the consequences and danger of debt in an earlier section we can appreciate the gravity of the situation confronting Jonathan Green on that day. He laid the state of his personal affairs before the meeting and confirmed their suspicions, they *'finding he falls short of Answering his Just debts.'* (3) However, Jonathan Green was *'willing to give up what he hath towards Discharging ye same.'* Because he was prepared to liquidate his assets by selling up such possessions as he had to pay off his creditors, High Flatts Friends were *'requested to assist in Drawing up a Letter of Request for his Creditors (to) take share of what he hath at some convenient time as soon as moneys can be made of what he hath.'* The Letter of Request carried a great deal of weight in a community. It was effectively a personal guarantee by local Friends to local creditors that they would ensure that all debts would be paid off. High Flatts Meeting intended to stand fully behind Jonathan Green in his attempts to make good his debts. Unfortunately, Jonathan Green was being less than honest with local Friends. Two months later at a MM held at High Flatts the tragic story of Jonathan Green, his wife Ann and their young children, began when the following minute was made:

'This meeting having again under their Consideration ye affairs of Jonathan Green & finding he has not Delt fairly with us in giving in the accounts of his Debt, but is Involved farr beyond what we expected & the account he gave us, And moreover we find that he has unrighteously hid his affairs which is afflicting to this meeting And we think it our Duty to give forth a paper of Denial against Jonathan for such practices...' (4)

The full extent of Jonathan Green's debt had not been revealed by him and this had inevitably come to light. It is almost certainly the case that he did not dare to reveal the full extent of his debt for fear that he would be disowned immediately. No doubt he had harboured personal hopes of settling the undisclosed debt without Friends knowledge. Whatever his motives for concealment he had acted dishonestly with Friends by not disclosing the real extent of his insolvency and thus, as a natural consequence, he came to be disowned.

At this point it is important to reveal that Jonathan Green had, in fact been, a devout and devoted member of the Society serving locally in several capacities. On a number of occasions he was a representative of High Flatts Meeting to MM. He was also appointed as a representative of MM to QM. Richard Ellis was his regular travelling companion and we must assume, because of events that are to be recounted shortly, that the two men were or became close personal friends. We know very little about Jonathan Green. He married an Ann Wilcockson in 1713. The fact that he was able to go to MM and QM would tend to suggest that he was relatively well off. His income must have been sufficiently substantial to enable him to take time away from his labours to participate in the Society's affairs. How he came to fall into debt is something that has also proved elusive and is particularly mystifying considering his apparently impeccable background amongst local Friends.

So far we have regarded debt simply as an offence against religious principles. Yet there is a dimension that we have not fully explored. In the secular world of that time the inability to settle with creditors could lead to a prison cell. Attached to this possibility was the very serious matter of what could happen to a family in such an event. Jonathan Green appears to have honoured his debts in full but at the expense of reducing himself and his family to abject poverty. His wife and children seemed to have come under some considerable distress as this MM minute of nearly a year later recounts:

'Joseph Firth requests the advice of this meeting relating to the relief of Jonathan Green's family being under necessitys for food & raym. (raiment) *through mismanagement in it & aid that has reduced them thereto, to which it is agreed that Highflatts Meet: do enquire further into their case and we shall be willing to give some assistance as need requires for their present relief.'* (5)

Jonathan Green's denial did not include his wife Ann or their children. They were not held responsible for his failure to remain solvent or for his dishonesty with Friends. Local Friends considered it their Christian duty to keep themselves informed of the Green's circumstances and act if the circumstances resulted in distress: this they did. Joseph Firth returned from Pontefract with instructions to ascertain how best High Flatts Friends could help Ann Green and the children and by the time MM met again a plan was available for consideration:

'The poore condition of Ann Green the wife of Jonathan Green being laid before this meeting & there being some small children towards their Relief, friends agree to make a Collection amongst such as are able & willing hearted in Each meeting for the buying them a Cow which Contribution when made to be brought up to our next monthly meeting for friends to consider how to dispose thereof.' (6)

Nor was this the only help that Ann Green was to receive. Elizabeth Crowder, shortly before she married, visited the family and *'laid down 10s for Some goods when Jonathan Green was broken up by his creditors in pitty of sd. wife & children.'* She had bought *'such household goods yt. could not well be done without'* to ensure that they continued to have some semblance of comfort. Richard Ellis further gave account that:

'...ye Cow formerly purchased for ye Wife & Children of Jonathan Green do report yt. said cow did not suply them well with milk & ye sd. Rich.(ard) sould her at Markit for the sum of £2 13s 0d And that Richard Ellis & Joshua Sanderson having laid out for divers things for the Relief of sd. Wife & children 11s 8d out of ye sd. cow price.' (7)

It is during this period that Joshua Sanderson began to take a greater personal involvement in the Greens affairs and continued to do so even after the couple had removed from the locality. Richard Ellis, as we can see, had also proved to be the proverbial 'friend indeed.' Both men were prominent Quakers in this area. Joshua Sanderson of Midhope Hall was a particularly affluent Friend and was in a favourable position to look into and after the problems of the family. Richard Ellis was probably a descendant of one of the first families that had embraced Quakerism in the locality. His established friendship with Jonathan Green led him to personal endeavour on behalf of the distressed family. Like Joshua Sanderson he too would be in some position to help.

Towards the end of 1728 Jonathan Green and some of his family moved out of the area to within the confines of Breach MM, *'for his more conveniance & maintaining his family.'* (8) We must assume that his departure had been partially caused by his reduced circumstances in the world and that he desperately needed to get away to make a fresh start somewhere else. Once again, whatever his motives were, he was in need of a certificate of removal for his wife Ann and their children. A Testimony of Denial had formally been issued against him during the 6th Month of 1726. However, it seems that he was still maintaining his Quaker beliefs even though disowned for our local MM recorded the following minute towards the end of 1728:

'...this meeting refereth ye writing of some sort of a Certificate with said family of Jonathan Green to friends of Highflatts meeting that it may be so taken care of in the wording of it, that truth of friends may not come under reproach by ye same...' (9)

The phrasing of the above minute sheds light on the attitude of our local Friends and MM towards Jonathan Green and his family. Though they did not condone the debt that he had fallen into, nor his dishonesty with them about it, nor the suffering and distress that it had brought upon his wife and children, nevertheless they felt impelled to give a fair account of the man who had laboured with them in the cause of truth. No doubt they entertained hopes of readmitting him back into the fold at some future date. Until that time, however, they intended to make sure that the Friends of Breach MM should not be misled about his recent past.

When Jonathan Green removed from the area he does not seem to have taken all his children with him.

Nor did this signal the end of High Flatts and MM's involvement with his family. When MM convened the following month at Burton, Richard Ellis brought *'an account to this Meeting of ye Change about the Family of Jonathan Green So at present there remains in sd. Rich: hand 2s 7d for ye sd. family if occation demands.'* (10) When Jonathan Green left to seek employment he also left a son of the same name in the care of Richard Ellis of Wooldale. Richard Ellis appears to have made a decision to adopt young Jonathan and raise him for he reported to a MM held at Wakefield (in the 5th Month of 1729) that he agreed to:

'...keep sd. Jonathan with meat & clothing until he can attain to 20 years of age without any further Charges to friends and then to set sd. Jonathan at Liberty...' (11)

Just as things were beginning to show distinct signs of improvement for the Greens fate cruelly intervened. Towards the end of 1729 Pontefract MM received a letter from Breach MM concerning the family:

'This meeting having rec.d a letter from Breach Mo: Meeting concerning Jonathan Green's Wife & Children, her husband being dead desiring we should take care to Supply her necessities being already become Chargeable to their mo: meeting, & properly belongeth to us; Elihu Dickinson & Highflatts frds. are desired to give us an answer unto ye sd. Letter accordingly as they judge necessary on this Acct. the Mo: meeting discharges ye Expences of a Messenger going over to Breach on this Occasion if need require.' (12)

How and under what circumstances Jonathan Green died we do not know. Ann Green was now left on her own with the youngest children, far from home and her closest relatives, to fend as best she could. Technically, she still belonged to Pontefract MM even though her new MM was not lax in taking care of her immediate needs and those of the children. Rightly, however, it was the duty of High Flatts Friends to respond to the task of relieving her distress. The commitment to the young widow was continued. Joshua Sanderson *'happened to go & see sd. Ann & finding her in a poor condition did leave £1 1s 0d'* in the hands *'of Francis Tantam for her relief.'* (13) MM also responded quickly by drawing once more upon its stock of money to assist in the relief of the widow and her children.

Ann Green's tale of woe and sorrow had a happy, if slightly messy, ending. Just over a year later, in the 5th Month of 1732, Joshua Sanderson reported to MM that Ann:

'...is soposed to have an inclination to marry, butt Breach Mo: Meeting (into which she at present resides) seems to put a stop to ye same until our monthly meeting, send them a few lines in order if we will oblige ourselves to take care to relieve her present children so if it is agreed yt. a Letter be sent & signed on ye behalf of our mo: meeting & ordered Joseph Firth & others at Highflatts meeting whom hee may so convenient to assist him to Draw ye same.' (14)

The matter appears to have been resolved quickly and satisfactorily for there the accounts concerning the family end. One would like to hope that Ann Green's life was lived in happier circumstances after the six years of trial and tribulation she had endured. Friends response to the problem was fairly extensive and ensured that the family was not left as a charge to the local parish. This, in any case, would have been wholly out of keeping with the nature of the Society and its responsibilties.

(1) MMMB 1726
(2) RDA 1834 p.274 No.14 1732
(3) MMMB 1726
(4) Ibid 1726
(5) Ibid 1727
(6) Ibid 1727
(7) Ibid 1728
(8) Ibid 1728
(9) Ibid 1728
(10) Ibid 1728
(11) Ibid 1729
(12) Ibid 1729-30
(13) Ibid 1731
(14) Ibid 1732

Caleb Roberts of Wooldale

Caleb Roberts (b.1672) was the youngest son of the same Thomas Roberts of Holmfirth who had been imprisoned for his Quaker beliefs in January 1661. At the age of 25, in 1697, he had married Mary Jackson of Bolton near Bradford (by whom he had ten children not all of whom survived).(1) At the end of 1729 when he was 57 he brought dishonour upon the family name and then placed the reputation of Friends into disrepute when he tried to avoid the discharge of his *'just debts'* by a rather devious means:

'Complaint hath been made to this meeting against Caleb Roberts of Wooldale that he hath run himself into debt may be soposed far beyond what he is Capable to pay (notwithstanding ye great Care that hath been upon Frds. minds & In Enquiring from year to year In to frds. dealings in comerce & trade which hath been made from family to family & all ways aforetime when frds. Enquired of him gave such acct. as he could Discharge his Just debt (tho' a (Jeloucie) was upon some minds he could not) And now hath Absconded himself & made over the effects to his son which is neither satisfactory to his condition nor to friends, Therefore this meet. requests both him & his son to appear at our next mo: meet. to give Frds. some satisfaction or otherwise they may further proceed as in ye Wisdom of truth may be seen meet And appoints Caleb Broadhead & Uriah Brooke to acquaint ye sd. son & desires him to acquaint his father.' (2)

By transferring possession of his goods and chattels to his son, then performing a disappearing act out of reach of his creditors, wily old Caleb hoped to save his estate at the expense of the creditors. From this account it appears that his debts had been mounting for some time. Having seen the results of Jonathan Green's late act of honesty in paying off his creditors and then reducing his family to poverty into the bargain, Caleb Roberts probably had no intention of allowing the same to happen to himself and his family. Such an act of dishonesty could not, naturally, be condoned by Friends given their strict dealings over matters of debt and insolvency. (See 'Insolvency and Non-Payment of Debts'). The dispatch of two notable Friends, particularly Uriah Brook, is most interesting. Uriah Brook was a very strict Quaker. He was well known for his attitude towards debt. (See 'Uriah Brook of High Flatts').

When the next MM convened at Burton in the 12th Month of 1729-30 the following information was passed back to it:

'The matter relateing to Caleb Roberts & son hath been discussed this day & ye results is that Frds. of or belonging Highflatts Meet. did go to ye house where sd. Caleb resides & sd. son do sheir unto Frds. a fair & perfect Acct. of all ye Debts of ye sd. Caleb (& to whome owing) as likewise to shew to sd. Frds. all ye effects that should ballance ye same as farr as sd. son is capable to give Account of...' (3)

Initially, the son was prepared to disclose the full extent of his father's debts to Friends. After all, it was his father who had contracted the debt and who was in trouble with the Society with regard to it. Since the father could not be located Friends were left with no choice but to lay the full extent of the discharging of the debt upon the son. We cannot be sure which of his sons was the one that came to be involved. (It may have been Thomas or Caleb but was probably not the youngest son, Joshua who was born in 1711). A second visit was made with these consequences:

'Jn. Broadhead gives Account to this Meet: that according to Frds. order severall Frds. of Highflatts meet: went to Caleb Roberts son to Enquire what Effects he had left towards ye discharge of his just debts, but he being by aside for fear of his creditors his son would give no Acct. of his fathers Substance or any satisfaction to the Meeting, he is desired once again to Come up to our next Mo: Meeting to satisfy Frds. in this matter Otherwise a paper of Denyall will be given out against him for refuesing to Discharge his just Debts as far as he is able.' (4)

When the son discovered that he would become liable for his father's debts he became less than obliging concerning the matter. Nor was there any sign of old Caleb who was still missing. It is no great wonder that Friends were once more dispatched to try and resolve the matter:

'The matter relating to Caleb Roberts...requests Frds. of Highflatts to speak to sd. Caleb as also to his son yt. if theyre Crediters may be paid & discharged as far as substance will Extend to, & sd. father & son are ordered to be at ye next mo: meet. ...' (5)

Neither the young Roberts nor the father seemed interested in appearing before MM. Nor did they intend to make good the debts. MM decided to persist with them a while longer.

'Frds. of their particular meeting are desired in ye Interim to Labour with him & his son to give up their all: in Equal proportion towards the discharge of their Just debt & for taking away ye reflection yt. is Cast upon them, as tho' they endeavoured by Concealing their Effects in not giveing a Just acct. of their debt, to defraud their Creditors, & if nothing is done herein towards ye satisfaction of his Creditors, then ye mo: meeting are left to their Liberty to give out a testimony against them as ye son with whom we have no unity in such disorderly practices.' (6)

'What price religious conviction?' was probably not a question deeply meditated upon by Caleb Roberts and his son. The son may have appeared unwittingly involved at the start of the whole affair but it was not long before he realized his own vested interest. Therefore, as an accomplice in this attempted fraud, he was held to be equally as guilty as his father. There can be little doubting that they knew what the inevitable consequence of their actions was likely to be. When the next MM assembled at High Flatts in the 4th Month 1730 neither father nor son attended to give Friends satisfaction over the affair. Uriah Brook, Richard Ellis and Joseph Firth of Lane Head were appointed to draw up a testimony of denial against the pair. As we can see not all Quakers were dyed the same shade of grey.

(1) MMMB 1697 & QBBREG1
(2) MMMB 1729
(3) MMMB 1729
(4) Ibid 1730
(5) Ibid 1730
(6) Ibid 1730

Joshua Woodhead of Mount

Early in 1743 Joshua Woodhead, the son of John Woodhead of Mount, formally acquainted High Flatts meeting of his intention of marrying Mary Walker, the daughter of Sarah Walker of Dewsbury. The parents of both parties signified their consent and the intention of marriage was duly minuted. (1) However, young Joshua Woodhead appears to have had an inexplicable change of mind concerning his impending marriage. To the embarrassment of High Flatts meeting he decided to stop the proceedings but he did not inform Mary Walker nor local Friends of his plan as this lengthy minute from MM held at Lane Head, in the 6th Month of 1744, reveals:

'Whereas Jos. Woodhead of Mount within the Compass of Highflats particular meeting haveing as appeared had an intention to marry a Young Woman within the Compass of Brighouse Mo: Meeting, and has appeared & gone through the Rules of Society with that Intention to marry sd. Woman, Yet notwithstanding as far as we find for reasons not Known to any of us, nor to ye young woman neither hath declined (as appears) his Intention, nor can we find by some that hath spoken to him concerning ye same Could not give any satisfaction, on yt. acct: So this day two Frds. by order of Brighouse Mo: Meetting appeared here & maketh complaint of ye unreasonablness of ye young man & way of acting & this meeting Can do no less than Joyn with them the fact is so pernicious to rules of Society, so this meeting appoints Joseph Broadhead, John Broadhead & Edw. Dickenson to speak to him about the appearance of his bad Conduct & if he do not give ye Frds. before mentioned Satisfaction then to order him to appear at our next Mo: Meeting to answer these what Frds. may propose to him.' (2)

Joshua Woodhead's motives may not have been apparent at this moment in time but there can be no doubt that they were distressing to his estranged fiancee, Mary Walker. They were equally perplexing to local Friends. The young man had good reasons for wanting to break-off his engagement and kept these a closely guarded secret until they eventually had to come to light. Terminating an intention of marriage, even employing a courteous method, was a very rare occurence indeed and definitely not *'good ordering'* nor in keeping with the 'mores' of secular society as a whole. To terminate such an intention, without a word being said, was both highly unpleasant and distressing for all involved. Marriage was a condition that was entered into with complete gravity and seriousness. Under these circumstances, in fairness both Joshua Woodhead and Mary Walker, Friends decided at the next MM held at Burton to fully investigate the matter. Representatives were dispatched to Brighouse MM to see what, if anything, had transpired there with regard to this distasteful affair.

'Josh.a Woodhead not appearing in this meeting as was requested by some of Highflats meeting, therefore ye matter being duly Considered in this meeting, and it is thought requisit that some Frd. or Frds. belonging Highflats meeting go over to Brighouse Mo: Meeting, in order to see and take notice What sort of Complaint is Judged in their mo: meeting book from the Young Woman and also her mother in order that our own proceedure against sd. Joshua's appearance of bad conduct may be of Safe ground. Edw. Dickinson & Joseph Firth are appointed to make Enquiry as above.' (3)

After the representatives had visited Brighouse MM they reported back their findings which were cryptically minuted as follows:

'...we have had some small acct. from ye Young Woman, which seems to request us to refer further proceedings against sd. Jos. a month longer.' (4)

The exact details of Mary Walker's *'small acct.'* are not revealed but we must presume that she was hoping for some further word of explanation from Joshua Woodhead in the following month. Pontefract MM agreed to wait and see how the situation developed. It seems that Mary Walker did eventually receive some kind of an explanation from Joshua Woodhead and allowed the marriage proceedings to be halted. For his misconduct in the matter Joshua Woodhead was about to be severely, and rightly, *'censured'* by the meeting — until the real motive for his ending the engagement came to be disclosed in Wakefield at the next MM.

'Notwithstanding we have shown much Christian forebearance towards Joshua Woodhead before we came to a final Determination to censure him for his very great Misconduct as Set forth in our former Minutes relating to his Late; yet as as we find by what our Friends of Highflats Acquaint us that Instead of Showing Tokens of Repentance he hath now added to his Offences by marrying a Person not of our Society and thereby apparently Shewn his great Insincerity & Impropriety in his indeavours to Impose upon this Meeting and We finding it our Duty to preserve the solemnity of that Branch of Discipline relating to Proceedings before Mo: Meeting respecting Marriages Do now for the said offences Desire our Friends of Highflats (which is the Meeting the said Joshua frequented) to draw a Testimony of Denyal against him & bring it to our next Mo: Meeting.' (5)

A Testimony of Denial was issued the following month at Pontefract.

How did Joshua Woodhead come to be involved in such an unpleasant episode? No actual details survive but a working hypothesis based on certain sound assumptions might lead us to the following scenario. The parents would most likely have brought the idea of marrying a suitable young Quaker woman (Mary Walker) to the young man's attention. Match-making was a common enough practice in this period. Joshua Woodhead may have already been involved with a woman of another *'persuasion'* but felt that a marriage out of the Society would be out of the question. He may thus have decided to go along with his parents suggestions concerning Mary Walker. The existing romance with the unknown woman must have suddenly blossomed around the time of the public announcement of his forthcoming marriage to Mary Walker. In such a situation he would be confronted with a formidable decision about his future. Now whether this existing romance was 'pure', or there was a slight matter of an unwelcome and untimely pregnancy necessitating a hasty Church marriage, can only be an surmised. However, it could be the rational explanation for Joshua Woodhead so abruptly ending his engagement with Mary Walker.

(1) MMMB 1744
(2) Ibid
(3) Ibid
(4) Ibid 1744-5
(5) Ibid 1745

Uriah Brook of High Flatts

Uriah was a son of Joshua Brook (1654-1737). He was born in 1683, married Elizabeth Broadhead (daughter of Caleb Broadhead of Wooldale) at Totties Hall in 1711. They had five children: three were born at Totties, Daniel (b.1712), Sarah (b.1714) and Hannah (b.1716). The youngest children were two sons who were born at High Flatts: John (b.1720) and Joseph (b.1722). (See 'Joseph Brook of Wooldale'). Uriah had a brother Epaphras who married Martha Broadhead (Uriah's wife's sister) also at Totties Hall. Uriah Brook's name figures prominently in the second Pontefract MM minute book and in local PM minutes and was quite clearly a Friend of some consequence. His advice was often sought particularly on matters concerning finance.

We are fortunate to have a copy of a remarkable pamphlet printed by Thomas Smart, bookseller of Huddersfield in 1804 entitled: *'A Short Account of the Inward Exercises of Uriah Brook. Late of Highflatts; with a Prayer Written by Himself. To which are prefixed Testimonies concerning him.'* From this we are able to build up a picture of this Friend from his own words and those of his family.

Uriah Brook had deep religious experiences in his earliest years as he recounts:

'The Lord who at Times visited me in my Childhood, (and more particularly when I was about Eight Years old), was pleased to reach unto me in a more abundant Manner and manifest his Love and Goodness, when I was Eighteen Years of Age.'

These experiences were to prepare him and give him strength as in his late teens *'I had a deep Exercise to go through.'* Uriah Brook does not tell us what this *'Exercise'* was but it was obviously a very low period in his life as he relates of *'the inexpressible Sorrow and Trouble that was upon me in those Days'* and of *'the many subtle Snares and Temptations the Enemy laid before me.'* However, he overcame these trials and says *'let me never forget the kindness of the Lord unto me in the Days of my Youth.'*

He relates to us how he came to marry Elizabeth Broadhead. It seems that when he was still young his mother had suggested *'that E.B. a sober young Woman, Daughter of honest and religious Parents, would be a suitable Wife for me.'* However, Uriah was determined to make up his own mind as at first he did not follow his mothers advice, the advice being reiterated by his father after his mother's death. He tells us that *'I did not find Freedom in my own Mind; for I thought I could have been well contented, to have sojourned out my Days in a single state.'* Eventually, Uriah had a change of heart and married Elizabeth Broadhead telling us that *'I found Drawings in my own Mind that way'*, although, *'Yet still I was not hasty or forward, but took great Deliberation...for I sought unto the Lord for Counsel and Direction.'*

Uriah Brook appears to have been fairly introverted and solitary spending much of his time in reading and meditation: *'I was much inclined to Reading in my young Years, for I Loved to read the Holy Scriptures, and other good books.'* Henry Dickinson said of his father-in-law *'he loved Solitude, and spent most of his leisure Hours in private Retirement.'* His other son-in-law, William Earnshaw, describes him as *'a Man of a meek and quiet Spirit'*, being *'quick to hear, but slow to speak.'* His retiring nature seems to have applied to Meeting as well as in Henry Dickinson's words *'although He was a diligent Attender of our religious Meetings...he did not appear in public Testimony, yet his Heart caused many melodious sounds to proceed therefrom, to the Strengthening of the Weak and Comforting the Living.'* His wife Elizabeth tells that *'He dearly loved to go to the Quarterly Meetings at York: He went more than thirty times, though he lived near forty miles off.'*

He had strong opinions on various subjects including debt. Henry Dickinson relates that *'when he heard of Friends falling short of paying their just Debts said, that might have been prevented by being frugal and industrious.'* It is not surprising that he was one of the Friends appointed by MM to try and sort out one of the most serious cases of debt recorded. (See 'Caleb Roberts of Wooldale'). William Earnshaw tells us that *'he was often concerned on the Account of the Discipline in the Church, that it might be kept up.'* He had a care for the world he lived in, as testified by his children: *'He was one that used this World as though he used it not — not abusing it.'* Uriah's prayer at the end of this booklet shows the deep affection and care that he had for his children and concern that they should be guided through the troubled times that they would face as he had in his youth. He prays *'O Lord...I pray thee meet with them in thine own Way, and in thy own Time, and bring them to be acquainted with thee.'*

Uriah Brook died in 1758 at age of 75 and was interred in High Flatts burial ground. His wife Elizabeth recorded: *'He was well beloved by his Friends and Neighbours.'* Elizabeth Brook was to survive him and live into her nineties, a well respected minister of the Society. We can leave Uriah Brook by quoting two further sections from his own account of his life. The first extract hints at a touch of humour in the character of this strict but thoughtful Friend: he cannot have missed the play on words contained therein. The second shows his very deep and clear insight into the nature of religion.

'I have met with many bitter storms, and Strong Temptations of various Sorts...But, at Times, I have been favoured with a Brook by the Way, the streams whereof make truly glad the City of God.'

'One Time, having my Mind religiously concerned I thought I saw clearly there but few entered into the Kingdom of Heaven, who had not passed through great and manifold Tribulations, and Abundance of Exercises, Sorrows and Afflictions.'

Joseph and John Broadhead of Wooldale

When Henry Jackson (II) died in 1727 he left a legacy in his will *'to be put out upon Interest or laid out from time to time in keeping the Meet.g House at Wooldale in good Repair.'* (1) By the direction of this will Joseph and John Broadhead (the sons of Caleb Broadhead of Wooldale) were appointed to administer this legacy. They were *'sound Friends'* who were well respected by the local Quaker community and could be relied upon to *'imploy the same in exicution & performance of the said Trust.'* Joseph was a clothier of means. His wife, Ann, was a devout woman and a recorded minister (See Appendix (13)) who was to have a Testimony written about her upon her death. (See Appendix (10)) Both brothers served their PM and MM dutifully in varied capacities.

In 1760 a complaint was brought by *'some Friends of Highflatts'* before MM being held at Wakefield that month concerning the administration, *'security'* and care of this legacy.

'...said Friends think 30 pounds of said Legacy is not properly secured And in perusing and considering the Clause in the will and Considering the Circumstances relative thereunto this Meet.g thinks that the said Joseph & John Broadhead ought to submit the affair to this Meet.g whose Opinion is that the said Joseph & John Broadhead must either give such a Security for said 30 pounds or take such Security for the same as this Meeting approve.' (2)

The exact details of the mysterious clause are not revealed but the *'Circumstances relative thereunto'* become quite obvious when the age of the two brothers is considered. Joseph (1687-1771) was seventy-four and John (1691-1775) a slightly younger seventy. Even though the two brothers were to live until they were both eighty-three it was clearly becoming a matter of some concern to younger Friends. Should the two brothers have died suddenly then the unsecured £30 might have been completely lost. Although many Friends enjoyed longevity the eighteenth century was not a time when it was common for many to reach their biblically allotted *'three score and ten.'* The time had now arrived when the matter of the trusteeship and £30 needed to settled. Unfortunately, the matter was not going to be cleanly and amicably resolved as was usually the case in such circumstances. No immediate action was taken at Wakefield. The matter was referred to the next MM to be held at Pontefract.

At Pontefract a decision was reached by MM that the two brothers *'shold submit to the Judgement of Friends.'* William Leatham, Samuel Dickinson and John Wilson were requested to visit Joseph and John concerning the matter. When they reported back the following month it was already becoming evident that an easy resolution of the matter was not likely. MM heard that *'Joseph and John refused to meet them at any other place then (sic) Wooldale Meeting House.'* This refusal did not appear to have gone down too well. Representatives of MM were sent to inform *'the said Joseph and John that they intend to wait upon them at the said place about 9 on the Morning of the Monthly Meeting to be next held there.'* Two months later, when MM assembled at Wooldale, the matter was still far from resolved. According to the minutes:

'As to the affaire of Joseph & John Broadhead Some Friends Mett, Agreeable to ye Appointment but it is Still Referr.d to our next and at ye Request of Joe:Broadhead one of ye Parties, if ye Affaire Cannot be made up before our next all ye Appointed friends are Desired to meet at Lainhead ye 9th hour on ye meeting Day to have a further hearing & Report of it.' (3)

When the next meeting was held at Shepley Lane Head the affair had to be deferred yet again. The Broadhead brothers, seemingly intransigent, decided not to appear. It was beginning to seem to some Friends that perhaps the *'unsecured'* £30 might never be *'secured'* again. It was this refusal to co-operate that had many Friends puzzled as to why the two brothers did not want to relinquish their trusteeship. The answer was as plain as the two elderly Quakers involved: the two brothers did not like to think that, after all these years, they were no longer able to fulfill their committment to the Society, the meeting and the late Henry Jackson. No doubt they felt far from old. No doubt they also objected to the high-handed manner in which the whole affair was being handled.

At this juncture the proceedings became irrate as this thinly disguised minute of the 9th Month 1760 discloses:

'...this Meet.g having long Laboured with them in a Spirit of Love & Meekness and done all that seems to be in our power, diverse Friends having visited them from remote parts of it, in order to have prevailed upon them to give or take Security for the above mentioned Sum of £30, for which Land security hath been offered to them but cannot prevail with them either to part with the Money or to Submit to a few impartial Friends or to refer it to our Qr. Meet.g to Settle according to the Rules of Friends but on the contrary have treated diverse Friends with unbecoming Language and seems to set the Love and Care of this Meet.g at nought and the said John being present & refusing to give this Meet.g security for the £10 which belongs Wooldale Mtg. or to pay into said Meet.g from whence he received it, as the said £30 is all in Johns hand this Meet.g appoints Caleb Marsden John Broadhead (of Mearhouse) and Wm. Radley to know whether he be willing to resign his part of the Trust to the direction of this Meet.g...' (4)

Caleb Marsden's visit *'did not meet with desired success'* but one of the other two local Friends reported that *'in their last visit Joseph gave some expectation that the £10 would be paid in.'* Highly contradictory yet not inexplicable. John Broadhead of Mearhouse (situated close to Wooldale) would have been received more sympathetically than either Caleb Marsden of Birdsedge or William Radley of Shepley. In the meanwhile, 'in absentia', MM had taken it upon itself to let three unnamed Friends from QM make an *'Award in writing'* upon the matter and present it to Joseph and his wife, Ann. At this juncture, an indication of the division and ill-feeling that was already occurring, became evident when an as yet unnamed Friend made allegations against the clerk of MM:

'...a certain Member of their Meet.g in a publick Assembly gave forth some unbecoming Reflections on the Clerk of our last Mo. Meet.g as to the Minute concerning Jos.h & John Broadhead were not the Act of this Meet.g but an Arbitrary proceeding of the Clark which this Meet.g conceives to be an Untruth & great Reproach upon the Dignity & Solemnity of this Meet.g...' (5)

The meeting immediately dispatched Tobias Mallinson, John Wood and Abraham Beaumont to deal with *'the Abuse.'* Caleb Marsden was also labouring further with the two elderly brothers but with no success for he reported at Burton in the 11th Month *'that there appears no probablity of reconciling them to pay the Money according to the Arbitration of the 3 friends from York.'* MM also felt distinctly annoyed by the stubborness of the two brothers because it threatened *'to give out a Testimony of Denial against them.'* The Testimony was not issued *'in Compassion to their years and out of a tender regard to Joseph's wife.'* Also there appeared to be some extenuating *'Circumstances relating to John Broadhead.'* Had the matter continued then no doubt the Testimony would eventually have been issued. The meeting decided that *'in the mean while Joseph & John are to be regarded as Members out of Unity with this Meet.g...'* A copy of this minute was sent to them. The unnamed Friend who who earlier intervened in the affair turned out to be Joseph Brook of Wooldale. He was the youngest son of Uriah Brook (See 'Uriah Brook of High Flatts' & 'Joseph Brook of Wooldale') and a nephew of Ann Broadhead. Joseph was obviously not particularly repentant as according to those who visited him he appeared to be very *'disaffected and very unsensible of the Offence given to this Meetg.'* Josiah Cookson and Samuel Dickinson were sent to visit him *'to make him sensible of the bad consequences that may attend his Contempt of this Meetg.'* Being a good 'plain Friend', as the few extracts of his missing account book tend to show, Joseph bit his tongue and apologized in person to MM. He said *'that he was sorry that he had given Occasion against him (the Clerk) and intended to be more careful for the future to do the like.'*

The two Broadhead brothers, now having been shown the *'Award'*, decided that they were not going to be put out of unity by MM. In their opinion the 'underhand' method of employing QM members to pronounce judgement without a hearing was certainly unfair treatment. These two cantankerous old Quakers informed MM by letter in the 3rd Month of 1761 that they intended to *'apealle to the Quarterly Meeting aganst (sic) the proceedings of this Monthly Meeting.'* (6)

William Leatham, John Wilson and Samuel Dickinson were appointed to speak to the Broadhead brothers. Quite what transpired in their meetings we can only guess. Surprisingly, the following month, when the meeting convened at Pontefract, we learn that John Broadhead at the *'...solicitation of & request and by direction & appointment of this Meet.g hath paid into this Meet.g the sum of £10 given to him and his Brother Joseph by the late Henry Jackson.'* The meeting went on to record rather lamely *'...it was some misunderstanding that the said Joseph & John Broadhead heretofore refused to give this Meet.g the above satisfaction.'* Further, the meeting received the two brothers back *'into their former unity.'* The £10 was made the responsibility of Joseph Firth of Shepley Lane Head with John Broadhead of Melton House and Joshua Marsden of Birdsedge as the new trustees. There the matter ended.

That Friends could be divisive on matters such as this reveals their human imperfections. The two Broadhead brothers cannot be held entirely guilty for this disquieting episode. Their role was almost definitely contributive. The wisdom of their years should have led to better conduct on their part. Giving in gracefully to old age may not have been one of their stronger virtues. In this instance the rather officious pressure of MM cannot be neglected. A Friend like Joseph Brook of Wooldale, whilst a relative of the two men, was not likely to have commented upon the situation without some just cause. One cannot help but wonder if John Griffith, upon his visit just two months later, read the minutes concerning the matter during his YM visitation. Perhaps, it was this and other more observable phenomena that led him to make his famous and powerful observation.

(1) MMMB 1761
(2) Ibid 1760
(3) Ibid 1760
(4) Ibid
(5) Ibid
(6) Ibid 1761

Joseph Brook of Wooldale

Joseph Brook was the youngest son of Uriah. (See 'Uriah Brook of High Flatts'). He was born in 1722 at High Flatts. During his life he kept an account book which contains numerous short comments on what he was buying and other related matters. Although the authors have been unable to trace this work some of the entries were quoted in an article in 'The Sunday Magazine' for February 1905 entitled 'The Quakers of Early Times' by Isabel Maude Hamill. Some of these quotations are used in this section to help us to build up a picture of another generation of Brooks connected with Wooldale and High Flatts. The first entry reads:

*'31st 3mo: 1748. Cost 1s 6d.
Joseph Brook his Book.
I desire not great riches, but such as I
may get justly, use soberly, distribute
Cheerfully, and Leave Contentedly.'*

The book is described as being in a good state of preservation (1905), bound in calf with a brass clasp. Joseph moved from the family home early in his life as he records coming to:

'Wooldale to be boarded, and is to pay 2s a week for bord and hous room and is to have bate for being away a whole Day or more and I were a way 14 days this year and I paid 2s for hors to Highflats, £5-4s and 2d.'

A Joseph Brook married Mary Roberts in 1765 but this could possibly refer to his first cousin who had the same name. However, this is unlikely. There are numerous references to his wife including some referring to doctors fees:

'8-6 Mo: Robert Cannely of Manchester 3 bottles to Cuer my Wife, gave 2s 6d, and when Cured is to have more 3s, but it did Little good.'

Joseph finally records his wife's death as follows:

'18-6 Mo: 1794. My Dear Wife Departed this Life and Was buried the 22nd of the Same; and it was a favoured meeting at the same time and I have cause to beleve that She is hapy. Cofin 26s. a table Covered 11s.'

Their children included John (b.1773), Sarah (b.1768), Mary (b.1770), and Hannah (who died aged 15 in 1781). Elizabeth, Esther and Joseph died in infancy after 3 weeks, 8 days and 4 days respectively. It is possibly to one of these that this sad comment applies: *'Pd. Sose Bour (Susan Bower) for Laying ye child 6d, for Coffin 1s, for grave-making 6d, 2s in all.'* On the following line the doctor's fee: 10s 6d for bringing the short-lived child into the world.

During the same year that his wife died, Joseph Brook appears to have had trouble with his landlord. The exact nature of this trouble is not made clear but revolves around the landlord's refusal to accept some rent when it was offered to him by Joseph Brook.

'Was at Landlord's and had the same witnesses as before, but he would not be seen and his wife would not have it...Landlord came and brought Constable and Bailiff to make Distress and we paid him the Hole years rent, that is 14-0-0, and the Constable and the Bailiff besides.'

In her article Isabel Maude Hamill records that the landlord was eventually made to pay £5 1s 3d for wrongful distraint.

Like his father, Uriah, he was a well respected Friend and a frequent attender not only at MM but further afield as the following entries show:

'Pontefract Monthly Meeting on foot with W.E. and there was Lucy Eckroyd and a young woman Rebecca Smith, friend from Gloucestershire, and had such a sence given her of the stait and staits of ye members of ye meeting, as several thought they had not heard ye like delivered before, I was with her at 6 Meetings, before York Quarterly Meeting.'

'At Macclesfield Yearly Meeting, Which was to a good degree of satisfaction, and was on foot, Cost 12s.'

We know that during this period of his life there were many visitors to our local meetings including Friends from America who gave *'abundance of good Councel and advice.'* (See Appendix (16) and 'The Visit of John Griffith'). Joseph also gave considerable financial support to Wooldale Meeting House as he records for 1782 that he *'Paid a second time 2-7-6 towards Wooldale Meeting house...'* This would have been at the time of the major alterations and enlargement carried out in 1782-3. He kept careful records in his account book of any borrowing and lending of money. One wonders whether his father, Uriah, who had such strict opinions on debt, would have approved. Included is the following entry:

'Lent Samuel Bowers 5-0-0, he Hath a Wood Legg and I Have his note for it.'

One wonders if poor Samuel Bowers had to mortgage his wooden leg for the loan and would Joseph have taken it from him had he been unable to repay the debt? More plausibly the note was concerned with the loan rather than the wooden leg! Other transactions also have brief and rather 'strange' comments appended such as, *'We are stright, but I ow 2d now'* and *'I remain debter, but now it is Reckoned and Paid.'* His precision and attention to detail was not confined to money matters only, as the record of his daughter's birth shows:

'Sarah Do. was born on the 20th of 6th 1768 About 20 minits after four of the Clock in the morning on the Second Day of the week.'

The final entries in the book are in different hands, according to Isabel Maude Hamill, mainly recording family births and deaths including one by his son, John for the 10th of the 5th Month 1809:

'My dear Father departed this Life and was buried 13th of the same aged near 87 years. John Brook.'

Joseph Brook seems to have shared his deeply abiding faith with his father, Uriah. He frequently acknowledged God's goodness and his own failings, even during the hours of his labours, always remembering that in his daily life that there was a higher nature: *'Oh! How I was visited with Divine goodness, I had cause to rejoice'* and *'This day there was hard strugglings.'*

It is interesting to follow the story a little further and to quote a paper that was to be read in conjunction with John Brook's will:

'My chief reason for my not having divided the whole of my Property into three equal parts — is because I should not like my Property in Pellane to be sold — on account of its being so near the Meeting House.

I should like my Nephew Robert not to make a sale at all but to com and take things as the are — If he can make it convenant or som Friend that it may be a House for Friends to com to, and I hope and desire he will do his best for it to be continued to be so. I hope that all my near and Dear relations will be satisfied with my having don so. as I have left my three sisters the whole or nearly so of what my Dear Father left me, and I was 36 years old when I had it. So that I hope and desire youl all be very <u>Loving</u> and grable one to warde another, for that is the way to be happy both in this world, and in that which which is to com.

I am with Dear <u>Love</u> to you all.

John Brook.

Pellane 16th of 1st month 1838.'

John Brook had no children which partly explains this document. The house referred to is Pell Croft, adjacent to Wooldale Meeting House, and John Brook's nephew was Robert Walker. This is the remarkable story of the continuing care and concern of one family through several generations and their links with Wooldale and High Flatts Meetings. In John's note the desire for fairness within the family and his attention to detail and care for the Meeting is as apparent as that exhibited by his father, grandfather and probably great-grandfather before. The house was passed down through Robert Walker to Joseph Walker, both of whom were prominent members of Wooldale Meeting in later years. The family remained at Pell Croft until Joseph Walker died in 1940. In fact the house remained in Quaker hands until the mid 1950's. During this long Quaker occupation parts of the original grounds were transferred at various times to the meeting house as additions to the graveyard.

George Lee of Wooldale

One of the problems that local Friends faced was the arrival of newcomers professing to be good Quakers. George Lee was such a Quaker. He came from Sheffield within the boundaries of Balby MM (c.1755). No one appeared too certain about his reasons for coming to this locality but it was not very long before they became suspicious.

As an outsider and a newcomer he was visited as soon as local Friends became aware of his arrival. Those who visited him reported back that he had informed them that he was *'not certain Yet of Settling with us, But when so intends to Bring a Certificate as Soon as maybe after.'* (1) This was rather contrary to form. The next PM was not entirely happy with George Lee's explanation. The lack of an accompanying certificate would have further heightened suspicion. Was George Lee who and what he professed to be? Why, exactly, had he left Sheffield? Had he left under a cloud? John Broadhead and William Earnshaw were appointed to invite George Lee along to the next meeting *'in order to satisfy Friends Concerning his late removal from Sheffield to us as yet having no Certificate.'*

No details are given of what happened between the visit made by John Broadhead and William Earnshaw and the next PM minute mentioning George Lee. A certificate of removal was obtained according to MM minutes of the 12th of the 2nd Month 1756:

'Highflatts Friends brought to this Meetg. a Certificate from Balby Monthly Meeting setting forth that George Lee a Member of their Meetg. was a sober Person of an Orderly Conversation; & in Unity with our Society whilst amongst them & the same being read & accepted is sent by Joshua Marsden to be recorded:' (2)

However, if we read the following minute taken from PM dated the 4th of the 2nd Month 1756, just eight days before the above mentioned MM, we discover that there is something distinctly at variance:

'We have received a Certificate on Behalf of Geo. Lee from Balby Monthly Meeting to ours sent our Representatives. But George having resided Some latly w.th us, And his Conduct hath not been altogether to Friends satisfaction.' (3)

George Lee does not appear to have left Sheffield under a cloud: on the contrary. The certificate from Balby MM lauds his praiseworthy manner of life. However, this does not appear to have been the finding of local Friends as we can see from their minutes. Whilst George Lee might have left his MM with a spotless record he had somehow not managed to sustain it on his arrival here. As he was now within the province of Pontefract MM it was up to local Friends as to how they decided to deal with him. Another visit was made to George Lee *'Concerning his Late misconduct'* to determine what course of action should be undertaken. The Friends responsible reported back that they had *'Some Degree of hopes that he will walk more agreeable for the future.'* (4) No further action was taken: Friends, presumably influenced by his certificate, gave him the benefit of the doubt on account of his good character reference from Balby MM. His certificate of removal, despite his recent misconduct, was placed before MM held at Wakefield on the 2nd Month of 1756. Local Friends must have reasoned that this misconduct might be just a temporary abberation caused by the circumstances of having moved into a new locality among strangers.

Nothing more appears in the minute book during the ensuing years until 1767. Then George Lee appears once again. *'Complaint is made to this Meeting of the bad conduct of George Lee which in several respects hath been very scandalous, & brought great reproach upon Truth & us as a people.'* (5) The overseers were sent to see him and let him know that he could have *'the Liberty to clear himself from such complaints if he can...'*

George Lee did not bother to turn up. He must have decided to make the break with the Society for good because he continued to misbehave. The following PM minutes disclose that *'fresh complaint being made of his misconduct in drinking to excess This Meeting apprehends there is no hopes of his being reclaimed...'* (6) The years between 1755 and 1767 are tantalizing when it comes to evaluating George Lee's life among local Friends. Did he reform and then 'slip' from the straight and narrow path of plain living? Or did he simply amble along the thin dividing line between acceptable and unacceptable conduct? He could well have been a thorn 'tolerated' by local Friends for all those years. Why did he succumb again to delinquent activities? Or, had he already, on leaving Balby MM, decided to begin making the break? Or was the rupture caused by local events of which we are not aware? We shall never know but we may now appreciate why certificates were issued with respect to persons coming into a new meeting. We may further appreciate of what limited use these certificates of removal could also turn out to be.

Friends in the locality had given George Lee a second chance to make good his initial misconduct shortly after arriving in the area. They may well have given him more. This is a purely unsubstantiated supposition but one that is not unreasonable given Friends tolerance in the case of George Cartwright (See 'The Unnecessary Frequenting of Alehouses'). They had hoped that he would *'walk more agreeable'* but they had been proved disappointingly wrong.

(1) PMMB 1755
(2) MMMB 1756
(3) PMMB 1756
(4) Ibid
(5) Ibid 1767
(6) Ibid

John Haigh of Moor Royd Nook, High Flatts

What happened when a couple wished to get married but could not obtain their parents consent? Did they just simply decide to marry out of the Society of Friends? Or was there another alternative? Under the usual circumstances there was no alternative. However, in 1762 John Haigh and Hannah Dickinson (daughter of Enoch and Mary of Thurlstone) used an unusual ploy. This ploy seemed to have worked to their advantage.

It was the practice for both parties parents to signify their consent either by being present when an intention of marriage was made public, or by submitting an attested written note if they could not attend. To openly make a declaration of intention to marry before a meeting without such parental consent was certainly not a step to be recommended. (See 'Marriage & Marital Difficulties'). According to the minutes this is what the erstwhile young lovers did ...

'...John Haigh & Hannah Dickenson laid their Intention of Marriage with each other, before our last meeting, but the meeting cou'd not accept thereof, as their appearance was without the Consent or Allowance of Hannah's Parents, yet nothwithstanding they laid their Intention before our last Mo. meeting, but that cou'd not Accept thereof for the above Reasons, but appointed 3 frds. of this Meeting to treat w.th the said Jn. Haigh & Han. Dickenson & also w.th the young woman's parents, which they accordingly have done, The said Jn. Haigh & Han. Dickenson hath this day delivered into this Meeting a paper of acknowledgement for their unwise proceedings & desires Friends to pass by their Offence, which paper is to be sent to Mo. Meeting. They again in this Meeting signified their Intentions of taking each other in Marriage, her Parents in writing signified their allowance thereof...' (1)

John and Hannah's happiness looked likely to be thwarted. The young woman's parents did not like or want this particular match for their daughter. As later events will reveal their judgement in this matter was to prove impeccable. No consent, no marriage. Neither John nor Hannah were prepared to tolerate this deplorable lack of approval. So they took a bold course of action fully realizing that there would be consequences and repercussions. They announced their intention to marry without that required consent in full knowledge of the likely consequences. The meeting must have received quite a shock at this very unprecedented step. They were turned down just as they had probably forseen. One can imagine the uproar and anguish in the Dickinson household. The embarrassment of their daughter's action would not easily be lived down. The parents found themselves with no recourse but to reluctantly consent to this marriage in order to save face. It is worth noting that the parents consent, done 'in absentia', was via a note (even though they lived locally enough to be present). John and Hannah must have anticipated that they would need to prepare a *'paper of acknowledgement'* for their misdeed. This they appear to have readily done. Accepting a reprimand for their offence appears to have been worth it to get Hannah's parents to consent. The fact that the meeting let them off so lightly might appear to testify to a personal desire to allow the two young people to get married. Certainly, if that was the feeling, then the meeting would not have felt too happy about what was going to happen after their marriage. Hannah's parent reservations concerning John Haigh were not without grounds. He was quarrelsome, idle and untypical of Friends to be found in the local meetings.

Nearly two years later John and Hannah found themselves involved in yet more trouble when Caleb Marsden and John Broadhead paid them a visit.

'The above Frds. also report that they w.th some friends Visited Jn. Haigh & his Wife, & took the opportunity to enquire into their Situation & made proposals of giving them a Little Money. But instead of receiving any or taking friends advice mixt kindly Expressed their disrespect to Friends as were cause of much uneasiness to the Visitors...' (2)

There would be nothing unusual in Friends visiting recently wedded couples. They would be visiting to ensure that the young couple were managing materially as well as spiritually. They found that the couple were not managing at all well. It must have been all the more surprising when the generous offer of financial help was so abruptly rejected by John Haigh. Knowing John Haigh's mettle the prospect of receiving charity might not have been so welcome. In these circumstances the meeting decided to send out a very weighty band of Friends to deal with the forthright John Haigh. Tobias Mallinson, Joseph Shaw and William Radley paid him a visit. No doubt John Haigh and his wife expected to be revisited because the records show that:

'The Friends appointed to revisit Jn. Haigh & his Wife, Report their Visit was more to their Satisfaction than they expected, & that Jn. & his Wifes behaviour to the friends that visited them last Month had been a matter of great uneasiness to 'erm. The overseers are desired to have them under their Notice.' (3)

After this incident John Haigh kept himself out of further trouble for some years. Hannah gave birth to five children at their home at Moor Roid Nook between 1762-1773. (4) She and her young children appeared to have had a far from easy life. Despite the fact that John Haigh was a clothier by occupation it is clear that he was too lazy to make good. Local Friends frequently helped the family out for the sake of Hannah and the children. This all proved to no avail. She died at the age of 36 in 1774 leaving John Haigh to bring up the three surviving young children. He almost immediately abdicated responsibilty for bringing up his two daughters. Compassionate Friends from High Flatts Meeting took over their upbringing. Young Joseph, his son, went away to William Earnshaw's of Totties to receive some schooling. Even so the shiftless father was incapable of making sufficient of a living to pay towards the upkeep of his son. This eventually forced William Earnshaw to take action by referring the matter to MM. The meeting agreed to give William Earnshaw:

"1 2s...towards the Expence of Joseph Haigh's boardage. And it is agreed likewise to pay for sd. Joseph's Boardage another Month...' (5)

Friends were then sent to speak to John Haigh and *'to examine into his capableness to assist in supporting his sd. Son...'* They were far from impressed by the encounter. In the opinion of these Friends *'...it would not be proper to trust'* young Joseph *'with his Father, who is a Person indolent and exceptionable in his Conduct.'* Upon this advice MM decided that the young boy should continue *'with William Earnshaw, on the same Terms as before.'* MM also decided to ask Friends *'...if any Members, or Meeting can propose any easier Method of maintaining him..'* to let them know as soon as possible. Assistance came from an unexpected quarter:

'Joseph Haigh of Ebson house in Highflatts Meeting is willing to take the above mentioned Boy Joseph Haigh for three years, and find him all Necessaries, being allowed by this Meeting One Shilling A Week for that time; and at the Expiration of the said Term of Three Years, he is to take him as an Apprentice, till he be twenty one years of Age, without any Apprentices Fee to which this Meeting agrees, and proposes paying him Quarterly.' (6)

Joseph Haigh of Epson House (7) was possibly John Haigh's younger brother although the evidence linking the two is not at all clear on this point. (Two John Haigh's were born in 1738 — one being an only child). This might explain the charitable act. Equally, Joseph Haigh of Epson House may just have been a distant kinsman. With the assistance of MM he was willing to take over from William Earnshaw until the boy was ready to become an apprentice. William Earnshaw could be excused the responsibility as he was now advancing into old age and would shortly remove to Lancashire.

John Haigh managed to survive in membership for just a few month more until the second month of 1778. His testimony of denial makes interesting reading and is quoted here in full.

'John Haigh of Ingbirchworth was born of Parents in Profession with us the people called Quakers and joined himself in Marriage to one of the same Profession yet not with the entire approbation of her Parents but in condescention to and in hopes he might make a more industrious Husband than they apprehended he would they assented thereto: He and his Wife lived together many Years and had several Children, but his Conduct was far from being agreeable notwithstanding he was frequently advised to more Circumspection, yet Friends out of regard to his Wife and children frequently administered to their Necessities until the decease of his Wife; soon after which for the welfare of his Children and that he might not be overburthened with them some neighbouring Friends took two and the meeting provided for the Third: he had only then himself to provide for: in this manner he was situated severall Years, in which time it was thought he might have something to spare towards supporting his children and easing Friends; for which he was applied to, but nothing co'd be had from him tho' he gave some expectation of doing something, but instead there of he hath exceedingly abused sundry Friends by giving them bad language, and hath of late neglected attending our Religious Meetings. Such a course of Life being much inconsistent with the Rules of our Society we can have no Unity therewith, and therefore we hereby disown him from being a Member thereof...' (8)

One cannot help but wonder if the young twenty-four year old Hannah Dickinson, who challenged her parents prudence over her choice of husband as well as Quaker marriage conventions, would have made the same choice if she could have forseen the future? Did she live a miserably unhappy twelve years of married life before dying? And what of the young children she left behind? Elizabeth, the eldest daughter, gave birth to an illigitimate child in 1788 and was disowned. (See 'Loose & Disorderly Conduct'). To what extent was that 10-11 year old child in her formative years influenced by a lack of real parents? It was indeed fortunate that there were few rogues like John Haigh within the Society. All the more surprising then that local Friends tolerated his conduct and attitude as long as they did.

(1) PMMB 1762
(2) Ibid
(3) Ibid
(4) The five were: Eizabeth (b.1763), Hannah (b.1765), Ann (b.1766), Joseph (b.1768) and Thomas (b.1773). Ann and Thomas died within their first year.
(5) MMMB 1776
(6) Ibid 1777
(7) Variously referred to as Epsom, Epson, Hebson: now called Ebson House.
(8) MMMB 1778

Elihu Dickinson the Tanner

There were two prominent Elihu Dickinsons living in High Flatts during the eighteenth century: they were identified as 'the Tanner' and 'the Clothier'. The two Elihus were cousins, (see 'The Dickinson's of High Flatts'), and both frequently worked together on matters relating to the Society. Both were succesful men in their daily lives.

Elihu Dickinson the Tanner was the son of Elihu Dickinson and Mary Aldham and the grandson of Elihu Dickinson and his second wife, Sarah Kay. Elihu Dickinson the Clothier was the grandson of Elihu Dickinson and his first wife, Mary Firth, and the son of Edward Dickinson and Ann Greenwood. The two Elihu's were clearly distinguishable in daily life for the Clothier wore the normal Quaker *'drab'* whilst the Tanner, in keeping with his profession, dressed entirely in leather. Physically, Elihu the Tanner was described as *'a dapper little man, conspicious in hair powder, light gaiters and white stockings.'* (1)

The Tanner married twice. His first wife was Sarah Sutcliffe who came from within the compass of Brighouse MM. They had six children. According to a letter written to Joseph Wood by Richard Crafton of London, on the 19th December 1772, the Tanner had married a woman of some substance.

'I was pleased to hear Elihew Dickinson the Tanner was so well married I think he has taken a great deal of pains for a Wife & I doubt not but he will make a very good Husband. I think him a very Cleaver Industerous Young man. He tells me his wife's Fortune is Ten Thousd pounds...' (2)

Following the death of his first wife he married Elizabeth Rothwell who, according to a rather vague tradition, gave Denby Dale its name. (Prior to this time it had been known as Denby Dike Side).

Elihu Dickinson was by all accounts quite a character. He was a man of considerable business acumen who in addition to being the owner of a successful tannery diversified his interests to include being a farmer, corn miller, timber and stone merchant, colliery proprietor and land valuer. This same man also managed to attend Huddersfield Market by eight o'clock in the morning, whatever the season, even though it was ten miles away. In 1792 he was known to be working coal pits at Fulshaw but it is not certain whether he had started these or indeed owned them. He was certainly working coal pits at Denby Dale in 1799.

Elihu Dickinson was in many ways symptomatic of the new breed of Quaker business men who were to leave their mark on that century. Although Elihu cannot be counted amongst the Darbys of Coalbrookdale, or the Tukes of York, or even the later Rowntrees, Cadburys, Lloyds or Clarks, there can be little doubt that he typified the drive and energy necessary to be successful. Despite his highly active life as an entrepreneur and as a leading member of High Flatts Meeting he managed to live to a ripe old age. The following extract was recorded in a newspaper report concerning a case being heard at York Assizes:

'One of the witnesses for the plaintiff was Mr. Elihu Dickinson, a most respectable and venerable-looking old gentleman of the Society of Friends, who in his profession of a land-valuer had been employed to inspect the farm occupied by the plaintiff and to estimate the allowances to which he was entitled by the custom of the country. His testimony, delivered with a precision and good sense which we have seldom witnessed, was

strongly in favour of the plaintiff's claim; and he wound up the whole by declaring that judging from his own long experience there could not be a custom more beneficial to all parties than that insisted on by the plaintiff. Mr. Scarlet: Will you allow me, Mr. Dickinson, to ask how old you are? Witness: I am now in my eightieth year. (The appearance of Mr.D. betokens a hale and happy man of about sixty; and his clear eye and ruddy cheek present no small contrast with the care-worn parchment visages of most of the learned gentlemen by whom he was surrounded). Mr. Justice Bayley: Ah! Mr. Scarlet, this land valuing is a far better occupation than the law. (A laugh).' (3)

He served High Flatts Meeting in the capacity of an elder and was frequently called upon to deal with both matters of Quaker discipline and finance. However, even he does not appear to have been totally beyond reproach as the following letter from his contemporary, Joseph Wood the minister, reveals:

Newhouse 6th Mo. 4th 1798

Respected Friend
Elihu Dickinson

The respect that I bear thee & thine engages me in the cross to my own inclination as a Man to write unto thee; having heard several times of late of thee having been overtaken with drinking to excess. I am sensible that thou art very much exposed to temptations of this kind in the way of thy business, in the world, & as thou advances in years, I apprehend it may steal on thee at unawares; But, this dear friend makes it more necessary for thee to set a double watch. I believe thou loves the Society of which thou art a member, & those who are concerned to walk uprightly therein; Indeed I have thought thou has at all times manifested it towards me a poor unworthy creature which it hath greatly encouraged me to write unto thee that, thou may be strengthened to withstand these temptations, which if overtaken with thou knows wounds the cause, brings great & heavy distress upon the faithful, loses thy authority over thy children & servants, hurts thy own health, & greatly endangers the eternal welfare of thy immortal part. I would therefore in all tenderness of a Brother & fellow member of the same religious Society, tenderly intreat thee to consider these few hints, & guard against being inadvertantly drawn to take more liquor than is really useful & as this is the case a hope attends my mind that thou will experience preservation in the hour of temptation. I am with real respect to thee thy truly well wishing friend
Joseph Wood

For Elihu Dickinson
Tanner of Highflatts' (4)

Elihu Dickinson the Tanner died in 1829 apparently active to the end. During his lifetime he built and resided at Mill Bank House in High Flatts which later became a 'Home for Inebriate Women'. The Dickinson estates were sold in March 1875 upon the death of Herbert Camm Dickinson and included Mill Bank House and adjoining buildings, Thread Mill Farm at Birdsedge and Dearn House Farm near High Flatts.

(1) Quoted in 'The History of Penistone' by J.N. Dransfield p.136-137
(2) Joseph Wood Collection. Misc. Letters.
(3) Ibid (1).
(4) Joseph Wood Memorandum Book No.12

Elihu Dickinson the Clothier

Elihu Dickinson the Clothier, like his namesake, contemporary and cousin nicknamed 'the Tanner', was a Friend of considerable property, wealth and influence. Even so, his wealth and position in local society made him no more immune to personal tragedy than anyone else.

In 1781 he married Martha Beaumont, a young woman described as *'naturally of an high lofty & turbulent disposition'* who had been *'esteemed a good servant except for her disposition'* by those several families for whom she had worked. She was the daughter of Abraham Beaumont of Deershaw *'a friend of lowish circumstances'* in the world and the darling of his eye. Apparently, she was *'very much indulged by her father who always manifested a particularity to her.'* According to Joseph Wood she possessed *'very little education'* but despite this *'demeaned herself in other respects as to gain the esteem of friends.'* Despite these failings she was successfully courted by the prosperous Elihu Dickinson who seems to have been blind to these failings. Initially, in spite of reservations, the marriage seemed destined to be a successful match. Elihu Dickinson was an active and valued member of the Society of Friends attending MM's as a representative as well as being an elder of High Flatts Meeting. Shortly after their marriage Martha also became very active in meetings for discipline but not, it appears, *'from a real concern of the heart.'* This was largely because *'she had married a man of great property & had thereby a greater opportunity of attending meetings for discipline than many of her Sisters had.'* Even with this knowledge of her, Martha Dickinson was allowed, through the good auspices of Friends, to take up *'appointments of divers kinds'* in the *'hope for better things.'*

Martha Dickinson proved to be a veritable whirlwind of activity *'as was painful to the sensible friends who were engaged with her.'* Although *'much suitable counsel & advice'* was given to her, which she appeared to accept, all proved not to be right. This, it seems, was not to be discovered until it proved to be too late. Joseph Wood recounts that *'we flattered ourselves with a hope that in time she might come to be truly useful.'* She was first appointed as an overseer and not long after that as an elder. It was very soon after her appointment as an elder that the trouble began.

'Soon after which a friend who was in the Station of an Elder came to Superintend the School at Ackworth, he not knowing her as well as us gave her very unsuitable encouragement, by which that past, which ought to have been slain upon the cross was strengthened. How needful it is to attend to the Apostles Advice 'Not to believe every spirit, but try the spirits whether they be of God.'' (1)

Precisely what form this *'encouragement'* took is not specified. However, it seemed to awake the darker side of her character resulting in what can only be described as a form of nervous breakdown. This began to manifest itself in meetings for worship with attempts at ministry that rapidly degenerated into extravegent outpourings with unpleasant consequences.

'She soon lost herself getting quite into a Self exalted, wild Ranting state mixed with a degree of derangement, by seeking to comprehend things above her capacity which had always been weak. Thus she became very troublesome to friends & made much disturbance in our meetings.' (2)

Unpleasant as this outbreak of ranterism was to the meeting it also had its unpleasant consequences upon Elihu Dickinson and the rest of his family and household. In a letter written to Joseph Wood in the 11th month 1799 we learn that he had ceased to attend MM because of his wife's conduct when there. Also that his life at home was no longer his own and that all mail addressed to him was subject to her scrutiny if casually left within her reach *'...for she has always a liking to see all that comes or goeth.'* To avoid her prying he confessed that *'I have no opportunity of writing a letter when she is at home nor nothing else in my own house. But if I have anything to write that I have an objection of her seeing I take pen, Ink & Paper unknown into the Meetinghouse for to do it.'* His lowness of spirit is clearly evidenced in the following lines from the same letter:

'I seem to have no comfort at present in no one thing, nor in the enjoyment of anything here below, for everything seems as I think sufficiently tarnished in my view but that is best known to him that knows all things. I may say at present & has been for some time that Life seems a burthening to me for many times think at morn that I do'not know how to get the day over cannot avoid weeping sometimes a great part of the day & being asked by several what troubles me, I cou'd hardly have told them, if I had an inclination to have done so, for I am a Poor low dejected mind...' (3)

When he adds that *'I have at present something of a nervis complaint...'* we begin to realize how serious a problem it had become. A little further on in the letter he discusses the possibility of sending his wife to The Retreat in York. This he is dissuaded from doing, for in the opinion of his wife's sister, she does not appear *'a propper object for the Retreat...'*

Friends had recognized early that there was such a condition as mental illness that required treatment rather than incarceration as was more typically thought necessary in society at large. The Retreat at York had been founded to deal humanely with people suffering from mental illness. Yet, even with Friends enlightened attitude to mental health care and treatment, Friends still considered it something of a disgrace to send one of the family to such a place. From Elihu Dickinson's letter it becomes obvious that he is willing to grasp at any straws to avoid sending his wife away:

'I sometimes think that if friends was to pay her a Visit by the order of the Monthly Meeting & deal very plainly with her & tell her what the consequences wou'd & must be if she did not alter her conduct & be still & silent when there, but if I was asked who they must be I shou'd be at a loss to advise, for I now do'not know of one since Mercy left ne(i)ther Man nor Woman in our Mo. Mtg. that stands in a favourable light with her.'

In an earlier letter to Elihu Dickinson from Joseph Wood we are made to appreciate the kind of sympathy that was extended towards him:

'I may truly say my spirit, according to my measure nearly sympathizes with thee, I am frequently led secretly to breathe, that thou may be supported under them, so as not to sink too low in thy spirits, or injure thy health, & I believe as a Man & a christian it is thy duty to endeavour to bear thy heavy affliction as patiently as thou can.' (4)

The brunt of dealing with the Dickinson's problems fell upon Joseph Wood's broad and strong shoulders. As the weightiest Friend and most respected minister at High Flatts he repeatedly had to deal with Martha Dickinson. In a letter dated the 28th of the 6th month 1800 we read of:

'The abundance of labour which hath heretofore been bestowed upon thee, & the little effect it appears to have had, is cause of discouragement from attempting anything further of the kind, were it not that I feel my mind covered with Pity & compassion for thee...' (5)

And further on in the very same letter:

'O that thou be favoured to be still, and know the Lord, & then thou would be better acquainted with thyself, & instead of taking his great & Sacred Name in vain, Thou would sit down in thy own shame & thy confusion would cover thee, In this state there would be some hope that the power which brings order out of confusion would do this great & absolutely needful work in thee...'

These words had no effect for, on the 5th of the 7th month 1800, we read in another letter to her that:

'...since I last saw thee thou hast been fighting with thy Brother S:Haigh in the milling close, & that the blows thou gave him with rod where heard by People who were several closes distante. If this be true is it not astonishing that thou canst be so far deceived as to imagine thou art favoured with a discovery into the states of others, & Commissioned to Preach that Gospel which breathes Peace on earth & good will towards all Men...' (6)

The rantings in meeting continued: *'she became very troublesome to friends & made much disturbance.'* MM was forced into *'discharging her from the offices of overseer and elder'* in the hope that this might bring about some change but it was to no avail. Joseph Wood relates that *'she continued to grow worse & worse...that there was no fastening the most weighty advice upon her.'* Had it not been for the fact that Friends had realized that Martha Dickinson *'had thrown herself into a degree of derangement'* she may well have been disowned *'by their testifying against her extravagent & ridiculous behaviour.'* In the end Elihu Dickinson had no recourse but to send his wife to The Retreat. She had become so *'exceedingly troublesome both in meetings, & her own family as well as amongst her Neighbours'* that there was no longer an alternative. Sadly, although the treatment she received in York appeared to bring about some improvement, she did not stay long enough. No sooner was she released from York than she *'became as bad as ever.'* Worse still, Martha Dickinson became *'sport for the unthinking youth.'* MM directed Joseph Walker to write to her concerning her continuing misconduct.

Shelley Paddock 7th mo 17th 1800

Respected Friend
Martha Dickinson

I am under the necessity of informing thee, that thy conduct having given considerable pain & it being weightily considered by the Overseers To which they have jointly & unanimously agreed that for the future, If thou do not keep thy seat in meetings silently & in good behaviour thou must not be allowed to attend them. I believe thou hath been favoured repeatedly with many tender admonitions, from faithful friends; which if thou had taken due heed thereto it would have been an inducement to a lasting peace unto thy own mind & satisfaction to thy well-wishing friends. I am thy Respected Friend

Joseph Walker.' (7)

A very typical incident of this period appears to have happened on 3rd of the 5th month 1805 and involved Joseph Wood once again.

'This day as I was going into the Meeting I heard her voice before I opened the door & understood afterwards that John Bottomley had been desiring her to behave in a becoming manner, She continued talking after I got in & all the way as I went to my seat, in a wild enthusiastic manner. I shook my head at her & spoke prettily to her desiring her to be still but, without effect. Whereupon I took her by the arm & led her out of the meeting where I reasoned a little with her respecting her behaviour & desired her to stop at home she promised she would, & I return'd into the meeting where my mind was deeply humbled under a feeling sense of the continuation of divine regard towards us...' (8)

In 1817, Edward Dickinson, Elihu Dickinson's son, committed suicide at the age of 31. (See 'Daniel Collier and Edward Dickinson'). To what extent his mind had been affected over the years by his mother's behaviour we will never know. There is certainly an indication that his sister, Mary, was affected and had a difficult home life as a result of her mother's condition. Elihu Dickinson died shortly after his son in the same year *'aged about 76.'* Martha Dickinson survived her husband by thirteen years, dying at the age of 78 in 1830. Joseph Wood wrote the following testimony concerning Elihu Dickinson the Clothier:

'I think I may add respecting the deceased, That he had been in declining state of health for upwards of half a year before his change, but at last was unexpectedly removed. He was a very due attender of our religious meetings to the last, & though he might not have had the five talents committed to his care, it may be said of him as our Saviour said of the Woman Mark C:14.v:18 'She hath done what she could.' So I believe he was concerned to do what he could do for the Society freely, by whom he was much beloved, & his death lamented, & his services therein will be much missed. In respect to his character amongst men he was a quiet & peaceable neighbour, a man of uprightness, integrity & strict punctuality in all his dealings. A considerate Landlord not oppressing his Servants but endeavouring to do unto others as he would wish to be done by. I conclude with desires that those who succeed him may go & do likewise.' (9)

(1) Joseph Wood Memorandum Book No.23
(2) Ibid.
(3) Letter from Joseph Wood Collection.
(4) Joseph Wood Memorandum Book No.14
(5) Ibid.
(6) Ibid.
(7) Joseph Wood Memorandum Book No.13
(8) Ibid (1)
(9) Joseph Wood Memorandum Book No.36

Daniel Collier and Edward Dickinson

During the eighteenth and first half of the nineteenth century Meetings for Worship rarely lasted less than two hours and could last as long as four hours. There could be very long ministry given in the form of testimony, prayer and supplication. This would usually be based on one or more biblical quotations. Quaker meetings also seemed to have a drawing power to those who were members of other Churches. Joseph Wood in his writings records many such instances. At a meeting at High Flatts in 1804 he records:

'...a great many People of other Societies attending far more than usual except on some special occasions...'
(1)

People from other *'persuasions'* often came on more public occasions particularly for burials or when there was a visiting *'Publick Friend'* of note. Methodists are frequently mentioned as visiting Quaker meetings. To what extent Friends visited Methodist meetings is less clear. The very nature of a Quaker meeting could lend itself to abuse and several accounts of unsavory behaviour are recorded at local meetings.

Daniel Collier's (1742-1803) behaviour at High Flatts caused the overseers of the meeting to write him a stern letter in 1794 suggesting that if he could not behave himself during meeting he would be better staying at home. Joseph Wood's account of the event relates how Daniel Collier, a clothier, was in his younger days a fine example of a well behaved Friend. (2) He was a regular attender at meetings and spent much of his free time in reading and writing religious pieces. He had married Mary Dickinson of Balby MM in 1766 and they had a son. His wife had died when the boy was about two and Friends had given him financial help for a number of years until his son was old enough to work. It was then that the trouble started as it appears that Daniel Collier was quite happily living on charity. When this was withdrawn he began to slander Friends. Joseph Wood recounts how:

'...many friends out of compassion visited him & laboured abundantly to make him sensible of the error of his ways...'

This was all to no avail. He began to cause disturbances in meeting and on his way to and from meeting. Again, Friends seemed to put up with his behaviour for a time. At length the overseers wrote to him. Having received the letter:

'...he appeared much disturbed & getting a stick with a white Cloth ty'd upon the end thereof came as he had frequently done before & stood before several of our houses calling & abusing us who had never done him any wrong...'

It appears that his behaviour deteriorated, with him suffering severe bouts of depression. Joseph Wood visited him on a number of occasions. At the meetings he was full of remorse for his bad behaviour. Friends felt it was unwise for him to be alone in this condition and arranged for him to move to Susanna Kay's at Park as his only son, Joseph, had removed to Manchester. Friends ensured that Daniel Collier had some work and that he was well fed. Despite all efforts made on his behalf by Friends his mind still remained disturbed. One afternoon in 1803 he went missing and could not be found. Next day Joseph Wood recounts:

'...we arose pretty early & tho' the morning was very wet 7 of us went & sought the Woods where he was found by Benjamin Beever my servant, in husbandry having put an end to his own existence by a small rope fastened to a small branch of a tree...' (3)

An inquest was called and the jury brought in a verdict of *'Lunacy.'* Joseph Wood in his account of the event quoted from John Ch.12, v.35: *'Yet a little while is the light with you; walk while you have the light, lest darkness come upon you; for he that walketh in darkness knoweth not whither he goeth.'*

There was a similar tragedy a few years later in 1817 at High Flatts. This concerned Edward Dickinson, the son of Elihu Dickinson the Clothier, a young man of about 31 years. Joseph Wood's account runs as follows:

'It was...betwixt 7 & 8 o Clock in the evening when he committed the fatal act in the corner of the middle close on the back of the Windmill' (There was a windmill for grinding corn at this time at High Flatts). *'And after bleeding there a considerable time he went home of himself which was very admirable after losing such a large quantity of blood.'* (4)

Despite some signs of recovery he died seven days later. The Coroner and Jury found that for a time previous to the event he had been in a *'...disordered state of mind...'* Joseph Wood goes on to describe the subsequent events attending the burial:

'...such a multitude of people assembled before the interment, that it thought prudent to keep the Meetinghouse doors locked until that service was performed. After the corps was interred I requested the People not to crowd the Relations of the deceased but wait until they got into the Meetinghouse & then as many as were disposed to attend the meeting & could get in might have their liberty. The Meetinghouse was very much crowded & betwixt 2 & 300 stood without that could not get in, & great numbers went away that could not get near...at the close of the meeting which held about 3 hours I informed the People the meeting was about to conclude, desiring them to withdraw in a still quiet manner...'

Meetings of 100 or more were not uncommon at High Flatts at this time but this gathering may well have broken all records. Perhaps it was the morbid fascination of the suicide of the son of a prominent and influential local family that caused the interest? It appears that particular family was afflicted with more than its fair share of suffering. (See 'Elihu Dickinson the Clothier').

(1) Joseph Wood Memorandum Book No.23
(2) Joseph Wood Memorandum Book No.6
(3) Joseph Wood Memorandum Book No.18
(4) Joseph Wood Memorandum Book No.35

The Last Disownment [1]

Consideration of disownment in the first half of the nineteenth century had taken up much of MM's time. Report was brought in during 1861 that there had been 85 disownments within Pontefract MM during the preceding thirty years:

Marrying out	47
Immorality	13
Insolvency	13
Fraud and dishonesty	7
Non-attendance at meetings	3
Intemperance	1
Holding different relgious views	1

Friends were appointed to visit these 85 in 1861 and enquire into their circumstances. It appeared that most of the visits were favourable from both sides and it was suggested that a continuing watchful concern should be kept. The present circumstances of the 85 were reported:

Dead	18
Abroad	15
Re-instated	5
Attending meetings	16
Attending other Churches	13
No place of worship	12
Nothing known	6 (2)

Towards the end of the nineteenth century the discipline of the Society gradually began to relax. No longer were Friends disowned for marrying out of the Society. By the end of the century it was only in the most serious cases of misconduct that disownment occured. The Society was gradually coming to the realization that its image to the outside world was not the most important consideration. Care and help for those in need, which had always been present, became of increasing importance.

The last disownment that concerned a member of Wooldale or High Flatts Meetings well illustrates the need for this change in attitude. This sad case was certainly not dealt with in the most sensitive way. Although the final outcome, within the bounds of another MM, redeemed the Society to some extent the original dealings did not present the Society in its best light. The time had come for a radical change in attitudes. The Quaker discipline had very nearly caused the death of the Society.

The particular episode concerns Alfred Morris and his family, members of Wooldale Meeting. (For reasons that will become apparent the true identity of the family cannot be revealed and an assumed name is used). Alfred Morris had met his wife to be at Rawdon School where they had both been pupils. Both their parents were *'connected'* with Friends. This probably implies that their parents had been disowned from the Society for marrying out. Rawdon School was established for the children of such parents.

Alfred Morris's association with the Society seemed fated from the start. The couple jointly applied to Pontefract MM for membership in 1869. The Friends appointed to visit them brought in their report, which although supporting the Morris's application, was not as enthusiastic as some. After *'careful consideration'* Friends decided to defer their decision. Two Friends were requested to pay Alfred Morris a further visit. Again the report brought in to MM was favourable, the interview being of a *'satisfactory character.'* The decision was again deferred. It was not till three months after this that MM came to a decision. The minute records that the meeting was *'not prepared to accede...at present'* to their application.

The implication that some Friends had doubts about Alfred Morris's character are strengthened by events that happened exactly twelve months later. In the 2nd month 1871 his wife, Frances Morris, applied for membership by herself. In the following month the Friends appointed to visit her reported that they had no *'hesitation in recommending her application to the kind regard of the Monthly Meeting.'* MM acceded and in the 3rd month 1871 Frances Morris became a member.

For a number of years local records remain silent concerning the Morris family. The reason for this becomes apparent as it is recorded in the Wooldale List of Members that in the 2nd month 1878 Alfred Morris, an attorney's clerk, removed from Huddersfield to Wooldale. It appears that after his refusal of admittance to membership from Pontefract MM he had attended Huddersfield Meeting and gained admittance to membership through Brighouse MM.

Alfred Morris's career in the law seemed to prosper for a time as by 1883 he was listed in the membership records as a solicitor. For a period of five years between 1890-1895 he removed to High Flatts before returning to Wooldale. Whether this was caused by strained relationships between Alfred Morris and the meeting or for other reasons we are not told. However, there is reference in MM minutes to a letter that he wrote to MM in 1895 before removing back to Wooldale. We are not informed of the contents but three Friends were appointed:

'...to confer with the parties who have knowledge of the matters referred to therein and either report to this meeting or take such steps as may seem to them desirable.'

No further mention is made of the matter in MM minutes and thus it appears the problem was resolved either by the appointed Friends or the subsequent removal back to Wooldale.

It is not until 1898 that the full extent of Alfred Morris's problems are revealed. An overseer from Wooldale requested that MM enquire into the circumstances surrounding his failure *'to meet his pecuniary liabilites.'* In the 11th month 1898 a full report was brought to MM. He had started his own practice as a solicitor in 1887. From the start it appears that his expenditure had been in excess of *'what his actual income justified.'* He and his family had been living on credit. In 1890 he had been involved in a serious railway accident which compelled him to withdraw from practice for fifteen months. He never fully recovered from the accident as he was *'liable to attacks of illness and mental weakness & excitement'* following the event. Despite *'considerable compensation from the Railway Co.'* his expenses were still too high. The report continues:

'It is quite probable that it was in consequence of the accident that he did not at an earlier date realize and fairly face his true position and take steps to apply a remedy.'

The Official Receiver had become involved in the case. It transpired that during the preceding five years the income from his business had been £1428 and his expenses £4117. Sums of money that had been received on account of his clients had been mixed up wth his own private bank account and used for family expenditure. It was only in the final few months that he claimed to realize the seriousness of the situation.

In the 12th month 1898 *'a serious charge of delinquency in money matters having been proved'* MM issued a minute of disownment. Part of that minute was phrased as follows:

'We regret the position in which our friend has placed himself, but we feel bound to uphold the necessity of integrity in trade and all outward concerns, that opportunity may not be given for reproach against our Society.'

This sentence is most revealing. Despite expressions of sympathy the blame was put very much on Alfred Morris's shoulders. This was despite the earlier report that had recognized that the effects of the accident had contributed largely to the state that he had got into. One can perhaps imagine many individual Friends being in sympathy with Alfred Morris. However, once the MM, started to consider the problem, its past based on strict discipline took over.

The detailed facts of this incident will now never be known: perhaps MM's original doubts about Alfred Morris's suitablity to become a Friend were correct? Or, perhaps, they showed their inablity to deal with this type of situation? Whatever the facts this was certainly a turning point and never again was the old discipline to be applied in such a blinkered way.

The ending to the story was not quite as bad as it might have been. During 1898 Alfred Morris and his family removed to Bradford and began attending meeting there. In 1905 he applied to be re-admitted to the Society. Brighouse MM, of which Bradford is a constituent meeting, contacted Pontefract MM for their reaction. Brighouse informed Pontefract that for the past eight years Alfred Morris's conduct had been exemplary and that he had done nothing that *'would reflect discredit upon the reputation of our Society.'* They also stated that they felt that he had *'deeply repented of his misdeeds.'* Friends of Pontefract MM replied that they knew of no reason for objecting and left matters to the discretion of Brighouse MM. Hopefully, Alfred Morris was to live out the rest of his life in happier circumstances in the care of Bradford Friends.

(1) MMMB 1862-1870, 1870-1879, 1890-1900, 1900-1908. Wooldale List of Members 1867-1901.
(2) MMMB 1861

Joseph Wood of Newhouse — 'Fisher of Men'

'The Quaker of the olden time!
How calm and firm and true,
Unspotted by its wrong and crime,
He walked the dark through.
The lust of power, the love of gain,
The thousand lures of sin
Around him, had no power to stain
The purity within.'

John Greenleaf Whittier

Joseph Wood was born on the 15th February 1750 on the 50 acre farm of Newhouse near Birdsedge and High Flatts. He was the oldest of seven children raised by Samuel Wood and Susannah Walker. (See 'The Woods of Newhouse'). From the age of seventeen he began to keep a journal of his travels, as well as a comprehensive account of his correspondence with numerous Friends, that was to span the rest of his life. Certain extracts from Joseph Wood's journal were published many years ago in a book written by J.Travis Mills: 'John Bright and the Quakers'. However, his fifty-five year long journal and correspondence has never been published and has remained virtually unknown outside his descendants family circle. In Joseph Wood the Religious Society of Friends has its own Samuel Pepys. Quite possibly his detailed record of Quaker life between 1767 and 1821 is unrivalled.

It would be impossible to do justice to Joseph Wood within the scope of this book: his life story is deserving of a book in its own right. Yet something of his story must be recounted for he was more than just a diarist. Joseph Wood was the quintessence of a Quaker of the Quietist age and one of its finest blooms. The authors are entirely in agreement with the sentiments expressed by J. Travis Mills:

'In holiness of life, in unquenchable zeal for the spread of truth, and for the salvation of individual souls, he was surpassed by few in his day.

His was a small orbit, but within its range he showed once more that holy courage triumphant over every weakness of the flesh and spirit which was so conspicious a characteristic of the early Quakers, and which through the ages has never been left without witness among their spiritual sons.' (1)

Joseph Wood received his education at the nearby boarding school in High Flatts. (See 'James Jenkins at High Flatts') and followed in his father's footsteps as a farmer and clothier. It was during his teenage years that Joseph Wood became deeply spiritually aware:

'In his youth he gave way to some of the vanities incident to that period of Life but when approaching manhood, he was happily brought under the sustaining power of Truth and often humbled in great contrition of soul before the Lord. During this season of deep inward exercise, he has since related that once in his extremity being out in the Fields in the Night he exclaimed 'Lord what shall I or whither shall I go?' The answer in the secret of his own Heart was as intelligible as if spoken to his outward Ear. 'Whither wilt thou go have not I the words of Eternal Life?' Soon after he attended a neighbouring Meeting when a Ministring Friend who was a stranger stood up in testimony with the very words which he had received as an answer to his inquiry and who afterwards enlarged upon the subject in a manner suited to his state of Mind. This circumstance yielded him both consolation and great encouragement.' (2)

At the age of seventeen he commenced his extensive travelling with a visit to the Northern Yearly Meeting at Macclesfield held in the 4th month 1767. In the ensuing twelve years he travelled to GM's, QM's, MM's and PM's in Derbyshire, Nottinghamshire, Cheshire, Lancashire, Cumberland, Westmorland, Durham, Wales and his native Yorkshire. In 1775, the only time in his long life, he attended YM in London. In the period before he became a minister he made over 50 separate journeys and came into contact with many of the *'Publick Friends'* of his day. Amongst those with whom he had friendly, close, or very close acquaintance were Abiah Darby of Coalbrookdale, Esther Tuke of York, Thomas Colley of Sheffield, Isaac Sharples of Hitchin, Samuel Spavold, Tabitha Mariot, Tabitha Hoyland, Hannah Wigham of Northumberland (later of Pontefract), and John Cash. Undoubtedly they had more than a passing influence upon him in those years. As a youth he had also met with John Woolman. (See 'John Woolman'). Joseph Wood's record of that meeting, coupled with the other influences, set him on his remarkable path as a 'fisher of men'. Later in life he would establish another close relationship with the great travelling preacher, Thomas Shillitoe.

Joseph Wood never married. He appears to have made a conscious decision to devote himself to *'the labours of the Gospel'* sacrificing personal happiness and the opportunity of having children of his own. His committment to his faith and the ministry remained total.

At the age of twenty-nine, in 1779, this very tall, broad, fair-haired Yorkshire farmer became a minister of the Gospel. Amongst the first to counsel him at the start of his long and hardworking *'gospel labours'* was Esther Tuke. They had been acquainted for quite a number of years and he was a regular visitor to the Tukes home in York. Before entering into the ministry he had been frequently charged with making the arrangements for Esther Tuke's 'evangelizing' meetings in Yorkshire and Derbyshire. His gift in the ministry led him to become one the most powerful preachers of the Quaker message in his day.

In the prime of life he gave up his profession as a clothier to devote himself to the Lord's work. His labours were ceaseless. His powers as a preacher were magnetic. His converts to Quakerism included persons of every age, status and degree of learning and were large in number. He toiled not only at his own meeting in High Flatts but in all the nearby towns and villages of West and South Yorkshire as well as further afield. One of his converts, John Yeardley, writes:

'To attend a Monthly meeting he would leave home on foot the Seventh day with John Bottomley, also a Friend and a preacher and at one time his servant, for some neighbouring meeting. He would occupy the evening with social calls, dropping at every house the word of exhortation or comfort. The meeting next day would witness his fervent ministry. In the afternoon they would proceed to the place where the Monthly meeting was to be held the following day, which they would attend, filling up the time before and after with social and religious visits... On his return home from these services he would spend the day in an upper room, without a fire even in the severest weather, writing a minute account of all that had happened.' (3)

Joseph Wood had a sound rather than scholarly education. Yet this in no way disadvantaged him for he was *'deeply versed in the things of God.'* In public gatherings and meetings he was granted the gift of speaking eloquently to the condition of those present. Relying upon prayer and the leadings of the Spirit he proved himself *'a veritable master of assemblies.'* (4) Joseph Wood's *'...testimony was not with enticing words of mans wisdom but in demonstration of the Spirit and of power.'* John Yeardley recollected:

'I attended another public meeting appointed by Joseph Wood at Middletown. I think it was the most extraordinary time I ever knew. My friend bore a long and powerful testimony to the tendering of many present. If I ever forget it while in my natural senses I fear I shall be near losing my habitation in the truth, for it was as if heaven opened and the Most High poured down his blessed spirit in an unbounded degree.' (5)

Elizabeth Yeardley further testifies to his powers as a preacher recalling a visit to Westmorland and Lancashire in which:

'J.W. was very much favoured all the time he was in those parts. He really appears endowed with astonishing powers.'

In a Testimony written to his life we are informed *'that he was eminently gifted and was often favoured in an extraordinary manner to explain to the people Scripture Truths; and his ministry on these occasions was often attended with the powerful blazing influence of the Spirit to the convincement of many.'*

If Joseph Wood was a gifted preacher and a *'master of assemblies'* he was also gifted in speaking to individuals and making converts in less formal circumstances. (See account about Joshua Schofield in 'Quakers and Luddites'). His gift was extended to discern the spiritual condition of those he encountered and to speak to it in a *'tendering'* manner. An apocryphal tale was often recounted by John Sadler of High Flatts Meeting towards the end of the nineteenth century:

'A young woman said to herself going to meeting, 'What am I going to meeting for? To hear the same old sermon by Joseph Wood!' Joseph Wood rose as usual and commenced, 'What matter thought it is the same old sermon'. The old story is ever new. The young woman was startled and a new light came to her.'

When not engaged in meeting people he wrote letters to his friends and acquaintances and general epistles to Friends, attenders and the newly convinced within the MM. Typical of such epistles was one written 'To the newly Convinced Friends in High Flatts Meeting' on the 10th day of the 10th month 1777.

'It hath oftens run thro' my mind to write a few lines to you sincerely desiring your growth in the blessed and unchangeable Truth: In the first place therefore suffer me to intreat every individual of you frequently to call to mind and esteem it as a great privilege that the Almighty was pleased in great loving kindness to visit your souls in a peculiar manner, by drawing you from the barren mountains of an empty Profession, from the many Lo here's and Lo there's and setting you under his own divine and heavenly teaching by convincing you of the sufficiency of that Light which enlighteneth every one that cometh into the world.' (6)

In 1802 we have another such letter entitled 'An Epistle in Tender Love, by Joseph Wood of Highflatts. To the Newly-Convinced at Barnsley':

'Beloved friends — I have felt my mind drawn, under the pure influence of gospel love, to write you; and though I am fully sensible that your words are spirit and life; may every mind gather unto that light which flows through him unto the hearts of all mankind, during the day of their visitation; and, by your obedience to its manifestations, know a passing through the many outward and shadowy observations, unto him who is the substance of all types, and end of all shadows.' (7)

When not engaged in travel or in the direct work of the ministry he taught numerous local people to read and write. As late as 1806 he was prepared to undertake the personal tuition of James Birchall of Ingbirchworth writing the following in a letter to him:

'Altho' I fully concluded in my own mind never to undertake to instruct another young man in learning; but finding thou was desirous to learn, & knowing the great disadvantage those are under who cannot read the scriptures of Truth, & feeling compassion for thee that thou wast deprived of this privilege. I found a willingness raised in my mind to afford thee what instruction lay in my Power, more especially as thou appeared so desirous, & no other seemed willing to undertake the arduous task...I thought when my mind was first concerned to write to thee, it would be better to speak what I had to say to thee, as if I wrote, thou could not read it; But as times & seasons are altogether in the Lord's hand it is 'He that openeth, & no man shutteth; & shutteth & no man openeth.' Therefore feeling mine heart inlarged with love towards thee, & a sincere desire for thy welfare, in time & in eternity; I took my pen & wrote simply what opened; believing the same Power which engaged me to write, would make way for a suitable time to read it unto thee...' (8)

Newhouse was naturally a haven of hospitality to any travelling Friend. Visitors were always plentiful and Joseph Wood's company much sought. In a letter dated the 9th month 1815 Samuel Lloyd wrote: *'...I should like very much to see thee and enjoy thy cheerful and instructive company.'* In December of that same year he further wrote:

'I would very much like to be one of the party assembled around thy blazing fire, but would prefer still more to ramble with thee into the Country with a summer's sun and enjoy thy interesting company. I should in the course of my travels get into thy neighbourhood, whether winter or summer, I intend to seek thee out and witness the peaceful dwelling wherein thou dwells, and learn from thy pleasant but humble mansion not to covet riches, but rather better things.' (9)

Thomas Shillitoe was another eminent visitor to Newhouse. Joseph Wood recorded his first visit, on 4th of the 4th month 1807, in these revealing words:

'...Our friend Thomas Shillitoe of Tottenham in Middlesex who was on a religious visit to friends in these parts, came to my house very unexpectedly not thinking myself worthy to receive such a guest under my roof he travelled on foot & was an example of true self-denial; got to my house pretty early, & his company was truly acceptable to me.' (10)

That first visit was the meeting of kindred spirits. When Thomas Shillitoe came to live near Barnsley the two men became personal friends often visiting each others homes. In the years following they frequently worked in close unison sharing common concerns. (See 'Quakers and Luddites'). Although an 'evangelizer' of the Quaker message he was not one of the new breed of Evangelical Friends that were beginning to appear like Stephen Grellet or John Joseph Gurney. Joseph Wood was an archetype of the Quietist era: *'he was sound in Doctrine and bold in delivering plain Truths without wavering from the christian faith.'* The extent of his plaines and adherence to the Quietist tradition can be readily gauged from just two of many incidents in his long life. The first of these transpired during a journey to Warmsworth MM in the 10th month 1773. Whilst staying at the Queen's Head in Epworth he enquired about local Quaker meetings in the vicinity. He was informed that there was such a meeting at nearby Beltoft and that there were two families living in fairly close proximity to it. He was directed to the home of a Friend called William Read, who happened to be away at the time, but was hospitably greeted by his wife and daughters and invited to breakfast on the morning of the meeting:

'On ye 10th of Week according to Promise I went to Breakfast to our Friend William Reads where I met with a kind Reception but the Morning being very Wet & Stormy when Meeting time came I understood none of them was for going I askt the Reason they told me they did not use going on Rainy Days at which I was sorry & told 'em I thought at going, they said if I went I should find Nobody there for as None liv'd very near the Meeting so they Never attended but when the Weather was tolerable good finding things thus low amongst 'em I thought I could maybe reach the Afternoon Meeting at Thorne they Prest much for me to stay telling me it was very unlikely for me to set out upon Account of the Rain & that I should be very Welcome at their House I told 'em when I was hearty I did not think the day of the Week well spent if I did not get to some

Meeting accordingly I set out betwixt 10 & 11 & left these Fair-weather worshippers without being at their meeting tho' with some Reluctance...' (11)

The second incident transpired on the last evening of his visit to the Northern YM held at Bolton in the 4th month of 1774. Joseph Wood was staying at the King's Head Inn in Deansgate with several Friends. They had gathered in his room for a leave-taking and small Meeting for Worship when:

'...a considerable number of people who had been at the meeting & were collected together in a Room beneath us began to Fiddle & Dance, which brought a great exercise upon my mind accompanied with a concern to go down & speak to them, which after some reasoning I gave up to being join'd by Alice Eccleston a Publick friend from Freckleton meeting. When we got into the room, we stood still in awfull silence before them for sometime, & then taking the young Man by the Arm that was Fidling, I desired him to be still, as I had a few words to say to them, which he immediately comply'd with; I then told them that our coming to this Town was entirely upon a religious account, & in love to that part in them that must never die, & as their behaviour in the meetings had been satisfactory to us & commendable to them, we much desired that their behaviour might continue so that we might leave the Town in Peace but if we should be the means of drawing many People together upon this solemn occasion & (k)now when the meetings were over they should stay drinking & spending their precious time in vanity at an Alehouse it would not only bring Sorrow & trouble upon our minds but very much hurt their own Souls, so that I desired them to desist or words to that effect, After which Alice Eccleston had a few seasonable words to them, & they then told us they would do so no more & seem'd to be affected with what was delivered to them, & we return'd with the Answer of Peace in our own bosoms.' (12)

Joseph Wood's testimony speaks of him *'being zealously concerned for the proper support of discipline in our religious Body'* but yet he was not without sympathy or understanding for those confronted by that unbending discipline. Shortly after entering upon the ministry, whilst attending a QM held at York in the 6th month of 1780, he was visited several times at the home of Joseph Awmack by William Baiston. William Baiston was a young man who had become recently convinced but who was faced with a difficult decision. He had sought out Joseph Wood for advice because:

'...of some entanglement he had got with a young Woman before he left the Methodists, which now appeared to lie heavy upon him, he being afraid to break his engagement with her, & afraid to go to a Priest, O that all young men would be careful to seek unto the Lord for counsel in the beginning of this great & weighty affair, & move in his Wisdom, then would they be preserved from many troubles which those who follow the counsel of their own will bring upon themselves. I thought this was a strait place to advise in, yet my Spirit felt a secret sympathy with him believing he was concerned to act conscientiously.' (13)

Joseph Wood certainly never shirked his responsiblities with regard to the maintaining of the discipline. Within his own MM *'he gave active service in this important branch of Church Government.'* When words of admonishment needed to be spoken he was well able to speak in *'a plain close manner to the unfaithfull professors of Truth.'* Equally, Joseph Wood *'had the word of consolation to the rightly exercised unto whom he was a nursing Father.'* (See 'Elihu Dickinson the Clothier'). There were few ministers in those days who would have had the temerity to admonish an elder of their own meeting about the dangers of drink and frequenting alehouses as Joseph Wood had cause to do. (See 'Elihu Dickinson the Tanner'). In lesser men the authority which he commanded on those occasions *'might indeed be considered by some as too great an assumption of power..'* However, *'...his superior qualifications for the service and the manifestly good effects which resulted from his labours'* were testified to by his MM which further added scripturally: *'it is by their fruits we are to know them.'* (14)

Even with his totality of commitment to God Joseph Wood had time to enjoy the ordinary everyday pleasures of life. He liked a pinch of snuff which he kept loose in his coat pocket. He was frequently in receipt of snuff-boxes as gifts from Friends, there being over 50 at Newhouse upon his death, which he somehow never quite managed to use. During the course of his long walks to QM's, MM's, PM's and public meetings he would regularly call at an inn and enjoy some *'Rum & water'* or drink *'a quart of mulled ale.'* Every account of his journeying contains details of the inns at which he stopped for refreshment as well as of how much he had paid, drunk and *'tarried'* in each along the way.

In the latter years of his life his health began to decline but *'His Zeal increased with his Years and he became more and more abundant in his Labour for the promotion of the Christian cause, and he was frequently out travelling on Truths service.'* Between the age of 68 and 70 he managed to undertake and thoroughly document all the following journeys:

1818

2nd Mo. Knaresborough MM & adjacent mtgs.
2nd Mo. Mtgs. at Ossett & Dewsbury.
3rd Mo. QM at Leeds.
4th Mo. Mtg. at Hoyland Swaine.
5-7 Mo. Lancashire, Settle MM, Yorkshire, Lancashire.
7th Mo. GM at Ackworth
8th Mo. Mtg. at Lumbroyd
8th Mo. Balby MM, Lincolnshire, QM at York.
11th Mo. Mtg at Gawthorp.
12th Mo. Mtg. at Barnsley.
12th Mo. Visit to the House of Correction (Wakefield).

1819

2nd Mo. Mtgs. at Pontefract & Brighouse
3rd Mo. Mtg. at Thornhill Edge & QM in Leeds.
5th Mo. Mtg. at Thurlstone.
5th Mo. Visits to Norwich, Norfolk, Lincs, Derbyshire, Suffolk.
8th Mo. Mtg. at Hoyland Swaine.
10th Mo. East & North Ridings of Yorkshire, QM at York.

1820

2nd Mo Mtg. at Ing-Birchworth.
3rd Mo. QM at Leeds.
4th Mo. Coalbrookdale (Shropshire), Balby MM, Public Mtgs. at Wolverhampton, Wednesbury, Sutton Coldfield, Castle Donnington, Tickhill & Conisborough.

About a year before his death he wrote: *'this day I have attained the Seventieth Year of my Age may the remainder of my Days be so devoted to the Lords Service as when the solemn message of death is sent I may have nothing to do but render up my account with joy.'* (15) On the day before he died he appeared in ministry for the last time at his own beloved meeting of High Flatts with the following words from the Old Testament: *'We are journeying unto the place of which the Lord said I will give it to you; come thou with us and we will do thee good, for the Lord hath spoken good concerning Israel.'* Joseph Wood died at 5 o'clock the following morning on the 26th of the 3rd month 1821. He was aged seventy one years. Sixty Friends belonging to Pontefract MM signed the Testimony to the life of this remarkable man.

(1) 'John Bright and the Quakers' J.Travis Mills
(2) Jospeh Wood's Testimony — Pontefract MM 1822.
(3) Ibid (1)
(4) 'Memoir of John Yeardley'
(5) Ibid
(6) Joseph Wood Correspondence
(7) Armistead's Selected Miscellanies
(8) Catherine Walton Collection
(9) Joseph Wood Correspondence
(10) Joseph Wood Large Memorandum Bk. No.25
(11) Joseph Wood Small Notebook No.3
(12) Joseph Wood Small Notebook No.4
(13) Joseph Wood Small Notebook No.13
(14) Joseph Wood's Testimony — Pontefract MM 1822.
(15) Ibid

Monthly Meeting at High Flatts (1910)

John Wood and Family at Newhouse (Circa. 1875)

Wooldale Meeting House

High Flatts Meeting House

Former Lane Head Meeting House

Site of Lumbroyd Meeting House

Sheephouse

Judd Field

Midhope Hall

Former Hoyland Swaine Burial Ground

Meal Hill

Totties Hall

Langley Brook

Strines

Joseph Walker and Family at Pell Croft (Circa. 1895)

Lane Head House (Circa. 1896)

Joseph Wood (1750-1821)

Edward Henry Burtt (1849-1922)

Joseph Firth V (1814-1873)

Sarah Firth (1811-1892)

Jackson Gravestones (Wooldale F.M.H.–Hall)

Jackson Gravestones (Wooldale F.M.H.–Gallery)

O THOU TRETCHEROUS ROGUE JOHN WOOD OF NEW
HOUSE DENBY DALE I MAKE THIS THAT THOU REST
NOT NIGHT NOR DAY BUT BELIKE THE WATERS
OF THE TROUBLED SEA TOSSED TOO AND FROO
WITHOUT A RESTING PLACE AND THAT THOU
CANNOT SLEEP NIGHT NOR DAY NOR THAT
THOU CANNOT DIE UNTILL THOU CONFESS
THE WRONG THAT THOU HAS DONE ME TG
AND J G AND MY FATHERS HOUSE BY
AIDING AND ASSISTING A FORGED WILL
AND ROBBING HIM AND ALL HIS
SONS OUT OF LAND AND MONEY
SIGNED IN THE MIGHTY NAME OF GOD
AMEN

John Wood Curse *(Front)*

57	38	29	70	21	6	15	54	5
6	58	79	30	71	22	63	14	46
47	7	59	80	31	72	23	55	15
16	48	8	40	81	32	64	24	56
57	17	49	9	41	73	33	65	25
26	58	18	50	1	42	74	34	66
67	27	59	10	51	2	43	75	35
36	68	19	60	11	52	3	44	76
77	28	69	20	61	12	53	4	45

John Wood Curse *(Back)*

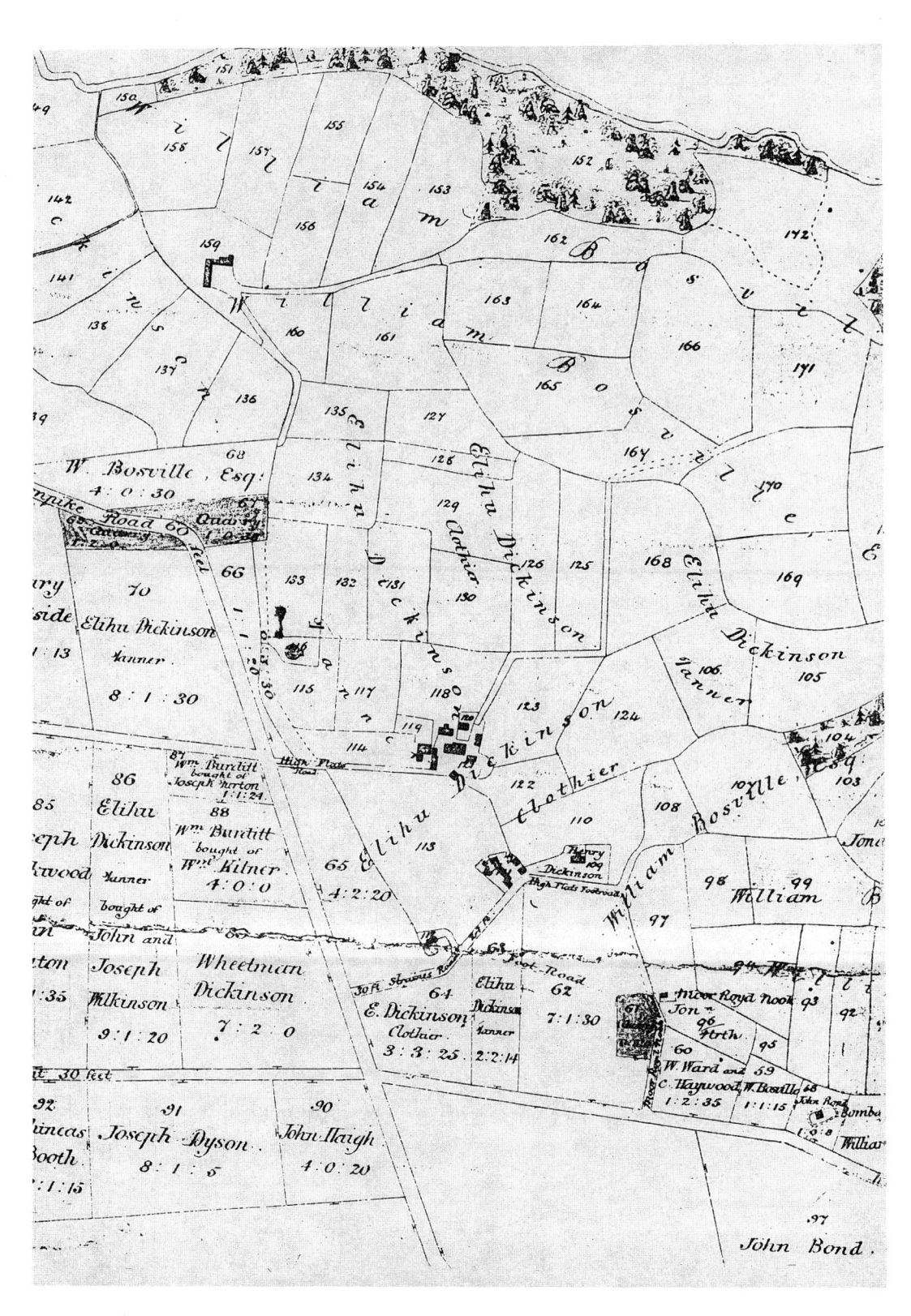

Denby Dale & Clayton West Enclosure Map–High Flatts Detail *(By kind permission of WYAS-Kirklees)*

Quakers and Luddites

In the early years of the nineteenth century, one of the most respected and celebrated local Friends, Joseph Wood came to the forefront of Quaker activity in this area. He had become a personal friend of the most prominent *'Publicke Friend'* of that period, Thomas Shillitoe, who for a time settled in Durkar. It is almost entirely due to their detailed journals that we are able to have a clear picture of Quakers 'at work' in the aftermath of the Luddite disturbances in the West Riding.

Thomas Shillitoe had visited the area for the first time in 1807. On this occasion he recorded in his journal attending meetings at Lumbroyd (See 'Lumbroyd Meeting House') as well as High Flatts and Wooldale:

'First day morning walked to Highflatts, attended the meeting which was very large; in the afternoon walked to Wooldale to attend a meeting at five this evening, which was largely attended, and closed under a precious sense that the Divine regard was hovering over us.' (1)

It was probably whilst on this first visit that he made the decision to move to Yorkshire. During this first visit he also attended meetings at Huddersfield, Brighouse, Halifax, Gildersome, Rawden, Bradford and Dewsbury. He seems to have been affected by the transformation that he witnessed taking place as the momentum of the Industrial Revolution became intensified. His comments upon visiting Paddock Meeting in Huddersfield appear to bear this out:

'If my view of the state of the membership of our Society there are correct, the precious seed of the kingdom sown is buried in many hearts under the rubbish of the surfeiting cares and concerns of this present life.' (2)

The outlook was just as gloomy in the other burgeoning centres of industrialization. Joseph Wood and other Friends at High Flatts had witnessed numerous removals of members in the past ten years to within the compass of Brighouse MM, especially to Huddersfield with its frenetic growth. After the Luddite disturbances there in 1812, which had resulted in violent acts culminating in the murder of the influentially powerful mill owner, William Horsfall, both Joseph Wood and Thomas Shillitoe wished to visit the families in the area that had suffered in the tragic aftermath with the execution of those Luddites involved. Joseph Wood recounts the circumstances that led to his involvement in these words:

'After their execution a concern came upon my mind to pay a religious visit to families & near connections of the Sufferers, but I thinking it so unusual a thing to engage in, endeavoured to reason it away, but the more I reasoned, the more my concern increased, so that in the 2nd month at our Monthly meeting; having previously acquainted Thomas Shillitoe therewith whom I found under a similar concern, I spread our united concern before friends which being solidly weighed, & many testimonies borne of friends unity therewith, the meeting gave us the following minute... Our esteemed Friends, Joseph Wood & Thomas Shillitoe laid before this meeting a concern they have felt to pay a visit to the Families or near connections of those persons who have lately suffered at York, & who reside in Huddersfield & its neighbourhood. And this meeting after solidly considering their proposal, feels unity with the friends in their prospect, & leaves them at liberty to proceed as way may open.' (3)

Thomas Shillitoe's account of how this unusual concern arose within him differs little in essential details but his reasons for wishing to undertake the visit are more explicitly outlined:

'...my mind was brought under such feelings of sympathy with the widows and fatherless children of the sufferers, that I believed I should not stand acquitted in the sight of my Divine Master, unless I was willing to go and sit with them in their families; and yet the prospect of such a service felt humiliating to the creature, beyond words to describe. Understanding my friend Joseph Wood of Highflatts meeting, was under a similar exercise, in the Second-month we spread our united concern before our Friends, on which the meeting gave us a minute to proceed therein as truth opened our way.' (4)

The certificate granted to the two ministers was duly prepared by Robert Whittaker, clerk of MM. Joseph Wood set out for Huddersfield at 2 o'clock on the afternoon of Saturday 27th of the 2nd month 1813. Travelling via Shepley and Farnley he reached the home of his relative, Joseph Mallinson, in

Longroyd Bridge at 5 o'clock. Thomas Shillitoe set out the following day and walked from Barnsley to Paddock Meeting House where he met up with Joseph Wood in time for Meeting for Worship. After dining at the home of John and Pheobe Fisher of Springdale they commenced their visit being accompanied by two local Friends: John Fisher and Abraham Mallinson.

The lives and working conditions of people moving into the new industrialized urban areas would never again be the same. The Luddites were a reaction to one aspect of these changes. The introduction of new machines by mill owners to quicken and improve production and thereby profits increasingly deprived weavers of their jobs. Many groups of unemployed textiles workers in Nottinghamshire, Derbyshire, Lancashire and Yorkshire banded themselves together in covert Luddite gangs. Their aim was the destruction of these new machines in the hope that their former employment could be regained. In the Huddersfield area the Luddites were led by a young man, George Mellor, a cropper of Longroyd Bridge, who lived very near to Paddock Meeting House. In April of 1812 one hundred and fifty Luddites committed the largest local disturbance by attacking William Cartwright's Rawfold Mill at Liversedge. The attack was successfully resisted by the mill owner, some of his servants and two soldiers but resulted in the deaths of two of the Luddites. One of the local mill owners in Huddersfield, William Horsfall, threatened to deal with any such attack on his property by installing cannon loaded with grapeshot. The scene was thus set for a local tragedy with far reaching and unsuspected consequences. Looking for revenge for the deaths of the two Luddites at Liversedge, George Mellor and three companions planned the ambush of the truculent and violently inclined mill owner. As William Horsfall rode home from Huddersfield market on the afternoon of April 28th, 1812, he was mortally wounded at about 6.15 by George Mellor and his three accomplices, William Thorpe, Thomas Smith and Benjamin Walker.

The four young Luddites departed the scene of the crime at the junction of Blackmoorfoot Road and Dryclough Road, leaving Horsfall dying, hid their guns, and later met up with one another at the 'Coach and Horses' Inn at Honley in the evening. The murderers remained undetected despite a £2000 reward being offered. It was only when one of their number, Benjamin Walker, turned King's evidence and betrayed the other three, that they were brought to justice. Walker receive a pardon and the £2000 reward offered. As a result of his information sixty six Luddites were rounded up and put on trial. Charged with murder, robbery and the wilful destruction of property and machinery, seventeen were sentenced to death by hanging, six were transported for seven years to the penal colonies in Australia. On the 13th January 1813 the convicted men were publically executed in York, still wearing their leg irons, before the largest crowd every assembled in the county for such an event. Army detachments kept the entire proceedings under control. Never before had so many convicted men been hanged at a public execution. (5)

It was in these circumstances, following the aftermath of this violence, that Thomas Shillitoe and Joseph Wood set out to visit the families of these men. They first visited the house of Jonathan Dean in Longroyd Bridge who had *'suffered'* (been executed) for rioting, *'the widow's mind appeared under very great distress with her helpless, fatherless children, the oldest child being about eight years, the youngest not more months old.'* She had been left with five children to be brought up. Friends were deeply moved by the suffering they encountered on this very first visit, prompting Thomas Shillitoe to record *'all that was alive in us and capable of feeling for her, plunged as she was in such accumulated distress, we felt to be brought to action.'* The next house they visited was that of the widow and three children of John Walker where they found more distress and suffering. *'The feeling of distress awakened in my mind, in sitting down with this family, were sad that I was tempted to conclude human nature could hardly endure to proceed with the visit before us'*, was Thomas Shillitoe's comment. After tea at John Fisher's, despite the unhappiness they had already encountered, they proceeded to the home of the parents of George Mellor, the Luddite ringleader.

'We sat with the parents, who are living a respectable line of life. In this opportunity we had fresh cause to acknowledge holy help was near, furnishing matter suitable to the deeply-tried and affected state of mind in which we found them; whilst we endeavoured to be upon our guard that nothing escaped our lips, that should be the means of unnecessarily wounding their feelings. Our visit was thankfully received by both parents, and, as we afterwards understood, was like a morsel of bread at a time when they appeared almost ready to famish. The father acknowledged, the melancholy circumstances had brought their minds into such a tried state, that they had concluded to move to some other part of the country; but our visit had tended to settle them down again in their present place of residence.' (6)

Also present at the Mellors, according to Thomas Shillitoe, was John Wood who had employed the young Luddite in his cropping shop. Joseph Wood's account differs. (John Wood was not related to Joseph Wood). The first day's visiting concluded the party had supper at John Fisher's, where Thomas Shillitoe lodged that night. Joseph Wood went back to Joseph Mallinson's.

The next day the party went to Lockwood to visit the widow of Thomas Brook, as well as meeting his two brothers who had been in York castle with him but had eventually been freed. From the township of Lockwood they proceeded to Huddersfield and visited the childless widow of James Haigh of Dalton Fold who, according to Thomas Shillitoe, *'appeared to have a clear view of our motives for taking the steps which we did, expressing in strong terms, the gratitude she felt for our visit.'* The young widow was staying at the home of an Edward Walton where she had a room having removed from her former home. The party then paused at the home of a prominent local Friend, Robert Firth, where they obtained refreshment before continuing their journey.

A little later that same morning they arrived at the home of the parents and two sisters of William Thorpe, one of the convicted murderers of William Horsfall, where they were initially not so well received until their intentions were made apparent. Then they dined at Abraham Mallinson's before continuing. In the afternoon, stopping briefly along the way to see another local Friend Thomas Wilson of Greenhouse, they walked to Cowcliff. There they visited the widow and children of John Ogden. After this visit they made their way to Joseph Firth's of Toot Hill where they arrived *'betwixt 6 & 7 o'clock'* and lodged that night.

On the third day, this time accompanied by John King and James Lees, two Friends from Brighouse Meeting, they went to Sutcliffe-Woodbottom in Hipperholme to *'sit with the parents of Thomas Smith'* and his sister whose husband had *'suffered'* for rioting. Thomas Shillitoe recounted that a rather strange incident transpired involving Joseph Wood.

'At the time I was engaged in addressing the company, a young man opened the door, came in and immediately left again; on which I felt a stop against proceedings, and was obliged to request the young man might be sought for to give us his company, which taking place, I was able to proceed. This young man's mind so wrought upon in the opportunity, that it became evident to all present. After having closed what I had given me for the family, my mouth was again opened with nearly these words: 'It is not in man that walketh to direct his own steps aright, the Lord alone must have the ordering of them, who does at times order our steps, but we know it not; which appears to me to have been the case this day with the young man who came in amongst us.'; after which, my companion (Joseph Wood) addressed him in a very feeling manner. After the opportunity was over, he walked with us a short distance: his mind appeared much broken, and under a remarkable visitation. He told my companion, he had been apprehended with the rest of the prisoners, and confined in the castle, but was discharged on bail; that he was twenty two years of age, and his name was I— S—; that he knew nothing of our being in the house, nor could tell what brought him there, as he had no business with the family.' (7)

The mysterious I—S— was actually a young man called Joshua Scholefield. It is interesting to compare Thomas Shillitoe's account with that of Joseph Wood's regarding this incident. According to Joseph Wood:

'It was a time of remarkable favour, & remarkable circumstance took place therein, a young man a neighbour when my companion was appearing came in, as soon as we saw him we were both of us struck with his appearance; when he saw us sit he turned back & the Son in law followed him, my companion then enquired who he was & was informed, he was one of the prisoners who was discharged on Bail, he then desired he might be called in, he came & sat down, the power of Truth eminently overshadowed him, my companion went on with what was before him to the family, & when he had done, my mouth was opened from, It is is not in man that walketh to direct his steps aright but a good mans steps are all ordered of the Lord, (Proverbs 20:24) observing that our steps were sometimes ordered by Providence, when we knew it not, & this appeared to me to be the case with the young man who had dropt in amongst us at this time. I then proceeded as matter opened before me unto him, he was much broken & tendered, & a remarkable time of visitation it was to him. After the opportunity he went a little with me, told me his name was Joshua Scholefield, that he was in the 22nd year of his age, & that he knew not of our being there until he came into (the) house, nor knew not why he came there at that time. We parted in very near affection with each other, & I hope it was a time to him that will be lastingly remembered by him.' (8)

Certainly a remarkable incident and one that confirms Joseph Wood's abilities as *'a fisher of men.'* This would not be the last encounter between Joseph Wood and Joshua Scholefield as we shall see. The single discrepancy in the account revolves round which of the two Quakers actually used Proverbs 20:24. Joseph Wood was almost certainly the one who was led to use this Scriptural quotation since he usually wrote up his accounts of events either on the same day or very shortly thereafter. Thomas Shillitoe wrote his account many years later and his version is peppered with slight inaccuracies relating to a variety of details particularly names. His recollections of the precise details had probably been dimmed with the passage of time. From the Smiths home they went, according to Joseph Wood, to dine at the home of John Pool, a Methodist preacher.

Later that day they travelled to Skircoat Green to visit Nathaniel Hoyle's widow and seven children. They were accompanied by Thomas Dearden of Halifax Meeting whom Joseph Wood described as *'a friend under convincement.'* Thomas Shillitoe wrote about the Hoyle's: *'their situation to us appearing to be a very pitiable one.'* The party then proceeded to James Hay's widow who was *'not twenty one years of age'* and had *'two children'* according to Thomas Shillitoe. At this meeting they were joined by Joseph Hay and his wife, the widow's inlaws, in whose house the young woman now lived. Joseph Wood now recounts that:

'From hence we set out for Joshua Stansfields of Handgreen 2 miles, & Joseph Hey expressing a desire to speak with me accompanied me nearly thither, & then returned; his company was very agreeable to me, he being I believe a truly pious man, & a Local preacher in the Methodists Society; & having had to express my belief in the opportunity that he had discharged his duty to his son & therefore was clear, I was confirmed in the Truth thereof, in our conversation together, & we parted under a near sympathy, & tender regard for each others welfare.'

That night the party, with the exception of Thomas Shillitoe, lodged at Joshua Stansfield's. He went to stay with his mother who was living in the vicinity. On the fourth day they went to breakfast at Elizabeth Stansfield's and then moved on to Sowerby Bridge to visit the widows and families of Joseph Crowther of Luddenden and William Hartley (who had left eight children). The Hartley household was in particular distress. The mother had died about *'36 weeks before'* and her orphaned children were now being cared for by their grandparents, the parents of William Hartley. Afterwards they returned to Joshua Stanfield's to dine before going on to *'North-dean in the township of Elland.'* There they met with the widow of John Hill and her infant child. The widow recounted how:

'...the night he was taken, he was forced out of his bed by the gang; that she ran after him half a mile without any of her upper garments upon her, until they obliged her to return, threatening to blow her brains out if she followed them.' (9)

John Hill's brother had been similarly implicated in the disturbances that happened that night. It appears that he was a religiously disposed young man of very good character who helped his mother maintain their small farm. The mother was distraught at the prospect of losing her other son, against whom there was a warrent issued and a search being made. Before the party left, they assured her:

'...on account of the general good character we had received of the young man, and the manner of his being taken away, we would lay his case before the magistrate who granted the warrent and use our influence to obtain permission for him to return home 'with safety'.' (10)

They next visited the widow of Job Kay and her seven children finding *'great poverty, her numerous children, without any visible means for their support.'* Joseph Wood adds to Thomas Shillitoe's comment that the widow *'appeared in a very tryed state both inwardly & outwardly.'* Leaving this cottage *'of woe and misery'* they continued on to Halifax, with the exception of John King who returned home, walking the three miles to the town by seven o'clock. There they visited Joseph Wood's cousin, Joshua Smith and had tea. Joseph Wood lodged there the night and the rest of the party took up their quarters at John Pool's.

On the fifth day a small Meeting for Worship was held with a few Friends of Halifax at which the young man Joshua Scholefield appeared once again. (No mid-week meeting was held in Halifax at this time. This meeting had been specially appointed). According to Joseph Wood as John King was making his way to Halifax that morning he happened to pass by Joshua Scholefield's place of work. John King informed the young man of the meeting that morning and he *'laid down his tools, went home & cleaned himself, & came with him.'* At this Meeting for Worship Thomas Shillitoe records that:

'...in addition to Friends, we had the company of several not professing with our religious Society; amongst them I— S—, the young man before mentioned, whose mind was again so reached during what was communicated, that he trembled so much he could not hide his state from the meeting, although it was evident he endeavoured for it. He afterwards settled in the neighbourhood of a meeting of Friends, became a steady young man, manifesting attachment to our principles, and regularly attended our meetings.' (11)

Joseph Wood's account is manifestly more detailed and evocative at this point. It was a small meeting that day. There were only twenty five persons present that morning at 10 o'clock. Seven or eight of these *'were People of other Societies.'*

'The Power of Truth eminently overshadowed this meeting to the tendering of the hearts of many. Joshua Scholefield eminently felt the effects thereof which caused him to tremble exceedingly, that altho' he endeavoured to hide it he could not conceal it from the meeting. I had a long testimony to bear therein from 1 Cor: C:14. v:20. In malice be ye children, but in understanding be men. Thomas Shillitoe had two pretty long times next, the first from Eccle: C:9. v.11. The race is not to the swift, nor the battle to the strong. & the other time from Psalms 110 v:3. Thy People shall be willing in the day of thy Power... The meeting held upwards of 2 hours and a half. I took Joshua Scholefield after meeting to dine at Cousin Smiths & after sitting with him a while there, I went to cousin Elihu Steads, were all our company din'd. After dinner I return'd to Joshua Scholefields with whom I had some agreeable conversation, & for whose welfare I felt very deeply interested.'

In the afternoon they began the return journey to Huddersfield. On the way back, travelling via Salterhebble, Elland and Blackley, they stopped at Longwood in the hope of visiting Benjamin Walker *'the informer'* but he was not at home. They left a message with his father asking if he would meet them at Joseph Mallinson's in Longroyd Bridge the following day. Walker complied with the request arriving at Joseph Mallinson's home at 8 o'clock in the morning.

'Fifth day, agreeable to our request, Benjamin Walker met us. On entering the room, he appeared to us raw and ignorant; with such apparent self-condemnation in his countenance, we thought we had not before witnessed; as if he felt himself an outcast, and thought a mark of infamy was set upon him; newly-clad, as we supposed, from the money he had received, as the reward for having discovered his accomplices in the murder, for which they had suffered. We could not but anticipate the deplorable situation he would find himself in, when the means of keeping up his spirits were all exhausted. On taking his seat, his mind appeared much agitated, and, during the opportunity, he was unable to sit with ease to himself on his seat. After a time spent with him in quiet, a door of utterance opened, whereby we were enabled faithfully to relieve our minds towards him, although he did not manifest anything like a disposition to resent what we had to offer him; but little if any appearance of tenderness was manifested. The opportunity to us was the most distressing we had experienced; feeling, as we were enabled to do, deeply on his account, lest his mind was getting into quite a hardened state, and that his case would become a hopeless one; yet not without some reason for believing, that in the opportunity we had with him, things had been so closely brought home to him, that he would not soon be able to wholly to cast them away again. When he went away, those who were in the room through which he passed, observed to us, his countenance was pale and ghastly, and his joints, as it were, so unloosened, as if they were scarcely able to support his body. We advised him not to go into company, but to return directly home, which, we afterwards heard, he attended to. The feelings of suffering we were introduced into on his account, will not, I believe, soon be forgotten.' (12)

Joseph Wood passed very little comment on this meeting beyond recording the very same observation that Walker seemed to take little heed of what was said to him. Walker did become an outcast shunned by all who knew of him. This Luddite Judas became a password in his own lifetime for treacherous betrayal. His ill-gotten reward, worth a very substantial amount in that age, proved of little help since he apparently never received anything but a small fraction of the total amount. In his old age he became a recipient of outdoor relief from the Huddersfield Guardians. Yet it is a sign of Friend's care that they would not exclude him from their visitation, even though they failed to *'speak to his condition.'*

Friends led by John Fisher and Robert Firth had already met with Joseph Radcliff of Milnsbridge House, the magistrate responsible for *'scourging the Luddites,'* as the party had begun their visitations, to explain to him the nature and purpose of the visitation *'lest any unfavourable construction should be put on it.'* Therefore, when Thomas Shillitoe and Joseph Wood went to speak to him about what they had seen they were cordially met by Joseph Radcliff and his wife. True to their words they raised the case of John Hill's brother as they had promised to do. Their intercession worked. The Magistrate was persuaded to suspend the warrant against the young man on the proviso that he appeared in person before him. He would then be at liberty as long as he continued to live in a *'quiet, orderly manner.'* Far more importantly, the Friends drew Joseph Radcliff's attention to the plight, poverty and distress that they had witnessed on their local journeyings. It was on these matters that the Quakers intended to use their utmost influence.

'...I also laid before the magistrate, which was the deplorable situation of the widows and children; there appearing no other prospect but that they must, by degrees, sell their household furniture to procure subsistence, they informing us, none would employ them; some refusing through prejudice, and some through fear of being suspected to countenance the proceedings of their husbands whereby the parish workhouse must soon be their only resource, if no speedy remedy was applied. This, from the view I had of the subject, was to be dreaded; the children, from the company they would associate with, being likely, on every slight offence, to have reflections cast on them, on account of the conduct, and disgraceful end of their father: thus held in contempt, the danger was, the minds of the children would, by degrees, become hardened, and they, thereby become unfitted for usefulness in society. After thus expressing my views, and my desire that some mode should be adopted to educate, and provide for the children, until they attained an age fit for servants and apprentices, and to aid the earnings of the widows whilst they remained single, and proposing for his consideration a plan for these purposes, which suggested itself to my mind almost daily of late, I felt discharged from these subjects, which had pressed heavily upon me.' (13)

The magistrate appeared to take these words kindly for they parted in friendship. The lengthy detailing of this particular concern not only helps to establish the relationship that 'plain Friends' had with their community but illustrates their attitude in this time of sweeping changes towards social unrest and social injustice. Studying the plan that Thomas Shillitoe formulated we are made aware of the enlightened and almost modern thinking that Friends had at this time with regard to the alleviation of hardship and suffering. As the century wore on, this enlightened humane attitude arising from their Christian faith would increasingly come to the fore. We cannot neglect these positive steps that were taken so early on within this area. Although Wooldale and High Flatts meetings were still to be considered essentially rural they were quite clearly affected by the growth of social evils in the nearby industrial centres. Wooldale Friends would see the quickening of this industrialization in and around their village more so, perhaps, than at High Flatts. Nevertheless, their awareness of what was happening would be all too clear as they kept in close contact with the meetings at Paddock and Brighouse. Nor could they ignore the prevalent distress and poverty that at this time was visible everywhere.

After seeing Joseph Radcliffe the two Quakers went on to visit the families of other Luddites. Amongst the families they visited were those of Joseph Fisher's of Briestfield, John Lumb's of Thornhill Edge and John Swallow's of Emley. Joseph Wood and Thomas Shillitoe parted at the home of Benjamin Stead on the 7th of the 3rd month their religious visit completed. Joseph Wood wrote:

'And being now quietly sat down in my own habitation, reaping the fruits of obedience, even the rich reward of Peace; I may add. That altho' the exercise attending the service in which we had been engaged was great & the Sufferings we had to bear heavy in a feeling sympathy with the suffering families, yet it was eminently manifested that he who put forth, went before, & in a remarkable manner prepared our way.'

They travelled again in the spring of 1817 on a common concern. This time in the cause of temperance to visit the alehouses of Barnsley.

Thomas Shillitoe continued to journey throughout England and overseas to Ireland, Europe and America visiting Kings and Emperors. Joseph Wood confined himself to this nation. Thomas Shillitoe left us his highly evocative journal, a window onto our local past, without which our historical view would be so much diminished. Joseph Wood also kept his own extensive journal but one that has remained almost unknown. Yet one cannot help but feel that their close friendship made them ideal travelling companions in this labour. That one, without the other, might not have had the strength of his convictions to perform these visitations so thoroughly. Without the 'openings' of Thomas Shillitoe, and the tender words of Joseph Wood, could the highly wrought Joshua Scholefield have achieved peace of mind? One cannot help but feel that their compassionate vists to all the distressed made and left some lasting impression.

As for Joshua Scholefield the story did not end there. He corresponded with Joseph Wood and later came to visit him and stay at Newhouse. The young man eventually removed to Leeds and began a new life in that city... However, that, as the proverbial saying goes, is another story.

Postscript

The visits to these families are particularly interesting and revealing in the relationship that existed between the Quakers and the Methodists. As far as it has been possible to acertain all the families visited belonged to the Methodist fold. The Luddites appeared to have been essentially from this denomination: the absence of Luddites from other denominations being quite noteworthy. Relations between the Methodists and Quakers have yet to be explored. The links and connections between Methodists and Quakers are likely to reveal that they had much more common ground and purpose than ecclesiastical and social history has hitherto supposed. Joseph Wood, for example, knew many Methodists in the region and frequently held public meetings in their meeting houses. He also corresponded with them. The simple historical fact that Friends stayed with a leading Halifax Methodist figure, John Pool, on their religious visit point to something more interesting than simple hospitality.

(1) 'Journal of the life of Thomas Shillitoe' Vol.I pub. London 1839 Ch.IV p.57
(2) Ibid Ch.IV p.58
(3) Joseph Wood Small Notebook No.51
(4) Ibid (1) Ch.XI p.184
(5) A detailed account of the Luddite disturbances in the Huddersfield area & the Horsfall murder can be found in 'A History of Huddersfield & its vicinity' by D.F.E. Sykes pub. 1898 Ch.13 p.281-289
(6) 'Journal of the life of Thomas Shillitoe' Vol.I pub. London 1839 Ch.XI p.185
(7) Ibid Ch.XI p.187
(8) Joseph Wood Small Notebook No.51
(9) Ibid (1) Ch.XI p.188
(10) Ibid
(11) Ibid
(12) Ibid
(13) Ibid (1) Ch.XI p.191

James Jenkins at High Flatts

We have a first hand account of High Flatts between 1764-1767 from James Jenkins (1753-1831) when he was a pupil at the Quaker boarding school in the hamlet. He was the illegitimate son of Zephaniah Fry (1715-1787) and Ann Jenkins, a servant in the Fry household in Bristol. At the age of nine he was sent to London to be a servant at the home of John and Frances Fry. Then in 1764, at the age of eleven, he was nearly sent to America but a last minute change of heart saw him sent to:

'...a cheap poor boarding-school at Highflatts...It was then kept by Joseph Shaw who was so far qualified for a Schoolmaster as to write a pretty good hand, but, 'farther, this deponent saith not.' (1)

James Jenkins records how he was sent, from London, with a wagon but had to walk most of the 190 miles. Unfortunately, the wagon driver forgot to drop him off at High Flatts and he arrived in Huddersfield. They managed to find someone who agreed to take him to High Flatts but who promptly went off to spend his fee on beer. The story continues:

'Near the Market-place, lived a Friend whose name was ---Firth, and tidings having been taken to him that a little quaker-boy was lost, and sat crying in the market-place, he came, and kindly took me to his house.' (2)

---Firth arranged for him to be transported, with his luggage, up to High Flatts for 1s 6d which was all the money James Jenkins by now had left.

James Jenkins has bequeathed to us a vivid description of the High Flatts that he found in 1764:

'Highflatts is a village about midway between Barnsley, and Huddersfield situated by the side of a moor, or common which was then fourteen miles in length, and in some places half as broad.' He records in a return visit in 1799 that... *'many acres had been inclosed...'*

'Nearly all the inhabitants of the village of Highflatts and its immediate vicinity were Friends; the occupation of some of them was farming, but by far the greater number were engaged in the manufacture of woolen-cloth...'

'Most of the many Friends who lived in these parts, and indeed the people generally, were poor, simple, uneducated rustics, but of innocent lives, and not a few sustained characters for piety...' He compares this to the rural Kingswood (Bristol) that he knew *'...where most of the people were exceedingly poor, and exceedingly wicked.'*

'The dialect of the Country is barbarous, and some of the words so little English that none but a Yorkshireman can understand...'

The above comments should be taken in the context of his upbringing. Although brought up as a servant it would have been in the affluent surroundings of the Fry family in London.

The school itself consisted of fifty boys and was held in the *'pretty large Meeting-house'* at High Flatts. The meeting house *'was mostly well filled.'* Most of the boys were boarded *'at the farm-house of Edward Dickinson and lived well ...'* (probably Low House Farm). James Jenkins, with five others, however, boarded at Joseph Shaw's. This was apparently not a pleasant experience as Joseph Shaw *'...loved money more than doing justly by his boarders...'* or *'he had probably imbibed an idea ...that pinching care is favourable to study...'* Joseph Shaw was *'...a convinced Friend, having been first powerfully reached by Joseph Milnthorp's ministry at a time when he was under preparation to fill a Yorkshire Curacy...'* James Jenkins description of his diet reveals the extent of the frugality displayed towards him:

'Hard oaten-cake, and thin oatmeal gruel was generally our breakfast; our dinner, oaten-cake with a little butter spread thereon with water to drink; small thick-crusted pies with a few raisins in them; and in the winter we frequently dined on Oaten cake broken into the intolerably salt liquor in which hung-beef had been boiled for the master, and mistress.'

This very poor diet he blamed as the origin of a mild type of scurvy that he suffered from. The salt liquor made the boys drink a lot of water to quench their thirst with the following consequences:

'...and because we so drank, our beds were found wet in the morning, and because they were so found, we were not only much scolded, but our poor pittance of a penny per week pocket money, was stopped as a fine.'

The boys were driven to supplement their diet by other means:

'We now, and then, <u>borrowed</u> a few potatoes from the fields of Edward Dickinson without his knowledge or consent.'

James Jenkin's lot improved through his own ingenuity during the latter part of his stay at High Flatts. He was apparently very good at his school work, especially in arithmetic. Joseph Shaw made use of this by using him *'...in setting, and examining the sums of other boys...'* In fact, he made him his deputy when meetings caused his absence. James Jenkins turned all this to his advantage for, by concealing his fellow pupils' errors, his school mates repaid him by pilfering bread for him from Edward Dickinson's.

The other Friend for whom James Jenkins had little regard was Joshua Marsden *'...a friend who lived at Birds-hedge near Highflatts...'* He conveyed the boys letters to the Post Office in Huddersfield, but only those approved of by Joseph Shaw. Joshua Marsden is described as:

'...a reputable manufacturer of woolen-cloth, and being 'wise above his fellows' was, in a Society point of view, the chief disciplinarian; the great man of the district.'

James Jenkins records with a certain amount of un-Quakerly glee that both met their just ends and came to poverty:

'...Shaw lent to Marsden, on Interest I believe the whole of his property...who failing: at the same time they both became servants at Leeds...' (3)

The rest of the Friends in the area James Jenkins seems to have held in very high regard:

'We had two ministers also at Highflatts with whose earnest communications we were frequently favoured, Henry Dickinson was an excellent man and (his illiteracy, and condition in life considered) ministered with great propriety of language, and connection of argument; There was too, the meek, the loving, the every way good, old Bessy Brook, whose affectionate address to us, 'the dear, rising youth' I have often remembered; she sometimes preached to us four times in the course of two hours for being feeble, said but little at a time, and often without standing up; She lived to extreme old age, and it used to be said of her that she was thus able to address her daughter, 'Arise daughter, go to thy daughter, for thy daughter's daughter, has got a daughter.' ' (4)

He explains how meetings were '...held by turns, here (High Flatts), Shipley-lane-head...and Wooldale...' Of William Earnshaw of Wooldale he says:

'...a man of excellent character and one of our constant Ministers who died in 1802, aged 84, during the three years of my stay in this country, I do not recollect his omitting to preach but once, and then, at the conclusion of the (meeting) he made an apology for the omission...'

One thing he noted, although he thought it was a habit from past generations, is described:

'Not having observed it in other places it is to me a singular circumstance that the ministering Friends of these parts when preaching, tremble greatly: perhaps a slight convulsive motion may be a better description...'

We hear also of visiting ministers such as Joseph Milnthorpe who '...was in person so corpulent, that he used to pass sideways into the Meeting-house...'

On a return visit to the area in later life he comments on the numerous new mills being erected, mainly for the finishing of cloth. He stayed with his old school friend John Firth at Lane Head and noted: 'the beauty of some of them (the views) were greatly obscured, by the smoke which arose from the numerous manufactories.' However, at High Flatts, where he was entertained by Elihu Dickinson, he found very little altered. On remembering his period at this boarding school he posed the question: 'If such an unlearned seminary could deserve the appelation of a boarding school?' If nothing else he seems to have gained his love of literature from the school including 'balled-poetry.' He remembered that Pope's 'Essays on Man' was introduced to the school while he was there: he read it '...on evenings whilst other boys were at play.'

(1) 'Records and Recollections of James Jenkins' Edited by J.William Frost
(The whole of this section is drawn from this source)

(2) This unknown Firth may have been Thomas Firth (d.1782) who had removed to Huddersfield.

(3) Joshua Marsden was disowned by MM in 1782/3.

(4) Henry Dickinson of Strines was the son-in-law of Uriah and Elizabeth Brook. (See section 'The Dickinson Families'). Elizabeth (or Bessy) Brook lived to be 90 and died at Strines.

THE GROWTH OF CONCERN
Education

George Fox supported and encouraged the development of education amongst early Friends. His enlightened vision extended beyond the promotion and provision of a purely academic education. He envisaged a broad education that would include more practical and useful subjects providing a solid grounding for later life. His ideas found ready acceptance which in later times enabled Quakers like Joseph Lancaster (of Monitorial School fame) to become one of the leading educationalists of his day. Thus from the earliest days of the movement Friends have always been involved in education regarding it as an essential foundation upon which to build a future.

Very little is known about the earliest provisions for education in the area except that they did exist. Examining both MM and PM minute books from 1672 to 1772 discloses that the Friends entrusted in the keeping of these records became increasingly more literate with each succeeding generation. Increasingly too one notes fewer Friends having to sign with a mark — an indicator of the levels of literacy in the late seventeenth and early eighteenth century.

Generous bequests, provided by Friends like Joseph Milnthorpe, enabled poorer parents to have their children educated. In 1769 we have the following minute:

'By acct. from last Mo: Meeting we understand there is some money in hand, being the interest of a sum of money left by Joseph Milnthorpe for the Education of poor friends Children; this Meeting apprehends there are several proper objects for a part thereof within the compass of this Meeting...' (1)

MM agreed to pay for the sons of John Haigh (See 'John Haigh of Moor Royd Nook, High Flatts') and Matthew Broadhead of New Mill to be educated. Friends were also diligent in inspecting the progress of the children receiving financial assistance:

'The Friends appointed to visit the Families of Poor friends Reports, that they have gone thro the Visit to good satisfaction, That they have inspected their state and found them comfortably provided for; that their Children appear to partake of necessary learning according to their respective Ages...' (2)

Within our own area the provision of which we have details was the boarding school at High Flatts run by Joseph Shaw in the mid-eighteenth century. (See 'James Jenkins at High Flatts'). Prior to the formation of this school local Quaker based education appears to have been conducted by individual members of the meetings like William Earnshaw of Totties. Further afield, within the area of Pontefract MM, Ackworth School was established in 1779 *'for the education of children whose parents are not in affluence.'* In 1831 Rawdon School (between Bradford and Leeds) was established for the large number of children of parents who had been disowned for marrying out of the Society but who had remained in association with their meetings. The school's doors were opened in 1832.

Regular collections towards funds for Ackworth and Rawdon were made both at Wooldale and High Flatts. Local Friends did what they could to assist some of their poorer children to have an education at these schools:

'The following Contributions hath been brought in towards Procuring Ann, the daughter of Thos. Dickinson one year's education in Ackworth School amounting to £1 17s 6d.' (3)

'The representatives are desired to request on the Monthly Meetings committee on money matters £2 13s 9.5d being the expense of Clothing for Edmund Priest in order to him going to Ackworth School.' (4)

In the early part of the nineteenth century there was also a wider concern for education in other countries. Collections for the *'Promotion of Education in Greece'* (1830) and *'...the education of the African race...'* (1838) are recorded. (5) However, Friends also had a concern for education in the locality. John Wood and Joseph Firth were instrumental in founding the Birdsedge Village School. The drive to provide education for children and adults was at its most active in the period from 1830 to the early 1900's and came in the form of First Day and Adult School provision.

(1) PMMB 1769
(2) (H)PMMB 1797   (4) Ibid 1838
(3) Ibid 1798   (5) Ibid

Quaker School Days — A Letter from Ackworth

Ackworth School
9th Mo. 16th 1830

Dear Parents;

Being about to write a few lines to you, I may inform you that I am in good health. I like Ackworth very well. I began to cipher in the Square root a few days since, and I set the sums down in the ciphering book which I brought from home with me, Thomas Brown thinking it better for me to do so. I hope I have made some improvement in setting down. I should like some good strong white leather lashes, and some thin ones to make whips of, to whip tops: The Boys here are very fond of this play, and it tends much to keep them warm; The shed in which they whip them is 5 or 6 yards broad and 20 or 30 long. John Walker wants a boy every seventh day afternoon to help him in the kitchen. I have been twice, and I have been once to mangle: a Boy goes to mangle every fourth day afternoon. I have been once to the washing-mill which the first table boys take in turns: we go on third days at 5 o'clock in the morning, and do not again join the other Boys till twenty minutes after 7 in the evening: we have our meals in the kitchen. I have not got much more to say at present. I should like to see some of you at the Monthly Meeting, but I fear I shall not. Please to give my dear love to my brothers and sisters.

I remain your affectionate Son,

William Wood. (1)

(1) William Wood (1818-1847) son of Robert and Sarah Wood of Moorbottom, Shelley. (Later resident at Newhouse). Letter written in a very neat hand. Catherine Walton Collection.

First Day Schools

First day schools were set up for the education of local children. The Friends First Day School Association (FFDSA) brought together those working for both children and adults with the establishment of the National Adult School Union in the early 1900's. First Day classes at High Flatts were held for children on a Sunday as early as 1834:

'John Firth having suggested to this Preparative Meeting, whether, there could not with propriety, Something in the way of a first day school, be held in this Meeting house which after a little consideration it is thought desirable that friends generally may have it under their care...' (1)

This first school lasted until 1847 (the year of John Firth's death) when report was made:

'That the school has been carried on up to about 12 months ago when in consequence of there not being a sufficient number of efficient teachers to conduct the school satisfactorily — it was deemed necessary that it should be suspended — & the sanction of the meeting is therefore requested for the school to be given up entirely at present.' (2)

A full report was lodged on the activities of the school. It had started with about 35 pupils but soon increased in size till the average attendance was about 50 each week, both boys and girls. When it was forced to close through lack of good teachers only two of the children on the books were not receiving some other form of instruction. This makes an interesting comparison with the 35 original pupils in 1835 of whom 33 were **not** receiving any other form of education. It was also reported that a total of 104 boys and 86 girls had received tuition. (3)

The inventory of books belonging to the school shows the type of subjects studied. As one would expect Bibles, copies of the New Testament and associated Scripture study books were predominant. The other books consisted of various spelling and vocabulary primers as well as general lesson books.

A second First Day School was started in about 1865. We have a detailed record book covering the period 1866-1877. (4) In 1866-67 there were 43 boys and 31 girls each being divided into four classes. There were both morning and afternoon classes at which there could be up to 8 male and 4 female teachers in attendance. A ticket system was operated to reward pupils: ten tickets were equivalent to 1d and when a pupil had saved up enough tickets a suitable book was purchased. This was usually a Bible or a copy of Bunyan's 'Pilgrim Progress'. Teachers conferences were held regularly at either High Flatts, Lane Head or Newhouse. At the meetings, at which there was an average attendance of 14, a paper was usually presented for discussion. Topics included: 'Temperance', 'Prayer', 'Pleasures of Teaching' and 'Good accommodation as a Help to good behaviour'. This latter paper was unanimously supported as the teachers felt that the meeting house was not really suitable for the school. They requested Joseph Firth to see if other arrangements could be made. This search for better accommodation finally came to an end in 1877 when new school rooms were opened at what is now 'Three Wells', a private house, situated above the Meeting House. The families that were most involved in the running of the school and frequently appear in the records are the Firths, the Woods and the Dickinsons. Representatives were also sent to the annual FFDSA conference held at Ackworth.

At one of the teachers' conferences a paper was presented which was entitled *'A few remarks on the advantages of Penny Savings banks in connection with First Day Schools.'* This led in 1868 to the formation of 'High Flatts First Day School Penny Savings Bank'. Rules were carefully laid down with provision of pass books and an interest rate of 5% per annum to encourage the children to save. The subject of Temperance was also frequently discussed and encouragement was given in the establishment of Bands of Hope in connection with the schools.

The problem of school discipline is certainly not exclusive to the present. In 1869 we hear that: *'The rambling and mischievous habits of children between meeting and school time has been brought before the notice of this meeting.'* Two teachers were appointed to overlook them during the dinner hour. Later in the same year: *'A paper has been read by John Sanderson raising the question as to whether we allow the children too much liberty between school times & it is thought that forbidding them to go beyond the gates of Joseph Firth's yard might be attended with good results. It is further resolved that they shall be forbidden to play at hide & seek.'*

At sometime between 1877 and 1899 the High Flatts First Day School had to close due to declining numbers. In 1899 there was an unsuccessful attempt to restart the school. (5)

Wooldale also had its First Day School although it was on a smaller scale than that at High Flatts. This started in the late 1800's and continued until the early years of this century. In 1903 it had eleven pupils and one teacher. (6) Declining membership during the next sixty years at both meetings saw little provision for children. The creation of a state system of education effectively ended the need for such schools. The nature and purpose of First Day schooling began to alter. In keeping with the needs of the times the First Day School finally came to an end.

In recent years at both meetings, activities for children of the meetings have again been organized. At Wooldale there is now a thriving Children's Meeting. The emphasis is no longer on the basic skills of literacy or numeracy. There is also less emphasis on formal Bible study than previously. Quaker thought, history and heritage are still covered. The older children discuss such typical topics as 'The Meaning of Silence' and 'What it means to be a Quaker today?' An appreciation of more topical issues and problems seen from a Quaker perspective are also included. Younger children are introduced to themes like 'Friendship', 'Caring' and 'Sharing' as well as broader topics concerning nature and the environment.

(1) (HF)PMMB2 1834
(2) Ibid 1847
(3) Ibid
(4) First Day School Record Book 1866-77.
(5) (HF)PMMB3 1899
(6) (W)PMMB 1903

Adult Schools

The Society of Friends was strongly represented in the founding and running of Adult Schools. These schools reached their peak of popularity towards the latter end of the nineteenth century and during the early years of the twentieth century. They have been described as: '...*groups which seek on the basis of friendship to learn together and to enrich life through study, appreciation, social service and obedience to a religious ideal.*' They were originally started to teach poor people to read and write. This moved on to Bible study and finally into various social activities, these always being rooted in religious ideals with a strong emphasis on Temperance. The Quaker influence in the movement was evident in the organization which encouraged the running of the schools by the participants and free discussion and exchange of views. (1)

Many of the Adult Schools used Friends Meeting Houses for their premises and local Friends often undertook the organization and teaching. Wooldale and High Flatts were no exception in this respect. The school at Wooldale opened its doors in 1905:

'Permission is asked for the use of the Meeting House by the Adult School Organization who offer to pay a proportion of the cost of cleaning the premises and to leave things in order for the Meeting for Worship.

The use of the Meeting House is willingly granted on that condition by this meeting for first day morning.' (2)

In 1906 it was reported that there were 34 on the books with an average attendance of 19 with four or five Friends occasionally taking part. In 1907 permission was granted for the Adult School to hold two regular meetings. The school continued for some years but its running was probably affected by the Great War. It was finally recorded in 1921 that there was no longer an Adult School; this despite an attempt in that same year to restart it which met with a poor response.

The High Flatts Adult School started in 1908 in the Meeting House. One of the beliefs of the Adult School Movement was that for people to really know each other they should spend a holiday together. To this end the Adult School Union organized outings and began summer schools as well as setting up Guest Houses. The Rest House (later called Guest House) at High Flatts was one of these to be started by the Yorkshire Adult School Union. It started by using Three Wells, the same premises above the Meeting House, that had earlier housed the First Day School. During the 1920's a number of improvements were made to these premises to make them more comfortable. However, in 1925 the building was sold to William Tuke Robson and it became necessary to find new premises.

Strines, the former home of Henry Dickinson and his descendants, had just been bought by Alfred Blakely the Chairman of the Rest House committee. He offered the use of Strines as the site of the new premises. The property was in a poor state of repair and the estimated cost of rebuilding was in excess of £1500. The Yorkshire Adult School Union felt that this scheme was too costly and eventually the three cottages comprising Strines were demolished. Two old army huts were purchased from Woodhouse Grove School at Apperley Bridge and re-erected on the site. The full cost of the scheme was £1100 and included the cost of the land. The Rest House now became known as the Guest House. Guests in 1927 were charged 7s 6d for board and lodging for the first day and 4s 6d for every subsequent day. The caretaker was paid 10s 0d per week and provided with food and a place of residence. He received a bonus of 6d per visitor for the first night and 3d for subsequent nights. The money for the new Guest House had largely been borrowed and there appears to have been some difficulties in raising the money to repay the loans. In fact it was sometime before the Yorkshire Adult School Union were prepared to take on the responsibility of the new premises. In the meanwhile it was run by a Management Committee. (3) In the 1930's the Depression came and support for the Guest House waned. The premises were eventually sold to Barnsley Corporation who used it as accommodation for evacuees during the war. The two High Flatts Quaker families most involved with running the Guest House were the Sadlers and the Cooks.

The main activity of Strines Guest House was as a centre for conferences, summer schools, weekend discussion groups, in addition to accommodating individual visitors..We have the records of one of these groups that came and spent a weekend at the old premises in August 1915. (4) These *'pilgrims'* were a group of twelve men and included: Albert Holliday (President of the Yorkshire Adult School Union), Norman Holliday (*'Botanist, Scientist, Artist and lecturer. Quiet at bed times. Makes good coffee.'*), Bert Crosby (*'Handy in the kitchen'*) and Alfred Greenwood (*'A backward bachelor'*). Their groceries for the weekend cost them 18s 5.5d. Sam Cook, their host and a member of High Flatts Meeting, remarking on the social evils of the towns saw a future for this type of gathering:

'If (the Rest House) provides a spiritual home, or at least a spiritual atmosphere for those who cannot be bound by creeds and sectarian beliefs, but this does not seem to me to be enough, and here is one of the things that I believe we in the country could do better than anybody else: viz. to provide hospitality and entertainment for those who wish to get away for a short time into the fresh air of the country, and the sunshine of the lanes and fields.'

The various pilgrims left their own personal written recollections of this weekend. The following is a part quotation from one of these:

'An old fashioned hamlet (High Flatts) in an out-of-the-way place, and yet not far from the busy haunts of men who are toiling day by day for the bread that perisheth. What memories flash across the mind when we think of the weekend we spent there, and the heart to heart fellowship that we enjoyed so much? O that we had more opportunities of refreshing. How much closer we get to one another and learn to understand more of our place in the world... On Sunday morning... some attended the Friends Meeting at which two of our party spoke. In the afternoon we attended the Adult School where Norman Holliday gave a talk on 'The evolution of a mother' being a splendid contribution to the Bible Lesson on 'Mary of Nazareth' which followed. By invitation we were joined at tea by 20 local Friends, after which we sang 'What purpose burns within our hearts' and Whittier's Hymn 'Dear Lord and Father of mankind' was read by Henry Dixon.'

One can see implied in these contributions that the Rest/Guest Houses were of great value in those days. The urban working class would very rarely have the opportunity of getting out into the country. Working hours were long and conditions poor. The age of cheap personal transport available to all still remained some years away. With the advent of education for all and the reduction in Church attendance the Adult School Movement gradually declined leaving only a few schools in urban areas.

(1) 'The Adult School Movement' G.Currie Martin
(2) (W)PMMB 1905
(3) Rest/Guest House Minute Book 1920-1929
(4) MS 'High Flatts Pilgrimage — The Chronicles of Common Men'

Poor Relief and Charities

Friends have a long tradition of poor relief and association with charity work. This involved not only assistance to Friends but also in the wider world. The need for assistance must have been at its most necessary in the troubled years preceeding the 1689 Act of Toleration. As we have seen in the first part of this book Friends were liable to long terms of imprisonment, fines and confiscation of belongings including the tools of their trade. The remaining members of a family affected in this way would have needed all the support and assistance from their meeting that they could receive. Even after the Act of Toleration Friends suffered considerably over the non-payment of tithes.

It was primarily the responsibility of MM to provide funds for poor relief. However, there was also assistance provided directly from QM. Additionally, each PM did what it was able for its own members. As local PM minutes prior to 1752 are not extant we need to turn to MM minutes for further detail. Throughout the earliest records there are numerous references to sums of money being either given or loaned, depending on circumstances, to Friends in distress. In 1681, High Flatts Friends were involved in providing relief to one of their number who had suffered a term of imprisonment:

'Whereas Friends of High Flatts meeting at the request of Tho: Crowder of our meeting and upon serious consideration of his presant Condition, and he haveinge beene a sufferer For truth hand some of under(signed) to lend hime three pounds untill such time as he shall be Inabled to pay it a gaine, so Friends of that meetinge have already laine down the money wodded a gree and condesende that they sheere be rermbursed at 3 seperaet paymente at 3 ekewall times of money some.' (1)

Even after the times of persecution there were still many needy Friends who required assistance. This often continued over a number of years. When a needy person had been identified they became known as an *'object of charity'*: this was not a derogatory term but a simple statement of fact. The section on Elizabeth Morehouse clearly illustrates the care Friends gave to their less fortunate members. In the section on Education we have seen that this was one of the areas where Friends were most able to help. They ensured that the poorer children did get some form of education. Friends were regularly appointed to visit the poor families in the meetings and to report back. Visiting Friends were mindful of the conditions surrounding these poor families. When the children came of an age to be employed serious consideration was given to the necessity of continued support. Other factors, such as the price of provisions, were also carefully taken into consideration.

Those in need farther afield were also helped wherever possible. We read of sizable collections towards *'the relief of the distressed in Jerminy.'* When the Irish Potato Famine was at its worst in 1847 High Flatts collected £56 7s 6d and Wooldale £18 9s 0d.

More immediately in 1826 an operation of relief was mounted in the township of Denby. This was not directly under the control of High Flatts Friends as other local people, including the clergy, were involved. A meeting for *'taking into consideration the state of the distressed poor within the said Township'* was held in May 1826. Elihu Dickinson the Tanner was in the chair. Other Friends at the meeting included Richard Dickinson and John Firth. The problems had mainly been caused by the change in the textile industry as outlined further on. It was noted that many were engaged in the manufacture of fancy goods. At the meeting it was reported that in Denby there were 127 poor families consisting of 664 individuals. This made up approximately half the population of the township. Of the 664:

        55   — 'wholly employed'
        145   — 'Partially employed'
        208   — 'unemployed'
        256   — 'Children under the Age of 10 Years'

The average earnings of these people was calculated at 1s 7.5d per week each, which included sums paid out by the Overseer of the Poor to weavers and those working on the public highways. The meeting resolved that a subscription should be raised to help. Also a copy of their report was sent to the *'Fund in London for the relief of the distressed Poor in Yorkshire and Lancashire.'* (2)

In 1842 at QM in the 9th month the 'Distress in the Manufacturing Districts of Yorkshire' was brought to the attention of Friends. An address was prepared and circulated throughout Yorkshire Friends. This reported that: *'Pale, emaciated, cold and hungry without sufficient clothing, without beds, and almost without any furniture; the industrious labourer, the skilful artisan is feeling the sickness of heart which springeth from 'hope long delayed'.'* Subscriptions were soon raised and within a few months over £1000 was available for distribution. One of the first grants made was for the High Flatts area:

'At a meeting of the Committee held 12th of 12th mo. 1842...An application through John Firth for the Chapelry of Denby-Cumberworth, Skelmanthorp, Clayton & High Hoyland was read and considered and the Treasurer was requested to remit £100 to John Firth for that district.'

Only large industrial towns and cities such as Leeds and Sheffield received larger amounts (£300) than this substantial grant. Many of the other country areas receiving much smaller grants: e.g. Lothersdale (£30) and Addingham (£15). (3)

Friends of Wooldale Meeting were also involved in this major relief programme. It is detailed in PM minute books as *'the relief of the distressed operatives in the parish of Kirkburton and Graveship of Holme.'* The textile industry locally had been through a period of depression since the loss of the American market and the financial crisis of 1826 when prices had tumbled. It was at this time that the textile trade was moving out of the home and into the mill. The traditional hand operations of spinning and weaving were being transferred and also coming under power. This caused considerable hardship particularly amongst the hand-loom weavers also known as *'operatives.'* In the first month of 1843 £50 was received from the Friends Relief Committee in York which Wooldale Friends set about distributing. The surrounding area was divided into five divisions:

(1) Townend, Red-Row, Mythom Bridge, New Mill and Thurstonland.
(2) Wooldale, Totties and Paris.
(3) Cliffe and Underbank.
(4) Scholes, Jackson Bridge and Hepworth.
(5) Fulstone

Each division was allocated a portion of the £50 and received help in the form of '...*food as Oatmeal & Flour except in extreme cases of destitution as regards clothing & bedding.*' Report was made that the following number of families had been relieved:

Division 1	52 families
Division 2	100 families
Division 3	96 families
Division 4	100 families
Division 5	74 families

Thus in total 422 families had been relieved: a considerable undertaking. This was not the end of the relief programme. The following month a further £25 was received which was similarly used to relieve 349 families. Then again in the third month another £25 was used to relieve 361 families. (4)

Over the years there have been various Charitable Trusts associated with the meetings. (5) By giving or leaving sums of money or property Friends were able to ensure that there would be funds available to help the less fortunate in the future. The main charity that has provided the most assistance over the years is the Priestroyds Trust. It still operates today with a reasonable income. The 1735 trust deed allows the trustees:

'*...with yearly profits...to relieve & succour such poor people belonging to High Flatts & Wooldale Meeting as shall stand in need of succour & relief according to their wisdom & discretion without any other restriction or limitation whatsoever.*'

The origins of the trust go back to the seventeenth century and concern two closes of land that were rented from John Firth by John Wadsworth in 1673. This land was in Denby-Dike-Side (now known as Denby Dale). It was officially handed over by deed of gift in 1681 by Elias Morton of Simhill in Thurgoland. The orginal trustees were Henry Dickinson of Sheephouse and John Couldwell of Simhill. Also combined into the same trust was £20 left by Henry Jackson III (1680-1727) and £10 from Joseph Bayley of High Flatts. Following the Cumberworth Enclosure Act in the early 1800's another two closes of land at Upper Cumberworth were added to the trust. All the land was rented out and the proceeds used by the trust. The original two closes of land known as Upper Priest Roids and Lower Priest Roids contained about 8 acres.

Gradually, various sections of the land were sold off over the years and the proceeds invested. The Lancashire and Yorkshire Railway Company bought part of the land and Denby Dale Station now stands on the site. The railway line itself passed over the land. There were also beds of both coal and fireclay under the land. Thus it was an exceedingly valuable plot that brought in good rents and a high price when sold. The main part of the land was sold to Joe Kitson in 1879 for £1,200. He had already been renting it and carrying out his business of the manufacture of sanitary pipes and fire bricks. The land can still be easily identified today as the railway viaduct in Denby Dale crosses it and Naylor Bros. pipeworks is the successor to Kitson's business

Throughout Wooldale and High Flatts minute books there are frequent references of money used for poor Friends out of the rents received from Priestroyds. Down the years it has provided welcome support to many. However, the trustees were also sympathetic to adverse conditions affecting the tenants. For instance in 1832 they returned half a years rent due to the low price of produce. (6)

Elihu Dickinson the Tanner left a cottage (Shepley Bar House) and land in Shepley '*for the benefit of poor widows, infirm and past labour, being Quakeresses and members of the High Flatts Preparative Meeting, as the assembled members of the said Meeting should think fit.*' The cottage was rented out on an annual rent ranging between £4 and £6 until it was sold in 1896 for £220. The money was invested and the proceeds continued to be available for distribution.

Other monies for a variety of purposes have been left at various times. These have included £20 left by Henry Jackson II (1633-1710) for trustees *'to put forth to interest — the yearly profit thereof to be distributed ... unto the poor of the hamlet of Wooldale.'* Money has been left towards the upkeep of Wooldale Meeting House by J.B. Woodhead (£40) and Henry Jackson III (£10). Thomas Earnshaw left £10 for the poor of High Flatts Meeting. Property has also been left. The Allot family left Quaker Cottage at High Flatts as a caretakers cottage during this century. In 1940 Joseph Walker left Pell Croft and three fields to Wooldale Meeting. During the war it was used to house evacuees and Holmfirth Urban District Council paid an annual rent of £40. After the war the house and land had to be sold under the order of the Charity Commissioners. The Mortmain Act prevented it being held as an investment. The proceeds of the sale, £1,340, were invested and used towards the running costs of the meeting.

Although many of these gifts by todays values are, in monetary terms, more or less worthless they have served their purpose over the years. They have helped to ensure that the poor of the meetings have been cared for by Friends.

(1) MMMB 1681
(2) Catherine Walton — Misc. Papers.
(3) Proceedings of the Relief of Distress in the Manufacturing Districts of Yorkshire.
(4) (W)PMMB 1831-1843 & 1843-1851
(5) Details of Charities from various sources
        — Minute Books
        — Charity Records
        — 'Endowed Charities (West Riding of Yorkshire)'
        — 'Quaker Charities' HMSO 1899
(6) (H)PMMB 1812-1853

Upholding the Peace Testimony

'I told the (Commonwealth Commissioners) I lived in the virtue of that life and power that took away the occasion of all wars and I knew from whence all wars did rise, from the lust, according to James's doctrine... I told them I was come into the covenant of peace which was before wars and strifes were.' (1)

This statement by George Fox in 1651 can now be seen as the start of the testimony by which many Friends are recognized today. His personal statement was followed in 1661 by the famous corporate declaration by Friends to Charles II which stated: *'We utterly deny all outward wars...'* (2) The peace testimony has been the most enduring of all the Quaker testimonies. It should be understood that Quaker testimonies are a reflection of the thoughts and attitudes of Friends and not a directive instructing Friends what they should believe or how they should behave. As early as 1666 local Friends were echoing George Fox's sentiments. Henry Jackson II, while in Warwick Prison, stated that his *'...Principle is to live peaceably with all men..'* (See 'Henry Jackson II'). (3)

Local Friends were constantly reminded of their duties in these matters when faced with answering the Queries:

'Do you bear a faithful Testimony against Arms and paying Trophy money, or being in any manner concerned in the Militia, Privateers, Letters of Marque or in dealing in Prize goods as such.' (4)

Specific minutes were made when there were particular conflicts occurring such as the Stuart uprising of 1745:

'We have this day Rec'd a paper which Came from our Last Quarterly meeting, Intimating the Care which should be upon ye minds of Frds. (viz) not to bear or Carry Arms, being yt. our Lord and Saviour Jesus Christ Testified against such practices, ye sd. paper being read in this meeting & ordered that Copies of ye same be sent Every particular meeting.' (5)

Friend's concern was more for the relief of the effects of any such conflicts:

'...we have sent £2-3-6 for the Releife of Poor Suffering friends by ye late Rebellion...' (6)

Friends were liable to be called up for service in the militia during times of conflict. The wealthy were able to hire a substitute to avoid being called up. Friends would not normally, as a matter of principle, expect anyone else to do what they themselves were not prepared to do. Thus they were often confronted by the law as in the case of John Firth in 1776 at the time of the American War of Independence:

'John Firth, son of Joseph Firth of Lanehead, aforesaid being allotted to serve in the Militia and for refusing, or hiring a Substitute, William Goodlud Constable of Shepley, by virtue of a warrant Granted by H. Zouch & (?) Milns Justices & Gamaliel Milner Deputy Lieutenant on the 14th of the 5th Month 1776 made distress on the goods of his father (said John not being a Householder) and took Seven Bushels of Wheat & two bushels of Malt worth £2-6-0d.' (7)

In 1796-97 during the course of the Napoleonic Wars Joseph Dickinson was admonished for being:

'...concerned with his Brother in Providing a Substitute to serve in the Militia and that his Conduct on that occasion and under some respects have been reproachful.' (8)

The other misdemeanour that Friends sometimes fell foul of was failing to uphold their resistance to paying special military taxes, for example *'the rate for the Cavalry.'* Joseph Woodhead of Wooldale Meeting when confronted with this in 1800-01 by MM rather smugly replied that as the cavalry had been dissolved any money paid could not be used by them! Friends did not accept this explanation as they pointed out that the money was being used to pay off arrears. Joseph Woodhead did not appear to be moved by these arguments and having made his formal reply the matter was allowed to drop:

'Had I thought that the Money had really gone for the bearing of Arms etc. or the expenses said to be accrued for that purpose, I should not have paid it. And had I known the Case then as well as I have since done I should have let them do as usual.
Joseph Woodhead.' (9)

Until the turn of this century all that really had been necessary to maintain the peace testimony was individual commitment to resistance to military service and payment of any specifically military taxes. The whole concept of war changed with the outbreak of the First World War (1914-18). No longer did war affect relatively small groups of people. Many nations, from most of the world's continents, were now involved. Large numbers of the civil populations of the warring countries were engaged in the 'war effort' in some capacity or other and there was conscription.... In later years, as the media became more widely available to ordinary people, it was not possible to escape the reality of war. For the peace testimony to be viable in these changing circumstances it became necessary for it to be adapted to the times. It became more political and active in practice: a matter for the Society itself to make witness to rather than leave to individual Friends.

Locally Friend's concern was shown a number of years before the 1914-18 war broke out. In 1903 Wooldale Friends obtained copies of a memorandum condemning military training to distribute to local school managers. In 1909 High Flatts Friends passed a minute which they sent on to their local MP Henry J. Wilson:

'In view of the deplorable demand for increased armaments, and the spread in this country of the war spirit generally, this Meeting desires to place on record its unabated and unswerving adherence to the conviction which Friends have always felt that war is utterly opposed to the teaching of Christ: and therefore unlawful for Christians.' (10)

Henry J. Wilson, who had represented the Holmfirth Division since 1886, was a Sheffield man who had many links with Friends. In March of 1909 he had written deploring the defection of several members of the Armaments Protest Committee as a result of persecution by the party leaders. As both meetings had greatly diminished in numbers and were becoming elderly during the two World Wars very few members were faced with the problem of conscription. One member of Wooldale Meeting, G. Edward Burtt, undertook service in the Friends Ambulance Unit (FAU) in the 1914-18 war. At the start of the Second World War (1939-45) Wooldale Friends distributed a large number of copies of the peace pamphlet 'Will War Bring Peace?'.

(1) JGF
(2) Ibid
(3) 'Extracts from State Papers relating to Friends 1654-72' Edited by Norman Penney.
(4) Quoted in PMMB 1752-1768
(5) MMMB 1745
(6) Ibid 1747
(7) Catherine Walton Collection
(8) MMMB 1796
(9) MMMB 1800-1801
(10) (H)PMMB 1909

Local Friends and Politics

There is little or no direct evidence of local Friends involvement in politics during the eighteenth century. Such involvement as was to arise, with well known national figures like John Bright and the Pease family, would be stimulated by the social conditions created as a result of the industrialization process. However, it is evident that Yorkshire Friends were not afraid to express views of a highly overt political nature as at least one such comment is to be found copied out in the back of the Wooldale PM minute books and is dated the 3rd month 1801:

'The Ruin or Prosperity of a State depends so much upon the administration of its Government, that to be acquainted with the merit of a Ministry, we need only observe the condition of the People. If we see them obedient to the Laws, prosperous in their industry, united at home and respected abroad, we may reasonably presume, that their affairs are conducted by Men of experience, abilities and virtue; if on the contrary we see an universal Spirit of Distrust and dissatisfaction, a rapid decay of trade, dissensions in all part of the empire, and a total loss of respect in the eyes of foreign Powers, we may presume, without hesitation, that the government of the country is weak, distracted and corrupt.

The multitude in all countries are patient to a certain point. Ill usage may rouse their indignation and hurry them into excess; but the original fault is in Government.'

This most untypical entry was a strong indictment in its own day. These words remain as a timeless truism, relevant now as then, for any age or nation.

High Flatts Sanatorium

In 1886 a Home *'intended for the restoration of inebriate women of the working and middle classes'* was started, on Quaker owned property, at the house built by Elihu Dickinson the Tanner at High Flatts: Mill Bank House. (1) This Home for women was largely run by women and the greater part of the support and donations came from women. The long running testimony of Friends on Temperance ensured the strong involvement and support of the women Friends of High Flatts and Wooldale Meetings. Miss Wood of Newhouse was one of the joint secretaries in 1895. There was strong support from other Churches as the scheme came under the auspices of the Yorkshire Women's Christian Temperance Union. The Home continued to run into the early years of the present century.

One can do no better than quote the rules of the establishment verbatim to reveal the attitudes toward alcoholism in those days (1895).

'(1) The Applicant on becoming an inmate of the Sanatorium will be required to conform to the regulations of the Institution, and to perform the duties, industrial or otherwise, that may be assigned to her.

(2) The Committee reserve to themselves the power to accept or refuse applications, and to dismiss any patient who may become unfit for the Sanatorium or who may refuse to conform to the Rules, or for general misconduct.

(3) A residence of two years is strongly recommended and no care can be received for less than twelve months.

(4) Inmates will be required to abstain from all intoxicating drinks and drugs, to give up possession of all money, keys, and valuables: also not to go beyond the premises and grounds unattended without permission.

(5) Terms:- Patients doing needlework for the Home 10s per week; a limited number assisting in cleaning and cooking, 7s 6d per week; those who can clean, cook and wash, 5s per week. Payment in advance, quarterly or monthly, will be required.

(6) Yorkshire Applicants, and those nominated by subscribers of £1 and upwards, will have the preference of admission; Patients from other Counties pay an entrance fee of 10s, 15s and £1, according to the rate of payment.

(7) No immoral woman can be received.

(8) No one subject to fits, or suffering from any mental or infectious or serious complaint can be admitted.

(9) Visitors are not to give any article to the inmates, but to place the same in the hands of the Superintendent.

(10) Suitable and sufficient clothing must be provided for each patient by her friends during her residence at the Sanatorium.

N.B. — An agreement to abide by these Regulations must be signed by each patient on her admission.'

Today alcoholism is regarded as an illness caused by addiction. Except in the very early stages of treatment of severe cases patients are made to live in and face up to situations in the outside world. This includes being placed in situations where alcohol is freely available. In the early days of the High Flatts Sanatorium it appears that the *'inmates'* were regarded as completely responsible for their own failings and were shut away to keep them from further temptation. However, it does seem that patients were well treated as during 1895 a number of former patients were recorded as returning to the Sanatorium to help and encourage those undergoing treatment. It should be remembered that homes to treat alcoholism were comparatively uncommon. Most sufferers would remain without any form of help becoming more dependent on alcholol and open to the many associated problems. The worst cases would find themselves locked away in mental institutions often for long periods. The Sanatorium committee supported the call made by the Inspector of Licenced Inebriate Homes in his 1895 address to extend and simplify the legal powers to commit and retain inebriates in Homes.

The Sanatorium appears to have been unable to cope with the worst symptoms of alcoholism as one patient had to be *'removed to a Lunatic Assylum, and we were compelled, with much regret, to dismiss two others for insubordination; these extreme measures being necessary to maintain order and discipline in the Home.'* These particular patients *'were admitted in a state of very great excitement, arising from the excessive use of stimulants, and required more restraint and personal care than we were able to give.'* In reviewing the success rate over the preceeding three years before 1895 it was reported that certainly eighteen and probably more of the forty who had left had resisted *'the old temptation'* and were doing well. A fifty percent success rate can be considered fairly satisfactory. Even today many sufferers have to undergo further treatment at a later date.

In 1895 there were fourteen patients: five from Yorkshire, the rest from other parts of the country as far away as London and Cheltenham. The Home was obviously well known. From the financial statement the fees from the patients only covered about two thirds of the running costs which totalled £450 per annum. The balance was made up from donations collected throughout Yorkshire although the largest proportion actually came from the immediate vicinity of High Flatts. The patients needlework was also sold at a profit to supplement funds. Report was given of a very successful open day and garden party for members of the various branches of the Yorkshire Women's Christian Temperance Union.

The Home was firmly established on religious principles:

'The struggle is no doubt in many cases difficult and prolonged, but our experience proves that many are, through the mercy and loving kindness of their Heavenly Father, enabled permanently to overcome the temptation, and return to spend many happy years in their own homes, gratefully acknowledging the protection which sheltered them when they were too weak to stand alone...and some for whom we have trembled on their departure, have proved as shining lights, having been enabled out of their own bitter experience to reach out a helping hand to others.'

(1) Tenth Annual Report of the High Flatts Sanatorium for Women (1895). (Much of the material quoted in this section has been taken from this report).

FRIENDS AT WORK

Occupations

Local Friends of the seventeenth and eighteenth century tended to engage in farming or the manufacture of woollen textiles. It was not uncommon to find them combining the occupations of farmer and clothier. Considering the vagaries of the Pennine climate and nature of the land this was hardly surprising. The Woods of Newhouse were typical of families that worked both as independent clothiers and farmers. (See 'Woods of Newhouse'). To their name could be added those of the Marsdens of Birdsedge and Shepley, the Dickinsons of Thurlstone and High Flatts, the Broadheads of Wooldale and Mearhouse and many others. The Firth family of Shepley Lane Head, on the other hand, were a farming family that expanded into malt-processing and land ownership. It was as maltsters and landlords that the Firth family made its fortune over successive generations.

Those who solely engaged in the occupation of a clothier tended to be a comparative rarity until the later years of the eighteenth century. The onset of the Industrial Revolution and the gradual ending of the domestic system of textile manufacture resulted in a greater degree of specialization. This, in itself, contributed to the decline in the size of the meetings as Friends removed to the new industrial centres to make use of their specialist skills. (See 'Removals from High Flatts and Wooldale').

Although a great number of Friends continued to be engaged in farming or textile manufacture well into the nineteenth century the change in the pattern of occupations had already commenced. The number of Friends involved in retailing, for example, steadily increased. George Chapman (1745-1811) and Daniel Broadhead (1755-1825) of Penistone, John Pickford (1770-1823) of Cumberworth and Robert Broadhead (1752-1826) are all listed as shopkeepers. A greater diversity in other occupations is also noted with local Friends working as masons, carpenters, cloggers, millwrights, tanners, tailors and tallow chandlers. There can be little doubt that the educational opportunities available to Friends children at Ackworth and Rawdon schools led to many entering the professions during the nineteenth century.

The last quarter of the nineteenth century saw Friends engaged in professions like medicine and the law. Yet, even with such diversification, farming and textiles (or textile related occupations) still remained the dominant forms of employment in this locality in 1900. Allowing for the steadily declining numbers this pattern remained essentially unchanged until after the Second World War.

As membership began to increase once again in the 1970's the traditional pattern of occupation finally came to an end. Today, hardly any members are involved or connected with farming or textiles at either of the two meetings. Following a wider national trend in the Society the single largest occupation pursued by local Quakers is that of teaching with every level of education being represented. Other forms of employment also follow the national trend. Friends and attenders come increasingly from professional backgrounds.

Wood and Burtt

The Quaker owned textile firm of Wood & Burtt provided employment in the Totties, Wooldale and New Mill districts for nearly a century. From the mid-1800's to the mid-1900's, this small firm of woollen spinners, at Ford Mill in Totties, was a successful and thriving enterprise. (1)

The Wood and Burtt families were both members of Wooldale Meeting and made major contributions towards the life of the meeting during that period. When the meeting was at its lowest ebb, during the early/mid 1900's, it could well have closed down entirely. During that period the membership of Wooldale Meeting was largely made up of and sustained by various members of the Burtt family. This did have the effect of distancing the meeting from the locals at that time. One of the present members, who was brought up in Wooldale village during the 1940's and 1950's, remembers an air of mystery surrounding the meeting house. When, as a young man he first started attending the meeting, his work mates reaction were that he should not go there as it was *'the bosses chapel.'* Most of the working population in the village attended one of the two Methodist chapels. The phrase *'Burtt's chapel'* was also used by the locals in reference to the meeting. The only real sign of activity was the one day each year when MM was held. This was always referred to as the *'Quaker feast'* by the locals, thinkng it was a similar annual event to these held at the chapels.

The Wood family had been Quakers for a number of generations. (See 'The Woods of Newhouse'). Their early connections were mainly with High Flatts Meeting since the family home had been at nearby Newhouse. The particular branch of the family which helped to found the firm that became Wood & Burtt lived at Ford House. It was within a few yards of his home that Alfred Wood I (1820-1894) was to build the mill that he appropriately called Ford Mill.

Edward Henry Burtt (1849-1922) came to the district from Welbourn in Lincolnshire. He was a member of an old established Quaker family. The Burtts were of farming stock and owned considerable acreage in their native part of Lincolnshire. They are to be found mentioned in the earliest records of many local meetings such as Brant Broughton. Edward H. Burtt's father was Edward Burtt of Welbourn (1822-1887) who was renown for breeding red short-horn cattle known as *'Burtt's Welbourn Short-horns.'* Quite why Edward H. Burtt decided to move to Wooldale from Lincolnshire is unknown. One can surmise that, perhaps, two factors lead him to West Yorkshire. The first may have been the possible association between the two families in the textile trade: the Burtts probably kept sheep as well a cattle and may have sold fleeces to the Woods for their trade. The second factor may have been their mutual committment to the Society of Friends and contact at a Friends school. The story of how Alfred Wood I and Edward H. Burtt became partners is revealing and fascinating in the light that it sheds upon that Quaker practice of taking apprentices.

Alfred Wood I built Ford Mill in 1862. (1) Even after the mill was built some of the work continued to be done for a time in the attics of Ford House. It is likely that Alfred Wood had carried on his trade for some years before the building of the mill and initially needed to continue work at his home as well as in the new premises. In the 1860's, Edward H. Burtt, in his teens, left his Lincolnshire home and is recorded in 1867 as an *'Apprentice with Alfred Wood.'* (2) He appears to have learned his trade quickly as just three years later in 1870 he is recorded as a *'Manager'* (3) and then in 1872 as a *'Manufacturer'* (4). This last description is the same as that given to Alfred Wood I. By 1874 Edward H. Burtt was married to Annie Pickard and lived at Whinney Bank Farm which, along with Totties Farm and surrounding land, was owned by the mill. The Burtts later moved to Tenter Hill where they lived for over 70 years. Edward H. Burtt was appointed a J.P. for the West Riding in 1895 and he was a member of the Wooldale and Cartworth School Board for eighteen years. As a clerk to Pontefract MM *'he conducted the business with efficiency and painstaking care.'* He was a member of The Retreat Committee and *'he attended their meetings with unfailing regularity.'* The testimony to his life relates that:

'It is as a wise counsellor, as a Friend of sound and balanced judgement that he stands so high in our esteem...Many a diffcult problem seemed to become surprisingly simple after hearing a few well chosen words spoken by him.' (5)

In the 1870's Alfred Wood I handed over his part of the business to his son, Fredric. Fredric Wood, who built and resided at Woodfield, emigrated to California in 1916. Alfred Wood's other son, young Alfred (1868-1955), also joined the firm but only after some family disagreement. Whatever the disagreement was about it lead to young Alfred Wood going out to South Africa. Whilst out there he was caught up in the Boer War. Badly wounded by a spear through the intestines, the story recounts that, he had to tie himself to a tent post for some weeks until the wound healed. On returning from South Africa he joined the firm and built and resided at Shaley Dene. He was later joined by Edward H. Burtt's son, George Edward Burtt (1884-1977), after he had obtained a 1st Class Honours Degree in Economics, Physiology & Chemistry at Victoria Universty (Manchester). G. Edward Burtt's career at the mill was interrupted for a time during the First World War when he served in the Friends Ambulance Unit in France.

Despite a severe fire in 1906 the business thrived and employed over 100 people during the first thirty years of this century. There were various extensions made to the premises which even necessitated the diverting of the road between Wooldale and Totties. Water had to be pumped uphill from the dams by a windmill but following the dyehouse extension and the need for an increase in the supply of water other arrangements had to be made. The firm decided upon an unusual solution to their water shortage problem. They called in a Mr. Chesterman of Hereford who was a water diviner. He appears to have found water in a field close by which was then pumped to the dyehouse. This supply of water had unexpected consequences. Many of the mill's employees learned how to swim in the mill dam which was made available for their use. So too did quite a few members of Wooldale Meeting who would regularly go after Sunday Meeting for Worship. The water was warmed by the heat from the steam and processing.

The firm started as worsted and yarn spinners and manufacturers but came to specialize in woollen spinning. The firm was known for products such as Turkey Rug Wool which was a forerunner of the home made rug kits now so successfully marketed by Readicut. The firm also produced Green Tie yarn which was exported in large quantities to China as well as various fancy yarns, coloured nepps, carpet yarns and knitting yarns including a line called Abb Yarn. Abb Yarn was an oiled yarn sold mainly to the fishing ports for the hand knitting of water repellant fishermans jerseys. Wood & Burtt's employed buyers to purchase fleeces. The fleeces came mainly from Yorkshire and Derbyshire farms (including a regular supply from the Chatsworth House Estate) but some wool was also purchased from New Zealand and Australia. The buyers had to visit the farms themselves since in this period the Wool Marketing Board had not yet come into existence.

Wood & Burtt amalgamated with J. & J. Baldwin & Partners of Halifax in 1919 which subsequently became Paton & Baldwins. The firm grew into Coats Patons and is now one of the largest textile groups in the country: Coats Viyella, with its many international interests. All operations at Ford Mill finally ceased in the late 1950's and were moved to Wakefield. By this time Alfred Wood II had died and G. Edward Burtt had gone into retirement. Wood and Burtt was not the only Quaker textile firm in this area. One of todays most successful firms is that of Jonathan Thorp & Sons (Successors) Ltd. of Valley Mills, New Mill. Although no longer in Quaker ownership it was started by the Thorp family of Springwood House, New Mill, who were members of High Flatts Meeting

The firm of Copley Marshall Ltd. of Wildspur Mill, New Mill, also had Quaker connections. It was founded by J.F. Copley who invented and patented a number of processing machines. Various members of the Copley family became members of Wooldale Meeting.

The second generation of the Woods and Burtts are still remembered in the locality with affection by surviving employees. They were regarded as very good employers with a reputation for being honest and straight in all their dealings. They never took advantage of their position. Anything they had from the mill was always paid for and as directors they only took the same holidays as their employees. Alfred Wood II was technically very competant in his trade and did not tolerate bad workmanship. He was an astute businessman with a tough and independent streak: no doubt formed as a result of his experiences in South Africa. However he is also remembered for the great generosities and acts of kindness that he showed. One particular instance concerns the Holmfirth Flood of 1944. He was then an elderly man and hearing of the suffering and loss caused by the catastrophe gave Nurse Cartwright, the local district nurse, *'a fistful of £5 notes.'* He asked Nurse Cartwright to use her knowledge of those likely to be in most need and to share out the money amongst them, anonymously.

G. Edward Burtt was a tolerant, kindly and sympathetic man. He served the MM for many years as Treasurer. The two were contrasting personalities who in their very differences forged a successful partnership. Both men were dog owners and brought their animals to work. Apocryphally, Alfred Wood's dog sat on his desk and growled at any one who came near while G. Edward Burtt's dogs sat placidly and peacefully under his desk. Perhaps, the dogs reflected their masters temperaments.

(1) Much of the information for this section was kindly supplied by Frank Lindley of Stoney Bank, New Mill who was employed all his working life at the Wood & Burtt Mill.
(2) Wooldale PM List of Members 1867-1901.
(3) Ibid
(4) Ibid
(5) MMMB 1923

THE FAMILIES

The decendants of many of the original families that made up the membership of these meetings either no longer reside within their vicinity or even belong to the Religious Society of Friends. David Bower and his mother, Ruth Bower, are the only surviving present day members of Wooldale Meeting who are descended from the local Quaker families of the past. In one way or another, through the different branches, they are related by varying degrees of closeness and distance in kinship to the Burtts, the Brooks, the Woods, the Pickards, and the Broadheads of Wooldale. By the marriage of their ancestor, Robert Broadhead of Wooldale to Mary Kay in 1714, they can claim a connection to Wooldale Meeting stretching back to the Quaker dawn and Gervas Kay of Fulstone and Meal Hill.

The descendants of families like the Woods, the Woodheads, the Pontefracts of Thurstonland, the Brooks of Wooldale and High Flatts and others, who are still Quakers, are scattered far and wide. In the course of writing this history correspondence has been received from descendants living as far away as the United States and New Zealand.

A considerable number of factors have prevented the inclusion of details about many of the families mentioned in this book. One of the chief constraints was that faced by all authors, namely the space available. Some, like the Marsdens of Shepley, Birdsedge and Ing-birchworth, the Haighs of Wooldale and Shepley, the Brooks of Huddersfield, the Beaumonts, the Bottomleys and the Mallinsons would have proved almost impossible to detail due to a lack of information. Others, like the Brooks of Wooldale and High Flatts along with the Walkers receive attention within the narrative. Families, like the Pontefracts with their Quaker origins in this area, have had to be mentioned only briefly at this juncture since they removed to meetings in other parts of the country and so their stories fittingly belong elsewhere. (William Pontefract, their ancestor, was a convinced Friend who entered into membership of the Society during the early 1800's probably influenced by the preaching of Joseph Wood and Thomas Shillitoe. In 1819 he married Sarah Haigh of High Flatts, the daughter of Samuel Haigh. However, apart from their son Joseph, who was a member of Wooldale until his death in 1883, the other children moved away from the area. Joseph Pontefract's daughter, Matilda, by removing to within the bounds of Brighouse MM in 1884 after her father's death, severed the family link).

As one of the principal families, the Jacksons, have been detailed in the early chapters it was felt that brief histories of several other families needed inclusion. The choice was eventually narrowed down to: the Dickinsons of High Flatts, Sheephouse and Thurlstone, the Firths of Shepley Lane Head, the Woods of Newhouse and the Broadheads of Wooldale. The choice of these families was based on their very long associations with the meetings and the role played by each over successive generations. The extent to which information was available upon each of the families was also a major factor in the selection process. The necessity of identifying different branches and members of the families in relation to each other in the course of the book was also an important consideration. Finally, it was felt that the families selected should be representative of the area and the meetings attended by our plain country Friends of the past.

The Dickinsons were selected because of their many branches and the number of individuals mentioned within the pages of 'Plain Country Friends' that were guaranteed to confuse readers. They were also a major influence within the meetings for over two hundred years from the Quaker dawn. The Firths were included chiefly because of the confusion their ancestors have wrought upon local history. Their long association with Shepley Lane Head as both an early meeting house and a place of residence, and their later influence upon High Flatts Meeting in the nineteenth century made their inclusion almost a prerequisite. The Woods of Newhouse serve as a backdrop to that most illustrious member of their family and these local meetings: Joseph Wood. Without his detailed records this book would indeed have been a poorer offering. The Wood family also represents, although not uniquely so, that enduring continuum which has maintained the Quaker Way over successive generations to the present. The Broadheads complete the group as a Quaker family representative of the Wooldale membership from about 1670 to the early decades of the nineteenth century.

The Dickinsons of High Flatts, Sheephouse and Thurlstone

The Dickinsons of High Flatts

The ensuing sections are descriptive rather than anecdotal. Their aim is to help clarify, as simply as possible, the various relationships within the family over successive generations without confusion.

There appear to have been two distinct branches of the Dickinson family residing in Denby and High Flatts during the mid-seventeenth century. One of these, that of John Dickinson, can be traced quite clearly. The other branch, that of Henry Dickinson of High Flatts, (not to be confused with his namesake at Sheephouse near Penistone), is poorly documented.

Henry Dickinson of High Flatts

Henry Dickinson, a linen weaver at Denby, was a contemporary of John Dickinson of High Flatts and Henry Dickinson of Sheephouse. (Whether the three were related is unclear). Henry is recorded as having at least two sons but he may have had more: both Joshua (b.1661) and Joseph (1663-1667) are clearly recorded as his sons. A second Joseph (b.1665) is also attributed to Henry Dickinson but this could be a transcription error when the births and deaths register (QBBREG1) was compiled. A Henry (b.29/12/1667) is also a possible son but no extant evidence links the two.

John Dickinson of High Flatts

John Dickinson (d.1687) is a shadowy figure about whose life very little can be established. A John Dickinson is mentioned in the earliest surviving minute belonging to Pontefract MM. Dated the 5th day of the 4th month 1672 it mentions him *'disbursing 10s to John Swift of Denby.'* This John Dickinson was the father of Edward Dickinson (1654-1716) and David Dickinson (1665-1727) from whom two distinct Dickinson genealogies can be mapped. He had other children besides: Judeth (b.1657), who was named after her mother, Sarah (b.1660), Matthew (1663-1677) and Jonathan (1669-1670). The family genealogy of Edward Dickinson and David Dickinson, the younger brothers of John Dickinson, are well documented.

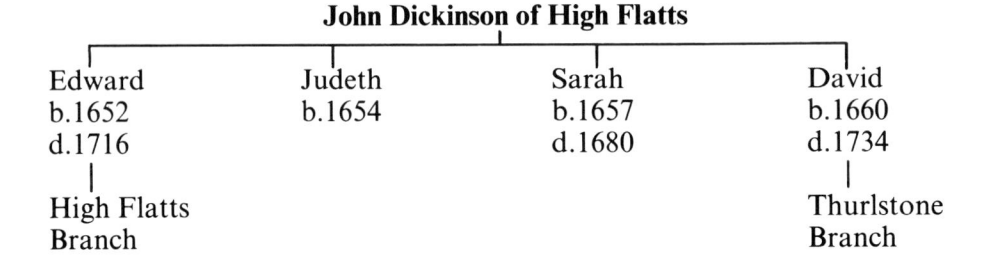

John Dickinson of High Flatts

Edward	Judeth	Sarah	David
b.1652	b.1654	b.1657	b.1660
d.1716		d.1680	d.1734
High Flatts Branch			Thurlstone Branch

The Descendants of David Dickinson

David Dickinson was a clothier and is recorded as having married Martha Horsfall of York in 1691. They settled at Birkhouse where their children are recorded as having been born.

David Dickinson I m. Martha Horsfall

Sarah	b.1692
David	b.1694
Mary	b.1695
Edward	b.1700 m.1727 Ann Jepson (1)
Lydia	b.1702
Enoch	b.1708 m.1734 Mary Ellis (2)

(1)

Edward Dickinson m. Ann Jepson

(Resided Hoyland Swaine)

Martha	James
b.1728	b.1732
	(m.1758 Hannah Kay) (1A)

(2)

Enoch Dickinson m. Mary Ellis

CLOTHIER

Sarah	b.1735
Hannah	b.1736-7
Benj.	b.1738
Thomas	b.1740 m.1769 Hannah Roberts (2A)
Enoch	b.1743
David	b.1746 m.1769 Martha Haigh (2B)

(1A)

James Dickinson b.1732-d.1818 m. Hannah Kay b.1735-d.1818

CLOTHIER

(Resided at Folly between Thurlstone & Ingbirchworth)

Sarah	b.1759
James	b.1761
Edward	b.1763
Ann	b.1766
John	b.1768
Samuel	b.1771
Caleb	b.1773
Joshua	b.1777
Hannah	b.1780

(2A)

Thomas Dickinson b.1740-d.1797 m. Hannah Roberts b.1749-d.1794

CLOTHIER

(Resided at Belroyd/Bellroid nr. Scouts Dike and Folly)

Jonathan	b.1771
Amos	b.1772-d.1779
Esther	b.1774
Mary	b.1775
Gideon	b.1777-d.1779
George	b.1779-d.1782
Hannah	b.1783
Thomas	b.1785-d.1785
Elizb.	b.1789-d.1792

(2B)

David Dickinson II b.1746-d.1819 m. Martha Haigh b.1747-d.1810

CLOTHIER

(Resided at Mill Walk, Thurlstone)

Elihu	b.1771-d.1776
Lydia	b.1773
Ruth	b.1775
Susanna	b.1778
Martha	b.1780
Elizb.	b.1782
Elijah	b.1785
David	b.1787
Enoch	b.1790

The Descendants of Edward Dickinson of High Flatts

Edward Dickinson b.1654-d.1716 m. Sarah ? d.1712

Elihu Dickinson I b.1679-d.1748 m. 1705 (1) Mary Firth d.1708 (1)
                    m. 1715 (2) Sarah Kay   (2)

Ann Broadhead wrote this Testimony concerning Elihu Dickinson: *'Great was his concern for the prosperity of Zion and the good of souls, and earnestly did he long that the Church militant might be adorned with the gifts of the Holy Spirit, and that the name of the Lord Jesus Christ, her holy and heavenly Head might spread to the ends of the earth.'*

(1)

Edward Dickinson b.1708 m. 1740 Ann Greenwood

(Edward was the only of Elihu Dickinson I & Mary Firth)

Elihu	b.1741/2-d.1819 (the Clothier)
Edward	b.1743
Mary	b.1745
Ann	b.1747
Hannah	b.1749
Sarah	b.1757
William	b.1753

(2)

Elihu Dickinson II b.1716-d.1748 m. Mary Aldham

(Elihu Dickinson II and Sarah b.1723 were the only children of Elihu Dickinson I & Sarah Kay. Elihu Dickinson II died 2 weeks before his father).

Elihu Dickinson III (the Tanner) b.1745-d.1829 m. Sarah Sutcliffe b.1751-d.1790

(Resided at Mill Bank House, High Flatts. See section 'Elihu Dickinson the Tanner').

Mary	b.1774
Sarah	b.1775
Richard	b.1777 m. Ann (2A)
Hannah	b.1780
Susanna	b.1782
Elihu	b.1784-d.1812

(2A)

Richard & Ann Dickinson

(Resided at Mill Bank House, High Flatts)

Margaret	b.1817
Mary Ann	b.1818
Herbert Camm	b.1820

The Dickinsons of Sheephouse nr. Midhope

Amongst the earliest prominent Friends to be mentioned in Pontefract MM minutes is Henry Dickinson of Sheephouse. Henry Dickinson (1635-1719) married Anne Downing (1644-1720) of Midhope. Precisely when he and his wife became Quakers is not known. He was active in the service of Friends certainly from 1672 onwards frequently attending MM and performing a wide variety of duties including the disbursment of monies to those suffering from persecutions and/or in general need of relief. In the absence of Henry Jackson II, who was frequently away from home, Henry Dickinson of Sheephouse appears to have been a leading local Friend.

Henry Dickinson m. Ann Downing
YEOMAN FARMER

Samuel (b.1670)
Rebecca (b.1672)
Daniel (b.1673) m. Rachel Fisher of Bradnall (Derbyshire) (2)
Caleb (b.1676) m. Sarah Firth of Shepley Lane Head (1)
Benjamin (1678-1679)
Hannah (b.1680)
John (b.1684)
Rachel (b.1684)
Henry (b.1687)

(1)

Caleb Dickinson m. Sarah Firth

John (1712-1713)
Hannah (b.1708/9)
Joseph (1711-1713) Twin
Mary (1711-1712) Twin
Martha (b.1713)
Mary (b.1715)
Ann (b.1721)
Edward (b.1723)
Susan (b.1725)

Henry Dickinson (1710-1786) of Strines, High Flatts

This prominent and influential eighteenth century Friend was a clothier by occupation. He was the grandson of Henry and Ann Dickinson of Sheephouse and the son of Daniel Dickinson (1673-1727) and Rachel Fisher (1680-1720). Henry Dickinson married Hannah Brook (one of the daughters of Uriah Brook of Wooldale and High Flatts) in 1737. They settled in Woodnook near Denby Miln where their three eldest children were born before they removed to Strines. A Daniel Dickinson (b.1712) is recorded as having died at Strines in 1771. He was a younger brother of Henry Dickinson. There is some evidence to indicate that Daniel Dickinson was handicapped and was supported by Friends charity. Henry Dickinson was a recorded minister at High Flatts Meeting.

The Descendants of Henry Dickinson of Strines

Henry Dickinson Snr. m. Hannah Brook (b.1717-d.1791)

Hannah   b.1738
Henry   b.1743-d.1828 m. 1769 Hannah Green b.1747-d.1827 (2)
Joseph   b.1745
Jonathan b.1738
George   b.1752
Joshua   b.1755
John   b.1758
Judeth   b.1762

(2)

Henry Dickinson Jnr. m. Hannah Green

(Resided in Ingbirchworth)

CLOTHIER

Joseph   b.1769
Samuel   b.1771
Elizb.   b.1779
Sarah   b.1780
John   b.1782 m. Hannah (2A)
Jonathan b.1785 m. Alice (2B)
Henry   b.1789-d.1790

126

(2A)

John Dickinson m. Hannah

(Resided at Strines)

CLOTHIER

Ann	b.1806
Simeon	b.1807
Eliza	b.1819
Emma	b.1827

(2B)

Jonathan Dickinson m. Alice

(Resided at Strines)

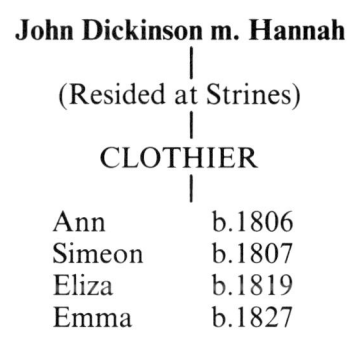

CLOTHIER

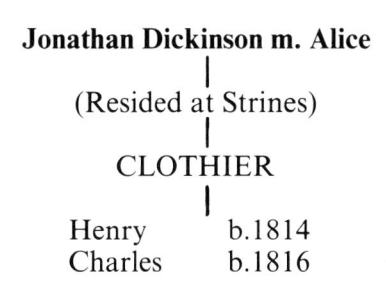

Henry	b.1814
Charles	b.1816

It seems that both John and Jonathan Dickinson continued to live with their wives and children at Strines after the death of their father, Henry Dickinson Jnr.

The Firths of Shepley Lane Head

At the Wakefield Quarter Sessions held in Barnsley on the 15 October 1689 John Firth (Shepley Lane Head), Edward Dickinson (High Flatts), Ralph Sanderson (Upper Midhope), John Charlesworth (Midhope Hall), Jonathan West (Midhope) and Caleb Broadhead (Wooldale), amongst others, were licenced to use their homes as dissenting places of worship. This John Firth, about whom little is known, has been frequently and wrongly confused with others of the same name living in the area. At least three John Firths are known to have been among the 128 who signed the petition to have a separate parish church in Holmfirth. Some examination of his forebearers is necessary to finally end nearly two centuries of erroneously recorded local history.

There were two distinct families bearing the Firth surname living in Shepley towards the end of the seventeenth century: the Quaker Firths of Lane Head, distinguished by their red hair and the Firths of Shepley Hall with contrasting black hair. The Shepley Hall Firth's claimed that the two families were not related. (1) The Lane Head Firths family tradition recounts that they were descended from James Firth who resided at Leak Hall, *'a fine old house'* situated between Denby Dale and Lower Cumberworth. James Firth had a son, John, who was baptized in 1597. This John Firth was the father of Thomas Firth of Leak Hall and the Quaker John Firth. (2) A John Firth of Cumberworth purchased Shepley Hall with all its lands from William Hepworth on the 12 June 1629. He died in 1682 at the age of 86 and his wife, Ann, died in 1694 at the age of 91. This same John Firth is the one that that has been erroneously confused with the Quaker and, according to local tradition, was compelled to direct a party of Parliamentarian troopers to Kirkburton Parish Vicarage. The troopers had been sent to arrest the staunchly Royalist Vicar, Rev. Gamaliel Whittaker. John Firth managed to escape into the undergrowth of Boxing Wood, which is between Shelley and Kirkburton. Despite a search until nightfall he could not be found. The Captain of the troop became so frustrated by the loss of his prisoner that, as he and his men passed the Vicarage at Kirkburton, he discharged his gun at the window when a light and a face appeared. The shot killed Hester Whittaker, the wife of the Rev. Gamaliel Whittaker, as she was descending the staircase.

Whittaker was arrested and imprisoned in Manchester where he *'died in a month of grief and ill-usage.'* This was because he was a Royalist supporter.

The Quaker Firths of Lane Head recount an intriguing but fancifully embroidered version of this same story. John Firth served as a soldier in the Civil War. Tradition relates that he *'was in a regiment raised by 'Boswell' of Gunfit Hall (Gunthwaite), some thousand strong, every man six feet tall without his shoes.'* (3) Whilst garrisoned at Nottingham he was convinced by George Fox's preaching and became a Friend. Whether this John Firth resigned his commission from the army is not noted but it appears that soon afterwards *'a John Firth became obnoxious to the Royalists.'* A Royalist cavalry detachment was sent from Halifax to arrest him but having received prior warning he hid himself for sometime in a quarry at Skelmanthorpe. The Royalist soldiers discovered him in hiding and arrested him on the 12 January 1644. From that point onwards the events are identical to the first version of the story.

The Quaker version of the story can now finally be laid to rest and dismissed from any serious study of the Firths of Lane Head. John Firth of Shepley Hall did not become a Quaker nor could he have been convinced by Fox at Nottingham since Fox was not imprisoned there until 1648 and the events transpired in 1643. John Firth the Quaker was not born until 1645.

The first, and generally accepted, version of the story has the merit of a more substantial hypothesis. This is based on the replacement of the ardent Royalist Vicar ten months earlier by a Rev. Daniel Clark *'to officiate as vicar in this parish...and to receive the profitts of the said vicaridge for his paynes, till further orders bee taken by both Houses of Parliament.'* In the ebbing fortunes of this bitter civil war, which reflected the ecclesiastical bias of both sides, Holmfirth was stormed by Royalist troops and Whittaker was re-instated to the dissatisfaction of the large number of dissenters in the area. When the tide turned once more in favour of Parliament the fate of Gamaliel Whittaker was sealed. Whatever the real truth of the tradition it sharply illustrates the divided religious, as well as, political consciousness of the period.

The Firths family history can thus be said to begin with the shadowy John Firth who was the father of Joseph Firth I. When exactly he became a Friend is a matter of pure conjecture but he is known to have been persecuted for his beliefs in 1683. (See 'Early Persecutions'). MM minutes between 1672-1700 make no mention of John Firth of Shepley Lane Head. Nor is there any record of his death although the probability is that may have died in 1694/5 when Lane Head had to be re-licenced under his son's name.

Joseph Firth married a Martha Haigh in 1678. He had three children. Joseph II (1684-1735) married Hannah Dickinson (1684-1765), who was the daughter of Edward and Sarah Dickinson. Mary married Elihu Dickinson in 1705 and Sarah married Caleb Dickinson in 1709. Joseph Firth II also had three children: Joseph III, Hannah and Thomas. Joseph Firth III (1711-1787) married Martha Greenwood (d.1763) from Langfield near Todmorden. Hannah Firth married twice: firstly, to Joseph Clark of Upper Haugh (by whom she had a daughter), and then to George Walker of Doncaster. Thomas Firth, the youngest son, married Mary Crosland of Oldfield Nook near Scholes. This Thomas removed to Huddersfield and both he and his son, Thomas Firth II, became influential figures in the development of Quakerism in the Huddersfield, Rastrick and Brighouse areas. (4) John Firth (1752-1830) was the only son of Joseph III. He married Ann Burrows in 1780. Together, they had four children: Jane (1783-1831), Joseph IV (b.1775), John (1790-1847) and Thomas (b.1797).

Joseph I is recorded as having licenced his house at Lane Head as a place of worship in 1695 (even though John Firth had undertaken the same in 1689). Little else is known of him other than that, in modern parlance, he kept a 'low profile' in the affairs of the Society. Joseph II and Joseph III were very much more active Friends. Throughout their lives they attended to the affairs of Lane Head as a meeting house and regularly travelled to MM and QM as representatives.

During the lifetimes of Joseph II and III the fortunes of the Firth family were amassed. They were farmers and there is no indication in the Lane Head/High Flatts branch of the family records that they were ever involved in the wool trade like many of the other Quaker families. Joseph Firth III ploughed with two yoke of oxen named respectively, Matthew, Mark, Luke and John. John Firth's occupation is given as that of Maltster. The Firths gradually became amongst some of the largest landowners in the vicinity of Shepley. They appear to have acquired a great deal of land during the common land enclosures of 1820. According to one historian they appeared to have got more land than many of their neighbours and became the subject of a popular saying of the time:

*'Firths o't' Lane Head and the Tinkers o' t' Carr,
Went up Nabs Cliffs as far as they dar.'* (5)

A map of the Shepley enclosures dating from 1829 showing the ownership of land reveals that there might well have been some truth to the allegation.

Thomas Firth I (1722-1782), the son of Joseph Firth II and Hannah Dickinson, established a business in Huddersfield as a drysalter. In his early days he resided in the town during the week, paying 3s 6d for his accomodation at the Horse Shoe Inn at the bottom of Kirkgate, then travelled home to Lane Head at weekends. Thomas Firth's drysalting business prospered and he became a very wealthy man. His hobby was the love of horses and he had the reputation of owning the best hunter in Huddersfield. By his wife, Mary Crosland, he had four children: Joseph (1786-1822), Grace (1758-1846), Robert (1760-1828) and Thomas (1762-1831) of Toothill. His story, and his children's stories, rightly belong to the history of Huddersfield but are here included to complete this history of the Firths of Lane Head.

John Firth II and his son Joseph Firth IV continued the family tradition but by their day Lane Head had ceased to be a meeting house. Their allegiance was inevitably towards the meeting at High Flatts where, as the influence of the Dickinson families declined, they became one of the leading Quaker families in the area. Ann Firth (1759-98) was the daughter of Edward and Ann Burrow of Foulstone in the compass of Preston Patrick Meeting in Westmorland. She removed with her parents to Bentham Meeting in Yorkshire in 1777 and thence to Otley. It was there that she married John Firth. She was described in the Leeds Mercury of June 1780 as *'the handsome young Lady with £1000 fortune.'* This fortune was not, however, received from the Burrow family. Some time after her marriage she was appointed clerk of the Womens Meeting, *'which service she discharged much to the satisfaction of Friends.'* Some time after this Ann Firth became an Overseer. In 1796, in company with George Chapman, John Bottomley and Joseph Wood, she engaged on a religious visit to the families of High Flatts Friends *'as were negligent in the due attendance of Week Day Meetings.'* She died of jaundice at the age of 39 and was interred at High Flatts. Her funeral, according to Joseph Wood who wrote her testimony, was attended by one of the largest gathering ever seen. The following extract from her testimony provides a pen sketch of this plain Friend.

'...her deportment was grave, weighty, and instructive intermingled with an innocent cheerfulness, which rendered her Company both pleasing and profitable. She filled up the several duties of life, with great propriety, being an affectionate wife, a prudent mother, not indulgent, but endeavouring to restrain her offspring from everything that might have had a tendency to corrupt their tender minds. A good neighbour and a kind friend, sympathetic with the afflicted in body and mind...a lover of the company of the faithful without respect of persons, adorning her profession by a consistence therewith in dress and demeanour. In a word she was a good example to all around her.'

John Firth III (1790-1847) was the second son of John Firth and Ann Burrow. After spending 4 years at Ackworth he was apprenticed to Godfrey Woodhead of Fulstone. He appears to have been the first of the Firths to become directly involved in the wool trade because he is described as *'a clothier of Foulstone.'* Together with his brother-in-law, Samuel Woodhead, he established a partnership in the textile trade. On the 18th September 1817 he married Mary Dickinson, the daughter of Elihu Dickinson the Clothier and Martha Beaumont, at High Flatts. After their marriage they settled at Low House in High Flatts until his death. They had no issue. (6)

During his youth he was described as being *'rough and boisterous'* but it appears that he experienced a gradual spiritual deepening *'so that in later life few men exceeded him in the exercise of Christian kindness and sympathy with the afflictions and trials of his friends.'* (7)

John Firth is remembered for establishing a First Day School in his own home for the boys and girls of poor parents in the neighbourhood. This First Day School ran for many years *'and was a marked influence for good on the character of the children who attended it.'* (8)

As an influential member of the local community he frequently used intermediaries to anonymously perform acts of charity to the needy so that neither they nor his family would know who was responsible. Renown for his *'good natural understanding, discriminating judgement and sound sense'* he looked upon himself as a custodian of his material possessions. John Firth III was regarded as a valued member of High Flatts Meeting: *'the gravity of his deportment and the weight of his spirit in meeting for worship were very instructive.'* Like his forebearers he resisted the payment of tithes and church rates and appeared three times in five weeks before the magistrates for neglecting to pay church rates in 1841. He died at the age of 57 after having suffered for some three years from a disease affecting the brain. Towards the end he had *'lucid intervals'* but the attacks which he suffered grew more intense and violent. He is buried at High Flatts.

Joseph Firth IV was a land agent and valuer. However, like his brother, he served an apprenticeship with Godfrey Woodhead to become a clothier but never took up the profession. He married Hannah Pickard (1786-1865) of Painthorp, Sandal Magna near Wakefield. Her testimony records that:

'Throughout her long life she was a member of Pontefract Monthly Meeting, serving for some years as an Elder, and for 18 years as a recorded minister...most valued for her faithful attendance at meetings for worship and for business affairs, and her judgement was greatly valued.' (9)

John III's and Joseph IV's younger brother, Thomas became a Tea-dealer. He first attended a dame school run by Dame Oxley at the bottom of Paradise Lane in Shepley before being sent to Jane Wood of Haddenley to be taught to read and write. For a short period after this he attended schools in Shepley, Shelley and Thurstonland. Later he attended a school at Kirkburton, run by the Curate of the church, walking three miles there and back to Lane Head every school day. After leaving the school at Kirkburton he spent two years at Ackworth at a cost of £18 12s 9d p.a. In 1811 he was apprenticed to Broadhead & Cudworth Tea-dealers of Leeds. Upon the completion of his apprenticeship he set up in business for himself in Kirkgate, Huddersfield and no longer resided at Lane Head. The business flourished and he realized a considerable fortune. For 25 years he was the local treasurer of the British & Foreign Bible Society and upon his retirement he was elected Vice-President for life as a mark of respect. This office had been held almost continually since its inception by members of the Society of Friends. (He succeeded his namesake Thomas Firth of Toothill, who in turn had been the successor of Robert Firth of Firth House). An active member of the Temperance Society, and a generous subscriber to its funds, Thomas Firth was fond of recounting how he had taken his last glass of wine on the day of Queen Victoria's coronation. During his lifetime he was a Director of the Huddersfield Savings Bank and one of the town's Commissioners concerned with Improvements and the Water Works. Upon his retirement he lived in Greenhead Road, Huddersfield, looked after by two elderly sisters who acted as his housekeepers. He died in 1879 at the age of 82, never having married, highly esteemed by his fellow townsmen and leaving a number of legacies to a variety of religious, social and educational charities.

Joseph Firth V (1814-1873), was the son of Joseph IV and Hannah Pickard. He was educated at Ackworth School (1826-28) and then joined his father's business as a land agent and valuer. From an early age he became involved in the Temperance movement and throughout his life upheld *'the principle of total abstinence.'* On the 10th September 1846 he married Sarah King of Rochdale and settled at Carr Hill until 1860 when they moved to High Flatts. He is recorded as becoming an elder of the meeting in 1863 and as a minister in 1869. It is said of him that *'he often acted as peacemaker, and was often sought as a safe counsellor.'* His home was always open to entertain Friends. He died, nineteen years before his wife Sarah, aged 58 at Harrogate.

Sarah King Firth (1811-1892) was the daughter of James and Rachel King of Rochdale. Her father was a cotton warp-maker. She became a recorded minister of Pontefract MM and the following description of Sarah King Firth provides us with a brief cameo of her:

'Her house at Highflatts was a well known centre of true Christian hospitality; and she was, whilst health and strength permitted, diligent in the exercise of the gift in the ministry which had been conferred upon her. Whilst sensible of the responsibilities which a position of influence entailed, she had humble estimate of herself; and that true poverty of spirit, to which the Divine blessing is attached, seemed often the covering of her mind.' (10)

The next of the Firth's to be mentioned was not born a Firth but was the son of Joseph Bottomley, a woolstapler of Westroyd in Shepley. Also called Joseph, he was born in 1842 at Dobroyd in Shepley. His mother was Ann Firth, the eldest daughter of Joseph Firth IV. He was educated at Ackworth Friends School. Later in life, and for reasons which still remain shrouded in uncertainty, he took his uncle's surname by Royal Warrant in 1873 thus becoming Joseph Bottomley Firth. It is likely that he became 'adopted' into the family. Joseph Bottomley Firth married Eliza W. Tatham, the youngest daughter of the Quaker Mayor of Leeds. They had two children: Mary Georgina Tatham Firth and Joseph George Tatham Firth. After attending Ackworth he studied Law at London University and was awarded an LL.B Degree in 1873. In that same year he was called to the bar and served on the North-Eastern Circuit. He was a member of the London School Board for Chelsea from 1876 to 1879. From 1880-85 he was the M.P. for Chelsea Division and then in 1888 he was elected as M.P. for Dundee. From 1876 to 1888 he wrote numerous speeches and publications concerned with the reform of local government in London. In 1876 he published 'Municipal London: or, London Government as it is, and London under a Municipal Council'. When the London County Council was formed in 1888 he was appointed its vice-chairman at a salary of £2000 a year. He died at the age of 47 on the 3rd September 1889 of a heart attack at Chamounix in Switzerland whilst taking a brief holiday. (11)

The last of the Firth's of Shepley Lane Head was Mary Firth (1826-1898). She was the daughter of Joseph IV and Hannah Firth. She was educated at Ackworth and then spent the rest of her life at Lane Head. Mary Firth's obituary in the 'Huddersfield Examiner' contained the following words:

'Her memory will be long and gratefully cherished not only by Friends, but by the inhabitants of the village generally, to whom she endeared herself. The poor especially found in her a true and sympathetic friend, and any appeal made to her for the relief of human suffering was sure of a cheerful and ready response. The beauty and excellence of her character was unconsciously revealed by her self denying efforts to brighten and better the lives of others. The causes of religion, education, temperance and philanthropy have lost in the death of Miss Firth a warm-hearted friend and generous supporter. Though loyal and true to the Society of Friends, she was most tolerant of other peoples opinions and methods of worhsip. There is no church or institution in the village but has been cheered by her genial presence and assisted by her manifold gifts... Her very presence was at once stimulating and inspiring.'

Upon her death Lane Head passed to her nieces, Mary Ann and Helen Wood, who used the house as a summer residence until 1920. The house finally passed from Quaker hands when Georgiana Firth Lowe and Joseph George Lowe sold it to William Hallitt of Huddersfield.

(1) MS Typescript 'The Firths of Shepley Lane Head' anon. (Firth?) lodged HDL and dated as 1878.
(2) KRP Vol.I See entries 10123 & 10279 John Firth married Elizabeth Senier May 1644. John, son of John Firth baptized 1645.
(3) The various versions of the John Firth story can be found in:
   (a) MS typescript above mentioned.
   (b) Henry Morehouses 'History of Kirkburton & Graveship of Holme'
   (c) KRP Vol.II Appendix ccxli.
(4) For a detailed study of the Huddersfield, Rastrick & Brighouse branch of the Firth family W. Newton Dawson's idiosyncratic book 'History on your doorstep' 1973 should be consulted. (See Chapter on 'The Firths & Fryers' p.165-190).
(5) Quoted in 'History of Penistone' J.N. Dransfield pub.1906 p.83-4.
(6) QBBREG1
(7) DQB and associated sources.
(8) Ibid.
(9) Ibid.
(10) Testimony of Pontefract MM 1892.
(11) KRP Vol.II Appendix cccxli

The Woods of Newhouse

The Wood family began its long association with Newhouse when Abraham Wood (1673-1747) of Wetherwood Hall married Rebecca Green (?1680-1744) at High Flatts Meeting in 1703. His grandfather was Abraham Wood (b.1624) of Shelley and his parents were John (b.1647) and Jane Wood (nee Haigh). (1) When his mother died his father remarried but did not survive his first wife for more than a few years. Upon John Wood's death, Grace Wood, Abraham's step-mother also remarried. At the age of about eleven the orphaned Abraham Wood was apprenticed by his step-father, Richard Mallinson, to Joshua Broadhead of Wooldale to learn the trade of a clothier. There is no evidence to show that the Woods were Quakers at this time but it is possible that Richard Mallinson may have been a Friend. (2) It is likely that young Abraham, if not brought up as a Quaker by his parents or step-father, probably became one under the influence of Joshua Broadhead (d.1715). After their marriage Abraham and Rebecca Wood settled at Newhouse with Joshua Green. (3) Joshua Green died at Newhouse in 1710 and Abraham took over the tenancy of the farm. According to family records he was granted a 21 year lease on the property by William Bosville at £14 0s 6d per annum. The rental records for Captain Bosville's Estate, Martinmas 1722, confirm this to be correct disclosing the half-yearly payment of £7 0s 3d by Abraham Wood to his landlord.

Abraham Wood, in keeping with many others in the locality, divided his time between running the farm and working as a clothier. In 1709 he signed an indenture with Bartholomew Hoyle of Cumberworth. This was for the usual seven years to teach the youth the trade of a clothier. Abraham Wood was a thrifty and hardworking Quaker who during his lifetime was in a position to loan sums of £200 to Edmund Knight of Sands (1734) and £400 to Joseph Broadhead (1745).

He and his wife had seven children: Mary (b.1704), John (1706-1791), Hannah (b.1708), Sarah (1710-1724), Joseph (1713-1742), Abraham (b.1716), and Samuel (1719-1791). When Abraham Wood died at the age of 74 Newhouse passed into the hands of his youngest son. Samuel Wood, like his father, was both a clothier and a farmer. He was formally apprenticed to his father to learn the trade of a clothier: an indenture being signed by them in 1713. Later in life he would apprentice his own son, Joseph, to learn the same trade from himself, just as his own father had done. Samuel Wood also proved to be such a good farmer that his landlord, William Bosville, offered him an indefinite lease on Newhouse for £24 a year. He thrived and prospered despite the fact that he *'was a heretic (dissenter) and as such was persecuted for the good of his soul, and so to prevent the loss of his soul his body was sent to York Castle for non-payment of tithes for 3 months.'* Upon his release from York he walked the forty miles to Newhouse and on arrival mowed a half-acre of land. This kind of industry he extended to his work as a clothier making 2 pieces of cloth each week — a considerable quantity in those days of hand-loom weaving. It was no wonder that, shortly before his death, he could remark *'he had spent his full hat of silver in fencing the farm.'* Considering the size of a Quaker hat and the value of silver we can assume that he had managed to accumulate a small personal fortune through his hard working life. Yet this energetic Quaker also made a point of allowing himself one holiday every year. When the harvest had been gathered and the nuts were brown and ripe he would take the day off to go *'nutting and would gather a bee-hive full of nuts.'* An anecdotal tale is also recounted about the pony owned by Samuel Wood to carry his finished cloth to market. Moggy, as this pony was called, was equal to any such animal in the neighbourhood but never allowed herself to be overburdened refusing to carry more than one piece of cloth at a time.

Samuel Wood married Susannah Walker, the daughter of Joseph Walker of Shelley Paddock, in 1747. They had seven children: Joseph the preacher (1750-1821), Samuel (b.1752), Sarah (1754-1757), Mary (1756-1776), Abraham (1759-1774), Susannah (1762-1787) and Rebecca (1766-1790). Joseph Wood inherited Newhouse from his father and continued to work the land as a farmer as well as following his father in the occupation of a clothier. As the life of Joseph Wood is recounted in another part of the book it is not necessary to dwell on this distinguished member of the family. Since Joseph Wood never married Newhouse passed on his death in 1821 to his nephew, Robert Wood.

Joseph's younger brother, Samuel, married Mary Firth of Shepley Lane Head in 1780. They settled in Netherend near Denby, a substantial stone house built c.1663. Like his brother he was also a clothier and specialized in the manufacture of a kind of cloth called 'Tammy'. Unfortunately, Samuel was more addicted to hunting and shooting than working at his trade. When he found himself in debt he was forced to leave the area and go to Ireland while his friends and relatives settled matters with his creditors. He eventually returned to the district and settled on a small farm of about 9 acres at Haddenley. This was given to his wife by his father-in-law, Joseph Firth of Shepley Lane Head, presumably to save them from further disgrace. Whatever Samuel's best intentions were for the future he seems to have found difficulty in maintaining them. MM minutes divulge that, in 1816, he had *'been in the practice of attending Publick Houses unnecessarily, and drinking to excess.'* He was cautioned on this count by MM and appears to have responded to the caution. Samuel and Mary Wood had four children: Jane (b.1781) who married William Grimshaw, Robert (b.1782) who inherited Newhouse from his uncle, Joseph who married Mary Andrews and John who married Olivia Watson. When Robert Wood died Samuel went to live at Newhouse with his son's widow and her children. He died in 1842 and seems to have been much beloved by his grandchildren.

Robert Wood was born at Netherend and is known to have attended Ackworth School in 1809. He married Sarah Earnshaw, the daughter of John Earnshaw of Glodwick Clough near Oldham. They settled at the Nook, Moorbottom, Shelley. Besides running a small-holding he was was also a successful clothier and shopkeeper. However, his business appears to have suffered in those years of distress that followed the Napoleonic Wars as the price of goods began to fall. Robert lived the last nineteen years of his life at Newhouse where his three youngest children were born. He and Sarah had nine children: Samuel (died in infancy), Mary (1811-56), Ann (1813-37), Jane (b.1815), William (1818-47), Alfred (1820-94), John (1822-96), Eliza (1824-47) and Maria (1827-94). Robert died at Newhouse in 1840 and was buried at High Flatts. His wife died at Stockport in 1858. Mary, his eldest daughter, married Thomas

Wheeler of Stockport. Maria, the youngest daughter, married Joseph Lingford. As space prohibits a full account of the descendants of Robert Wood only a brief resume of his two eldest sons descendants is included.

Alfred Wood and Elizabeth Marshall were married in 1845. (See 'Wood & Burtt'). Elizabeth was described as a *'very beautiful girl'* who broke the conventions of her day by wearing a white Quaker bonnet instead of the black or grey silk ones that were then 'de rigueur'. They had 12 children: eight survived, three boys and five girls. Fredric Wood (1849) married Agnes Graham in 1879. He and his family, except for his son Albert Graham, emmigrated to the USA because Fredric *'would not tolerate living under the government of Lloyd George.'* Albert Graham Wood married Margaret Sterry Ashby and their grandson, James Wood, is presently the custodian of Joseph Wood's voluminous journal and other writings.

Alfred Wood's other son, Albert (b.1851) married Ann Moon in 1875. They had five children. Marian (b.1876) became Principal of Havergal College, Toronto, Canada. Elizabeth (b.1878) married James Jackson, a solicitor and alderman of Northampton. Harold Marshall Wood (b.1881) emmigrated to Canada and Irene Wood (b.1884) married Alfred Lynn. Charles Albert Wood (b.1886) married Cristine Wood in 1919 in Bombay, India: they had three daughters, Freya (b.1921), Millicent (b.1923) and Evelyn Veronica (b.1930).

Kelley's Directory for 1867, in a list of tradesmen, describes John Wood of Newhouse as a farmer and manure merchant. However, according to a small trade leaflet dated February 1880, it appears that he dealt in a wide range of fertilisers: bone meal, boiled bones for grinding and in particular *'Peruvian Guano.'* John Wood continued the long family tradition of farming whilst his brother continued in the other long established family tradition of textile manufacturing. The age when it was possible to perform both had by now disappeared. John Wood was an active Friend and an upholder of Friends testimony against tithes and church rates. In the Huddersfield Examiner of June 11, 1853 he is mentioned as having refused to pay a rate of one penny in the pound to Denby Chapelry. He was a life long teetotaler and a member of the Temperance Society. As has been previously mentioned, together with Joseph Firth, he helped to found the Day School at Birdsedge. He is known to have taught at least one of his farm-hands to write and to have been involved on many occasions in local Quaker charity work.

Around 1855 he appears to have been granted a 99 year lease on Newhouse by the Bosville Estate on the proviso that *'he expend £500 in building a House and improvements thereon.'* According to a letter from his solicitor, John Dransfield of Penistone, he was advised to *'take the opinion of a clever counsel on this point...'* John Wood appears not to have heeded this advice and the present Victorian house is the result of these improvements. His attitude towards the legal advise he received confirms that he was scrupulously honest in all his dealings. He was a principled man of integrity, highly respected and generous. The original 'Newhouse' appears to have then been vacated and left to crumble. It was finally pulled down during the late 1970's, by its present owner, Mr. David Mallinson, having reached a ruinous state.

During the early part of the summer of 1986, whilst repairing a section of dry-stone walling near Newhouse, Mr. Mallinson uncovered an inscribed and deliberately concealed lead plaque (21cm x 21cm 8″ x 8″) bearing the following mysterious words:

'O thou tretcherous rogue John Wood of Newhouse Denby Dale I make this that thou rest not night nor day but be like the waters of the troubled sea tossed too and fro without a resting place and that thou cannot sleep night nor day nor that thou cannot die untill thou confess the wrong that thou hast done me TG & JG and my fathers house by aiding and assisting a forged will and robbing him and all his sons out of land and money signed in the mighty name of God

AMEN'

The authors have not been able to find out the story behind this strange curse and its message but it would seem to indicate that there were those who were prepared to attack John Wood in a most underhand manner resorting to some form of magic. The back of the plaque is inscribed with a matrix of numbers. The pattern is recognizable as a 9 x 9 magic square identified with the Moon and Saturn. The plaque was probably concealed after 1850 and before John Wood's death in 1896.

Whatever the intentions of the spell, with all its efforts to derive potency through numerical and astrological symbolism, they were a miserable failure. Nothing ever happened to John Wood. The weight of evidence overwhelmingly points against the originators of this deed. It would not have been in keeping with John Wood's character to forge a will and deprive a family of its inheritance. Those who knew him intimately, like his daughter-in-law, Evelyn, ('*a shrewd judge of character*') would easily have detected any disgraceful conduct. The identities of TG and JG are a complete mystery but it seems fairly clear that if they had any cause for genuine grievance they were certainly not prepared to confront John Wood openly about it and instead resorted to a well concealed malicious slur. Their actions speak for themselves: '*by their fruits ye shall know them.*'

John Wood (1822-1896) and Jane Firth of Shepley Lane Head married in 1845. They had three daughters, Mary Ann, Eliza, and Helen. Jane Firth died in 1850 and of her three daughters only Eliza married (Jonathan Jackson). Neither of her two children survived. John Wood remarried in 1857. He and Elizabeth Shepherd were married in Pardshaw Meeting House. By his second wife he had two sons. Walter Wood (b.1859) married Elsie Smith, an American, and settled in the USA. William Herbert ('*Will*') (1861-1902) married Evelyn Emily Bayes of London. (4) They had two children: Cristine (b.1895) and Robert (1898-1959). The story concerning Cristine Wood's name is also worthy of mention. She was rightly named Christine but her aunt, Rosamond Bayes, raised an objection. In true plain Quaker tradition she stated that '*no human being could be worthy to bear the name of Christ.*' The 'h' was dropped.

When William Herbert Wood died of typhoid his wife and family removed from Newhouse thus ending nearly two centuries of family association. After their departure Newhouse then passed for a short time into the hands of another Quaker family: the Sadlers. (5)

(1) Kirkburton Parish Registers record an 'Abraham Wood and Elizabeth Armitage maried xxth' May 1644. (10098)
(2) The Mallinson family were prominent friends during the 18th Century but are not recorded as Friends in the 17th Century.
(3) According to family records she was the daughter of Joshua Green of Langsett who was then resident at Newhouse. QBBREG1, however, disputes this and gives her as the daughter of John Green of Langsett.
(4) It is largely due to Evelyn Emily Wood that the history of the Wood family was thoroughly mapped. Her notes, with later additions by Freya Wood who kindly passed on the notes to the authors, made this section possible.
(5) Anne Roberts (d.1672), an early Friend, is also given as having resided at Newhouse. After her it was occupied by other Quakers: Thomas and Martha Parkinson. (Martha d.1697). Joshua Green appears to have taken over Newhouse after 1697.

The Broadheads of Wooldale

During the seventeenth century two families bearing the surname Broadhead are recorded in local Quaker annals. The influential Broadheads of Burton and Monk Bretton and the Broadheads of Wooldale. It is possible, but not proven, that the two families were related.

The Wooldale Broadheads commence their Quaker origins with Joshua Broadhead (d.1660). (1) According to available evidence Joshua Broadhead did not become a Friend. He was twice married. His first wife was Ann Rooley whom he married in 1633. A year after her death he married Dorothy Robuck (d.1670). His second wife appears to have become a Quaker since she is amongst the earliest Friends to have been buried at Wooldale. (See 'Wooldale Meeting House'). By his first wife he had four children: Mary (b.1636), Anne (1638-1655), Robert (1640-1674) and Martha (1643-1671). Robert Broadhead, the only son, vested the burial ground at Wooldale to the Society of Friends upon his death. Since he was interred at that same burial ground and because his step-mother, Dorothy, was also buried there it can be inferred that he too was a Quaker. Very little else is known about Robert Broadhead except that he married Phebe Newton in 1671 and they had one daughter, Martha (1673-1674), with whom that family line ends.

Joshua Broadhead's second marriage resulted in eight children of whom five survived into adulthood: Elizabeth (b.1648), Joseph (1650-1684), Caleb (1652-1740), Joshua (1655-1715) and Daniel (d.1735). Caleb, Joshua and Daniel Broadhead were all active members of the Society of Friends.

Joshua was a clothier by occupation and apprenticed the young Abraham Wood to learn the trade. (See 'Woods of Newhouse'). No details concerning his marriage have been located since he was married prior to 1680. (No intentions of marriage are recorded in MM minutes before this date and there is no subsequent mention). He was the father of Robert Broadhead (1684-1769) of Mearhouse and Matthew Broadhead (d.1713) of Rawcliff.

Caleb and Daniel Broadhead were also clothiers. Caleb married Judeth Dickinson in 1678 (See 'The Dickinsons'). Daniel married Elizabeth Sanderson of Midhope in 1690. Caleb Broadhead, like his brother Joshua, resided in Wooldale. Daniel Broadhead removed to Grice Hall in Shelley.

As the number of descendants of these three brothers is so considerable a full genealogical account cannot be supplied. (Suffice it to say that Joshua Broadhead's son, Robert of Mearhouse, had 59 grandchildren from 10 of his 11 children). Therefore, only a brief outline of the various family branches and their members is included.

Caleb Broadhead's children included: Elizabeth Broadhead (1683-1773) who married Uriah Brook (See 'Uriah Brook of High Flatts') and her sister Martha (b.1694) who married Uriah's younger brother Epaphras. The story of Joseph and John Broadhead has already been recounted (See 'Joseph and John Broadhead' for extensive details). No local history would be complete without mention of 'long livers' and so it is worth noting the following facts: Caleb Broadhead lived to be 88. His daughter, Elizabeth ('Bessy' Brook) died at 90, and her two brothers, Joseph and John, both lived until they were 83. (Their cousin Robert Broadhead of Mearhouse reached 85). The decendants of Joseph and John formed the Wooldale Broadheads.

Daniel and Elizabeth Broadhead had six daughters and one son: Joseph (1691-1747) of Standinghurst. All the subsequent members of the Standinghurst branch are descended from Joseph.

From Robert Broadhead of Mearhouse came the Mearhouse, Meltom House and Ridings branches through his sons John (b.1719), Joshua (b.1721) and Daniel (b.1730) respectively. His other two remaining sons, Robert (b.1728) and Joseph (b.1736), removed to Sheffield where they both became grocers. Joseph Broadhead's son, James Broadhead of Sheffield, later removed to Leeds. It is probably the case that the later Quakers bearing the surname of Broadhead, in both Sheffield and Leeds, are descended from these two sons.

Matthew Broadhead's eldest son, Joshua (b.1712), established the later Lydgate, Biggin and New Mill branches which find mention in this book.

The Broadheads were by far the largest family grouping within Wooldale Meeting. They easily outnumbered the Earnshaws, Brooks, Woodheads and Haighs. Their descendants continued to be part of the meeting until 1872 when Jane Broadhead was the last recorded Friend with that surname. Then membership records reveal that Charles H. Broadhead and his wife Sarah Ann and their two children, Kate and John Greenleaf, began attending Wooldale in 1893. The final connection with the meeting appears to have been as late as the 1940's when Kate Broadhead's name still appeared on the membership list, even though she had by 1941 removed to Mold in Wales.

(1) Information on the Broadhead Family of Wooldale has been compiled from a wide variety of sources. These include:

(a) KRP Vols. I & II.
(b) QBBREG1
(c) MMMB 1672-1800
(d) Details supplied by John Wynne of Leeds.

EPILOGUE

During the eighteenth century the power and influence of the Quaker discipline upon its members had grown. It began to appear as the *raison d'etre* of the Society. The original personal religious experiences of early Friends were to a large degree lost. As the nineteenth century dawned there appeared to be little change in local Friends attitudes towards the Quaker discipline. This rigid adherence to the extreme discipline of plainess and conduct was to see the Society shrink from the 60,000 adherents of George Fox's day to approximately 13,500 members by the mid-nineteenth century. MM business during the first half of the nineteenth century was essentially dominated by investigations into alleged cases of misconduct. The number of such investigations resulting in disownments, due to breaking the rules of discipline, appear to have been on occasion of epidemic proportions. By far the largest number of disownments were for marrying out of the Society. There were also numerous *'cases of difficulty.'* The decline in membership can largely be attributed to this excessive and stifling discipline. However, it is interesting to note that we have substantial evidence at High Flatts and Wooldale of a continued and close association of disowned members with their meetings. Joseph Wood records in 1814 the visit of Sarah Lamley from Worcestershire and Ann Fairbank of Sheffield to the families of High Flatts *'who pretty duly attend Meetings.'* Of the sixty families that they visited fourteen were *'...such as one or both of the heads of families were disowned but continue to attend Meetings.'* (1) High Flatts certainly appeared to have commanded a strong loyalty from local people even when the discipline had been broken.

The Society finally came to a realization in the 1850's that its self-inflicted stranglehold had to be broken otherwise it would destroy itself. Interestingly enough the initiative for this came from Yorkshire QM. By 1861 a complete revision of the Book of Discipline was agreed. At last a breath of freedom began to blow through the Society. Attitudes and actions did not, however, change with any rapidity. (See 'The Last Disownment').

This, too, was the period when relief work saw an expansion. Friends no longer solely confined themselves to immediate and local problems. During the nineteenth century there were notable instances of relief given to the Germans suffering as a result of Napoleon's territorial ambitions and the Irish whose national economy had collapsed when the potato crops repeatedly failed. (See 'Charities and Poor Relief'). There was also a greater local awareness of the wider consequences of the historical Quaker stance on peace. (See 'Upholding the Peace Testimony').

The nineteenth century was also the century of evangelicalism. Rooted in Methodism it soon spread into other Christian denominations including Quakerism. Evangelical Friends were in part born of a reaction to the Quietism of the previous century. No matter what influence evangelicalism appeared to have on the wider Quaker world it left local Friends virtually untouched and unmoved. Evangelical Friends like Stephen Grellet and Joseph John Gurney, who visited the area, made little if any impression upon them. The Beaconite schism of the 1830's, fired by the fervour of Isaac Crewdson of Manchester, also failed to have any effect locally. The orthodoxy of Quietism remained deeply ingrained. As late as 1870 there was a marked reluctance and suspicion of evangelical ideas. At Wooldale the notion of formal Bible study groups and the enforced use of the Scriptures was treated with considerable coolness as this minute indicates:

'We have read the minute of the M. Meeting requesting friends to take into consideration the question of meeting together for the reading & prayerful consideration of the Scriptures & consider to let it alone officially, we are informed that a few do meet together for this practice.' (2)

Similar reactions were recorded to similar questions: in 1879 no *'...definite action in the matter...'* (3) could be taken and in 1891 *'...no collective action in the matter...'* (4) could be followed. Finally, in 1896, after long discussions it was decided to allow the reading of a passage of Scripture at the start of Meeting for Worship.

There was also an increasing concern for education with both Wooldale and High Flatts becoming involved in schemes centred on their meeting houses. (See 'Education'). This was all part of a widening concern for the welfare and development of young people within the meetings. During the 1850's comprehensive reports from each of the PM's were sent up to MM detailing numbers of children and their situation. In 1857 High Flatts had ten boys and ten girls all of whom, excepting one, were living with their parents. The single exception lived with an employer. However, only six were actual members. Wooldale had one girl living with her parents and four boys living with their employers. All were members except for one boy. (5) Reading Meetings organized by High Flatts were also mentioned in 1857 which by 1858 had gained considerable support. Report was made that two regular meetings were held: one at High Flatts, the other at Shepley. One meeting was attended mainly by the young with an average attendance of about thirty. The other was attended chiefly by adults with an attendance of about twenty. (6) Public meetings were also organized in surrounding villages and towns like Skelmanthorpe and Holmfirth.

Radical changes, in both thought and action within the Society, appear to have been accepted very slowly, if at all, in the local meetings. The decline in membership with a marked conservatism, geared to maintaining rigid discipline amongst these inward-looking country meetings, probably ensured the loss of many potential Quakers.

The Manchester Conference of 1895 is recognized as a turning point in Quaker history. It was perhaps the most significant event in the movement away from the evangelicalism of the later nineteenth century to Quaker thought and attitude as we know it today. However, as often is the case, quiet rural areas like Wooldale and High Flatts were slow to react. There is little evidence in local records to show the renewal and liberalism that followed this conference. New ideas took time to be accepted. It was not till 1905 in Wooldale that the following happened:

'Having received a suggestion from Women Friends that in future our PM be held in joint session the clerk is instructed to write to clerk of womens meeting to welcome women Friends to join our PM's.' (7)

The number of members at High Flatts had been steadily declining for many years and continued to do so. Wooldale membership had shown a growth in the latter part of the nineteenth century but this began to level off and then decline well into this century. Both meetings had Adult Schools on their premises in the early 1900's. These were not to last long. Nor did there appear to be great involvement in the running of the schools by local Friends. The Triennial Reports that each PM submitted to MM at this time are revealing. The problem of the small meeting was highlighted by Wooldale in 1901:

'We have very greatly appreciated the Visits which have been paid under the auspices of the Quarterly and Monthly Meeting interchange of Visits Committee and think that they have seriously increased the amount of interest that is taken in Church affairs: it is doubtful whether Members of large meetings can fully appreciate the help that such visits are felt to be in country places even though there may not be much apparent result at the time.' (8)

The 1910 Wooldale Triennial Report detailed the decline in numbers attending. This had been chiefly caused by removals and had resulted in evening and midweek meetings being poorly attended. Shortly after the report these meeting were discontinued. Sadly, report was made of *'a lack of vitality amongst us. Also it was noted that sometimes meetings were held in complete silence.'* (8) A similar pattern of removals was noted at High Flatts:

'...the younger members are constantly moving away to the towns where they can make a better living.' (9)

In times of decline there tends to be reflection upon past times. The 1913 Triennal Report from High Flatts was very much in this reflective vein. They reported being discouraged as they recalled *'...large and prosperous meetings of former years and the many honoured Friends then resident who were valiant for the Truth.'* The report continued:

'And yet gathering here in the shade of those who have passed away, & the calm & quiet of the old Meeting House, something of their spirit still lingers, & we are permitted to feel that He who was the strength & stay of their lives is round about us still, ready & willing to minister to the various needs of each worshipper who is seeking communion with Him in spirit & in truth.' (10)

During the 1920's, 1930's and 1940's many times no representatives were sent to MM from Wooldale or High Flatts. When MM queried the reason for this in 1927 Wooldale replied, stating the facts very precisely, and with some irony:

'A letter from MM Clerk has been read on the question of non-attendance at MM's & the matter has been very carefully discussed. Our mtg. is a very small one & age, health & absence from home prevents half of our members from ever being at MM's. Of the few who can attend the chief reason that we have difficulty in sending reps. is because Friends so frequently have occupations or other engagements, though it was also realized that lack of interest played a considerable part.' (11)

During this century there was some effort to enliven the proceedings at MM. This was centred on the High Flatts gathering in June. The first weekend MM conference was held in 1910. All attenders and Friends in the MM were invited as well as Friends from more distant MM's. The following extract gives some indication of the weekend's events:

'...The response to the 370 invitations issued was large; over 50 settlers were in residence for all or part of the time, a much larger number being present during the daytime. ...The informal ten minute address's on 'Friends Witness to Truth' by Ernest Dodgshun, James H. Heighton, Ralph Nettleton and John Sadler were felt to be especially timely and servicable... ...Settlers were freed from further outlay than that incurred in their own travelling expense, the general cost of the weekend being met by a fund raised privately for the purpose. ...Wooldale Meeting and Adult School was attended by visitors on First day morning. High Flatts Friends gave themselves to the service of the weekend with zeal and self-forgetfulness. The many letters and personal testimonies received encouraged the impression that the helpfulness and warm-hearted fellowship experienced were felt generally to be very real...' (12)

These weekend conferences at High Flatts were repeated on a number of occasions over the following years although never quite on so large a scale.

It was during the 1950's that Wooldale and High Flatts Meetings were at their lowest ebb. In this period PM minutes make very uninspiring reading. They are purely a catalogue of duties pruned to the essential minimum. Wooldale reported in 1955 that on a number of occasions no one had been present at Meeting for Worship on a Sunday. One of our members, Edward Darke, recalls finding Wooldale in 1952:

'...As I stood at the gate and looked at the simple but impressive old building, surrounded and once hung by great trees, I felt an intruder... Inside we heard voices upstairs. So up the stone stairs we climbed and found three people, all elderly, sitting on the front of several rows of dark wooden benches. The three were Edward and Dorothy Burtt and Alice Stephens, they welcomed us and and we settled at a discrete distance and sank into a pondering quiet. ...Alice Stephens said how pleased they were to see us and added that she thought we should find Wooldale a quiet and stable meeting...'

At Wooldale in the late 1960's and early 1970's the decline was arrested and membership gradually began to increase and vitality return. The building was repaired and made more welcoming and attractive. Today it is a thriving meeting. There is a midweek Meeting for Worship once again as well as one each Sunday. There are also midweek meeting discussion groups and a regular twice monthly childrens meeting. Other activities revolving around the meeting include a walking group, music, organized holidays, day trips and young Friends activities. The story at High Flatts has been somewhat similar although at a gentler pace. Their membership has gradually grown over the past few years with those joining taking an active part in the life of the meeting. Gone are the days when meetings at High Flatts were only held on two Sundays in the month and the PM was given up in favour of an Allowed Meeting. The future for both meetings appears to be promising.

As the authors reflect on the fascinating tapestry of the past they cannot help but look forward into the future. What will the rest of this century and the next add to this story? Only present and future Friends will be able to determine the outcome. Will the new life and vitality that is evident in the two meetings today continue? As we reflect on our past special mention should be made of the families of this century (the Burtts and Stephens of Wooldale and the Cooks and Netherwoods of High Flatts), who, in times of decline, kept faith and provided that essential bridge between the Friends of today and the 'Plain Country Friends' of the past.

(1) Joseph Wood Memorandum Book No.34
(2) (W)PMMB 1870
(3) Ibid 1879
(4) Ibid 1891
(5) MMMB 1857
(6) Ibid 1858
(7) (W)PMMB 1905
(8) (W)PMMB 1901
(9) (W)PMMB 1910
(10) MMMB 1907
(11) MMMB 1913
(12) (W)PMMB 1927
(13) MMMB 1910

BRICKS AND MORTAR

A SUPPLEMENT

The Origins of Wooldale Meeting

There were Quakers in the area as early as 1654. Where they met is unknown but almost certainly it would have been in the private houses and barns of the early converts. During this period of Quaker persecution, imprisonment and confiscation of property was common and it was very difficult to meet openly. The earliest reference to Wooldale, or *'Woodaille'*, is recorded in a list of towns associated with Denby Meeting *'A qrterly meeting at Yorke, ye 18th Day of ye 1th Mo: 1668/9.'* (1) Precisely where Friends met in Wooldale cannot be stated with any certainty.

Henry Jackson held meetings at his various homes when not imprisoned. Totties Hall was certainly not used as a place of worship until after 1682-84, the date of its erection. The earliest PM minute book remaining is the Women's PM minute book (1713-42) where reference is made to meetings held at Totties, Sheephouse and Lane Head. Totties Hall is last mentioned as a meeting place in 1714. The first mention of Wooldale in this book is in 1720. However, the evidence in this and the next section points to a meeting place existing in Wooldale before 1689. This may have been on the existing site of the present meeting house or in houses adjoining the present property.

In attempting to trace the origins of Wooldale Meeting House the authors came across three local traditions. One of these had to be entirely discounted and no documentary evidence could be found to support the other two traditions.

The first tradition concerns Hill End Farm, above Snowgate Head, which is more than 350 years old. It has been used as a home, barn and weaving shed. It is known that local Luddites visited it in 1812. Over one part of the house is an upper room, now a bedroom, that has an outside doorway onto the hillside. Tradition has it that this room was used during the persecutions for a meeting place and that the 'secret' door was a quick means of escape onto the hillside. As early Friends were not in the habit of escaping, preferring to be arrested rather than leave their worship, this detracts from the credibility of the tradition. It is worth noting, however, that Hill End is in one of the areas that had the highest concentration of Quaker homes.

The second tradition brings us back into Wooldale and concerns a building behind a cottage in Lower Townend Road. This appears to have been two storey and once again tradition relates that the upper room was used as an early meeting place for Friends. On one wall of this building are some tall narrow recessed arches, the purpose of which has yet to be explained. The remains of this building can be seen from the back of the burial ground. Its very proximity to the graveyard makes it a possible site for a meeting place. The other building that could have been used is Pell Croft above the present Meeting House: this was a Quaker occupied house for many generations.

The third tradition turned out to have no substance. A group of buildings called 'The Heys' at Thongsbridge were reputed to be an old Quaker meeting house. On subsequent investigation they were found to date back to the nineteenth century. These buildings, consisting of a small chapel and a terrace of houses built as a self contained community, were originally built by a group of Primitive Methodists.

(1) JFHS Supplement 'Meetings in Yorkshire' p.33

Wooldale Meeting House

The present graveyard was vested in trustees in 1673 by Robert Broadhead (d.1674) of Wooldale:

'To and for the use of such people as walk in the feare of the Lord, in and about Wooldale, Holmfirth, and therewayes, and are com'only called Quakers, for a possession of burying place for them freely to burye their dead in forever. And to or for the intent and purpose that the same may remaine and continue for a possession of a burying-place for all such as out of conscience towards God, have separated from Idolatry and Idolized places, for them freely to bury in forever.' The deed, however, provides that in case 'at any time hereafter any default be found, or cause of forfeiture in law by reason of the uncertainty of its present use, then the said premises to remain to the use and behoof of the said trustees therein mentioned, and their heirs forever. To the intent that they and their heirs, etc., shall with rents and profits thereof, yearly relieve and succour such poore people as stand in need, according to their discre'cons successively forever.' (1)

However, by reference to the digest register of births and burials of Yorkshire QM refering to Pontefract MM it appears that the burial ground was in use earlier. There are five recorded burials at *'Wooldale'* prior to 1673:

>Sarah Batty, of Wooldale, buried 14/6/1664
>Sarah Roberts, buried 29/2/1667
>Dorothy Broadhead, of Wooldale, buried 23/6/1670
>Mary Foster, of Foulstone, buried 12/2/1671
>Martha Broadhead, of Wooldale, buried 27/8/1671

Sarah Batty was the wife of Richard who was imprisoned in York in 1660 and 1661 for refusing to swear the Oath of Allegiance. Dorothy Broadhead was Robert Broadhead's wife and Martha was his daughter. None of these five burials appear in the Kirkburton Parish Registers thus confirming that they were not buried on Church property. The earliest recorded burial for High Flatts is that of Elizabeth Crosley in 1690 and for Hoyland Swaine that of Benjamin Jackson in 1681. This makes the Wooldale burials the earliest recorded in the MM except for some at Burton. However, it should be further noted that in this digest the majority of the earliest burials have no entry under the heading 'Place of Burial'.

The graveyard is described in the title deeds as being, *'...by estimation Nineteen Rods in length and eleven rods in breadth and the same now enclosed with a wall lying and being at the lower end of a close called Pell Croft and adjoining upon the high road called Pell Lane...'* (2)

A rod in this context should be interpreted as a measuring rod or yard. Thus the original plot of land was approximately 19 x 11 yards in area. It can be assumed that this first acquisition covered the area to the immediate front of the meeting house. The first trustees were Henry Jackson, Henry Dickinson, Thomas Roberts and Thomas Ellis.

It is uncertain exactly when the first meeting house was built. The following evidence can be considered:

'At our Monthly Meeting at Burton this 10th day of ye 2nd month 1690 Joseph Kay of Meal-hill a member of Wooldale Meeting did this day publish his intention of Marriage with Elizabeth Ellis of Wooldale a member ye said Meeting...' (3)

This is the first mention that can be traced of *'Wooldale Meeting'* in MM minutes. Our next clue comes from the registration of dissenting houses of worship: this arose following the Act of Toleration (1689) which allowed the Quakers, and other sects, the right to follow their own forms of worship. We find recorded for 1689 the following:

'...Itt is Ordered that the houses of the said all persons herunder written viz. ...Henry Jackson...and one meeting house in Wooldale all of them within the sd. Rid. be recorded as places for Religious Worship...' (4)

So as well as Henry Jackson's house (Totties Hall) we know that there was a public meeting house in 1689 if not before. If we follow the registration of meeting houses the following entry for 1713 appears:

'It is ordered that the House lately built at Wooldale within the Graveship of Holme be recorded.' (5)

This also probably refers to our meeting house although in the entry the denomination is not mentioned nor is it linked with known Quakers such as Henry Jackson.

We need also to consider the evidence of Yorkshire QM records. There is listed in the volume of Sufferings for 1710-32, in reference to Wooldale, *'a new meeting house'* for 1713. In the Trust Property manuscript for 1856 it is recorded that the meeting house was *'conveyed to trustees by Henry Jackson of Totties in 1715.'* These points tie up with the Wooldale title deed of 1715:

'At this Court it was witnessed...that Joseph Broadhead...on the Second day of May last...surrendered...All that Messuage or Structure called the Meeting house and two stables belonging to the same and all those parcels of land in which the said house is built containing by estimation Forty five rods in length and nineteen Rods in Breadth...' (6)

We also know that the first recorded MM at Wooldale was held on the *'9th of the 7th month 1714.'* (7)

In conclusion we can say that, at the latest a meeting house in Wooldale was in existence in 1689. This incidentally pre-dates the oldest claimed public dissenting place of worship in the Holme Valley, the Presbyterian Chapel at Lydgate (1694) by at least five years. A meeting house was registered again in 1713. This could be because the 1689 meeting house was in another part of Wooldale or alternatively it was on the present site and, perhaps, substantially rebuilt, or because there was a change in trustees. The actual date of the title deed (1715) can be confusing as often meeting houses (and graveyards) were not transferred to trustees until a number of years after being established. It is also puzzling why both MM and the Women's PM are not recorded as being held at Wooldale until 1714 and 1720 respectively: there could be reasons for this such as Wooldale's remoteness or the original unsuitability of the building. We will probably never know the exact truth of events that led to the subsequent development of this meeting house over the next three hundred years.

It would appear that the original building occupied the same ground area as the present building, but probably being of a lower elevation. The evidence for this can be seen on the rear north wall where the top five courses of stone work are of a later period than the rest of the wall which is in the style of the late seventeenth century. (See Appendix (7)). This view can be supported by the lean-to building on the north wall (present kitchen and former hearse house). This was built prior to the 1783 rebuilding, according to its style of stonework, its roof line (before it was raised in the 1977 restoration) would have exactly met the lower roof line of the original building.

Towards the latter end of the eighteenth century it appears that the meeting house was in a bad state of repair as this minute from the 7th Month 1772 shows:

'Edward Dickinson with Jo. Marsden, Joseph Firth & Caleb Marsden with any other Friends are desired to view the ruinous Situation of part of Wooldale Meeting house, and make report to our next Meeting what they think would be best to do, & how the Chamber there & at Highflatts cou'd be enlarged for the better accomodation of the Women Friends.' (8)

However, they only appear to have patched the premises up as this minute of the 9th Month 1772 indicates:

'Joseph Firth reports the Friends appointed hath viewed Wooldale Meeting house and they think for the present twill be be best to get the most needful repairs done, & soon as convenient, & as to enlarging Place for the Women Meeting as ye Summer is far Spent will be best to suspend till next Spring.' (9)

In fact it seemed to be more urgent to build a hearse house which was completed in the Sixth Month 1777 at a cost of £9 15s 9d :

'Joseph Firth reports, that the place agreed to be Built in the Graveyard at Wooldale to keep the Hearse in, is now finished.' (10)

It was not until 1782 that Friends again considered repairs and/or enlargement as revealed in the minute of the 5th Month 1782:

'Elihu Dickenson reports that most of the Friends appointed have taken together a view (of) Wooldale Meeting house, and were of oppinion it wou'd be best enlarge as well as repair it, and in order the same may be done Elihu Dickenson, Godfrey Woodhead Jun. and Joshua Broadhead are desired to take an account what Friends are willing to give & make report.' (11)

Details of the subscriptions and expenses in the rebuilding can be found in Appendices (2) and (3). During a ten month period from the 8th Month 1782 to the 5th Month 1783 PM's were held at the other meeting houses due to the rebuilding. The main alteration to the building seems to have been in creating a higher structure so that a gallery could be inserted for use partly as a room where the women could hold their meetings for business. Also the present fenestration on the south wall would have been inserted, meaning the almost total rebuilding of this wall, the much smaller seventeenth century windows being replaced. The west gable wall appears to have been completely rebuilt above ground level as it incorporates oversailing courses which are not found in the Holme Valley prior to the eighteenth century (See Appendix (7)). This is supported by the discovery during renovations in the 1980's of seventeenh century gravestones serving as window lintels. This would only have been done after YM advices on the removal of gravestones in 1717, 1765 and 1766. Finally, the east gable wall in the main appears to be built on a plinth of an earlier date. The building has altered little since 1783 except for *'boarding'* of the floor. Around the turn of the last century the present screen separating the entrance hall from the main room was erected and the entrance moved from the middle window to its present position. At the same time a boiler house, replacing a central stove in the meeting room, was built as a lean-to building on the north wall (demolished in 1976). In recent years the main work has been restoration. The roof was completely replaced in 1976-77 and the kitchen modernized. In 1983-84 the outhouse (former stable) and mens toilet in the south-west corner of the site was converted to a childrens meeting room and a garden store. In 1985 the toilet extension was built which incorporated the old outside toilet building.

The land on which the meeting house and burial ground are sited were part of the Manor of Wakefield termed copyhold land. Whenever there was a change of ownership it had to be registered on the court roll. The Latin documents in the deeds record this registration (See Appendix 7b). This explains how, until as late as 1940, the Wooldale property had to be treated in a different manner to the rest of the MM property in respect of deeds and trusts. In 1940 the Manor of Wakefield issued a certificate relating to the *'extinguishment of Manorial Incidents'* on the property on payment of compensation of £4 17s 0d. This, in effect, was the surrender of all Manorial rights.

After the first plot of land was vested in trustees for a graveyard in 1673 for £1 10s 6d (12) there have been a number of additions to enlarge it to its present size. As the first two Mens Minute books are now lost we are unable to trace this development precisely. However, we do have the following record from the 10th Month 1817.

'Bought of Jonas Catwright piece of Land at the West end of the Meeting House at Wooldale, containing by measurement 580 yards...We give up to Jonas Cartwright all the materials of the old Hearse house...Jonas Cartwright doth hereby promise to make the place where the Hearse house stood, arable and even with the Burial ground...' (13)

One presumes that this hearse house is the one built in 1777 and not to be confused with the present day kitchen which is of seventeenth century origin and has been probably used as both stabling and as a hearse house during its lifetime. Towards the end of the nineteenth century there was a protracted dispute between the meeting and the Cartwright family over the ownership of a small piece of land. It was finally settled by the meeting abandoning its claim and William Cartwright building up the boundary wall. Then in the 12th Month 1855 the following minute is recorded:

'With reference to the minute of 3rd Month last respecting the desired alterations and improvements Robt. Walker proposed to give, devise and bequeath to Friends about 225 square yards of land from the bottom of his croft for the enlargement and use of the burial ground: on condition that other proposed alterations and improvements should be done and in accordance therewith, the Stable has been removed New Gates provided, and the wall brought up to them, the Wall at the far end of the graveyard has been raised, the Hearse and Hearse House and burrough Wall to some extent repaired & the cost of which (See minutes of the 8th Month) is about £25 13s 9d not including the Hearse the cost of which is £4 17s 5d towards which J.B. Woodhead agrees to give 30s, Ann Walker 20s and Highflatts Friends appear agreeable to give the remainder towards the repairs of the Hearse.' (14)

The actual cost recorded in 8th Month 1855 is:)

2 tenders 1/-	*2 s 0d*
Masons Bill	*£16 12s 6d*
Joiners Bill	*£4 10s 0d*
Carriage of Gates	*9d*
Lead for hanging	*5s 0d*
Blacksmith's Bill	*£1 3s 6d*
New Iron Gates	*£3 0s 0d*
	£25 13s 9d

This plot of land is in the top south-west corner of the graveyard; Robert Walker's croft being Pell Croft. The above minute of the 8th Month 1855 also states that the stable was removed. This was probably in the vicinity of the present gate-way. A stable (now the children's meeting room) was built on the new plot along with a gentlemans toilets (now the garden store).

The final addition to the graveyard was in 1914 when Joseph Walker gave a strip of 316 square yards along the north boundary. The north boundary wall was moved for this purpose. Joseph Walker died in 1940 and left Pell Croft with three fields, which had been in Quaker hands for many years, to the meeting. Unfortunately, at this time the meeting had its lowest membership and it was unable to find anyone to live there. The Charity Commissioners, under the Mortmain Act, refused to allow the meeting to hold the property as an investment. It had, therefore, to be sold off, realizing £1,340 which was invested and the interest used for the Meeting.

The arrangements for grave-digging were reported on in the 5th Month of 1844:

'James Booth Woodhead, Henry Marsden and Robert Walker report that they have examined into the present mode of grave making, but do not find any previous arrangement relating thereto, they therefore believe it will be more satisfactory to all parties that the price of a grave 5 feet deep in the centre shall be 3s 6d and one for a youth under 10 years of age 4.5 feet deep 3s 0d to which our present grave digger consents which arrangement this meeting approves' (15)

To anyone unfamilar with Quaker ways the graveyard does not resemble the usual Church graveyard with its variety of monuments (See 'Gravestones and Mourning'). However, we are fortunate to have the gravestone of Hannah and Tabitha, two of Henry Jackson's II infant daughters, who died of smallpox in 1682. This had been removed and laid upside down as a paving slab following the YM advices in the 1700's. Rediscovered in the early 1900's it is now in the entrance hall of the meeting house. Two further Jackson gravestones were discovered in the early 1980's during restoration work. The first line of each of the stones which would have said *'Here lyeth'* had been chiseled out, the stones being re-used as lintels above the gallery windows. They commemorated Hilikiah (1674-1684) and Tabitha (1682-1687).

In the meeting records we have a list of burials between 1820-87 and their positions in the plot of land obtained in 1817. There were a total of 140 burials with an average age of 51 years. It is worth noting how child mortalty declined during this period. In the last twenty years there was only one death of a child under ten, while in the first twenty years there were eight.

Throughout the minute books careful records are kept of expenses including the costs of caretaking as recorded in the 10th Month of 1757:

'...5s to Joseph Broadhead to Finde fewel Make ye fire Cleane ye House;
Open & Shut ye Doors & Windows at Wooldale Meeting house for ye Ensuing Year.' (16)

Other expenses are recorded, for example, in the 1st Month 1769 and the 9th Month of 1769:

'paid for a pair of Bellows for the use of Wooldale Meeting house 1s 4d
collection for the repairs of this mtg. house (..?..) £6 8s 6d.' (17)

A statement of accounts was usually presented once a year, for example the 11th Month 1820:

'Balance due to John Brook 11th Month 1819   £1 2s 10d

4th Mo: 22	Paid for Hearse repairing	11s 6d
7th Mo:	Some repairs	5d
9th Mo:	7lds Coals	6s 5d
10th Mo:	The Grave Yard levelling	5s 6d
	One Years Care of the Mtg. House	10s 6d

     £2 17s 2d

Rec'd for lent of Hearse for One Year   £1 11s 6d

Balance due to John Brook the 12th of the 11 Month 1820.   £1 5s 8d

(18)

Money received from the loan of the hearse, which was jointly owned with High Flatts, figures prominently in each years accounts. It is quite probably that the local Chapels would also have made use of it. There is an interesting reference to the sale of common land on the 11th month 1833: *'Rec'd of Nathaniel Booth for 6 perches of common land on Wooldale Cliff being the common right belonging Friends Burial Ground at Wooldale: £1 10s 0d.'* Later in the same minute: *'for 100 copies of Notices for public meeting Printing 10s 0d'* (19)

One can best conclude by quoting Henry Morehouse, whose comment on Wooldale Meeting House in 1861, could well apply today: *'The present simple and retired structure...is preserved with characteristic neatness.'* (20)

(1) Morehouse
(2) Appendix (7b)
(3) MMMB 1690
(4) West Riding Quarter Session Orders (Wakefield 10th Oct. 1689)
(5) Ibid (Halifax 16th July 1713)
(6) Appendix (7b)
(7) MMMB 1714
(8) PMMB 1772
(9) Ibid 1772
(10) Ibid 1777
(11) Ibid 1782
(12) Indenture 1673 — Friends Trusts
(13) (W)PMMB 1817
(14) (W)PMMB 1855
(15) (W)PMMB 1844
(16) PMMB 1757
(17) PMMB 1769
(18) (W)PMMB 1820
(19) PMMB 1833
(20) Morehouse

High Flatts Meeting House

As with the origins of Wooldale Meeting, High Flatts earliest days are uncertain. Tradition states that meetings started to be held during the Commonwealth period (1649-1660) in a barn which is on the site of the present meeting house.

QM sources reveal two maps of PM's and MM's in 1665 and 1669 both of which show Denby as a meeting. The PM minute books prior to 1752 are not extant but Pontefract MM minute books which start in 1672 also record Denby as a meeting, although the MM is of earlier origin. By 1678 Denby had disappeared from the MM minutes to be replaced by High Flatts. It seems reasonable to assume that although the name had changed the location of the meeting had not. High Flatts is in the township of Denby and only one mile from Upper Denby.

It was not till 1701 that the premises were handed over by *'Joseph Bayley of Highflatts in Denby'* to trustees: Henry Jackson III, Daniel Broadhead, William Priest, Caleb Roberts and Elihu Dickinson. (1) It is described as *'All that Newhouse lately Erected att Highflatts...containing three Bayes of building...'* with the provision that *'...another bay of building may be erected & adjoyned to the Westend of the said Newhouse...'* (2) This was to provide stabling for the meeting. The ground to the immediate front of the meeting house was for use as a burial ground. The various stages of building and later alteration can be clearly seen on the rear wall of the building. One section has the date 1697 and the initials J.E.B. (Joseph and Elizabeth Bayley) carved into a stone. This confirms the 1701 reference to a *'Newhouse lately Erected.'* Thus at the end of the seventeenth century it appears that the barn became a purpose built meeting house. It was shortly after this date that MM's began to be held at High Flatts.

The first addition to the High Flatts graveyard was in 1790 when 367 yards at 4d per yard was purchased from Elihu Dickinson the Tanner. For a few years prior to this High Flatts Friends had to be buried at Wooldale which caused some inconvenience. This was because the small plot of land to the front of the meeting house was full. (3) The new strip of land backed onto the rear of the meeting house and measured 54 feet in length by 60 feet in width. (4) In 1839 *'The burial ground at the back part of the Meeting being mainly full...'* a similar strip of land was purchased from Richard Dickinson measuring about 400 yards and costing approxmately £40. (5) In a short period of time this new plot of land was nearly full and so in 1874 a further extension of 427 yards was added to the immediate north of the existing burial ground. This land had been part of the Kitchen Croft adjoining Mill Bank House and was obtained from the trustees of the late Herbert Camm Dickinson for £32 0s 6d plus legal costs. (6) The final addition was in 1892 when a further section of the Kitchen Croft of 341 square yards was purchased from the trustees of the late Joseph Firth for £25 11s 6d plus legal costs. (7)

The advent of gravestones at High Flatts caused a certain amount of controversy. While YM (1850) had permitted the use of gravestones it was on the understanding, in all cases, they were to be provided and put down under the direction of the MM. Report was made in 1868 that Edward Brook had without the consent of the meeting placed gravestones over his mother's and brother's graves. A committee was appointed which recommended that the stones (which must have been of the flat type) should be covered over by sods. Naturally Edward Brook was not happy with this but despite his representations the stones were covered. (8) It was not until the 1874 extensions to the graveyard that gravestones were generally accepted. The sale of land was conditional on the Dickinson and Dearman families being allowed to erect stones over their ancestors graves. The size, shape and wording were agreed and the upright stones seen today in the graveyard have followed that pattern. (9)

In 1754-5 £89 3s 0d was raised for the *'repairs'* of the meeting house. This considerable sum of money was spent as follows (10):

	£	s	d
Masons Work	24	11	9
Stone Cost	6	12	2
Wood Cost	13	0	6
Carpenters work	5	18	6
Joiners work	9	13	4
Blacksmiths work	1	4	9
Glaising	1	15	0
Labourers Bill		4	11½
Rearing etc.,		1	4½
Joseph Firth's Bill	12	11	9
Jenkinson's Bill	2	4	6
Work done by the Subscribers	5	15	1
	89	3	0

No further details are given but almost certainly this would have been a rebuilding rather than mere repairs. Probably the building was considerably raised in height and a gallery added hence the reference to *'Rearing'* (a forerunner of scaffolding?). To put the cost in perspective the total cost of the land and building at Lumbroyd a few years later (1763) was only £69 11s 3.5d. In 1779 Friends were appointed to see if it would be possible to enlarge the meeting house so that it could *'contain both Men and Women's Meetings with convenience when our Monthly Meetings are held there.'* (11) No further mention is made of this so Friends must have decided to make the best use of their existing facilities.

In 1816 various alterations were done at a cost of £14 19s 3d. (12) Further repairs, including re-roofing, were carried out in 1831 at a cost of £53 11s 1d. The details of these costs included an allowance of 5s 0d for ale for the workmen. (13) Again in 1836 further repair and alterations were required costing £40 13s 5d including the purchase of *'an umbrella stand'* at £1 1s 0d. (14) In the following years various other expenses on the property were incurred including the *'boarding'* of the floor and alterations to the heating arrangements. In 1856 a serious case of dry rot was discovered and the flooring (wooden boards laid on top of stone flags) and the wooden panelling on the walls had all to be removed. The walls were then plastered and also covered with matting to a height of four feet six inches. (15) It appears that at this time the floor level was about two feet lower than the present level and thus underground. This would have caused the damp conditions that led to dry rot.

The various problems of dampness and lack of ventilation continued until 1864 when finally major repairs and alterations were carried out costing £235 19s 0d. While this work was underway meetings were held in *'Joseph Firth's corn chamber'* and in the school rooms. The present meeting house's appearance, except for the modern kitchen and toilets, is mainly the result of this work. The floor level was raised to above ground level and a wooden floor put down. The roof was removed and the walls raised about five feet. The stabling was converted into a cloakroom/kitchen and the room above the stable was added to the existing gallery. Arrangements were made to rent stabling from Joseph Firth for Friends horses. A porch was added to the front door. (16) It was probably at this time that the front wall of the meeting house was completely rebuilt and the present large windows added.

It was not till over a century later that it was felt necessary to have further major repairs and alterations done. Electricity had been installed during the 1970's. By the 1980's the membership of the meeting had begun to grow a little following many years when the numbers attending had been very small. It was thus decided that modernization and repair work should be implemented. This was completed in 1984 at a cost of £20,000. Work included the laying on of a water supply, the conversion of the old kitchen to a modern kitchen and toilets, provision of a damp course and various repairs to roof, windows, stonework, etc.,

The small hamlet of High Flatts was for many years completely populated by Friends and became known as Quaker Bottom. Most of the surrounding land and buildings known as the High Flatts Estate had been bought in the early days by the Dickinson family from the Bayleys. It then passed by marriage to the Firth family. This Quaker community was over the years a thriving centre of activity. There was the traditional occupation of farming which was often combined with the manufacture of cloth. There are remains of various buildings associated with these activities including a dyehouse to the side of Low House. In a corner of the field at the top of the lane leading down from the main road there was a windmill which was used for grinding corn. Elihu Dickinson the Tanner had a tan yard and there was Jubb's blacksmith's shop to serve the farmers and the nearby quarries which were owned by Elihu Dickinson.

It was not only the immediate vicinity of the meeting house that was occupied by Quakers. Many of the surrounding farms and cottages were owned and lived in by Friends. This influence that Friends had on the area spreading as far as Lane Head, Wooldale and Midhope should not be underestimated. Many of the former Quaker homesteads have been identified by the authors. (See Appendix (8)). At its peak High Flatts was very probably one of the largest country meetings in this part of Yorkshire. So large that in the 1770's Friends residing in and around Skelmanthorpe had to hold their mid-week meetings there rather than journey to High Flatts. Membership figures for 1861, when numbers had already started to decline, stood at 57 with a further 101 (not including children) attending but not in membership. (17) In comparison with other meetings in the MM this very high ratio of attenders to members is unique. It appears that a high proportion of the local population, Quaker and non-Quaker, considered High Flatts Meeting as the main place of worship in the district.

Within Pontefract MM High Flatts was certainly the largest and wealthiest of the PM's. This is borne out by the fact that from the earliest MM minutes from 1672 until the mid-nineteenth century the collections from High Flatts were always larger than, and often double, those of other meetings. When YM Epistles were distributed High Flatts always received most copies. Its importance is also confirmed in that prior to the establishment of Ackworth School with its iron safe all the MM deeds were kept in a box at High Flatts. An example of this concerns some money left by Mary Woodhouse for the use of MM in 1728:

'...which Bond is ordered to be kept in the Monthly meeting Box at Highflatts.'(18)

Part of the reason for the apparent size of High Flatts PM was that up until 1792 Wooldale was not a PM in its own right but was a part of High Flatts PM. Lane Head, Judd Field, Lumbroyd and Friends living in the vicinity of Lockwood and Longroyd Bridge had also been part of High Flatts PM at various times. However, in 1792 following a visit by Friends from QM to the various constituent meetings of High Flatts PM certain changes were made. Those Friends living near *'Parrack'* Meeting House (Paddock in Huddersfield) had their membership transferred to Brighouse MM. These were Robert and Jane Kaye with John Earnshaw their apprentice, Emmanuel and Hannah Brook and Frances Brook, widow of Richard. Wooldale became a distinct PM with a first day (Sunday) and fifth day (Thursday) meeting. Lumbroyd Friends were offered the choice of becoming a PM or remaining with High Flatts: they chose the latter. These new arrangements were found to be satisfactory as those Friends living near the particular meetings had experienced difficulty when PM's had been held at a distance from them. (19) Even after this split, based on the size of the collections, High Flatts still appears to have been the largest and the wealthiest of the PM's for a number of years.

(1) High Flatts Indenture 1701
(2) Ibid

(3) Joseph Wood Memorandum Book No.5
(4) PMMB 1790
(5) (H)PMMB 1812-1853
(6) (H)PMMB 1853-1900
(7) Ibid
(8) Ibid
(9) Ibid
(10) PMMB 1754/5
(11) PMMB 1779
(12) (H)PMMB 1812-1853
(13) Ibid
(14) Ibid
(15) (H)PMMB 1853-1900
(16) Ibid
(17) MMMB 1861
(18) MMMB 1728
(19) MMMB 1792

Hoyland Swaine

In the earliest MM minutes the name of Hoyland Swaine appears. In 1676 and 1678 collections were brought in from *'Hoyland Swaine meetinge.'* Hoyland Swaine can probably be taken to be the same meeting as High Flatts (then called Denby) as when Hoyland Swaine appears Denby does not. A little more confusion occurs when referring to the 1665 QM map of meetings where the name Hoyland is marked as a meeting. This is marked on the map in the position occupied by High Hoyland not Hoyland Swaine. This was perhaps an error by the map makers as on both the QM map and the list of towns associated with meetings for 1669 Hoyland Swaine replaced Hoyland. Meetings could, however, have been held in private houses at Hoyland as they almost certainly were in Hoyland Swaine.

In 1657 a burial ground was donated by Deed of Gift by *'Daniel Moakson'* of Hoyland Swaine. We know that the Moxon (or Moakson) family were involved in Quaker meetings because in 1660 John Moxon was arrested for being at a meeting. (See 'Early Persecutions'). Later Henry Jackson II was arrested for causing a *'riotous assembly'* at a burial at Hoyland Swaine in 1684. (See 'Henry Jackson II'). It is very probable that this burial ground was used for many of the earliest burials of High Flatts and Midhope Friends.

By the mid 1700's the burial ground fell into disuse. High Flatts had their own burial ground surrounding the meeting house. Lumbroyd Meeting House and burial ground had been settled in 1763 to serve the Friends in and around Midhope and Penistone. Hoyland Swaine remained in Friends care until 1821 when it was sold to John Burley a Hoyland Swaine blacksmith for £12 12s 0d. Conditions of the sale stated that it should not be dug more than one foot deep nor should there be any cock-fighting or bull-baiting. The proceeds of the sale were to be used for the upkeep of Lumbroyd Meetng House and burial ground. (1)

The authors have found some difficulty in tracing the exact site of the burial ground. It was reported in 1913 as being *'a garden...used in connection with the village inn.'*(2) At the top end of the village there were two inns in 1913 that are now private residences: the Brown Cow and the Blacksmith's Arms. It is thought probable that a plot of ground near the former Blacksmiths Arms is the most likely site. Set into the wall is an iron ring known locally as *'the Quaker Bell.'* There was also a small building next to the land that was thought to have Quaker connections that has recently been demolished.

(1) MMMB 1821
(2) John Sadler's Report on High Flatts Burial Grounds (1913).

Shepley Lane Head

Lane Head, like so many older properties, has various stages of development. Luckily many of the dates of the building work are still preserved today carved into the stones, including the letter 'F' standing for Firth — the Quaker family that lived in the house for a number of generations. The west side of the house was built in 1597 and enlarged in 1647 by the addition of the dining room and a bedroom above it. (1) When the Act of Toleration was passed in 1689 Lane Head was licenced for the first time by John Firth for the holding of Religious Meetings. (See 'The Firths of Shepley Lane Head'). In about 1695 a lean-to structure specifically for use as a meeting house was built at the back of the house by John Firth's son, Joseph Firth. In the Orders for the Quarter Sessions held at Rotherham in 1695 the granting of a new licence for Lane Head is recorded:

'...the House of Joseph Firth of Hallroyd Lane Head, in Shepley,...for a Meeting place for religiouse worshipp...' (2)

The re-licencing of meeting houses upon the decease of its then owner appears to have been common practice. Over the door into the garden is inscribed *'Memento mori'* (Remember dying).

In 1709 Joseph Firth married Hannah Dickinson and a further addition was made which absorbed the meeting house into a staircase and pantry and meetings were then held in a large sitting room known as the *'low room.'* There is also a reference to the meeting being held in the *'cellar chamber.'* This probably refers to the lean-to addition which now has windows partly below ground level presumably blocked up in the 1709 alterations.

A family tradition recounts that the stones used to pave the court were brought from Elland before the turnpike roads were built. This was quite a taxing and *'important undertaking'* given the state of roads in that period. (3)

MM were occasionally held at Lane Head: *'It is agreed ye next mo: meet. be held at Lainhead at Joseph Firth house'* (4) PM's were held at Lane Head fairly regularly. The last recorded meeting was held the 3rd Month 1768. It is uncertain whether Meetings for Worship continued at the house after this date but certainly the Firth family remained in residence for a number of generations playing a prominent part in our history. (See 'The Firths of Shepley Lane Head').

It is significant that PM's ceased at Lane Head shortly after the building of Lumbroyd Meeting House in 1763. The density of meetings in our small area had become too great.

No history covering three hundred years of religious buildings and graveyards would be complete without a ghost story! Our first tale occurs at Lane Head. The story is recounted that a member of the Firth family died very suddenly in meeting. Ever since, on the anniversary of the death, St. Valentine's Day, it has been reported that the ghost walks and strange noises are heard. (5) A further variation on this story recounts that a number of years ago when Diana Wood, then a little girl, visited Lane Head from the U.S.A. she encountered the ghost. She was not frightened at all thinking the apparition was another member of the household. Apparently this *'gentle ghost'*, a lady dressed in Quaker grey, emerged from a non-existant door and passed down the staircase. Another incident is remembered when a heavy horseshoe hanging from a stout peg in a wall mysteriously fell to the floor. There was no one near at the time. The string was unbroken. The peg was well secured and at such an angle that it would have been impossible for the horseshoe to fall accidentally. (6) It is not surprising that after so many generations of Friends living and worshipping in the house that images of the past may still be retained in the fabric of the building rather like a magnetic tape recording.

(1) 'Legends & Traditions of Huddersfield & District' P. Ahier p.197
(2) Wakefield Quarter Sessions Order Book.
(3) MS Typescript 'The Firths of Shepley Lane Head' anon. 1878
(4) MMMB 1731
(5) MS Typescript 'The Firths of Shepley Lane Head' anon. 1878
(6) Misc. Family Notes — courtesy Freya Wood.

Midhope, Sheephouse and Judd Field

This area was a Quaker stronghold from the mid-seventeenth century until the first half of the eighteenth century. The Midhope district is situated south of Penistone and is a collection of isolated farmhouses and hamlets on the valley sides of the River Little Don. We know that Quakerism had taken a strong hold on the area as we hear of various Friends being prosecuted under the Act of Uniformity in 1662. These included John Charlesworth, John Woodhouse and William Downing (or Downend), of Midhope Hall, members of the Ellis family of Midhope, Jonathan West of Oakes in Midhope and Ralph and William Wordsworth of Penistone. (1) Three other Friends in the district were also involved in a similar incident:

'In 1664 John Cooke of Midduphall, William Marsden of Hunchilbrige, and Henry Dickenson of Sheephouse, for being at a Meeting were committed to the house of Correction at Wakefield and detained there four weeks.' (2)

Later on we discover that at the Knaresborough Sessions in 1683 the following local Friends were on trial for not attending Penistone Parish Church: Henry Dickinson and his wife, Mary Marsden wife of Daniel, John Couldwell and his wife, George Trout and his wife, John Green and his wife, Margaret Haigh a widow, Ann Haigh, Margaret Blackburn, Jane Brownell and John Wordsworth. (3)

The reference to the various members of the Ellis family is interesting as their ancestor Elias de Midhope had been granted the Manors of Midhope, Langsett and Penistone in 1284.(4) Many of these Friends were probably convinced before 1665 and some, as we have seen earlier, before 1656 because some of the oldest MM records of births and burials relate to this area. Henry Jackson II had strong local connections as he resided at a house in the valley, Langley Brook, for a number of years. His influence amongst Friends and acquaintance with George Fox would have undoubtedly been a possible reason for the concentration of Quaker families in this area.

The 1665 QM map shows Midhope as being one of the villages attached to Denby (High Flatts) Meeting. For MM held the 4th Month 1686 a collection was brought in from *'Highflatts and Midup Meeting.'* (5) Similarly, for the 12th Month 1686 a collection was brought in from *'Highflatts and Shephouse Meeting'* (6) This indicates that there were meetings held at both these small collections of farms. The one at Midhope was probably held at Midhope Hall. This was only about 100 yards from the Manor House Chapel of St. James's. Like Wooldale and High Flatts, this area was no stranger to dissent. In this instance the area had clung to the Catholicism rather than accept Protestantism. In fact this defiance had caused the downfall of the Barneby family. They had held Midhope Manor since 1337 but finally had to sell it in 1622 largely due to the fines that were imposed upon them for their beliefs. It is possible that some, who had perhaps once been Roman Catholic and were not in sympathy with the Established Church, turned eventually to Quakerism. (7)

We come across our second ghost story at Midhope Hall. A lady told the authors (1986) that, one evening on going upstairs to her bedroom (which was in the oldest part of the house), she saw the head and face of a *'Quaker lady in a bonnet'* on the landing. The apparition smiled at her and vanished.

On the opposite side of the valley to Midhope Hall is a collection of buildings called Sheephouse. Ths settlement, dating from the Middle Ages contains the remains of a medieval monastic building. This would have been used during the summer months by monks when tending their flocks: hence Sheephouse. The monks were Cistercians from Kirkstead Abbey in Lincolnshire, known as the White Monks because their habits were of undyed wool. These monks had great influence in the area and organized the sheep-farming on a large scale. They had a Grange in Langsett during the thirteenth century known as Penisdale Abbey. (8) It was one of the branches of the prolific Dickinson family that occupied Sheephouse during the period that it was used for Quaker meetings. At the Barnsley Sessions on the 15th October, 1689 an order was made licencing the house of Henry Dickinson of Sheephouse. Also licenced were the houses of those in the area who had earlier suffered persecutions including some of the Ellis family and William Marsden of Penistone. (9) Sheephouse is mentioned again in 1714 in the first Women's PM minute book as a meeting place. Its Quaker connections finally ceased in 1864 when Samuel Coward, a member of the Society of Friends, died at the age of 87. Samuel Coward's estate was auctioned in June of that year and amongst the 360 acres of land was Sheephouse Farm.

The other farm that was used as a meeting place was Judd Field which is about a mile further to the west on the same valley side as Sheephouse. This was occupied by the Couldwell family and later by the Earnshaw family. Like Sheephouse, Judd Field has probably been occupied for a long time as the remains of a pack horse road passes by the house. It has been suggested that the track might even be of Roman origin. It appears that this farm was used as a meeting place at a slightly later time than Midhope Hall and Sheephouse. It was eventually replaced by Lumbroyd in 1763. We have the record of a licence being granted in the Quarter Sessions Orders from Rotherham on the 19th July 1710:

'It is ordered That the dwelling house of Joseph Couldwell of Juddfield Lane head in the prsh. of Penistone be recorded.' (10)

A word of explanation is necessary over the terminology *'Juddfield Lane head.'* This for a time confused the authors as it could be taken that *'Lane head'* referred to Joseph Firth's house at Shepley. The mystery was solved when a 19th Century OS map was consulted which showed directly under the name Judd Field the word *'Lane'* — referring to the pack horse road: this does not appear on the modern edition of the map. As Judd Field is on the brow of the hill that the track runs up it could well be described as being at *'Lane head.'* In the first Men's PM minute book that we have there appears the following entry for the 1st Month 1753:

'Godfrey Woodhead reports to this meetg. that ye repairs of Jutfield meetg. house hath amounted considerably of Late and This meetg. considers In a Little time to make a collection for or towards that Service.' (11)

And again for the 3rd Month 1761:

'N.B. our collection being less is occationed by Frds. of Judfield being excused, havg. their Meetg. house Rent to pay.' (12)

From the evidence one can perhaps imagine that the meeting was held in one of the farm buildings at Judd Field and that the Couldwells made Friends responsible for its repair and charged a small rent. Judd Field was still in the hands of Thomas Earnshaw, a Quaker, as late as 1803.

The other house in the district, although there is no direct mention of its use, is Langley Brook which probably hosted many meetings during the times of persecution. This was occupied for a period by the Jacksons and also by another Quaker family, the Greaves. There is even the possibility that this was the house that George Fox visited when he came to *'Henry Jackson's'* in 1669. Henry Jackson moved away for a time from Meal Hill when the Plague broke out in Hepworth in 1665.

All these various meetings came under the umbrella of High Flatts PM as did Shepley Lane Head, Wooldale (until 1792) and later Lumbroyd.

(1) 'Midhope Church' Michael Fitton & QBBREG1
(2) Besse's Sufferings Vol.II
(3) 'The Early History of Stocksbridge & District' Joseph Kenworthy
(4) Ibid
(5) MMMB 1686
(6) Ibid
(7) 'Midhope Church' Michael Fitton.
(8) Ibid (3)
(9) West Riding Quarter Sessions Orders
(10) Ibid
(11) PMMB 1753
(12) Ibid 1761

Lumbroyd

It was not until 1763 that Friends in the vicinity of Penistone and Midhope built a meeting house. Although strong in the area since the coming of Quakerism into Yorkshire they had always met in private houses. (See 'Midhope, Sheephouse and Judd Field'). MM held at Shepley Lane Head in the 8th month 1762 records:

'Highflatts friends informs this Meetg. that they are Building a Meetg. house, Near Penistone, being deprived of the place they are used to meet in called Judfield, & having made two subscriptions towards Erecting the same & falling short desires this Meetg. wou'd take it into Consideration, and Relieve them as they think proper.' (1)

Despite some difficulty in raising the required amount (£69 11s 3d) the burial ground and meeting house were completed in 1763. The land having been bought from a James Walton of Thurlstone in 1762 for £2 6s 8d. By far the largest contribution came from one local Friend: John Sanderson of Midhope who gave £6 5s 0d. The rest of the money came from individual contributions from Wooldale, High Flatts, Lane Head and Midhope Friends. There were also contributions from other meetings including £5 5s 0d from QM. The subscriptions and expenditure are detailed in Appendices (5) and (6).

Lumbroyd Meeting was to last less than a century and never became a PM choosing to remain a part of High Flatts PM. Thomas Shillitoe visited the meeting for the first time in 1807 and recorded:

'In the afternoon walked nine miles to Lumbroyd, a meeting being appointed to be held at five this afternoon: the snow being much drifted, made travelling on foot in this open country difficult, yet as I believe it was required of me to set this example, I was much helped to press through every obstacle I had to meet from time

to time, under a persuasion that if I refused to maintain my post in this respect, I might go home, as my divine Master would have no further service for me. This meeting is much striped (sic) of its members: if my feelings were correct, the life of religion is at a very low ebb here. I was led in a singular manner in the line of the ministry in this meeting, which is trying to nature; yet what a strength it is to the poor tried mind, after much exercising engagement, when those whose judgements we believe we may rely upon, and who are acquainted with the local circumstances of the members of a meeting, take us by the hand, accompanied with a language in confirmation that what we have to offer was applicable to the states of the people; which was the case at the close of this meeting.' (2)

A few years later in 1813 Joseph Wood comments in a similar vein:

'The meeting is considerably reduced of friends but several of other Societies attended today which is not usual at that place...it was a pretty open satisfactory meeting...' (3)

By 1840 PM minutes record in the 4th month that as the only two remaining members belonging to Lumbroyd were to move away MM should be consulted about the meetings future. MM appointed a committee which decided that the meeting should be kept open, the members of that committee to attend that meeting whenever possible. However, in 1847 Joseph Firth submitted a report on behalf of the committee to MM:

'There are five or six individuals who are in the practice of pretty regularly attending the meeting but considering all the circumstances under which it is held the pretty unanimous feeling of the friends present is; that the time is come for the Monthly Meeting to consider the propriety of discontinuing the holding of a meeting for worship there for the present unless the Monthly meeting feel itself strong enough to maintain a regular attendance of a greater number of substantial friends.' (4)

Sadly, it seems that the *'substantial friends'* were not able to support Lumbroyd and there were no more meetings held there. By 1858 MM heard that *'...the roof (was) in a state of dilapidation...'* and *'...that it might be best to take it down and plant the ground.'* (5) The materials were sold in 1859 to Thomas and Joseph Hawley along with several trees for £8 16s 0d and the ground planted. (6) The site was maintained and cared for by Friends well into the twentieth century. In more recent years it appears that the site must have been sold off to the adjacent farm.

(1) MMMB 1762
(2) Thomas Shillitoe's Journal
(3) Joseph Wood's Memorandum Book No.32
(4) MMMB 1847
(5) MMMB 1858
(6) MMMB 1859

The Origins of Friends Meeting House in Paddock

The Friends Meeting House at Paddock, Huddersfield, like Lumbroyd Meeting House, has its origins partially in the meetings at Wooldale, High Flatts and Lane Head. Numerically, there were never very many Quaker families within the Huddersfield vicinity until the onset of industrialization. The Brooks of Row in Lockwood were the most prominent Quakers resident in the locality but they belonged, at the beginning of the eighteenth century, to Wooldale meeting. Richard Brook of Row was recorded as having regularly resisted the paying of tithes from around 1706. (1) According to one local historian Lockwood was certainly a Quaker stronghold in this period. Park Road was then officially called Quaker Lane for very good reasons. (2) When Huddersfield began to change and grow into an industrial township Friends living in the vicinity of the town decided to have their own particular meeting. Living on the very periphery of an ill-defined border area between Pontefract MM and Brighouse MM Friends of Lockwood and Longroyd Bridge were nominally counted as belonging to the former. (Hence registration of births, deaths, marriages and sufferings in Pontefract MM records). It is likely that they attended meetings for worship at Wooldale but not High Flatts. In view of the distances involved in travelling to PM's and MM's held at High Flatts and further away it is not surprising that they began to attend PM's at Brighouse. The first mention of this severing of ties is disclosed by this minute from Brighouse MM in 1770:

'Brighouse Friends Reporte that a number of Friends families belonging to their Meeting, which is held at Different Places, & sometimes so Remote from said families that they could not conveniently attend but have for many years last past at such times met with some adjacent families of Friends belonging to Pontefract Monthly Meeting at some one or other of their Houses. But as Several of them have families of Children Growing, it is becoming inconvenient to some of said Houses to accomodate them as aforetime which have put them upon Building a House on Purpose to Meet in at such certain times as they have done heretofore and desires the concurrence & assistance of this Meeting therein To which this Meeting agrees and it is desired friends will carry the case to Each Particular Meeting & set a subscription on foot for the same.' (3)

Pontefract MM records for this period indicate a similar story:

'The Friends of Rowe side who belong to this meeting inform us that they with the friends of Brighouse Meeting with whom they meet when our meeting is held at High Flatts, propose, with the consent of ours & Brighouse Meetings to erect a new house on a piece of land near Longroidbridge which the Trustee for the Lord of the (?) & principal Freeholders have been so kind as to give for that purpose, wherein they propose Meeting every other first day as heretofore. This Meeting having considered the same, as also their reasons for so doing and finding no objections thereto desire this to be laid before our next Mo: Meeting.' (4)

Joseph Wood's recollections are in a similar vein. Returning from the General Meeting held at Whitfield in Lancashire in the 6th month 1770 he recorded:

'...Call'd at Paddock about a Mile above Huddersfield to View Friends Meetinghouse which was Building there on a Large Piece of Ground which her Call'd Lady Ramsden & the Freeholders of the Town had given to Friends for a Burial Ground & to Build a Meetinghouse...' (5)

Seven months later in September of that same year the minutes of a PM held at Wooldale record that:

'£11-13-0d hath been raised in this Mtg. towards erecting the New Meeting House near Huddersfield, which was given to our last Monthly Meeting.' (6)

The breaking of ties with the Friends of Lockwood and Longroyd Bridge was gradual rather than sudden. Ten years later in 1780 the following entry in the High Flatts PM minute book records:

'We are informed that the Friends of Huddersfield are about to transfer the Meeting House & Burial Ground at Paddock, the following being pitched upon for new trustees Thos. Horsfall, Wm. Cooper, Robt. Firth, Jn. Firth, Wm. Marsden & Richard Brook Jr.' (7)

The history of Paddock Meeting is beyond the scope of this work but it is worth mentioning that the Firths of Lane Head and High Flatts were among those who figured in the establishment of Paddock Meeting House. Thomas Firth (d.1782 — youngest son of Joseph Firth (II)) who married Mary Crosland and moved into the locality was one of those Friends instrumental in this venture. (8) When he died he was buried at Paddock having firmly established another branch of the family elsewhere. His son, Thomas Firth of Toothill House in Brighouse, was another prominent Quaker involved in the affairs of Paddock Meeting and Brighouse MM. (9) Aspects of their lives have been well documented in a variety of local sources.

Even though Paddock Meeting was now a part of Brighouse MM local Friends continued for some years to maintain and stay in close contact with Friends at Wooldale and High Flatts. ('Quakers & Luddites', 'Removals in the late 18th Century' and also 'The Firths of Lane Head'). The present Paddock Meeting House replaced the original and was built in 1830.

(1) MMBS c.1706
(2) 'History of Lockwood & North Crosland' by Brian Clarke. See opening paragraphs of chapter on 'Churches'.
(3) Brighouse MM Minutes 1770.
(4) PMMB2 1770
(5) Joseph Wood Memorandum Book No.0
(6) Ibid 1770
(7) Ibid 1780
(8) David Blamires 'A History of Quakerism in Liversedge & Scholes'
(9) W.N. Dawson's 'History on your doorstep' recounts interesting details of the Firth family involvement in the Huddersfield & Brighouse areas.

APPENDIX (1)

Table of Days and Months of the Calendar Year

Col.1	MONTH	Col.2
11th Mo.	January	1st Mo.
12th Mo.	February	2nd Mo.
1st Mo.	March	3rd Mo.
2nd Mo.	April	4th Mo.
3rd Mo.	May	5th Mo.
4th Mo.	June	6th Mo.
5th Mo.	July	7th Mo.
6th Mo.	August	8th Mo.
7th Mo.	September	9th Mo.
8th Mo.	October	10th Mo.
9th Mo.	November	11th Mo.
10th Mo.	December	12th Mo.

The system of dating was altered on the last day of December 1751 to comply with changes instituted by Parliament for regulating the calendar. From January 1752 the Quaker calendar moved into line with the rest of the country (although not in the naming of the months). Col.1 shows the equivalent Quaker month before the last day of December 1751. Col.2 shows the equivalent Quaker month as from the first day of January 1752. First Day was Sunday, Second Day was Monday, etc.

Additional note:

$$£1 (100p) = 240d \text{ or } 20s. \quad 1s (5p) = 12d$$

APPENDIX (2)

Taken from PMMB2 1768-1786
Subscription list for the enlargement of Wooldale Meeting
1782 — 1783

Column I   Column II

		Brought forward	£107:19:4
Joseph Firth	8: 17: 6		
Elihu Dickinson (1)	8: 15: 0	William Stead	1: 15: 6
Elihu Dickinson (2)	8: 11: 0	Joseph Stead	1: 14: 6
John Firth	8: 11: 6	Samuel Wood Jr.	1: 18: 0
Joseph Brook	8: 4: 6	Joseph Wood	1: 3: 0
Joshua Broadhead	8: 10: 5	Henry Dickinson Sn.	0: 17: 6
Godfrey Woodhead	8: 5: 6	John Chapman	1: 14: 0
Joseph Woodhead Jr.	4: 19: 0	John Wood	1: 1: 0
Thos. Roberts Jr.	4: 19: 0	Martha Radley	0: 10: 6
John Earnshaw	4: 2: 0	John Mallinson	0: 15: 9
Robert Kay	4: 2: 6	Jeremiah Smith	0: 7: 0

APPENDIX (2) (Continued)

Samuel Wood Sn.	3: 12: 0	Ann Green	0: 2: 6
Tobias Mallinson	3: 12: 0	Benjaman Stead	0: 7: 6
Joseph Roberts &		John Broadhead	0: 1: 0
Thos. Firth (3)	3: 3: 0	Joseph Woodhead Sn.	0: 16: 9
Daniel Broadhead	2: 16: 6	Jonathan Bottomley	1: 3: 0
Wm. Earnshaw (4)	2: 16: 6	Sarah Broadhead (7)	0: 15: 6
John Beaumont	3: 5: 0	Joshua Brook	0: 9: 6
Ann Dickinson	2: 2: 0	John Kirk	0: 12: 0
George Earnshaw	1: 11: 6	John Dickinson	0: 7: 0
Benjaman. & Jo. Walker	1: 14: 6	Henry Dickinson Jr.	0: 5: 0
Joseph Haigh (5)	1: 13: 6	Joshua Dickinson	0: 5: 0
Wm. Dickinson	1: 12: 11·5	Samuel Haigh	0: 2: 6
Sarah Broadhead (6)	1: 1: 0	Wm. Dyson	0: 5: 0
Thomas Firth	1: 11: 0	George Mallinson	0: 5: 0
	£107: 19: 4·5d		£125:13:4.5d

(1) the Clothier
(2) the Tanner
(3) of Huddersfield
(4) including his daughters
(5) of Ebson House
(6) Meltom House
(7) of Wooldale

Column III		Column VI	
Brought forward	£125:13:4.5d	Brought forward	£139:10:4.5d
Mary Bottomley	0: 5: 0	George Broadhead	0: 7: 6
Joseph Haigh (8)	0: 3: 0	Samuel Jebson	0: 7: 6
Hannah Knowles	0: 15: 9	Ather Jebson	0: 5: 0
John Horsfall	0: 15: 0	Abraham Bottomley	1: 5: 0
Wm. Haigh	0: 15: 6	Joshua Broadhead	0: 5: 6
Widdow Bottomley	1: 1: 0	John Haigh	1: 5: 0
John Roberts	0: 15: 9	A friend unknown	0: 16: 6
John Brook	1: 1: 0	John & Thos. Bottomley	0: 8: 0
Richard Brook Jn.	0: 13: 0	Benjaman Broadhead	0: 4: 0
Joshua Brook	0: 15: 6	Wm. Woodhead	0: 5: 0
Susanah Bottomley	0: 7: 6	John Bottomley	0: 3: 9
Elizabeth Roberts	0: 7: 6	Joseph Bottomley	0: 2: 0
Esther Roberts	0: 7: 6	Elizabeth Broadhead	0: 10: 0
Mary Roberts	0: 7: 6	Joseph Broadhead	0: 1: 0
Susanah Haigh	0: 7: 6	Jos. & Emmanuel Brook	0: 15: 0
Hannah Beamont	0: 7: 6	Ann Broadhead	0: 5: 0
Sarah Roberts	0: 7: 6		
	£139: 10: 4		£142 : 4: 7

The subscription for the enlargement was made on three separate occasions with a four fold collection. The information has been presented as it appears in the minute book.

(8) of High Flatts

APPENDIX (3)

Taken from the PMMB 1768-1786
(An account of the expense in enlarging Wooldale Meeting House 1782-83)

Richard Thorp Bill	101: 18: 0
Peter Haigh bill for Plank & Duch latts	3: 18: 3.5
Joseph Marshall for Plank	4: 1: 6
Joseph Barraclough for Joiner work	9: 6: 4.5
Elihu Dickinson for 18 Planks	4: 14: 6
A Gate to Huddersfield for Planks	0: 8: 5.5
Carrige of Boards & Rails to & from Killn Gates, & 1 Gate to Peter Haigh's for Plank	0: 5: 0
2 Load of Throughs from Whitewells & Getting	0: 6: 0
Joseph Firth lime for Eastend	0: 10: 6
Setting Range in Low room & Putting Wall	0: 18: 2.5
A Range for Chamber & Setting	0: 16: 0
William Haigh Putting Westend Wall	0: 14: 0
200 Bricks & leading for Pillars for Gallary	0: 13: 10
Wood for Gallary Bottom	0: 13: 0
Lead for Soddering Crooks	0: 2: 11.5
Blacksmith Bill	1: 6: 9.5
James Barrow bill for hinges glew etc.	0: 6: 1.5
Oil Paint Brushes etc.	2: 11: 4.5
14 days Painting at 1/9	1: 4: 6
Nails, Sprigs, Candles, Oil, & Whitting	1: 2: 1.5
Mason Bill for Burying yard Wall	8: 10: 6
2 Planks for Gates to ditto	0: 10: 6
Total Paid	142: 4: 7.5
Total Received	142. 4: 7.5

APPENDIX (4)

Taken from PMMB 1790
Subscription lists for the enlargement of High Flatts Burial Ground

High Flatts Division		Wooldale Division	
Elihu Dickinson	2: 2: 0	Sarah & Geo. Broadhead	–:10: 6
Enoch Dickinson (34)	–:–:–	Sarah Broadhead Jr. (31)	–: 1: 0
Martha Haigh (34)	–: 2: 0	Daniel Broadhead (32)	–:11: 6
Samuel Haigh (35)	–: 2: 0	Benjaman Broadhead (32)	–: 1: 6
Wm. Haigh (34)	–: 1: 0	John Wood Broadhead (32)	–: 1: 0
Samuel Haigh Jr. (34)	–: 0: 6	John Roberts (1)	–:10: 6
Elihu Dickinson (2)	2: 0: 0	John Beamont (1)	–:10: 6
Mary Dickinson (34)	–: 2: 0	Edward Dickinson (33)	–: 2: 6
Hannah Dickinson (34)	–: 1: 0	Joseph Brook (33)	–: 5: 0
Judith Dickinson (34)	–: 1: 0	John Brook (33)	–: 2: 6
John Dickinson (35)	–: 1: 0	Sarah Brook (33)	–: 1: 6
William Dickinson (3)	–: 1: 0	Mary Brook (33)	–: 1: 6
Joseph Haigh (34)	–: 1: 0	Thomas Roberts (33)	–: 5: 0
Joseph Haigh Jr. (34)	–:–: 6	Wm. Earnshaw (33)	–: 2: 6
Benjamin Haigh (34)	–:–: 6	John Clay (33)	–: 2: 6

Henry Dickinson (4)	–:–:–
Tobias Mallinson (5)	–:10: 6
Joseph Mallinson (34)	–: 3: 6
Samuel Wood & Son (6)	1: 1: 0
William Talor (7)	–: 2: 6
Samuel Jepson (8)	–: 2: 6
Samuel Wood (10)	–: 5: 0
John Firth (11)	1: 1: 0
Martha Radley (12)	–: 1: 0
Phebe Haigh (13)	–: 1: 6
John Bottomley (36)	–: 2: 6
Benjaman Walker (15)	–: 7: 0
Joseph Walker (15)	–:10: 6
William Dyson (16)	–: 2: 6
Hutchinson Dyson (16)	–: 2: 6
Judeth Dyson (16)	–: 1: 0
Mary Stead (37)	–: 2: 6
Benjaman Stead (37)	–: 5: 0
Anthony Hinsley (19)	–: 5: 0
Joseph Stead (21)	–: 5: 0
Ann Beamont (22)	–: 1: 0
John Chapman (23)	–: 1: 0
Wm. Chapman (22)	–: 1: 0
Joseph Priest (22)	–: 5: 0
John Priest (22)	–: 5: 0
	£11: 4: 6

Elizabeth Roberts (33)	–: 1: 6
Mary Roberts (33)	–: 1: 6
Wm. Earnshaw (33)	–:–: 6
Hannah Earnshaw (33)	–: 2: 6
Sarah Gouldthorp (33)	–:–: 6
Matthew Broadhead (9)	–: 1: 0
Matthew Broadhead Jr.(9)	–: 1: 0
Joshua Broadhead (9)	–:–: 6
Elizabeth Broadhead (9)	–:–: 6
Joseph Woodhead Jr. (14)	–:–:–
Godfrey Woodhead (14)	–:10: 6
Joseph Bottomley (14)	–: 1: 6
John Cooper (14)	–: 1: 0
John Earnshaw (17)	–: 5: 0
Joseph Broadhead (18)	–: 1: 0
Ann Broadhead (18)	–: 1: 6
Jonathan Bottomley (18)	–: 2: 0
Joseph Bottomley (18)	–: 2: 0
Thomas Bottomley (20)	–: 2: 6
William Bottomley (20)	–: 2: 6
Mary Bottomley (20)	–:–: 6
Sarah Bottomley (20)	–:–: 6
	£5: 1: 6

Lumbroyd Division

George Chapman (24)	–: 6: 0
Martha Woodhead (24)	–: 2: 6
Thomas Earnshaw (25)	–: 3: 0
Mary Sanderson (26)	–:–: 6
Thomas Earnshaw (27)	–: 2: 6
Jonathan Green (28)	–:–: 6
Benjaman Dickinson (28)	–: 5: 0
William Dickinson (28)	–: 2: 6
James Dickinson (29)	–: 1: 0
Joshua Earnshaw (30)	–: 2: 0
	£1: 5: 6
Lumbroyd Division	1: 5: 6
High Flatts Division	11: 4: 6
Wooldale Division	5: 1: 6
Total	£17:11: 6

Footnotes (indicating location & contributions in lieu).

(*) of High Flatts. 1 day with Team.
(1) of Totties
(2) Tanner. 1 day with Team.
(3) of Pughall. 1 day labour.
(4) of Strines. 1 day labour.
(5) of Wood. 1 day labour with Team.
(6) of Newhouse. 1 day labour with Team.
(7) of Newhouse.
(8) of Birdsedge.
(9) of New Mill
(10) of Haddenley
(11) of Lane Head. 1 day with Team.
(12) of Shepley.
(13) of Bankbottom.
(14) of Foulstone.
(15) of Paddock.
(16) of Woodhouse.
(17) of Shepley-Woodend.
(18) of Shepley-Woodend.
(19) of Skelmanthorp.
(20) of Thurstonland-Woodend.
(21) of Toppett.
(22) of Denby.
(23) of Denby. 1 day with Team.
(24) of Penistone.
(25) of Judfield.
(26) of Middop.
(27) of Langsett.
(28) of Thurlstone.
(29) of Folly.
(30) of Bellroyd.
(31) of Meltomhouse
(32) of Mearhouse.
(33) of Wooldale.
(34) of High Flatts.
(35) of High Flatts.
(36) of Silver Ing.
(37) 1 day labour
(38) of Shelley

APPENDIX (5)

Subscription list for the building of Lumbroyd Meeting House
(1763)

	First	Second	Third	Total
John Wood, Denby	–:10: 6	–:10: 6	–: 5: 0	1: 6: 0
Henry Dickinson	–:10: 0	–: 5: 0	–: 2: 6	–:17: 6
Tobias Mallinson Jr.	1: 1: 0	–: 9: 0	–: 5: 0	1:15: 0
Tobias Mallinson	1: 1: 0	–:10: 0	–: 5: 0	1:16: 0
Samuel Wood	1: 1: 0	–: 9: 0	–: 5: 0	1:15: 0
Caleb Marsden	1: 1: 0	–: 7: 6	–: 3: 9	1:11: 9
Joshua Marsden	–:10: 6	–: 7: 6	–: 3: 9	1: 1: 9
Joseph Firth, Son & Daughter	1: 1: 0	–:15: 6	–: 5: 0	2: 1: 6
William Radley	–: 5: 0	–: –: –	–: 2: 0	–: 7: 0
Hannah Firth	–:10: 6	–: –: –	–: 5: 0	–:15: 6
Joseph Walker	–: 3: 0	–: –: –	–: –: –	–: 3: 0
John Hobson	–: 3: 0	–: –: –	–: 1: 0	–: 4: 0
Daniel Broadhead	–:15: 0	–: 2: 6	–: 3: 6	1: 0: 0
John Broadhead, Meltam	–:15: 0	–:15: 0	–: –: –	2: 0: 0
Samuel Greenwood	–:15: 0	–: 5: 0	–: –: –	1: 0: 0
Abram Beamont	–: 5: 0	–: –: –	–: 2: 6	–: 7: 6
John Earnshaw	–: 7: 6	–: –: –	–: 2: 6	–:10: 0
Jonathan Bothamley Sn.	–: 2: 0	–: 1: 0	–: 1: 0	–: 4: 0
Abram Bothamley	–: 4: 0	–: 2: 0	–: 2: 0	–: 8: 0
John Bothamley	–: –: –	–: 2: 0	–: –: –	–: 2: 0
William Bothamley	–: 2: 6	–: –: –	–: 2: 6	–: 5: 0
Joseph Woodhead	1: 1: 0	–: 7: 6	–: –: –	1: 8: 6
Elizabeth Brook	–: 5: 0	–: 2: 6	–: 1: 0	–: 8: 6
Joseph Broadhead	–: 5: 0	–: –: –	–: 1: 0	–: 6: 0
John Broadhead	1: 1: 0	–: 5: 0	–: 5: 0	1:11: 0
Thomas Roberts, Jr.	–: 5: 0	–: 2: 0	–: 2: 0	–: 9: 0
Josh.Broadhead, Ridings	–:10: 0	–: –: –	–: –: –	–:10: 0
William Earnshaw	–: 5: 0	–: 2: 0	–: 2: 0	–: 9: 0
Caleb Broadhead	–:10: 6	–: 5: 0	–: 2: 6	–:18: 0
Robt. Broadhead	–: 5: 0	–: 2: 6	–: 2: 6	–:10: 0
Robert Kaye	–:10: 0	–: –: –	–: 2: 6	–:12: 6
Richard Brook	–: 5: 0	–: 1: 0	–: –: –	–: 6: 0
Jos.Brook, Wooldale	1: 1: 0	–: 9: 0	–:10: 6	2: 0: 6
Daniel Brook	–:10: 6	–: –: –	–: –: –	–:10: 6
James Radley	–: 2: 6	–: –: –	–: –: –	–: 2: 6
Godfrey Woodhead Jr.	–: 2: 6	–: 2: 0	–: –: –	–: 4: 6
Esther Broadhead	–: 2: 0	–: 1: 0	–: 1: 0	–: 4: 0
Martha Elinson	–: 2: 0	–: 1: 0	–: 2: 0	–: 5: 0
Rachel Broadhead	–: 2: 0	–: 1: 0	–: –: –	–: 3: 0
Joseph Beamont	–: –: –	–: 2: 0	–: 2: 0	–: 4: 0
Hannah Dickinson	–: –: –	–: 1: 6	–: –: –	–: 1: 6
Jos. & Sam Wood	–: –: –	–: 1: 6	–: –: –	–: 1: 6
Elihu Dickinson	–: –: –	–: 1: 0	1: 1: 0	1: 2: 0
Ann Dickinson Jr.	–: –: –	–: –: 6	–: –: –	–: –: 6
Sarah Broadhead Jr.	–: –: –	–: 1: 0	–: –: –	–: 1: 0

	First	Second	Third	Total
William Stead	–: –: –	–: 3: 0	–: 1: 0	–: 4: 0
Mary Roberts Jr.	–: –: –	–: –: –	–: 1: 0	–: 1: 0
Jona. Bothamley Jr.	–: –: –	–: –: –	–: 5: 0	–: 5: 0
Joseph Haigh	–: –: –	–: –: –	–: 2: 0	–: 2: 0
Joseph Priest Jr.	–: –: –	–: –: –	–: 1: 0	–: 1: 0
Joshua Earnshaw	1: 0: 0	–: –: –	–: –: –	1: 0: 0
Godfrey Woodhead Sn.	2:10: 0	1: 0: 0	–: 3: 0	3:13: 0
Enoch Dickinson	2:10: 0	1:10: 0	–: 3: 0	4: 3: 0
James Dickinson	1: 1: 0	–:10: 6	–: –: –	1:11: 6
Thomas Earnshaw Jr.	1: 1: 0	–: 5: 0	–: 3: 0	1: 9: 0
Jonathan Green	–:10: 6	–: 4: 6	–: –: –	–:15: 0
John Sanderson	5: 0: 0	1: 0: 0	–: 5: 0	6: 5: 0
Thomas Earnshaw Sn.	2: 2: 0	–: –: –	–: –: –	2: 2: 0
Benj. Dickinsom	–: –: –	–: 5: 0	–: 2: 0	–: 7: 0
Thomas Dickinson	–: –: –	–: 5: 0	–: 2: 0	–: 7: 0
Sarah Dickinson	–: –: –	–: 3: 0	–: –: –	–: 3: 0
Joshua Earnshaw Jr.	–: –: –	–: 3: 0	–: 1: 6	–: 4: 6
Elizabeth Earnshaw Jr.	–: –: –	–: 1: 0	–: –: –	–: 1: 0
Sarah Earnshaw	–: –: –	–: 2: 0	–: 1: 0	–: 3: 0
Esther Kaye	–: –: –	–: 1: 0	–: –: 6	–: 1: 6
Wm. Earnshaw Jr.	–: –: –	–: –: –	–: 2: 6	–: 2: 6
Sarah Woodhead	–: –: –	–: –: –	–: 2: 6	–: 2: 6
David Dickinson	–: –: –	–: –: –	–: 1: 0	–: 1: 0
Sarah Earnshaw Sn.	–: –: –	–: –: –	–: 1: 0	–: 1: 0
Doratha Green	–: –: –	–: –: –	–: 1: 0	–: 1: 0
Samuel Green	–: –: –	–: –: –	–: 1: 0	–: 1: 0
Joseph Shan	–: –: –	–: –: –	–:10: 6	–:10: 6
From Wakefield Mtg.	1:11: 0	–: 9: 6	–: –: –	2: 0: 6
From Burton Mtg.	1:10: 0	–: 9: 0	–: –: –	1:19: 0
From Pontefract Mtg.	1: 7: 0	–:13: 6	–: –: –	2: 0: 6
From Yorks. Qtly. Mtg.	–: –: –	–: –: –	–: –: –	5: 5: 0
From frds. meetings	–: –: –	–: –: –	–: –: –	2: 2: 0
From another friend	–: –: –	–: –: –	–: –: –	–: 5: 0

Total raised £69:11: 6

To raise the required amount for the building of a new Meeting House at Lumbroyd the meetings made 3 separate subscriptions in the course of 1763. Appendix (6) shows and account of the expenditure on Lumbroyd Meeting House. The individual amounts subscribed are also an interesting source in helping to assess the affluence of Friends in this area particularly when related to the other appendices concerning expenditure.

APPENDIX (6)

An account of the expense in building Lumbroyd Meeting House (1763)

The Ground where on the house is built with the Grave yard and other Ground thereunto belonging	2: 6: 8
The Lawyers Bill for making the Conveyance	6: 2: 9
The several sorts of Stone with Leading	13: 9: 0
The several sorts of Wood with Leading	11: 11: 6
The Masons Bill	17: 15: 5.5

The Carpenters Bill	3: 6: 8
The Joiners Bill	3: 16: 2
The Glaziers Bill	–: 16:10
The Labourers Bill	1: 5: 4
The Blacksmiths Bill	1: 18: 9
The Lime and Sand	3: 0: 6
The Expence in making the out Fence with the gates	4: 1: 8

Total Expense £69: 11: 3.5

APPENDIX (7)

Structural History of Friends Meeting House, Wooldale
(1977)

During the restoration of the Meeting House West Yorkshire Metropolitan County Council had the building surveyed by their Archaeological Unit. A copy of their findings was later sent to Friends and is reproduced here in full along with additional footnotes.

FRIENDS MEETING HOUSE, WOOLDALE (SE 15320908)

The Friends Meeting House at Wooldale is primarily a building of 1783, although it incorporates 17th Century stonework and was partially remodelled internally c.1900.

The building is four bays in length, of which the western 1.5 bays are occupied by a gallery supported on two tuscan stone columns, with a small outshot to the north. The north wall is apparently of late 17th Century date and incorporates a small square opening, now blocked, although it was heightened by five courses during the rebuilding of 1783. The western wall of the outshot can be seen to key into the northern wall of the main block, and would therefore appear also to be of late 17th Century date; the fact that its roof-slope extends as high as the original stonework of the north wall, but not as high as the five courses which heightened it, strenghtens this impression. (1) The west wall is almost certainly of 18th Century date; it includes a two-light window lighting the gallery and an inserted window, c.1900, which lights the space beneath the gallery. The chimney on this gable is probably, on the evidence of its moulded cap, re-used from the 17th Century building. This western gable wall is built of stonework with oversailing courses which, with the fact that the stonework does not course through with that of the outshot, strengthens the supposition that it dates from 1783, as oversailing courses have not been observed in the 17th Century buildings in the graveship of Holme. The eastern wall is apparently built on a plinth and bottom-four courses of 17th Century date, but with the rest of the wall built with the courses of oversailing stonework dating to 1783. The south wall includes a doorway at the western end of which the sides, but not the lintels, are of 17th Century date, but since much of the wall is obscured by ivy it is not possible to state whether the wall includes any 17th Century stonework or whether the doorway mentioned above is in its original position or has been re-used. However, the insertion of the four large windows which occupy this wall would almost certainly have necessitated its rebuilding. Evidence that the central window lighting the main portion of the hall was originally a doorway is missing from the exterior, but is confirmed by a breach in the plank 'panelling' of the interior.

The gallery is supported by four substantial, plain joints and is reached by a stone staircase. The gallery is fronted by a low partition with fielded panels dating to 1783 and is closed off from the main hall by shutters hinged from the ceiling which close onto the partition but which can be swung backwards against the ceiling over the gallery when the latter is in use. The walls of the gallery are lined along the lower half with horizontal planking, almost certainly dating to 1783, with a bench against the north wall. (2)

The main hall has an elders bench built against the east wall, fronted by a low screen of fielded panels, probably dating to 1783. The north wall is lined along its lower part with vertical pine boarding which probably dates to the c.1900 alterations, but the south wall has instead wide horizontal boards of 1783. The floor of the main hall is of narrow pine boards, probably dating to c.1900, and the area under the gallery which was, at that time, partitioned off from the main hall by a moveable panelled partition, has a floor of concrete.

The roof has now been entirely removed, except over the outshot: the new trusses, of queen-post construction with short king posts standing on the collars, are said to reproduce the form of the originals. This, together with the tusked-purlins which were stacked in the graveyard when the building was inspected, indicates that the roof dated to 1783 and did not include any earlier work.

The admittedly limited evidence available suggests that the original 17th Century building was probably of identical size, although lower, than the present meeting house, and that its foundations were re-used during the rebuilding of 1783. The reasons for the 1783 rebuilding may be connected with a desire to improve lighting by replacing the original fenestration with the present large, rectangular windows, but although the building is now an 18th Century one 17th Century material was retained where appropriate, including a fine, cross-boarded door decorated with nail heads in the south wall. (3)

19 Feb. 1977

(1) During the 1977 restoration the outshot's (kitchen) roof was raised over the five courses to the same slope as the main roof. (This was to improve facilities inside).
(2) In 1977 the bench was found to be infested with woodworm and the planking had warped due to damp. So these were replaced in a form to match the original as near as was possible.
(3) As this door is now rotten (1987) it is proposed to replace it with an oak door.

APPENDIX (7b)

Translation of the 1674 Latin document in the Wooldale Title Deeds

At the Court Baron of Christopher Clapham, Knight, Lord of the Manor of Wakefield held there the twenty fifth day of September in the twenty sixth year of the reign of our Lord Charles the Second by the Grace of God of England, Scotland, France and Ireland, King, defender of the faith, etc., At this Court it was witnessed by the oath of William Morehouse a tenant of the Lord that Robert Broadhead of Wooldale on the seventh of March last past before the date of this Court for divers good Causes and Considerations and for the formation of certain agreements and stipulations contained and specified in one part of the Indenture bearing the date of This surrender made between the said Robert Broadhead of the one part and Henry Jackson of Mealhill, Henry Dickinson of Shephouse, Thomas Roberts and Thomas Ellis aforesaid Yeomen of the other part surrendered into the hands of the Lord by his own hands one little close or parcel of land containing by estimation Nineteen Rods in length and eleven Rods in breadth as the same was enclosed with a wall lying and being at the lower end of a close called Pell Croft and adjoining upon the high road called Pell Lane and all Coals and Stones (And Mynes and Quarries) Walls & fences to the same belonging with the appurtenances in Wooldall aforesaid within the grieve of Holme and now or late in the tenure or occupation of the said Robert Broadhead or his assigns at an annual rent to the Lord of 3.25d and for which a Composition was made by a certain fine of the same to the behoof and use of the said Henry Jackson, Henry Dickinson, Thomas Roberts and Thomas Ellis and their heirs and assigns in trust for ever and to and for such uses and intents and purposes and for under such agreements and limitations as they mention and specify; appoint, limit and declare in the aforesaid Indentures as to no other use intent or purpose whatsoever which was granted to the said Henry Jackson, Henry Dickinson, Thomas Roberts and Thomas Ellis to hold themselves and their heirs for ever under the said trust and in the words and from aforesaid by the services according the custom of the Manor and they give to the Lord for fines of entry 3.25d.

Before me Thomas Whitaker Under Steward there.
Endorsed:-
Henry Jackson etc. Holme

Translation of the 1715 Latin Document in the Wooldale Title Deeds

THE MANOR OF WAKEFIELD At the Great Court Barons of the most honourable Montagne, Earl of Atingdon and the Reverend Father in Christ the Lord of Lords (?) Philip, Bishop of Hereford and Ralph Freeman, Knight, Lord of the Manor of Wakefield, held there on the 14th day of October in the Second Year of the reign of our Lord, George, by the Grace of God, now King of Great Britain etc. AT THIS Court it was witnessed by the oath of James Bower, a tenant of the Lords, that Joshua Broadhead of Wooldale, on the second day of May last before the Date of this Court surrendered into the hands of the Lords by their hands All that Messuages or Structure lately built in Wooldale called the Meeting House and two stables belonging to the same and all those parcels of land in which the said house is built containing by Estimation Forty five rods in length and breadth as the same is now divided lying and being in the grieve of Holme at the end of a field called Nabcroft and adjoining on Pell Lane in the North with the appurtenances to the same belonging or in any way appertaining or Being at the Annual Rent to the Lords of a halfpenny and for which a Composition was made by a certain fine of the same to the behalf and use of Joseph Firth, Caleb Broadhead, Ely (Elihu) Dickinson, John Broadhead (son of the aforesaid Caleb), Jonathan Green and Henry Jackson in the County of York and their heirs and Assigns in Trust to and for the uses mentioned, specified and declared in one part of an Indenture being dated with this present surrender and to and for no other use and uses whatsoever which are granted to the said Joseph Firth, Caleb Broadhead, Ely Dickinson, John Broadhead, Jonathan Green and Henry Jackson to hold to them their heirs and assigns in trust to and for the uses aforesaid and in the mode and form aforesaid. In the sevices according to the Custom of the Manor and they gave to the Lords for fine of entry 1.5d.

before me W. Emsall Under Steward there
Endorsed by: Firth & Broadhead, Holme

APPENDIX 8
Gazetteer — Surviving Quaker Houses

Whilst researching into this book the authors were able to locate and visit many of the houses and hamlets that were inhabited by local Quaker families. To help complete a more detailed picture of the past this short gazetteer is provided with brief facts relating to the places mentioned. All the places mentioned have Quaker connections pre-dating 1837.

KEY

BG = Burial Ground D = Demolished F = Former
H = Hamlet I = Inhabited MH = Mtg. House
PR = Private Residence U = Uninhabited

cer. = certainly inhabited in that year
f. = family connected with location
OS grid references quoted are from Sheet 110

Bellroyd PR/I (SE 229049)

f. Thomas & Hannah Dickinson cer. 1777
f. Joshua & Ann Earnshaw cer. 1792

Biggin 2 PR/I (SE 165098)

f. Joshua Broadhead cer. 1760
f. Jonathan & Alice Morehouse cer. 1785
f. Henry & Elizabeth Marsden cer. 1816
f. William & Sarah Morehouse cer. 1817-34

Cheesebottom PR/I (SE 280012)

f. Josiah & Elizabeth Couldwell cer. 1660-1703

Dobroyd PR/I (SE 184089)

f. Samuel & Harriet Bottomley cer. 1879

Ebson House PR/I (SE 178088)

f. Joseph & Susannah Haigh cer. 1785
f. Enoch & Tabitha Dickinson cer. 1822

Folly PR/I (SE 227047)

f. James & Hannah Dickinson cer. 1766

Height PR/I (SE 163114)

f. Thomas & Harriet Bottomley cer. 1814

Hollingreave PR/I (SE 161096)

f. Alice Morehouse cer. 1779

Judd Field FMH/PR/I (SE 239007)

f. John Couldwell cer. 1668
f. John Green cer. 1677
f. Josias Couldwell cer. 1694
f. Joshua & Hannah Earnshaw cer. 1777
f. Thomas Earnshaw cer. 1800
f. Job Jepson cer. 1832

Lane Head FMH/PR/I (SE 192089)

f. John Firth cer. 1689
f. Joseph Firth cer. 1709
f. Joseph Firth cer. 1786
f. John Firth cer. 1825
f. Mary Firth cer. 1879
f. Helen Wood cer. 1910

Langley Brook PR/I (SK 249990)

f. Henry Jackson I cer. 1669-1679
f. Edna Greaves cer. 1715

Meal Hill H/PR/I (SE 168070)

f. Henry Jackson I cer. 1665 and earlier.
f. Gervas Kaye cer. 1668
f. John Jepson cer. 1684
f Richard Middleton cer. 1710

Mearhouse H (SE 165080)

f. Joshua & Sarah Brook(e)
f. Robert & Mary Broadhead cer. 1711-36
f. Daniel & Hannah Broadhead cer. 1766-94
f. Benjamin & Lydia Broadhead cer. 1811-37

Meltom House PR/I (SE 168077)

f. Abraham & Ann Wood cer. 1746
f. John & Sarah Broadhead cer. 1757-1807

Mount PR/I (SE 177077)

f. Godfrey Woodhead cer. 1680 and earlier.
f. John & Sarah Woodhead cer. 1706
f. Joseph & Lydia Woodhead cer. 1731-40
f. Abraham & Ann Beaumont cer. 1757

Midhope Hall FMH/H/PR/I (SK 233995)

f. John Woodhouse cer. 1657
f. William Downend cer. 1660-70
f. John Charlesworth cer. 1667
f. Jonathan Woodhouse cer. 1732

Mill Bank House, High Flatts PR/I (SE 212075)

f. Elihu Dickinson (Tanner) cer. 1828
f. Herbert Camm Dickinson cer. 1875

Newhouse PR/U (SE 208078)

f. Anne Roberts cer. 1672
f. Mary & Thomas Parkinson cer. 1690
f. Joshua Green cer. 1710
f. Abraham & Rebecca Wood cer. 1722
f. Samuel & Susannah Wood cer. 1772
f. Joseph Wood cer. 1750-1821
f. Robert & Sarah Wood cer. 1830
f. John Wood cer. 1855
f. William Wood cer. 1892
f. John Sadler cer. 1911

Pell Croft PR/I (SE 153091)

f. Robert Broadhead cer. 1670
f. Joseph Brook cer. 1779
f. John Brook cer. 1837
f. Robert Walker cer. 1880
f. Joseph Walker cer. 1939

Ridings PR/I (SE 153094)

f. Joshua Broadhead cer. 1760
f. Elizabeth Woodhead cer. 1879-1911

Sheephouse FMH/2 PR/I (SE 244016)

f. Francis Couldwell cer. 1661
f. Henry Dickinson cer. 1667-76
f. Caleb & Sarah Dickinson cer. 1712-50

Shepley Woodend PR/I (SE 181096)

f. John & Rebecca Earnshaw 1745
f. Jonathan Bottomley cer. 1751
f. Abraham Bottomley cer. 1800

Sim Hill ? (SE 299018)

f. Elias & Margaret Morton cer. 1669-82

Strines, High Flatts H/U/D (SE 214074)

f. Henry Dickinson cer. 1752-86
f. John & Jonathan Dickinson cer. 1820

Totties Hall PR/I (SE 157082)

f. Henry Jackson II cer. 1684
f. Henry Jackson III cer. 1715

Wood PR/I (SE 218081)

f. Tobias & Susannah Mallinson cer. 1760
f. John Bottomley cer. 1820

Wooldale Hall PR/I (SE 152088)

f. Elihu Jackson cer. 1740

Further Places of Interest (associated with Quakers)

Birkhouse
Croft Nook, Shepley (SE 185091)
Ford Mill (SE 155084)
Greenhouse, Penistone
Gunthwaite Hall (SE 238065)
Hagg, nr. Honley
Hill End (SE 185085)
Hill Top, Fulstone
Leeside, Scholes
Moorside Nook, Denby
Park Head, Cumberworth
Pithouse, Shepley (SE 184091)
Silver-Ing, Emley
Springhouse, Wooldale
Toppitt, Clayton West
Upper Holmhouse, New Mill
Westroyds, Shepley (SE 183090)

APPENDIX (9)

Barbary Jackson Testimony

'Barbary Jackson the only Child of Matthew Lupton of Upper Breadley near Scipton in Craven was Borne of believing parents and though her mother dyed in her childhood her father tooke great care in her Education being a man of Considerable estate and when she grew up to about thee age of 14 or 15 the Enemie sought to puff her up in mind because of her fathers Estate in which she was likely to succed & so far prevailed to get sume nippings in her head, clothes & pletts at the ears thereof, tho not to that digre that many now professing truth wears, but the great & good god by his light & grace manifested thee Evil Seed thee Enemie had sown in her heart So that she would often say that when she heard any friend declare against pride Shee thought Shee was thee person Spoaken of, which continued untill She was visitted with the Smalll pox which was about thee 18th year of her age now the Lord who had mercyfuly followed her stroke home, Laying thee State of hir Soul before hir, which rought a godly Sorrow withe resolution that if it pleased the Lord to restore hir, Shee would be more careful for time to come & in mercy Shee was remembered & as soone as she could get out of the roome, hir first work was to Cutt hir head Clothes & bring them into as much plainess as posably She could, which occationed Some of hir intimate acquaintance tho of the same persuation to revile her with unbecoming words, nevertheless She kept Stedfast to him who had began the good work for they Carring on thereof to his own praise & her Souls good; & afterwards thro the good providence of God Shee was married unto Henry Jackson who lived togeither in true Love for the space of 14 years in which time She bore to him 7 Children 2 of whome died & She behaved her Self as a tender mother in Israel to thee gaining of the Love of many & perticulorly of thee poor. She allso Stood firme against the Payment of tythes and Steeple house Rates, and about 9 months before she died She was visited with some weakness which caused vomiting of most of what She tooke which Continued with her untill her dying day, during the time of her Ilness she uttered diverss sweet Expressions to the tendering of those present which for brevities Sacke are omitted in this maniscript; and after having recomended her Children to the Lord & her husband She departed in peace.

So we desire these may be taken notis of to be an additional Caution unto all our youth & young Women who may not yet be Comme out of Such thing, least they so far reject the Striving of the Lord; as to have repentance to Seek when it is too late.

(W)PMMB (1713-1742) Extract written during 1717.

The Haverford Colleges Document

The following document is part of the Quaker Collection lodged with the Harverford Colleges Archives. Henry Jackson's remembrances are in his own handwriting. How the document came to be lodged in the USA is a mystery.

'*Henry ye Son of Henry & Kathren Jackson was born ye 10th day of ye 6th Mo: 1680 Barbary ye daught. of Matthew & Martha Lupton was born ye 8th: 2nd Mo: 1684*

The said Henry & Bar. was married upon the 9th: 1st: Mo: 1713 Elizabeth the daught. of ye sd: Henry & Barbary Jackson was born ye 22nd: 1 Mo: 1704

A son borne unto ye sd: Hen. & Bar. Jackson upon ye 23rd: 6th: Mo: 1706:
    Buried upon ye 24th sd: Mo:
Henry ye son of Henry & Barbary Jackson was born upon ye 22nd day of ye 6th Mo:1708
...and died upon ye 10th: 8th Mo: following

Martha the daught. of Hen. & Barbary Jackson was born upon ye 25th: 10:Mo:1709
Mary ye daught. of Hen. & Barbary Jackson was born upon ye 6th: 10: Mo:1711
Hannah ye daught. of Hen. & Barbary Jackson was born upon ye 27th: 9th: Mo:1713
Ebenz. Jackson ye Son of Hen. & Barbary was borne ye 5th:12th:Mo:1715

1717:

Barbary Jackson my Loving Wife after shee had nursed Ebeneezer & wained him, was visited with weakness in her stummoch wth. awful vomitting of Most of what shee tooke, so that shee got little nourishment of it; wch: proved a Consumtion, & tho' shee tooke diverse medicines, by several Doctors: yet nothing reached to ye removing of ye Distemper and about two weeks before she died her Father lying very Weak; she was Desirous to (make) a Journey as with her life in her hands, she accomplish this about 24 hours before his death, to both their Satisfactions & about 2 weeks after, having Utterd diverse sweet expressions to her husband & having done her days Work in ye day time, she departed in peace, & is gone to her lasting rest prepared of God for righteous Souls, she died on ye 17th of ye 10th Mo: at her father's Matthew Lupton's house at Upper Breadley in Craven, & was buried at Friends Burial place in Lower Breadley ye 21st: of ye 10th: Mo:1717: The Lords power & favour his large hands being manifested to his Waiting Children this day. (The Lord almighty?) helps me so to walk as I may arrive safe at ye Port of Everlasting rest is ye fervant desires of my soul:
                          Amen & done
                          Hen. Jackson

Our Deare Father Henry Jackson Departed this Life of a (Pleurisy?) Fevore ye 22nd of ye 10th Mo:1727

In another hand

Ebeneezer Jackson, departed this Life the 19th of the 11th Mo. 1775 and was buried in Friends Burial ground at Farrfield the 23rd of the same.

APPENDIX (10)

Testimonies recorded in Yorkshire Quarterly Meeting Minutes.

Ann Broadhead

A Testimony from the Monthly Meeting of Pontefract in Yorkshire concerning Ann Broadhead.

We cannot give much Account of this our Dear Deceased Friend, before she came to reside within ye Compass of this Monthly Meeting which was about ye year 1727: Save only yet we Understand, She was one whom Divine Providence wa pleased Early to Visit, fitt & prepare for a Minister of his Everlasting Gospel & was drawn forth in ye Love thereof to Visit ye Meetings of Fds. in several of ye Nothern Counties. But since her abode with us, Her Concern Lay Chiefly in her own & some Neighbouring Meetings.

She was a diligent attender of Meetings for Worship & Discipline, & in ye time of Silence therein, Her Countenance was both Awfull & Weighty. In ye Exercise of her Gift, she was Clear Solid & Lively. She was a Nursing Mother in ye Church & more especially so, to those Young in ye Ministry, was one of a Tender & Affectinote Spirit & Charitably disposed Often Visiting & simpathizing with those under Affliction. Her Mild & Innocent Conversation & deportment Corresponded with ye Doctrine she preached which Engaged Frds. Love Exeedingly towards her. She was a Pattern of plainess & Humility.

The Indisposition of Body which Occationed her Death was of a long Continuance attended with great pain which endured with remarkable Patience for some years before Her Decease She was much Confined at Home yet her strong desire to be at Meetings made her sometimes Struggle hard with those Infirmities She Laboured under, In so much at time ye Meeting She belonged to was Favoured with her Company, Altho in much weakness Yet she was Strong in ye Lord & ye Power of his Might by which she was enabled to Bear, Several Living & Powerfull Testimonies to ye Truth, which made Lasting Impressions on ye minds of some who are yet Left Behind.

Towards the Conclusion of her time, she gave good Advice & great Encouragement to some yet Visited her Especially ye Youth, her Earnest desire being they might not only be through to ye knowledge of ye Truth, but also come to Witness ye Power thereof to Establish them in Righteousness & Holyness of Life.

She departed this Life on ye 1st of 6th Month 1763 & on ye 4th of the same was intered in friends Burying Ground at Wooldale, And we doubt not but she Enjoys the Reward of her Faithfull labours, her soul being at Peace with God in his Kingdom, where the Righteous Rest and Sorrowing is no more.

Aged 78 a Minister near 50 years. Signed In and on behalf of Pontefract Monthly Meeting held there the 8th of the 3rd Month 1764 By

John Broadhead	Elizb. Clarkson
Edwd. Dickinson	Elizb. Leatham
Jenny Dickinson	Margaret Dickinson
Sam Empson	Hannah Marsden
Joseph Milthorp	Jane Brone (Brown)
John Clarkson	Mary Burn
Wm. Leatham	Mary Booth
John Walker	Amelia Walker
Joseph Burn	Hannah Burn
John Brown	

Sarah Marsden

The Testimony of Pontefract Mo. Meeting in Yorkshire concerning Sarah Marsden with some dying Sayings Annexed.

Our Dear Friend aforesaid, was Born of Believing Parents within the perticular Meeting of Highflatts, in ye Year 1706; and was not only favoured with a Religious Education, but with ye Visitation of Truth in her Early days; & by Yielding Obedience to ye Manifestations thereof, became a Sober, grave, discreet Young Woman.

In the Year 1733 She Joined herself in Marriage to our frd. Caleb Marsden and was a diligent attender of Meetings for Worship & Discipline, Honestly Engaged to improve her time therein Insomuch, yet in ye Year 1749 It pleased the Lord to Call her to ye Works of ye Ministry, to which in great fear & tenderness of Spirit, She gave up to, She was not large in Testimony But her Ministry was Plain, Sound & Edifying, & such as had a right discerning, it was clearly Manifested yet She was a Disciple of Humble Jesus. She was not hasty but rather backward in ye Publick Appearance & Affraid as she said to awake her beloved till he pleased, but when She felt ye Holy Fire Burning, she offered her Gift, & when that abated She sat down ... In Meetings whereof ye Ministers of too many are more Intent upon Words, if not to a Witness of ye Mercy & favour of God in 'emselves, She was a diligent Labourer in both Spirit and a burthen bearer, her very countenance was both Awfull & Affecting to some (who) are yet left behind; & at times, when she found ye Spring to Lie Low Like ye Worthy Elders and Nobles of ye People in the days of Old She was concerned to dig with ye Staff ye Lord had given her, & sometimes break forth in Solemn Supplication to ye great Lawgiver if ye Well of Life might Spring up which at times it was the happy instrument of Effecting, to ye Consolation of Ye Lord & People; & altho her publick Service was not very extensive, yet she frequently Attended our Quarterly Meeting & was zealous for ye Cause of God & promotions of his truth upon the Earth.

She was naturally of an affable, Peaceable disposition, an Affectionate Wife, a Tender Mother & Weightily concerned to Train up her Children in ye Nature & Admonition of ye Lord; Kind to her Frds, Charitable to ye Poor, & in Humility, Self denial & Resignations to ye Divine Will, as also in industry & a Prudent Management of the Affairs of this Life, a good Example to all.

Her Last Illness was Long & serious which, She Endured with much Patience & Resignation saying 'My Body is full of Pain, yea more than I can well bear, O the sad state of those in my poor Weak Condition who want peace of mind, But forever blessed by my God who now upon my sick bed answering ye desire of my mind in giving me evidence of my Peace with him, having nothing to do, but bear with patience ye Painfull Afflictions that are permitted to attend me. I find in its work enough to struggle with Nature; One had need have nothing else to do; My Breathing & Travail of Soul hath often been to ye Lord that he would let me see my Duty, & give me strength to perform it. If I had my time to spend over again, I know not if I could spend it much better. I can truly say, I have never been forward in my Appearance in Meetings & other things relating to ye Society; But always in great fear which Sometimes hath been so great that I have been too backward & have hurt myself thereby.'

To some Frds. present said 'Dear Frds. stand in ye Lord fear not Man; come up in ye proper places & ye God of Peace will be with you & strengthen you to perform & come up in ye way of your Duty to him & one unto another, & so you will be preserved in ye pure Love & Unity of the One Spirit.'

At another time a Frd. call'd to see her to which she said, 'Thou or I have been very near one with another: O my Body is full of Pain! I am some times ready to say, Lord what have I done; O I want to be eas'd & disolved My stay here seems very long, at Morning I wish for Night, at Night I long for Morning, but yet Blessed be my God, I feel his hand is underneath, & he bears up my Spirit, or I could not tell how to endure my Affliction.

At another time being very weak, she said to her Husband & Children At ye time of my departure, be as still as you can, & feel for your selves & do not mourn to Excess for all will be well, Do not mourn for me, but rather Rejoice when I am Delivered from these Pains, for my Change will be (a) happy one.

One Evening lying very still those that that attended her thought had been going to depart, but after sometime She opend her eyes & seeing her Relations standing by her, She raised her voice in a surprising manner & said 'I am entirely sensible & behold you every one & glad I am to depart in Peace' & took her Solemn Farewell of all present, thinking ye time of her departure had been very near but she continued some days longer, most of which she lay very still in a quiet, Peaceable & Resigned Frame of Mind, Patiently waiting for her dissolution, And tho' her Voice was very weak yet she was heard to say 'O that my Sweet Redeemer would come & take me to himself, do not hold me but Let me go freely.

We are fully persuaded She finished her course well, & that She is at rest with the Righteous.

She died ye 8th of ye 8th Month 1762 And was decently interred ye 11th of the same in Frds. Burying Ground at Highflatts.

Aged 56 a Minister 13 Years. Signed in & on behalf of Pontefract Monthly Meeting held there ye 8th of ye 3rd Month 1764 by

John Broadhead	Elizb. Clarkson
Edwd. Dickinson	Elizb. Leatham
Henry Dickinson	Margaret Dickinson
Joseph Milthorp	Hannah Marsden
Wm. Leatham	Jane Brown
Saml. Emson	Mary Burn
John Walker	Mary Booth
Joseph Burn	Amelia Walker
John Brown	Hannah Burn

Read approved & signed in our Quarterly Meeting held at York ye 28th and 29th of ye 3rd Month 1764 by

Roger Shackleton

Sarah Earnshaw

Sarah Earnshaw Daughter of William Earnshaw of Totties in the Parish of Kirkburton who departed this Life the 20th of the 9th Month 1782 & was buried the 23rd of the same in Friends Burying Ground at Wooldale, Aged about 23 years, a Minister about 2 Years, of whom the Friends of Pontefract Monthly Meeting give the following account (viz) She was early favoured with the Powerful Visitation of Truth, and by Yielding Obedience there unto became a good example to the Youth amongst us; A Pattern of Plainess, Humility & Self Denial; a diligent attender of our Religious Meetings, and a Patient waiter in Spirit therein for the arisings of Life; Her appearances in the Ministry were not large nor very frequent, but as we believe she was careful to move under the direction of Divine Wisdom, were truly acceptable & she experienced a gradual growth in her Gift.

Henry Dickinson

Henry Dickinson of Strinds (Strines) near Highflatts who departed this Life the 17th of the 9th Month 1786 and was buried in Friends Burying Ground at Highflatts the 20th of the same aged about 76 a minister about 36 years; concerning whom the Monthly Meeting at Pontefract gives the following account viz. He was favoured with the powerful Visitation of Truth when Young and by Yielding Obedience therunto, his mind became weaned from his former companions and those Childish Sports and Pastimes in which he had much delighted, and was led to seek after and love (?) and a diligent reading of the Holy Scriptures. About the 40th Year of his Age he came forth in the work of the Ministry acceptably. He travelled not much abroad but was a diligent attender of our own and Neighbouring Meetings, even when under great bodily Affliction.

John Broadhead

Our Public friend deceased viz. John Broadhead of Wooldale who departed this Life the 21st of the 5th Month 1787 and was buried in Friends Burying Ground at Wooldale on the 24th of the same Aged about 22 years, having at times expressed a few words in Meetings for 3 years.

William Earnshaw

Quarterly meeting 3rd Month 1803 William Earnshaw of Wooldale a Member of Pontefract Monthly Meeting departed this Life the 14th of the 7th Month 1802 and was buried in Friends Burial Ground at Wooldale the 18th of the same aged 84 years, a Minister about 52 years.

APPENDIX (11)

Intentions to marry between 1680-1802

Recorded in the Monthly & Preparative Meeting Minute Books.

The following contain the names of those who have been identified as belonging to the group of particular meetings affiliated to High Flatts Meeting Wooldale, Lane Head, Midhope, Judd Field, Shephouse & Lumbroyd.

Godfrey Morehouse (of Mount)	Sarah Swift (of Denby)	07/10/1680
Francis West (of Midhope)	Elizb. Robuck (Sheffield)	03/01/1680
Joshua Brooke (of Mearhouse)	Sarah Oxley (Skelmanthorpe)	07/05/1681
Edmond Kay (of Fartown in Huddersfield)	Sarah Kay (of Meal Hill)	05/02/1683
Wm. Earnshaw (Bradfield)	Ann Roberts (W)	13/07/1683
John Box (Harlington)	Martha Woodhouse (Midhope)	08/11/1683
John Jepson (Meal Hill)	Elizb. Marsden (HF)	10/02/1684
Richard Brooke (Huddersfield)	Martha Marsden (HF)	12/05/1685
Wm. Marsden (of Birdsedge)	Martha Crossley	05/07/1685
Wm. Naylor (W)	Anne Benson (Ossett)	09/06/1688
Joseph Kay (of Meal Hill)	Elizb. Ellis (W)	10/02/1690
Danl. Broadhead (of Shelley)	Elizb. Sanderson (Midhope)	14/06/1690
Joshua Marsden (HF)	Bethene Scaife (Pontefract)	11/07/1690
Joshua Dickinson (of Sheephouse)	Mary Brookesbank	12/01/1690
Joseph Couldwell (of Midhope)	Martha Coldwell (Midhope)	14/03/1691
David Dickinson (Thurlstone)	Mary Horsfall (York)	12/09/1691
John Wilkinson (Midhope)	Martha Couldwell (Judfield)	10/06/1691
Thos. Parkinson (HF)	Martha Green (Newhouse)	10/06/1692
Joshua Priest (Denby)	Ann Brookesbank	12/05/1693
Gervase Seaton (Blyth)	Elizb. Jackson (Totties)	12/05/1693
Josiah Couldwell (Judfield)	Martha Marsden (Swinden)	03/07/1693
John Kenworthy (HF)	Alice Honare (Mankinghole)	14/04/1694
Thos. Parkinson (Thurlstone)	Mary Couldwell (Judfield)	09/05/1696
Josh. Brookesbank (of Gunthwaite)	Rebecca Dickinson (of Sheephouse)	12/12/1696
Caleb Roberts (W)	Mary Jackson (Bradford)	10/12/1697
Joseph Hobson (Holmfirth)	Sara Dyson (Holmfirth)	10/01/1698
Henry Marsden (Birdsedge)	Martha Marsden	11/11/1698
Joshua Sanderson (Midhope)	Grace Haigh (Halifax)	10/05/1701
Caleb Marsden (Birdsedge)	Mary Morehouse (of Mount)	14/06/1701
Arthur Brookesbank (Denby)	Ann Kay (of Row in in Huddersfield)	08/10/1702
John Priest (of Denby)	Sara Roberts (W)	14/11/1702
Joshua Marsden (HF)	Mary Durden	11/01/1703
Henry Jackson (Totties)	Barbary Lupton	12/06/1703
Richard Ellis	Martha Pearson	14/08/1703
John Woodhead	Sarah Morehouse	10/12/1703
Elihu Dickinson	Mary Firth (Lane Head)	09/06/1705
Danl. Dickinson	Rachel Fisher (Bradnall)	11/08/1705
Edw. Benson (Huddersfield)	Sarah Webster	11/05/1706

John Kay (Lane End)	Edith Walker	10/08/1706
Rich. Middleton (Totties)	Mary Broadhead	10/05/1707
Caleb Dickinson	Sarah Firth (Lane Head)	12/12/1707
John Dickinson	Mary Hague	12/12/1707
Joseph Firth Jr. (Lane Head)	Hannah Dickinson	13/08/1709
Uriah Brook (HF)	Elizb. Broadhead	11/11/1710
Matthew Broadhead	Mary Jessup (Jr).	11/11/1710
John Couldwell (Cumberworth)	Mary Couldwell (HF)	14/06/1712
Joseph Mosley (Denby)	Hannah Dickinson (Shephouse)	14/03/1713
Jonathan Green	Anne Wilcokson	10/10/1713
Robt. Broadhead (W)	Mary Kay	13/03/1714
Jn. Marshland (Quarmby)	Grace Dobson	10/12/1714
Benj. Downing (Midhope)	Edna Greaves (Langley Brook)	14/02/1715
Elihu Dickinson	Sarah Kay	14/03/1715
Joseph Brook (of Row)	Elizb. Garner	13/10/1716
John Earnshaw (HF)	Rebecca Green (HF)	09/03/1717
Robert Kay	Mary Priest	13/01/1717
Tobias Mallinson (HF)	Sarah Broadhead	05/01/1718
Joshua Hirst	Rachel Dickinson	14/06/1718
Epaphras Brook	Martha Broadhead	16/04/1719
Joseph Mosley (HF)	Hannah Broadhead	13/06/1719
Joseph Hobson	Sarah Charlesworth	11/12/1719
Isaac Latimer (Lane Head)	Rachel Kay (Wakefield)	30/09/1720
John Knowle (Knaresboro)	Tabatha Broadhead	12/02/1722
Geo. Wadsworth (Burton)	Hannah Roberts	10/08/1722
Joshua Earnshaw	Sarah Couldwell	03/05/1723
Richard Green	Mary Kay	06/02/1726
John Clark	Elizb. Key	02/03/1726
John Kay	Mary Wood	09/12/1726
Edward Dickinson	Ann Jepson	11/06/1727
Wm. Chadwick (Brighouse)	Elizb. CrowdeR	31/05/1728
Geo. Haworth	Mary Hine	10/04/1729
John Wood	Hannah Priest	01/02/1730
Abraham Beaumont	Ann Ellis	30/04/1731
Nathaniel Lister (Bingley)	Elizb. Jackson	02/06/1732
Caleb Marsden	Sarah Dickinson	06/12/1733
Enoch Dickinson	Mary Ellis	03/05/1734
Joseph Lister (London)	Martha Jackson	13/02/1735
John Marsden	Hannah Jackson	05/09/1735
Joseph Priest	Martha Woodhead	31/01/1736
Joseph Broadhead	Hannah Wood	05/03/1736
Wm. Bradley	Marg. Beever	28/10/1736
Abram Hague	Hannah Broadhead	04/03/1737
Joseph Hague (W)	Elizb. Jackson	06/05/1737
Joseph Woodhead	Lydia Dickinson	31/06/1737
Henry Dickinson	Hannah Brook	02/09/1737
John Arthington (Leeds)	Mary Jackson	04/05/1739
Geo. Cartwright	Ann Brooksbank	05/07/1739
Edward Dickinson	Ann Greenwood (Brighouse MM)	05/10/1739
Joshua Marsden	Tabitha Benson (Leeds)	02/04/1740
Samuel Brook (HF)	Mary Marsland	31/02/1742
Wm. Earnshaw (Woodhead)	Sarah Brook (HF)	30/04/1742
Geo. Haworth (Marsden MM)	Rachel Broadhead	01/02/1743
John Green	Sarah Woodhead	31/06/1743
Elihu Dickinson	Mary Aldham (Warnsworth MM)	04/11/1743
Joshua Woodhead	Mary Walker (Brighouse MM)	04/11/1743

Jn. Ellis (Woodhouse Mtg).	Mary Brooksbank	11/02/1744
Joseph Clark (Warnsworth MM)	Hannah Firth	09/03/1744
Arthur Jepson	Hannah Haugh	01/06/1744
Robert Aldham (Sheffield)	Sarah Dickinson	05/06/1744
John Hirst (Sheffield)	Martha Priest	08/07/1744
Joseph Hague	Ann Laws (Mankingholes)	25/09/1744
Jas. Standing (Brighouse MM)	Martha Brook	01/03/1745
Godfrey Woodhead	Martha Dickinson	05/12/1745
Simon Dyson (Brighouse MM)	Sarah Mallinson	02/05/1746
John Wright (Leeds)	Mary Broadhead	06/03/1747
Samuel Wood	Susanah Walker	04/09/1747
Jonathan Green	Mary Law (Brighouse MM)	03/12/1748
Jn. Broadhead (Meltomhouse)	Sarah Greaves	06/04/1750
John Earnshaw (Woodend)	Mary Broadhead	04/05/1750
Jn. Broadhead (Meltomhouse)	Sarah Greaves	06/04/1750
John Earnshaw (Woodend)	Mary Broadhead	04/05/1750
Joseph Wade	Susanah Dickinson	29/05/1754
Jn. Webster (Burton)	Rebecca Woodhead	03/07/1754
Jos. Broadhead	Ann Haigh	02/10/1754
Robert Kay	Jane Smith (Brighouse MM)	02/10/1754
Tobias Mallinson	Susana Howard (Mankingholes)	30/04/1755
Jo. Walker	Esther Dickinson	30/04/1755
William Radley	Mary Walker (Gildersome)	11/05/1757
James Dickinson	Hannah Kay	05/04/1758
Joshua Marsden	Hannah Hargraves (Settle)	05/07/1758
Thomas Roberts	Judith Broadhead	08/08/1760
Wm. Sutcliffe (Brighouse MM)	Sarah Broadhead	10/12/1760
Joshua Earnshaw	Hannah Dickinson	10/12/1760
Thos. Earnshaw	Mary Halley	01/07/1761
Matthew Broadhead	Martha Greaves	30/09/1761
Joseph Beaumont	Mary Wood	02/12/1761
Abram Bottomley	Martha Broadhead	02/12/1761
Wm. Bottomley	Hannah Beever	05/05/1762
Daniel Broadhead	Hannah Wood	04/08/1762
John Haigh	Hannah Dickinson	03/11/1762
Joseph Shaw	Elizabeth ??? (Settle)	06/04/1763
Benjamin Dickinson	Martha Earnshaw	31/08/1763
Caleb Broadhead	Ruth Jackson (Blyth MM)	31/08/1763
Jo. Brook	Mary Roberts	05/06/1765
Wm. Cooper (Brighouse MM)	Sarah Woodhead	05/06/1765
Robt. Crosland (Brighouse MM)	Mary Marsden	04/09/1766
Joseph Priest	Sarah Dickinson	02/10/1765
Daniel Collier	Mary Dickinson (Balby MM)	02/07/1766
Henry Dickinson	Hannah Green	01/02/1769
David Dickinson	Martha Haigh	04/10/1769
Thos. Dickinson	Hannah Roberts	01/11/1769
Samuel Haigh	Mary Beaumont	03/01/1770
Wm. Keene (Lambeth)	Martha Lister	—/03/1771
Joseph Haigh	Hannah Greaves	31/07/1771
David Dent (Thorne)	Ann Dickinson	05/09/1771
Elihu Dickinson	Sarah Sutcliffe (Brighouse)	21/09/1772
Jared Collins	Esther Haye	01/12/1773
James Broadhead	Hannah Woodhead	05/01/1774
Geo. Ellis (Balby MM)	Hannah Dickinson	12/04/1775
Godfrey Woodhead	Dinah Knowles (Knaresboro)	04/10/1775
Joseph Woodhead	Betty Booth (Wakefield)	03/04/1776

Jn. Earnshaw Jr.	Mary Lees (Marsden MM)	01/01/1777
John Chapman	Sarah Wood	05/02/1777
Samuel Wood Jr.	Mary Firth	06/02/1780
John Firth	Ann Burrow (Knaresboro)	09/04/1780
Michael Teal (Knaresboro)	Martha Dyson	04/06/1780
John Green	Hannah Earnshaw	04/03/1781
Geo. Chapman	Sarah Woodhead	08/04/1781
Elihu Dickinson	Martha Beaumont	07/10/1781
Benjamin Stead	Mary Brook	10/03/1782
Benjamin Walker	Hannah Broadhead	07/04/1782
Joshua Dickinson	Sarah Dickinson	08/09/1782
John Roberts	Hannah Beaumont	06/06/1784
John Kirk	Ann Green	04/07/1784
John Dickinson	Sarah Brook	04/07/1784
John Broadhead (Brighouse MM)	Hannah Knowles (HF)	14/10/1784
Benj. Lees (Marsden MM)	Esther Roberts (HF)	09/06/1785
Samuel Jepson (HF)	Sarah Earnshaw (HF)	08/06/1786
Joseph Lister (Burton)	Susannah Bottomley	13/07/1786
Joshua Earnshaw (HF)	Ann Haigh (HF)	01/03.1787
George Haigh (HF)	Sarah Dyson (HF)	09/08/1787
George Earnshaw (HF)	Ann Pickard (Ackworth)	12/03/1789
John Lees (Marsden MM)	Sarah Broadhead	11/06/1789
Thos. Bottomley	Hannah Lister (Burton)	13/08/1789
Robt. Sutcliffe (Brighouse MM)	Mary Broadhead (HF)	10/09/1789
Benj. Walker (HF)	Esther Metcalf (Notts. MM)	11/11/1790
Joseph Walker	Mary Brook	10/05/1792
Hutchinson Dyson (HF)	Mary Bottomley (W)	09/08/1792
Joshua Roberts (HF)	Judith Dickinson (HF)	09/10/1793
William Dickinson	Elizb. Broadhead (W)	19/01/1796
Henry Swire (W)	Mary Roberts (W)	12/03/1796
Geo. Broadhead (W)	Lydia Grimshaw (Thirsk)	09/03/1797
Robert Grist (HF)	Mary Dickinson (HF)	09/11/1797
William Bottomley (W)	Sarah Brook (W)	06/09/1798
Benj. Walker (HF)	Elizb. Collier (HF)	08/11/1798
Simeon Hunter (Pontefract)	Sarah Dickinson (HF)	11/07/1799
John Brook (HF)	Mary Pickard (W)	08/08/1799
Samuel Woodhead (W)	Jane Firth (HF)	18/01/1802

APPENDIX (12)

Incidents of Marriage out of the Meeting
1712-1801

Joshua Broadhead	1712	Ann Beaumont	1781
Ann Wilkinson	1724	James Brook	1782
Hannah Dickinson	1729	Ann Woodhead	1782
Mary Roberts	1731	Jonathan Brook	1782
Jo. Priest	1737	James Dickinson	1782
Hannah Sanderson	1741	Mary Walker	1783
Sarah Key	1743	Joseph Haigh *	1784
Sarah Dickinson	1745	Susannah Haigh *	1784
Ellin Whalley	1748	John Mallinson	1784
Hannah Broadhead	1748	Martha Bottomley	1786
Jennet Ratliffe	1752	Ann Dickinson	1787
John Beaumont	1762	Joshua Broadhead	1787
Elizb. Brook	1762	Edward Dickinson	1790
John Parkin	1763	David Broadhead	1790
John Priest	1763	John Dickinson	1792
Ann Earnshaw	1768	John Broadhead	1792
Sarah Brook	1770	Lydia Broadhead	1792
Martha Sanderson	1771	Joshua Earnshaw	1796
Wm. Earnshaw	1768	James Taylor	1797
Joseph Haigh	1775	John Walker	1797
Wm. Jepson	1776	Sarah Dickinson	1797
Dorothy Green	1778	Susannah Lister	1798
Joshua Haigh	1778	Hannah Broadhead	1798
Hannah Haigh	1779	Hannah Stead	1800
Sarah Radley	1779	Mary Stead	1801
Ann Jepson	1780		
Daniel Broadhead	1781		
Thomas Broadhead	1781		

There are 53 recorded disownments during this 89 year period. The peak point appears in the 1780's with 15 recorded instances. This is closely followed by the 1790's with 11 disownments.

* Joseph & Susannah Haigh were first cousins who did not have the right to be married amongst Friends. They chose to marry out of the Society of Friends.

APPENDIX (13)

Deceased Ministers 1709-1892

This abstract was compiled from Appendix (15) of 'Yorkshire Quarterly Meeting 1665-1966' W. Pearson Thistlethwaite (pub. by the Author 1979).

RECORDED MINISTER	LOCATION	DEMISED
Thomas Roberts	Wooldale	16/08/1709
Henry Jackson	Wooldale	22/10/1727
Sarah Marsden (Caleb)	High Flatts	08/08/1752
Ann Broadhead	Wooldale	01/06/1763
Elizabeth Brook (Uriah)	High Flatts	07/03/1773
Sarah Earnshaw	Totties, Wooldale	20/09/1782
Mary Dickinson (Enoch)	Thurlstone, High Flatts	01/08/1786
Henry Dickinson	Strines, High Flatts	17/09/1786
John Broadhead	Wooldale	21/05/1787
William Earnshaw	Wooldale	14/07/1802
Joseph Bottomley	Kirkburton, High Flatts	17/01/1820
Joseph Wood	Newhouse, High Flatts	17/01/1821
Hannah Firth	High Flatts	27/03/1865
Joseph Firth	High Flatts	28/08/1873
Godfrey Woodhead	High Flatts	11/02/1880
Sarah Firth (Joseph)	High Flatts	24/02/1892

APPENDIX (14)

Applications for membership from convinced persons

1774-1806

APPLICANT	YEAR	ACCEPTED NOT ACCEPTED
George Chapman	1774	A
John Chapman	1776	A
Jeremia Smith	1778	A
Sarah Morton	1778	A
Mary Dyson	1778	A
William Dyson	1779	A
his son	1779	A
2 daughters	1779	A
Joseph Stead	1780	A
his wife	1780	A
John Kirk	1781	A
Georgiana Carter	1783	NA
William Taylor	1783	A
Mary Lockwood	1784	NA
George Haigh	1785	A
his sister Phebe	1785	A
Sarah Golthorp	1786	A
John Brook	1792	A
Joshua Roberts of Shepley	1792	A
James Taylor *	1792	A
Henry Swire	1795	A
John Haigh	1795	A
Hannah Haigh	1795	A
John Pickford	1795	A
Frances Field	1801	A
Charles Hinchcliff	1806	A

* Joined on the third attempt

APPENDIX (15)

Removals to other Monthly Meetings 1787-1812

Brighouse MM		Balby MM	
Elizabeth Broadhead	1787	Hannah Earnshaw	1789
Joshua Brook	1788	Joshua Broadhead	1792
Sarah Brook		John Cooper	1793
Jonathan *		Ann Dickinson	1797
John *		Ann Stivenson	1797
Robert Fryer **	1789	Enoch Dickinson	1798
Thos. Dickinson **	1790	Mary Earnshaw	1798
Sarah Dickinson	1790	Jane Walker	1799
Joseph Brook **	1791	Hannah Dickinson	1799
Wm. Earnshaw **	1791	Sarah Haigh	1800
Ann Beaumont	1792	Sarah Earnshaw	1801
Mary Stead	1792	Joshua Jepson	1801
Hannah Stead	1792	John Wood	1801
Ann Broadhead	1793	Robert Grist	1802
Mary Dickinson	1793	& Wife	1802
Sarah Stead	1793	William	
Elizabeth Dickinson	1794	Rachel	
John Clay	1795	James Walker	1802
Betty Earnshaw	1795	Jane Dickinson	1802
Joseph Broadhead	1795	Deborah Broadhead	1806
Martha Dickinson	1795	David Dickinson Jr.	1808
Joshua Dickinson	1799	Phebe Hinchliffe	1808
& Wife		Mary Hinchliffe	1808
Gideon		Jonathan Dickinson	1810
Samuel		Hannah Dyson	1810
Edward		Susanna Mallinson	1810
Ann		Sarah Mallinson	1810
Edward Dickinson	1800		
Joseph Dickinson	1802		
& Wife			
Samuel Stead	1806		
Rebecca Stead	1806		
Sarah Haigh	1808		
John Wormal	1809		
Elizabeth Kirk	1809		
Geo. Mallinson **	1809		
Ann Stead	1810		
John Mallinson	1811		
John Adamson	1811		
Mary Adamson	1811		
Thos. Firth	1812		

To other Monthly Meetings		
Thomas Salterthwate	1789	Swarthmore MM
John Chapman	1791	Morley MM (Cheshire)
Sarah Chapman		,, ,,
Mary		,, ,,
William		,, ,,
Sarah		,, ,,
Juliana		,, ,,
Edward Wilson	1793	Knaresboro MM
Ann Dickinson	1801	Morley MM (Cheshire)
Martha Haigh	1803	Knaresboro MM
Edward Woodhead	1806	Pembrokeshire
Ann Roberts	1806	Marsden MM (Lancs).
Edward Earnshaw	1811	Marsden MM (Lancs).

Between 1787 and 1812 there were 81 individual removals from the Meetings at High Flatts and Wooldale. Most of these were to the rapidly developing new industrial urban centres to be found within Balby MM (Sheffield) and Brighouse MM (Huddersfield, Brighouse, Dewsbury, Bradford, Leeds etc.).

* Jonathan & John Brook were eventually disowned by Paddock PM (Huddersfield) according to Paddock PM first minute book.

** Recorded as moving to Huddersfield and attending Paddock PM. (First Minute Book)

APPENDIX (15b)

Members and Attenders: A Tabular Statement 1861-1987

	High Flatts		Wooldale	
YEAR	Mem.	Att.	Mem.	Att.
1861	57	101	34	25
1871	49	65	41	17
1881	36	36	40	13
1891	31	19	44	13
1901	28	22	33	10
1911	24	17	28	9
1921	24	17	21	6
1931	20	**	16	**
1941	20	**	14	**
1951	18	**	15	**
1967	14	**	8	**
1987	14	**	26	**

APPENDIX (16)

MINISTERING FRIENDS VISITING LOCAL MEETINGS 1719-1845

The following list of visiting Friends was compiled from three sources. The first source, entitled 'A Travelling Alphabet of Visting Friends', is part of Pontefract MM archive collection at Ackworth School. The other two sources are from the Joseph Wood Collection (Small Notebook No.1 and Large Memorandum Book No.38). All three original sources were chronologically compiled. This compilation has been arranged alphabetically to avoid undue repetition. The record of visitors is not complete. There is a gap between 1820 and 1842.

After 1792 only those Friends who visited High Flatts Meeting are recorded since in that year Wooldale became a separate PM. Lane Head and Judd Field were meetings only until approximately 1763. Some visitors came on more than one occasion in any given year but this is not indicated. The meeting(s) visited are coded as:

    Wooldale W
    High Flatts H
    Lane Head L
    Judd Field J

The order of meetings recorded is the order of visitation.

A

ABBOT, John	Hunts.	1793(H)
ABBOT, Mary	Northants.	1748(H)
ADAMS, John	Hull	1723(W)
ALDERSON, Alice	Kendal	1736(W) 1745(L)
ALDERSON, John	Westmorland	1759(W) 1763(W)
ALDHAM, Mary	Sheffield	1727(W)
ALEXANDER, Ann	Suffolk	1802(H)
ALEXANDER, William	York	1814(H)
ANDERSON, Thomas	Nr. Skipton	1722(WLH) 1723(W) 1724(L) 1725(W) 1726(W) 1727(W) 1728(H) 1729(W) 1732(W) 1735(W) 1736(W)
ANDREW, Peter	W. Jersey (N.America)	1755(L)
ANESKIN, Thomas	Northumberland	1718(W) 1720(WH) 1720(H)
ANESKIN, Thomas	Aberdeen	1723(HW)
ANNAL, Lydia	Nr.Chesterfield	1719(WL)
APPLEBY, Susannah	Shropshire	1802(H)
APPLETON, John	Lincolnshire	1724(H) 1728(W) 1731(W) 1732(L) 1736(L)
ARNOLD, Rachel	Chesterfield	1720(W) 1723(L) 1724(L) 1727(W) 1728(H)
ARNOLD, Rachel	Sheffield	1733(W)
ASHALL, James	Nr.Keighley	1720(W)
ASHBY, Richard	Thetford, Norfolk	1724(W)
ATKINSON, Aaron	Nr.Leeds	1719(W) 1720(W) 1721(W) 1722(W) 1723(H) 1724(W) 1725(W) 1726(W) 1729(W) 1730(W) 1732(L) 1733(L) 1734(W) 1737(H)
ATKINSON, Henry	Carlisle	1728(W) 1729(W)
ATKINSON, Joseph	Cumberland	1722(L) 1723(H)

Name	Place	Dates
ATKINSON, Sarah	Rawcliffe	1754(L) 1760(L)
ATKINSON, Sibylla	Lancaster	1737(W)
AULEY, Joseph	Bradford	1720(W)
AWLEE, Joseph	Hightown, Brighouse	1727(W) 1729(W)
AWMACK, Anne	York	1778(H)
AWMACK, Mary	York	1752(H)

B

Name	Place	Dates
BACKHOUSE, James	York	1745(H)
BACKHOUSE, William	Settle or Yelland	1722(W) 1723(W) 1752(H)
BADGER, Daniel	Nr.Bristol	1733(W) 1741(L) 1747(H) 1758(L)
BAINBRIDGE, Ralph	Northumberland	1784(H)
BAINS, William	Westmorland	1723(W)
BAKER, Anne	Thirsk	1744(H)
BAKER, John	Nr.Bristol	1740(H)
BAKER, John	Durham	1727(HL)
BAKER, Richard	Kent	1791(H)
BAKER, Thomas	Bishoprick	1723(W) 1726(W) 1728(W)
BANTLE, Benjamin (See Bartlet)	Bradford	1720(W) 1724(L) 1726(L) 1727(L)
BARBER, Joshua	Nr.Leeds	1721(W) 1723(W) 1727(W)
BARKER, Mabel	Thirsk	1749(H)
BARLOW, Elizabeth	Sheffield	1780(H)
BARNARD, Hannah	New York (USA)	1799(H)
BARNARD, John	Sheffield	1788(H)
BARTLET, Benjamin	Bradford	1728(H)
BAVINTON, John	Warwickshire	1750(L)
BECK, Ann Mercy	York	1752(H)
BECK, Sarah	Essex/Kent(?)	1759(W) 1763(W) 1782(H) 1784(HW)
BEEVY, Nicholas	Cumberland	1736(W) 1738(W)
BELL, John	Nr.Carlisle	1735(W) 1740(W)
BENINGTON, Mary	(?)	1843(H)
BENSON, Abigail	Lancashire	1754(W)
BERTWHISTLE, Margaret	(?)	1743(WH)
BERTWHISTLE, Mary	Rossendale, Lancs.	1725(W) 1727(W) 1729(W) 1732(L) 1737(W) 1740(LW)
BEWLEY, Mongo	Ireland	1728(W)
BICKERDIKE, Lydia	Westmorland	1721(H)
BIGOT, William	London	1730(W)
BINNS, Henry	Lancs.	1767(L)
BINNS, Isabel	Skipton	1766(H)
BINNS, John	Nr.Skipton	1735(L) 1736(W) 1737(L) 1739(H) 1743(W) 1750(L) 1759(H) 1760(H)
BINNS, Jonathan	Lancs.	1759(H) 1768(L)
BINNS, Joseph	Skipton	1766(H)
BIRKBECK, Deborah	Settle	1766(H)
BIRKBECK, Morris	Castleford	1785(W)
BIRKBECK, Sarah	Settle	1792(H) 1793(H) 1796(H)

BLAKE, Mary	Bridlington MM	1723(W)
BLAKEY, Elizabeth	Otley	1779(W)
BLECKLEY, Mary	Cambridgeshire	1805(H)
BLECKLEY, Sarah	Norfolk	1805(H)
BLECKLEY, William	Norfolk	1791(H)
BODYLIN, John	Hitchin, Herts.	1727(L)
BOONE, George	Warwickshire	1777(H)
BOWLES, Abigail	Ireland	1722(H)
BOWMAN, Henry	Derbyshire	1738(W)
BOWNAS, Samuel	Somerset	1720(H)
BRADFORD, John	Warwickshire	1729(W) 1733(W)
BRADFORD, John	Lancaster	1760(W)
BRADLEY, Lucy	Bristol	1755(L)
BRADLEY, Naomi	Cheshire	1719(W)
BRADY, Elizabeth	Ackworth	1782(W) 1783(H) 1784(H)
BRAGG, Margaret	Newcastle-u-Tyne	1803(H)
BRAITHWAITE, Joseph B.	London	1844(H)
BRANDWOOD, James	Lancs.	1773(H) 1777(H)
BRANTINGHAM, Mary	Durham	1798(H) 1803(H)
BRAYTON, Patience	New England, (USA)	1785(H)
BRIGHTMAN, Mary	Essex	1769(H)
BROADHEAD, Hannah	Leeds	1812(H) 1818(H)
BROOK, Joseph	Leighton, Beds.	1759(W)
BROOK, Mary	Leighton, Beds.	1759(W) 1775(W)
BROOKFIELD, William	Dublin	1725(W)
BROWN, Goody	Northants.	1732(W)
BROWN, John	Pontefract	1758(W) 1760(H) 1762(H) 1763(H) 1765(WL) 1766(WH) 1767(HL) 1768(H) 1769(H) 1770(H) 1771(H) 1772(HW) 1774(H) 1775(HW) 1776(HW) 1777(HW) 1778(W) 1779(H) 1780(H) 1781(HW) 1782(H) 1783(H)
BROWN, William	Pennsylvania	1753(W)
BUNTING, Joseph	Cumberland	1721(W) 1725(W)
BURGESS, Ann	Leics.	1802(H) 1814(H)
BURGESS, John	Leics.	1777(H)
BURNET, John	Lincolnshire	1730(LW)
BURROW, Jane	Otley or Westmorland	1778(H) 1779(W) 1780(H) 1781(H) 1785(WH) 1787(W) 1792(H) 1796(H) 1797(H) 1798(H) 1799(H)
BURTON, John	Nr.Kendal	1720(H) 1737(L) 1756(L)
BYRD, Rebecca	Dorset	1804(H)

C

CABY, Mary	Norfolk	1755(L)
CADWALLITER, John	Pennsylvania	1722(W) 1734(L)
CANDLER, Elizabeth	Norfolk	1785(H)
CARR, Eleanor	Settle	1720(H)
CARR, Thomas	Settle	1720(H) 1722(H) 1726(H) 1728(H) 1732(H)
CARRINGTON, Thomas	Pennsylvania	1776(W)

CASH, Thomas	Cheshire	1781(H) 1782(WH) 1787(W) 1801(H) 1804(H)
CHANSOM, John	(?)	1760(HWL)
CHARMAN, Sarah	Surrey	1813(H)
CHURCHMAN, John	Pennsylvania	1753(WJ)
CLAREY, Esther	Philadelphia, Penn.	1723(H)
CLARK, Asenath	N.America	1844(H)
CLARK, Dougan	N.America	1844(H)
CLARK, John	Rawmarsh	1722(H) 1726(H)
CLARK, Thomas	Somerset	1807(H)
CLARKE, Anne	Bridlington	1723(W)
CLOTHIER, James	Somerset	1751(LJ)
CLOUD, Joseph	N.Carolina	1803(H)
COCKIN, Ellin	Doncaster	1820(H)
COGGSHALL, Elizabeth	Rhode Is. (USA)	1799(H)
COLDWELL, Thomas	Durham	1719(H) 1724(H)
COLE, William	Norfolk	1755(WH) 1767(H)
COLLEY, Jane	Sheffield	1781(H) 1784(W) 1785(W) 1788(WH)
COLLEY, Thomas	Sheffield	1775(HW) 1776(H) 1777(H) 1778(H) 1781(H) 1784(W) 1785(W) 1788(H) 1790(H) 1791(H) 1792(H) 1793(H) 1797(L) 1798(H) 1799(H)
COLLIER, Robert	Brigg, Lincs.	1719(W) 1724(W) 1725(WL) 1726(L)
COLLIER, Robert	Pontefract	1727(H) 1728(W) 1730(H) 1731(W) 1733(W)
CONWAY, George	Southowram, Halifax	1767(W) 1777(H) 1778(H)
COOK, Charity	S.Carolina (USA)	1801(H)
COOKE, Joseph	Bucks.	1734(W)
COOPER, Mary	Brighouse	1731(W) 1732(W) 1736(W)
COOPER, Mary	Brighouse	1815(H)
COOPER, Sarah	Brighouse	1786(W)
COPELAND, Elizabeth	Leeds	1798(H)
COPELAND, Elizabeth	Hull	1814(H)
COPELAND, Margaret	Kendal	1726(W) 1728(H)
COPLEY, Mary	Nr. Halifax	1720(W) 1722(W) 1723(W)
CORBYN, Thomas	London	1761(H)
COULSON, David	Notts.	1750(W) 1751(LJW) 1761(H)
COWELL, Rebecca	Leeds	1725(W) 1736(W) 1744(W) 1752(L)
CROOK, Hannah	Pontefract	1722(H) 1725(W) 1726(L) 1728(L) 1733(H) 1750(H)
CROSFIELD, Jane	Westmorland	1748(W) 1764(H)
CROSLAND, Grace	Bighouse	1750(L)
CROTCH, William	Suffolk	1785(W) 1793(H)
CROTCH, William	Scarborough	1803(H)
CROW, William	Cumberland	1762(L)
CROW, William	Norfolk	1768(L) 1779(W)
CROWLEY, Ann	Middlesex	1806(H)
CROWLEY, Sarah	Hitchin, Herts.	1754(H)
CUNNINGHAM, William	Thirsk	1751(W) 1764(W) 1775(H)

D

DANIELS, James	Massachusetts Bay	1762(H)
DARBY, Deborah	Shropshire	1780(H) 1787(HW) 1791(H) 1804(H)
DAVIS, Joseph	Gloucs.	1770(H) 1774(W)
DAVIS, Mary	Somerset	1785(H)
DAVIS, Peter	Rhode Is. (N.America)	1748(WL)
DAWSON, George	Lothersdale	1760(W)
DEARMAN, Nathan	Thorne	1786(W)
DENT, Anne	Notts.	1780(H) 1781(H) 1782(H) 1783(H) 1785(HW) 1789(H) 1791(HW)
DENT, David	Suffolk	1799(H)
DENT, Hannah	Richmond MM	1723(W) 1726(H) 1731(WL)
DENT, William	Marr	1844(H)
DICKINSON, Elizabeth	Sheffield	1779(W) 1781(H) 1783(H) 1785(W) 1788(W)
DICKINSON, Mary	Sheffield	1751(L) 1752(L) 1753(L) 1755(L) 1756(H) 1757(H)
DILLWYN, George	New Jersey, USA.	1786(HW)
DINNIS, Elizabeth	Essex	1742(W)
DIXON, John	Nr. Swarthmore	1756(H)
DIXON, Mary	Auckland, Co.Durham	1753(H)
DOBSON, Thomas	Cumberland	1766(H)
DODGE, Phebe	Long Is. (N.America)	1752(L)
DODSON, William	Northants.	1771(W)
DONCASTER, Jane	Sheffield	1810(H) 1813(H) 1817(H) 1819(H)
DRUMMOND, Mary	London	1751(L)
DRUMMOND, May	Scotland	1749(W)
DRURY, Barbara	Cumberland	1779(H)
DRURY, Thomas	Cumberland	1736(W)
DUCKET, David	Cumberland	1766(H) 1767(W) 1774(HW)
DUDLEY, Elizabeth	London	1820(H)
DUDLEY, Mary	London	1820(H)
DUNN, Ellin	Cheshire	1763(L)
DUNNING, Ann	Ayton	1842(H)
DYMOND, John	Devonshire	1818(H)
DYSON, Mary	Rushworth	1719(W) 1731(W) 1732(W) 1740(L) 1742(WH) 1744(W) 1746(L)

E

EARNSHAW, Mary	Lancs.	1782(WH) 1787(W) 1794(H)
EARNSHAW, William	Wooldale	1792(H) 1793(H) 1794(H) 1795(H) 1796(H) 1797(H) 1798(H) 1799(H)
ECNODE, John	New Marsden, Lancs.	1719(H)
ECROYD, Tabitha	Marsden Ht. Lancs.	1753(L)
ELLAM, Sarah	Halifax	1721(H) 1725(?) 1728(W) 1731(W)
ELLERTON, Mary	Knaresborough	1719(H) 1727(H) 1729(WH) 1730(H)
ELLINTON, Mary	Hunts.	1740(W)

ELLIOT, Philip	London	1748(W)
ELLIS, Margaret	Pennsylvania	1753(H)
ELLIS, Mary	Gildersome	1795(H)
EMES, John	Oxfordshire	1745(W)
ENGLISH, Margaret	Castleford	1786(H) 1787(HW)
ESTON, John	Jersey (N. America)	1721(H)
EVANS, Elizabeth	Suffolk	1759(H)
EVANS, Robert	Devonshire	1727(HW)

F

FAIRBANK, Ann	Sheffield	1798(H) 1814(H)
FAIRBANK, William	Sheffield	1775(H)
FALLOWS, Ruth	Leics.	1775(H) 1781(H) 1789(H)
FARRINGTON, Abraham	Pennsylvania	1756(H) 1757(H)
FARTWHAIT(E) Thomas	Sheffield	1724(HW) 1727(H) 1728(LH) 1729(HW) 1730(H) 1731(HW) 1732(WL) 1733(W) 1735(H) 1736(H) 1737(W) 1738(W) 1739(H) 1740(H) 1744(LH) 1746(H) 1747(H) 1750(H) 1752(LH) 1753(HL) 1754(L) 1755(H) 1756(HW) 1757(H)
FELL, Deborah	Carlisle	1726(H)
FENN, John	Norwich	1765(L)
FIELD, Hannah	New York State (USA)	1818(H)
FIELDEN, John	Mankinholes	1725(W) 1727(LW)
FIRTH, Mary	Huddersfield	1772(H) 1773(HW) 1774(WH) 1775(WH) 1776(WH) 1777(HW) 1778(WH) 1779(HW) 1780(HW) 1782(W) 1783(HW) 1784(WH) 1785(H) 1786(W) 1787(HW) 1789(H) 1790(H) 1795(H)
FISHER, Elizabeth	Westmorland	1720(W)
FISHER, John	Thorne	1719(W) 1721(W) 1724(H) 1726(H) 1728(L) 1732(HW) 1737(H) 1749(W)
FLETCHER, Elizabeth	Derbyshire	1742(W)
FOOT, John	Knaresborough	1765(H)
FOSTER, Josiah	London	1842(H)
FOSTER, Richard	Scarborough	1845(H)
FOSTER, William	Middlesex	1807(H)
FOSTER, William	Dorset	1818(H)
FOSTER, William	Norwich	1842(H)
FOTHERGILL, John	Richmond/Wensleydale	1719(H) 1720(W) 1724(H) 1728(H)
FOTHERGILL, John	London	1777(H)
FOTHERGILL, Samuel	Warrington	1745(W) 1763(W)
FRANCIS, Elizabeth	Barnsley	1721(H) 1730(H)
FRANCIS, William	Barnsley	1720(H) 1721(W) 1722(HW) 1723(LW) 1724(WH) 1725(WH) 1726(HW) 1727(WL) 1728(WL) 1729(L) 1730(HW) 1731(HW) 1732(HW) 1733(H) 1735(W)
FRANKLAND, Henry	York	1728(WH)

FREEMAN, Edward	Herts.	1731(W)
FREEMAN, Henry	London	1757(H)
FROST, Esther	Whitby	1721(H)
FROST, Sarah	Herefordshire	1726(W)
FRY, Elizabeth	Essex	1818(H)
FRYER, Esther	(?)	1749(W) 1750(W) 1752(W) 1754(L) 1755(W) 1756(L)

G

GAYLORD, Susannah	Warwickshire	1787(H)
GILPIN, Margaret	Shropshire	1771(H)
GLAESTER, Dan	Cumberland	1725(W)
GOODWIN, Thomas	Pennsylvania	1763(W)
GOTT, Tabitha	Bradford	1751(L) 1758(W)
GOUGH, Mary	Westmorland	1748(W)
GRAENGER, Christopher	Wisbech	1724(H)
GRAHAM, James	Cumberland	1791(HW)
GRAY, Isaac	Herefordshire	1758(W) 1768(L)
GRAYHAM, Robert	Carlisle	1758(L)
GREEN, Jonathan	Langside	1720(WL) 1721(W) 1722(WL) 1723(WL) 1724(WL)
GREEN, Pricilla	Dunmow	1842(H)
GREER, Thomas	Ireland	1783(H)
GRELLET, Stephen	New York (USA)	1812(H)
GRIFFITH, John	Pennsylvania	1748(L)
GRIMSHAW, Jeremy	Rushworth	1719(W) 1720(H)
GRUBB, Robert	Ireland/Malton	1781(H) 1783(H) 1786(WH)
GRUBB, Sarah	Ireland	1783(H)
GUNNER, Anne	Suffolk	1748(H)

H

HADWIN Isaac	Lancs.	1812(H)
HALL Alice	Lancs.	1727(W) 1729(W) 1733(W) 1737(L) 1740(WL) 1743(W) 1748(H)
HALL Anne	Whitfield	1735(W)
HALL David	Skipton	1718(H) 1719(WH) 1720(L) 1729(W) 1735(L)
HAMMOND Henry	Lincolnshire	1765(L)
HARDIN Sarah	Kendal	1727(W)
HARDLOCK Mary	(?)	1744(W)
HARGREAVES James	Halifax	1723(L) 1743(L)
HARKER Mary	Wensleydale	1748(H)
HARPER Lisel	New England	1737(H)
HARRIS Isabella	Ackworth	1804(H) 1805(H) 1806(H) 1807(H) 1808(H) 1810(H) 1812(H) 1813(H) 1814(H) 1815(H) 1816(H) 1818(H) 1820(H)
HARRISON Charles	Lancs.	1748(W) 1750(H) 1752(W) 1753(W) 1754(L) 1757(L)
HARRISON Hannah	Ackworth	1820(H)
HARRISON Henry	(?)	1765(H)

HARRISON Jonathan	Lancs.	1759(H)
HARRISON Samuel	Lancs./Settle	1759(H) 1774(W) 1776(W)
HARRISON Sarah	Pennsylvania	1796(H)
HART Hannah	Pickering	1765(H)
HARTCLIFF Margaret	(?)	1752(H)
HARTLEY Margaret	Settle MM	1757(H)
HARVEY Robert	Old Meldrum Scotland	1754(H) 1760(L)
HASTINGS Garret	Dublin	1738(W) 1751(W)
HATTON Edward	Ireland	1781(H)
HAUG(H)TON John	Ireland	1741(W)
HAWKSWORTH Lydia	Bristol	1776(H)
HEATH Joseph	Warwickshire	1770(H) 1774(W)
HEDLEY Jonathan	Bishoprick	1722(W) 1724(W)
HELM John	Nr. Whitby	1737(W)
HESLAM John	Woodhouse Mtg.	1723(L) 1724(H) 1728(W) 1731(W) 1734(L) 1736(W) 1739(H) 1741(W) 1746(W) 1748(H) 1752(L) 1755(H) 1757(W)
HICKS Willott	New York	1820(H)
HIGGISON Edward	Hunts.	1757(H)
HOBSON Edward	Woodhouse	1738(L) 1739(L)
HOBSON William	(?)	1744(H)
HODGKIN John	Tottenham	1842(H)
HODGSON Jonathan	Settle MM	1774(W) 1775(H)
HOLBEM Benjamin	(?)	1734(H)
HOLBEM John	Sheffield	1741(HL) 1742(WH) 1744(W) 1746(W) 1747(W) 1748(H) 1749(WL) 1750(WH) 1751(L) 1752(HW) 1753(WH) 1754(HW) 1755(WH) 1756(HWL) 1757(H) 1758(HL) 1761(WH) 1762(WH) 1763(W) 1764(W) 1765(WH) 1766(L) 1768(H) 1769(H) 1771(W)
HOLME Benjamin	York	1720(H) 1721(H) 1723(H) 1724(W) 1728(W) 1729(W) 1732(HW) 1734(W) 1739(H) 1742(W) 1743(H)
HOLMES Elizabeth	Newcastle-u-Tyne	1753(H)
HOPKIN Ursella	Thirsk	1744(H)
HOPKINS Joseph	Brigg	1845(H)
HOPWOOD Samuel	Cornwall	1723(W) 1755(L)
HORN William	Pennsylvania	1763(W)
HORNE Susannah	Middlesex	1806(H)
HORNER Tabitha	Leeds	1726(H) 1732(W)
HORSFALL John	Greenhouse	1719(W) 1720(W) 1721(L) 1722(W) 1723(W) 1724(H) 1725(HWL) 1726(WH) 1727(WH) 1728(WL) 1729(LW) 1730(WH) 1731(HL) 1732(H) 1733(WH) 1734(HW) 1735(W) 1736(W) 1737(LH) 1738(W) 1739(L) 1740(W) 1743(W) 1744(H) 1745(H) 1747(HW)
HOTHAM William	Sheffield	1774(H)

HOWARTH George	Lancs.	1732(L) 1741(W) 1742(LW) 1743(HW) 1744(W) 1746(H) 1747(HW) 1748(HW) 1749(WL) 1750(H) 1751(W) 1752(W) 1753(H) 1754(L) 1755(LH) 1756(WH) 1757(H) 1758(H) 1759(H) 1760(WL) 1761(W) 1762(WH) 1763(W) 1764(W) 1765(W) 1766(W) 1767(L) 1768(H) 1769(H) 1770(H) 1771(WH) 1772(H) 1773(H) 1774(H) 1775(W) 1776(HW) 1778(H)
HOWARTH James	Lancs.	1801(H)
HOWARTH Martha	Lancs.	1784(HW)
HOYLAND Barbara	Woodhouse Mtg.	1796(H)
HOYLAND Elizabeth	Sheffield	1782(H) 1784(H) 1786(WH) 1789(H) 1790(H) 1793(H) 1800(H) 1812(H)
HOYLAND John	Sheffield	1782(H) 1784(H) 1789(H) 1790(H) 1793(H) 1800(H) 1804(H) 1812(H)
HOYLAND Margaret	Sheffield	1788(H)
HOYLAND Tabitha	Sheffield	1778(H) 1779(W) 1781(H) 1782(H)
HUDSON John	Blythe	1719(W) 1722(H) 1723(L) 1724(WLH) 1730(H) 1732(LW) 1733(W) 1734(H)
HUDSON Peter	Cumberland	1736(W)
HULL Henry	New York (USA)	1811(H)
HULL John	Middlesex	1811(H)
HUNT Nathan	N. Carolina (USA)	1820(H)
HUNT William	N. Carolina	1771(H)
HURD Benjamin	Knaresborough MM	1764(W) 1769(H) 1770(WH)
HUSTLER Christiana	Bradford	1778(H) 1784(H)
HUSTLER Sarah	Bradford	1800(H) 1812(H)
HUTCHINSON Elizabeth	Ireland	1735(W) 1748(L)

I

IMPEY William	Saffron Walden Essex	1742(L) 1752(WJ)
INGLE Mary	Westmorland	1778(H)

J

JACKSON, Joseph	Gildersome	1758(W) 1759(H) 1771(HW) 1772(H) 1773(H)
JACKSON, Joseph	Northumberland	1762(W) 1770(W)
JACKSON, Sarah	Lancaster	1728(H) 1734(H)
JACKSON, William	Pennsylvania (USA)	1804(H)
JENKINS, Mehetabel	New England, (USA)	1785(H)
JESSOP, Ann	N. Carolina (USA)	1787(H)
JOBSON, Rebecca	Lancs.	1726(W) 1729(L)
JOHNSON, Gervas	Ireland	1789(H)
JOHNSON, Matthew	Northumberland	1773(H) 1779(H) 1789(W)

JONES, George	Warwickshire	1786(H)
JONES, Rebecca	Pennsylvania (USA)	1784(H)
JORDAN, Richard	Virginia (N.America)	1729(H) 1733(L)
JOWITT, Robert	Leeds	1842(H)

K

KEITH, John	Scotland	1725(W)
KENDAL, Elizabeth	Essex	1737(H)
KERSHAW, Abraham	Nr. Halifax	1720(W) 1721(W)
KIDD, Benjamin	Nr. Settle	1722(H) 1725(L) 1733(L)
KING, Anne	(?)	1731(W)
KING, James	Northumberland	1769(H) 1775(W) 1778(W) 1783(H)
KING, John	Nr. Skipton	1719(HW)
KING, John	Cheshire	1730(H)
KING, Lawrence	(?)	1719(H)
KING, Margaret	(?)	1744(W)
KING, Mary	Leeds	1764(W)
KIRBY, Mary	Norfolk	1755(W)
KIRKHAM, John	Essex	1814(H)

L

LAMB, Robert	Rutlandshire	1728(L)
LAMLEY, Sarah	Worcestershire	1814(H)
LANGCASTER, Lydia	Kendal	1727(W)
LANGDALE, Margaret	Binglington	1719(W)
LARGE, Ebeneezer	Jersey (N.America)	1746(H)
LATIMER, Isaac	Wakefield	1725(W) 1727(HW) 1728(W) 1729(WL)
LAW, Anne	Balby MM	1742(H) 1750(L)
LAW, Esther	Chesterfield	1735(W) 1739(L) 1740(L)
LAYE, Sarah	London	1723(H)
LEADBEATER, Peter	Chester	1722(W) 1724(H)
LEAVER, Mary	Nottingham	1759(H) 1770(H) 1771(H)
LEES, Esther	Lancs.	1809(H) 1812(H) 1814(H) 1816(H)
LEWIS, Ellis	Wales	1719(W) 1722(HW) 1724(H) 1725(WL) 1727(L) 1728(L) 1731(W) 1737 (W) 1742(WH)
LEWIS, Margaret	Pennsylvania	1753(H)
LIGHTON, Deborah	Nr.Kendal	1731(W) 1746(W) 1747(W) 1760(L)
LLEDGAR, Elizabeth	Nottinghamshire	1742(W)
LONGMIRE, William	Nr. Kendal	1728(L) 1735(L) 1748(H)
LOYD, Mary	Birmingham	1844(H)
LUCAS, John	Norwich	1755(H) 1757(H)
LUDGATE, Hannah	Essex	1769(H)

M

MARIOT, Tabitha	Lancs.	1765(H) 1767(L)
MARRIT, Elizabeth	Mansfield	1738(H)
MARSHALL, Esther	Rawdon Mtg.	1775(WH) 1777(H) 1780(H) 1781(H)

MARSHALL, Pheobe	Rawdon	1771(H) 1772(H) 1773(W) 1776(W) 1779(H) 1780(H)
MARSHAM, Margaret	Suffolk	1742(W) 1748(H) 1759(H)
MARSLAND, John	(?)	1728(H)
MARTIN, Mary	Ireland	1724(W)
MASON, Anthony	Brigflatts	1756(L) 1763(W) 1770(H)
MASON, George	Gisborough MM	1750(L) 1752(H) 1758(H)
MASON, Mary	Settle MM	1796(H)
MASTERS, William	Staffs.	1814(H)
MATTHEWS, William	Pennsylvania (USA)	1786(H)
MATTHEWS, William	(?)	1844(H)
MAUD, Esther	Bradford	1764(H)
MELLOR, Matthew	Manchester	1730(W) 1731(H) 1735(H) 1736(H) 1737(H) 1738(HW) 1740(W) 1754(W) 1761(H)
MELLOR, Samuel	Derbyshire	1720(W)
MELLOR, Samuel	Manchester	1731(W) 1732(W) 1735(H)
METFORD, Joseph	Somerset	1806(H)
MILNTHORPE, Joseph	Painthorpe	1749(H) 1751(L) 1755(H) 1752(H) 1756(L) 1757(LH) 1765(H)
MINSHALL, Nicholas	Bawtry	1740(W)
MINSHALL, Rebecca	Pennsylvania	1736(W)
MOLINEUX, Othniel	Lancs.	1730(H)
MORRIS, Deborah	Pennsylvania	1772(H)
MORRIS, Sarah	Pennsylvania	1772(H)
MORTON, Elizabeth	Barnsley	1774(H) 1777(HW)
MOSS, Isaac	Manchester	1729(H) 1731(H) 1738(W) 1741(L) 1744(L)

N

NEAL, Samuel	Ireland	1781(H)
NICHOLSON, Rachel	Scarborough	1719(LHW)
NICKLETON, Thomas	N. Carolina	1750(H)
NORRICE, John	Norfolk	1743(W)
NORTH, Benjamin	Leeds	1786(W)

O

OGBURN, Anne	Bristol	1725(W)
OLIVER, Daniel	Newcastle-u-Tyne	1813(H)
OXLEY, Joseph	Norwich, Norfolk	1758(W) 1760(W) 1762(W)

P

PAISLEY, Mary	Mt.Mellick MM	1748(L)
PALMER, Elizabeth	Nottinghamshire	1742(W)
PARK(INSON), Alexander	Lancs.	1743(H) 1747(L)
PARKER, Charles	Bentham Mtg.	1800(H)
PARKINSON, Thomas	Hull	1779(W)
PATRICK, Jacob	Netherdale Mtg.	1737(W)
PAYNTON, Katharine	Worcestershire	1761(H) 1767(L)
PEARSON, Jane	Cumberland	1779(H)
PEARSON, Mary	Cumberland	1762(H)

PECKOVER, Edmund	Norfolk	1756(H) 1760(LWH)
PEMBERTON, John	Philadelphia	1753(WJ)
PENGILLEY, Anne	Exeter	1725(W)
PENNET, Seth	Gisborough MM	1764(W) 1773(W)
PHILIPS, Katharine	Cornwall	1776(H)
PICKARD, Samuel	(?)	1842(H) 1843(H) 1844(H)
PINDER, Joshua	Oustick MM	1748(H)
PLUMLEY, Esther	Glastonbury	1725(W)
POE(LAND), Peter	Lincs.	1720(W) 1725(W)
POWEL, Benjamin	Suffolk	1750(HJ)
PRIESTLEY, Thomas	Settle MM	1777(W)
PRIESTMAN, Barbara	Pickering Mtg.	1778(H)
PRIESTMAN, Thomas	York	1800(H)
PRINCE, George	Devonshire	1751(W)
PROCTOR, Joseph	Lancs. & Yarm	1760(WH) 1762(L) 1770(H)
PROUD, Mary	Hull	1778(H)
PROUD, Robert	Thirsk MM	1751(L) 1775(H)
PUMPHREY, Thomas	(?)	1842(H) 1843(H)

R

RAINS, Jonathan	Sunderland	1743(W)
RAINS, Margaret	Lancs.	1743(W) 1767(L)
RANSOME, John	Norfolk	1760(L)
RANSOME, Joseph	Norfolk	1755(WH)
RANSOME, Joshua	Norfolk	1760(W) 1765(L)
RANSOME, Mercy	Herefordshire	1794(H)
RAPIER, Elizabeth	Bucks.	1775(W)
RATCLIFFE, Isaac	Sheffield	1772(H)
RATHBONE, William	Lancs.	1777(H)
RECK, Elizabeth	Norfolk	1754(W)
RECKITT, William	Lincs.	1767(H)
RICHARDSON, Anne	Cumberland	1751(W)
RICHARDSON, George	Newcastle-u-Tyne	1813(H)
RICHARDSON, Isaac	Scarborough MM	1769(H)
RICHARDSON, Isabel	Whitby	1762(H)
RICHARDSON, John	Gisborough MM	1725(W) 1728(L) 1729(W) 1730(H) 1768(W)
RICHARDSON, Joseph	Gainsborough	1738(H) 1746(L)
RICHARDSON, Mary	Richmond MM	1723(W) 1726(W) 1731(W)
RICHARDSON, Mary (Jr.)	(?)	1734(H)
RICHARDSON, Nicholas	Gisborough MM	1775(W)
RIDGE, Alice	Westmorland	1764(H)
RIDGEWAY, Mary	Ireland	1771(H) 1780(H) 1802(H)
RISHTON, Anne	Rossendale	1728(L)
RISHTON, James	Lancs.	1727(L) 1732(L) 1741(W) 1743(W)
ROBERTS, Elizabeth	Suffolk	1754(W)
ROBINSON, Amos	Wensleydale	1736(W) 1742(W)
ROBINSON, Elizabeth	Wensleydale	1760(L)
ROBINSON, George	Rutlandshire	1750(WL)
ROBINSON, Jacob	Holderness	1723(W) 1729(W)
ROBINSON, John	Thirsk MM	1751(L)
ROBINSON, Mary	Cumberland	1773(H) 1776(H)
ROBSON, Elizabeth	Durham	1815(H)
ROBSON, Isaac	(?)	1842(H)

ROGERS, Joseph	Markham, Notts.	1722(W)
ROOKES, George	Dublin	1725(W)
ROTHERFORD, Mary	Sheffield	1779(W) 1781(H) 1786(W) 1798(H)
ROUTH, Alice	Wensleydale	1748(H) 1753(W) 1767(W)
ROUTH, Richard	Manchester	1788(HW)
ROUTH, Sarah	Manchester	1741(L) 1745(L)
ROW, Joseph	London	1761(H)
ROWLINSON, Jane	Lancs.	1745(H)
ROWNTREE, Rachel	Pickering	1814(H)
ROWNTREE, William	Malton MM	1769(H)
ROWNTREE, William	Pickering	1814(H)
ROYSTON, Anne	Rossendale	1725(W)
RUTTER, Thomas	Bristol	1777(H)
RYLEY, Anne	Halifax	1753(L)

S

SALKEILE, William	Suffolk	1721(H)
SANDERS, George	Whitby	1814(H)
SANDS, David	New York (USA)	1804(H)
SAUL, Joseph	Cumberland	1791(HW)
SAWKILL, John	Pennsylvania	1726(W)
SCANTLEBURY, Thomas	Sheffield	1814(H)
SCATTERGOOD, Thomas	Pennsylvania	1799(H)
SCOTT, John	Nr. Leeds	1723(WL) 1727(W) 1734(L) 1741(W) 1746(H) 1749(W)
SCOTTICK, John	Northumberland	1720(W) 1722(W)
SEATTON, James	London	1743(L)
SEBOHEME, Benjamin	Bradford	1842(H)
SEBOHEME, Esther	Bradford	1844(H)
SEEKINGS, John	Birmingham	1843(H) 1844(H)
SEVITT, Mary	New Jersey	1801(H)
SHACKLETON, Sarah	Ireland	1798(H)
SHARPLESS, Barbara	Settle	1773(H)
SHARPLEY, Isaac	Hitchin, Herts.	1756(L)
SHAW, John	Kendal	1721(W) 1729(W)
SHILLITOE, Thomas	Middlesex/Barnsley	1807(H) 1810(H) 1812(H) 1815(H) 1816(H) 1817(H) 1818(H)
SHIPLEY, Elizabeth	Pennsylvania	1843(H)
SHIPLEY, Hannah	Staffordshire	1763(L) 1766(L) 1782(H)
SHIRES, Sarah	Nr. Bradford	1728(W) 1731(W) 1733(W)
SHORTHOUSE, Mary	Warwickshire	1814(H)
SIGSWICK, Jane	Nr. Settle	1720(H)
SIGSWICK, Stephen	Settle	1722(W) 1732(H) 1751(H) 1753(L)
SLATER, John (Jr.)	(?)	1742(W) 1745(L)
SLATER, Mary	Skipton	1722(H) 1723(W) 1725(HW) 1726(W) 1728(W) 1731(W) 1737(W) 1744(W) 1747(L) 1751(L) 1752(H) 1754(H)
SLATER, Tabitha	(?)	1751(L)
SLATER, Thomas	(?)	1750(L)

SLATER, William	Skipton	1722(H) 1726(W) 1728(W) 1730(L) 1734(H) 1736(W) 1739(H) 1741(L) 1747(W) 1750(L) 1752(L)
SMITH, Henry	Wellingborough	1721(L) 1734(W)
SMITH, Joseph	Nottinghamshire	1720(W) 1725(W)
SMITH, Joshua	Painthorpe	1750(L) 1751(H)
SMITH, Martha	Doncaster	1800(H)
SMITH, Mary	Norfolk	1740(W)
SMITH, Rebecca	Gloucs.	1763(W)
SMITH, Samuel	Pennsylvania	1790(H)
SMITH, William	Doncaster	1813(H)
SMITHSON, John	Westmorland	1783(HW)
SNEASDALLE, Richard	Lincs.	1750(W)
SOWERBY, William	Ackworth	1781(H) 1782(H) 1783(H) 1784(HW) 1785(H) 1786(HW) 1787(H) 1788(HW) 1790(HW) 1791(HW) 1792(WH) 1793(H) 1794(H) 1795(H) 1796(H) 1797(H) 1798(H) 1799(H) 1801(H) 1802(H)
SPAVOLD, Samuel	Kent	1744(H) 1749(W) 1756(L) 1768(H) 1774(H)
SPEAKMAN, Phebe	Delaware	1779(H)
STAINTON, Daniel	Philadelphia	1749(W)
STANDIN, Ely	Norfolk	1771(H)
STANDIN, James	(?)	1726(W) 1728(W) 1729(W) 1731(W) 1732(W) 1735(L) 1740(W) 1743(W)
STANNILAND, Thomas	(?)	1726(H)
STANSFIELD, Anne	Keighley Mtg.	1767(W)
STEPHENS, Samuel	Ireland	1728(W)
STERRY, Mary	London	1797(H) 1803(H)
STONES, John	(?)	1735(W) 1740(H)
STONES, Margaret	(?)	1735(W)
STORER, John	Nottinghamshire	1751(L) 1753(W) 1755(W) 1757(W) 1761(L) 1770(LH)
STORY, Thomas	Carlisle	1729(?) 1731(W) 1732(L)
STORR, Anne	Chesterfield	1763(L) 1771(H) 1774(H)
STORR, Caleb	Stockport	1720(W) 1726 (H) 1727(W) 1731(L) 1733(W) 1734(H)
STORR, Joseph	Chesterfield	1722(W) 1733(W)
STORR, Katharine	Chesterfield	1722(W) 1726(W)
STOTT, Samuel	Suffolk	1750(JH) 1760(H) 1767(H)
SUMMERLAND, Anne	Shropshire	1771(H) 1787(H)
SUTCLIFFE, Anne	(?)	1749(W)

T

TALBOT, Sarah	Delaware (USA)	1798(H)
TATE, Mary	Cottingwith Mtg.	1799(H)
TAYLOR, Isaac	Helmsley Mtg.	1814(H)
TAYLOR, Joseph	Durham	1719(H) 1743(W)
TAYLOR, Joseph	Thirsk MM	1764(W)
TAYLOR, Sarah	Manchester	1753(L) 1764(H) 1771(H) 1781(H) 1785(H)

TAYLOR, William	Manchester	1737(H)
TEAL, Martha	Otley	1781(H) 1783(H) 1785(H) 1787(WH) 1788(H) 1789(H)
THISTLETHWAITE, John	Leeds	1820(H)
THOMPSON, Abigail	Westmorland	1724(W)
THOMPSON, Edward	Handsworth-Woodhouse	1732(L)
THOMPSON, Jonah	Westmorland	1728(L)
THOMPSON, Thomas	Hitchin, Herts.	1720(H)
THORNBURY, Thomas	N. Carolina	1771(H)
THORNHILL, Martha	Ackworth	1842(H) 1843(H) 1844(H)
THORNTON, James	Pennsylvania	1788(HW)
TOFT, Joshua	Leek, Staffs.	1724(L) 1729(H) 1733(L) 1738(L)
TOMLINSON, Agnes	Preston, Lancs.	1728(L) 1735(H) 1741(W)
TOPPER, James	Marsden Ht. Lancs.	1731(L)
TOUSE, Timothy	(?)	1736(L)
TOWNSEND, Deborah	London	1794(H)
TOWNSHEND, John	London	1767(H) 1791(H)
TRICKET, Catharine	Sheffield	1786(WH) 1798(H)
TUBBS, Robert	Isle of Ely	1753(L)
TUKE, Esther	York	1774(H) 1778(H) 1786(WH)
TUKE, Henry	York	1785(W) 1792(H) 1802(H)
TUKE, Sarah	York	1779(W) 1782(H)
TUKE, William	York	1770(WH) 1786(W) 1800(H)
TURNER, Elizabeth	Poole, Dorset	1758(L)
TYLER, Edward	Bristol	1724(W) 1733(WL) 1739(W) 1744(W)

U

UPSHIRE, Katharine	Essex	1720(W)
URWUM, Anne	Cumberland	1726(W)
URWUM, John	Carlisle	1725(HW) 1732(W)

V

VALENTINE, Robert	Pennsylvania	1782(H)
VEFFE, Hannah	Cumberland	1720(W)

W

WAKEFIELD, George	Northumberland	1763(W)
WALKER, John	Hightown	1725(W) 1726(W) 1728(W) 1730(L) 1732(H) 1735(L) 1738(H) 17409(L) 1756(L) 1763(H)
WALKER, Robert	Gildersome	1754(W) 1756(L) 1762(W) 1763(W) 1770(WH)
WALKER, Robert	Netherdale Mtg.	1814(H)
WALN, Nicholas	Pennsylvania	1784(H)
WALTON, Edward	Nr. Newcastle	1762(L) 1763(W)
WANE, John	Whitby	1721(H)
WARDELL, Lance	Sunderland	1724(W)
WARDELL, Robert	Sunderland	1741(W)
WARING, Elizabeth	Thirsk	1732(H)
WATSON, Jane	Ireland	1771(H) 1780(H)

WATSON, Mary	Ireland	1797(H)
WAUGH, Mabel	Allendale	1756(H) 1760(LW)
WEATHERHEAD, Elizabeth	Wensleydale	1767(W)
WHALLEY, Jeremy	Rawden	1733(W) 1735(W)
WHEELER, Daniel	Sheffield	1814(H)
WHITE, Benjamin	Pennsylvania	1809(H)
WHITE, Esther	Pennsylvania	1743(H)
WHITE, Joseph	Pennsylvania	1761(H)
WHITE, Sarah	Ackworth	1782(W) 1783(HW) 1785(H) 1786(H'V)
WHITE, Sarah	Cheshire	1788(H)
WHITEHEAD, Thomas	London	1748(W)
WHITESIDE, William	Rawcliffe	1719(W)
WHITLEY, Elkanah	Rushworth	1719(W) 1720(W) 1722(W) 1723(H) 1725(W) 1726(W) 1728(W) 1729(W) 1731(W) 1733(L) 1734(W) 1735(L) 1736(W) 1738(W) 1740(WL) 1742(W) 1746(LH) 1747(W)
WIGHAM, Cuthbert	Northumberland	1760(W)
WIGHAM, Dorothy	Northumberland	1769(W)
WIGHAM, Hannah	Northumberland (Later Pontefract)	1769(W) 1776(H) 1780(W) 1781(H) 1782(H) 1783(WH) 1785(W) 1786(H) 1787(W) 1788(H) 1790(H) 1791(H) 1792(WH) 1793(H) 1794(H) 1795(H) 1796(H) 1797(H)
WIGHAM, John	Scotland	1800(H)
WIGHAM, Mabel	Northumberland	1766(W) 1767(L)
WILLIAMS, Martha	Monmouthshire	1766(W)
WILLIAMS, Michael	Lynn, Norfolk	1725(W) 1728(L)
WILLIS, Robert	New Jersey	1772(H)
WILSON, Christopher	Cumberland	1732(W)
WILSON, Deborah	Kendal	1736(W) 1752(L)
WILSON, Elizabeth	Nr. Kendal	1720(W) 1724(W) 1726(H)
WILSON, Henry	Trawdin, Lancs.	1737(W) 1743(W) 1748(L) 1750(L) 1754(W) 1760(HW) 1762(W) 1765(H) 1769(H) 1778(W)
WILSON, Jonathan	Nr. Kendal	1741(W)
WILSON, Jonathan	Lancaster	1756(HW)
WILSON, Rachel	Westmorland	1745(H) 1766(H)
WILSON, Roland	Northumberland	1722(W)
WINDLE, William	Nr. Skipton	1723(W)
WINN, Rachel	Scarborough MM	1764(W)
WINTER, Martha	Nottinghamshire	1775(H)
WOODHEAD, Dinah	Wooldale	1792(H) 1793(H) 1794(H) 1795(H) 1796(H) 1797(H) 1798(H)
WOOLMAN, John	New Jersey	1772(H)
WRIGHT, Ellen	Liverpool	1766(W)
WRIGHT, Joseph	Clifford Mtg.	1775(H)
WRIGHT, Rebecca	New Jersey (USA)	1785(H)
WRIGHT, William	Hunts.	1737(HW)
WRIGHTSON, George	Skipton	1760(H)

Y

YARNALL, Mordecai	Pennsylvania	1755(H) 1757(H)
YATES, John	Nr. Brighouse	1722(L) 1726(W) 1727(H) 1732(W)
YEARDLEY, John	Scarborough	1842(H)
YEARDLEY, Martha	Scarborough	1842(H)
YOUNG, Peter	Herefordshire	1733(W)
YOUNG, Rebecca	Shropshire	1787(W) 1791(H)

BIBLIOGRAPHY

Abbreviations of Archives, Collections & Libraries

ASA	Ackworth School Archive
BRO	Brotherton Library
FHL	Friends House Library
FT	Friends Trust Ltd.
HAV	Haverford College Collection
HDL	Huddersfield Central Library
HFL	High Flatts MH Library
Pvt.	Privately owned
WDC	Wooldale MH Collection
WAK	Wakefield County Records
YAS	Yorkshire Archaeological Society

Manuscript Abbreviations

ATF	An Alphabet of Travelling Friends 1736-1770	ASA
(HD)PMMB	Huddersfield PM Minute Books	BRO
(HF)PMMB	High Flatts PM Minute Books	ASA
MMBS	Pontefract MM Book of Sufferings	ASA
MMMB	Pontefract MM Minute Books	ASA
MMDRC	Pontefract MM Denials, Removals & Certs.	ASA
MSS Collect.	MSS Collection	FHL
PMMB	PM Minute Books	WDC
QBBREG1	Births & Burials Digest	ASA
(WD)MLB	Wooldale Membership List Book 1868-1900	WDC
QBBREG	Quaker Births & Burials Register	ASA
(WD)PMMB	Wooldale PM Minute Books	WDC
(WD)WMMB	Wooldale Womens Mtg. Minute Book	WDC
WMMB	Womens Mtg. Minute Book	ASA
YQMMB	Yorkshire Quarterly Mtg. Minute Book	BRO
YQM Sufferings	Yorkshire QM Sufferings (Tithes)	BRO

Manuscript Sources — Description

ATF	ASA
(HD)PMMB 1792	BRO
MMBS 1672-1793	ASA
MMDRC 1675-1766	ASA
MMMB 1672-1970	ASA
PMMB 1752-1812*	WDC
QBBREG1	ASA
(WD)PMMB1 1792-1813	WDC
(WD)WMMB	WDC
WMMB1 1713-1787	ASA

*PMMB Preparative Mtg. Minute Books for Wooldale, High Flatts & Lane Head Mtg. Houses until 1792. Two Volumes of PMMB pre-1752 are recorded as having been lost during 19th Century. PMMB From 1792 is also (HF)PMMB.

Non-abbreviated MSS collections

The following MSS Collections are all private collections loaned to the authors during the course of their research.

Joseph Wood Collection

1. Small Notebooks 1-63
2. Large Memorandum Books 1-37
3. Misc. Correspondence & Papers

Catherine Walton Collection

1. Misc. Correspondence & Papers
2. Photograph Collection

Miscellaneous Sources

John Sadler's Report on High Flatts Burial Ground 1913 (HFL)
Rest/Guest House Minute Book 1920-1929 (HFL)
High Flatts Pilgrimage — 'The Chronicles of Common Men' (Pvt).
Proceedings of the Relief of Distress in the Manufacturing Districts of Yorkshire. (BRO)
Harverford College MS 1717-1775 Harverford College, USA (HAV)
West Riding Qtr. Sessions Orders (WAK)
'10th Annual Report of HF Sanatorium' (1895) (Pvt)

Other Sources

DQB Dictionary of Quaker Biography FHL

Printed Source — Abbreviations

RDA = 'Rules, Discipline & Advices' (See 'Printed Quaker Sources')
JGF = 'The Journal of George Fox' ed. John Nickalls (1975 edition).
Besse's Sufferings = (See 'Printed Quaker Sources')
Thistlethwaite = (See 'Printed Quaker Sources')
KRP = Kirkburton Parish Registers (See 'Printed Non-Quaker Sources')
Morehouse = (See 'Local Histories')
JofFHS = Journal of Friends Historical Society
CFPESofE = 'Christian Faith & Practice in the Experience of the Society of Friends'